ETHICS IN THE CONF~
OF MODER~

Alasdair MacIntyre explores some central philosophical, political, and moral claims of modernity and argues that a proper understanding of human goods requires a rejection of these claims. In a wide-ranging discussion, he considers how normative and evaluative judgments are to be understood, how desire and practical reasoning are to be characterized, what it is to have adequate self-knowledge, and what part narrative plays in our understanding of human lives. He asks, further, what it would be to understand the modern condition from a neoAristotelian or Thomistic perspective, and argues that Thomistic Aristotelianism, informed by Marx's insights, provides us with resources for constructing a contemporary politics and ethics which both enable and require us to act against modernity from within modernity. This rich and important book builds on and advances MacIntyre's thinking in ethics and political philosophy, and will be of great interest to readers in both fields.

ALASDAIR MACINTYRE retired from teaching at the University of Notre Dame in 2010. He is the author of the award-winning *After Virtue* (1981), and his other publications include two volumes of essays, *The Tasks of Philosophy* and *Ethics and Politics* (both Cambridge, 2006), *Edith Stein: A Philosophical Prologue 1913–1922* (2005), and *God, Philosophy, Universities: A History of the Catholic Philosophical Tradition* (2009).

ETHICS IN THE CONFLICTS OF MODERNITY

An Essay on Desire, Practical Reasoning, and Narrative

ALASDAIR MACINTYRE

CAMBRIDGE
UNIVERSITY PRESS

CAMBRIDGE
UNIVERSITY PRESS

University Printing House, Cambridge CB2 8BS, United Kingdom

Cambridge University Press is part of the University of Cambridge.

It furthers the University's mission by disseminating knowledge in the pursuit of
education, learning and research at the highest international levels of excellence.

www.cambridge.org
Information on this title: www.cambridge.org/9781107176454

First published 2016
Reprinted 2018
First paperback edition 2020

Printed in the United Kingdom by TJ International Ltd. Padstow Cornwall

A catalog record for this publication is available from the British Library

Library of Congress Cataloging in Publication data
Names: MacIntyre, Alasdair C., author.
Title: Ethics in the conflicts of modernity : an essay on desire,
practical reasoning, and narrative / Alasdair MacIntyre.
Description: New York : Cambridge University Press, 2016.
Identifiers: LCCN 2016021890 | ISBN 9781107176454 (hardback)
Subjects: LCSH: Desire (Philosophy) | Ethics. | Philosophy and social sciences. |
BISAC: PHILOSOPHY / Ethics & Moral Philosophy.
Classification: LCC B105.D44 M33   2016 | DDC 170 – dc23
LC record available at https://lccn.loc.gov/2016021890

ISBN 978-1-107-17645-4 Hardback
ISBN 978-1-316-62960-4 Paperback

A shaoghail, tha sinn ann g'a aindeoin;
Tha a'ghriosach theth fo'n luaithre fhathast.
George Campbell Hay

Contents

Preface

This essay is divided into five chapters. In the first the questions initially posed about our desires and how we should think about them are questions that plain nonphilosophical persons often find themselves asking. When, however, they carry their attempt to answer these questions a little further, they find that they have, perhaps inadvertently, become philosophers and that they need some at least of the conceptual and argumentative resources which professional philosophers provide. So their enquiry, like this one, becomes philosophical. But philosophy in our culture has become an almost exclusively specialized academic discipline whose practitioners for the most part address only each other rather than the educated layperson. Moreover, those same practitioners have for the last fifty years been harassed by the academic system into publishing more and more as a condition for academic survival, so that on most topics of philosophical interest there is by now an increasingly large, an often unmanageably large, body of literature that has to be read as a prologue before adding to it one more item. Readers should be warned that my references to this literature are selective and few. Had I conscientiously attempted not only to find my way through all the relevant published writing in the philosophy of mind and in ethics but then also to explain how I had come to terms with the claims advanced by its authors, I would have had to write at impossible length and in a format that would have made this essay inaccessible to the lay reader for whom it is written.

Nonetheless, I have worked my own way slowly and painfully – the pain is sometimes, although far from always, the pain of boredom – through what matters in that literature and, if I have readers who are professional philosophers, they can be assured that if I make no reference to a vast body of published work, including their own, it is because nothing in it has given me reason to abandon or to modify the views here expressed and the arguments here advanced. My readers are invited to think their way through my extended argument on their own terms, whatever those terms may be. My primary aim is not to secure their agreement, since whether I do so or not depends in key part on the convictions and assumptions that they bring with them to their reading, but rather to invite them to redefine their own positions in the light of the case that I make.

The enquiries of the first chapter lead to a philosophical impasse, to a confrontation between two rival and incompatible positions, that of expressivism and that of a certain kind of Aristotelianism, two sets of theses and arguments about the meaning and use of 'good' and about the nature of goods, the protagonists of which are unable to provide sufficient reasons for their critics and opponents to change their minds. It matters that from each of these two rival standpoints the relationships between desires and practical reasoning is understood very differently and that the impasse, although theoretical, has important implications for practice. Is there then any way of moving beyond it? My strategy in the second chapter is to turn to another kind of enquiry, one in which I consider some social and historical contexts in which philosophical theorizing on relevant issues has functioned and of how it has functioned in those contexts. I take particular note of how such theorizing may sometimes function so as to generate misunderstandings in ethics and politics by disguising the social and economic realities of particular times and places. I note too that the remedy for such theorizing is, in part at least, better theorizing, theorizing that has the power to make us aware of those same realities. Examples drawn from Hume, Aristotle, Aquinas, Marx, and others provide a first step in rethinking the relationships between philosophical theorizing and everyday practice so that it becomes possible to pose as yet unasked questions about the conclusions at which I had arrived in the first chapter, questions that concern the relevant features of the distinctively modern moral and social contexts in terms of which, so it turns out, we need to understand the rival philosophical claims that I had discussed.

The third chapter of this essay, therefore, is a historical and sociological account, albeit a bare and skeletal one, of key features of the social structures and social life of advanced modernity in the course of which morality took on a new and peculiar aspect and from which the present form of the opposition between the two philosophical standpoints that I discuss in the first chapter emerged. I argue that we can understand how and why the morality peculiar to the modern world, the morality that I name 'Morality', has functioned as it has, only if we consider it in relationship not only to the political, economic, and social structures that are distinctive of modernity but also to characteristically modern modes of feeling and desiring. I argue further that we can understand expressivism adequately only by considering both how it provides a subversive critique of Morality and the limitations of that critique. Those limitations, which turn out to be limitations of expressivism as a theory, are identified in the course of discussing the claims of three notable critics of Morality, Oscar Wilde, D. H. Lawrence, and Bernard Williams, a philosopher whose enquiries were informed by an unusual awareness of the historical and social contexts of those enquiries. It is Williams who does most in enabling us to understand the present situation of the reflective agent and the alternatives that she or he confronts, in part by his insights, in part by the issues that his work raises but is unable to resolve.

In the fourth chapter I am able to return to the original philosophical enquiry, but now with resources for better understanding and for moving beyond the impasse at which we had arrived, not only because I have now been able to identify where it is that expressivism succeeds and where it is that it fails, but also because I am now able to supply a more adequate account of what it is to advance rational justifications in the contexts of practice. The discussion of Williams' views had already thrown important light on what is at stake in our contemporary situation in either accepting or rejecting a NeoAristotelian standpoint in ethics and politics. This fourth chapter is therefore principally a fuller exposition of NeoAristotelianism, and more specifically of Thomism, in its relationship to the moral, political, and economic limitations and possibilities of the contemporary social order. My argument is designed to show that it is only from a Thomistic Aristotelian perspective that we are able to characterize adequately some key features of the social order of advanced modernity and that Thomistic Aristotelianism, when informed by Marx's insights, is able to provide us with the resources for constructing a contemporary politics and ethics, one that enables and requires us to act against modernity from within modernity. Its conclusion is that a certain kind of narrative is indispensable for understanding the practical and the moral life.

The fifth and final chapter exemplifies this thesis by providing a biographical study of the relationship of theory to practice and of desire to practical reasoning in four very different twentieth-century lives, those of the Soviet novelist, Vasily Grossman, of the American judge, Sandra Day O'Connor, of the Trinidadian Marxist historian and political activist, C. L. R. James, and of the Irish Catholic priest and political activist, Monsignor Denis Faul. It was from such as them, quite as much as from Aristotle, Aquinas, and Marx, that I learned to understand both the unity of political and moral enquiry and its complexity, in that its subject matter is at once philosophical, historical, and sociological. One moral to be drawn by anyone who shares my conclusions is that the present organization of the academic disciplines is inimical to such enquiry.

I am all too aware of having attempted both too much and too little: too little because of the need to engage with adversarial positions in greater depth than I have done, too much because of the extensive ground that I have covered. One consequence is that I have had on a number of occasions to make the same point in different contexts. Readers who are understandably irritated by these repetitions should note that the alternative would have been to refer them too frequently to other passages in the text, so disrupting their reading. Some of the theses that I assert and some of the arguments that I advance repeat, revise, correct, or replace theses asserted and arguments advanced in my earlier books and articles, so that I could have cluttered the text with references to these earlier statements, but it seems better not to do so.[1] I am also happy to acknowledge my debts first of all to those institutions who have provided me with much needed and much appreciated academic hospitality since I retired from teaching in the Philosophy Department of the University of Notre Dame: Notre Dame's Center for Ethics and Culture and its Maritain Center and London Metropolitan University's Centre for Aristotelian Studies of Contemporary Ethics and Politics. I am most grateful for the remarkable generosity of those colleagues in a number of universities who read and commented on an earlier draft of this book: Joseph Dunne, Raymond Geuss, Kelvin Knight, and Elijah Millgram, each from a standpoint significantly different from my own. I learned a great deal from them, although not as much as they may have hoped. I also owe a considerable debt to Jonathan Lear, Jeffery Nicholas, and John O'Callaghan, who commented incisively on particular passages, and to the two readers for the Cambridge University Press for their identifications of errors and unclarities. I am especially grateful to my copyeditor, Jacqueline French. Earlier versions of some parts of this book were read to seminars at London Metropolitan University. I could not have had better critics than those who participated in those seminars and to them too I am immensely grateful. I scarcely need to add that the flaws and errors that remain are mine.

Let me also acknowledge a very different kind of debt. In philosophy it is only rarely that anyone or any argument has the last word. Debate almost always continues, and this is notably so with the topics and issues with

[1] I must, however, note that in Chapter 4 parts of sections 4.6 and 4.7 were originally published as parts of my "Philosophical Education Against Contemporary Culture," in *Proceedings of the American Catholic Philosophical Association* 87 (2013): 43–56, and parts of section 4.12 as parts of my "Ends and Endings," in *American Catholic Philosophical Quarterly* 88, 4 (Fall 2014): 807–821.

which I am concerned in this book: how normative and evaluative judgments are to be understood, how desire and practical reasoning are to be characterized, what it is to have adequate self-knowledge, what part narrative plays in our understanding of human lives, and what it is to understand these matters from a Thomistic perspective. Each of the positions to which I am committed puts me at odds with philosophers of insight, penetration, and wit who will remain unpersuaded by my arguments. To them I am very much in debt, since it is they who have forced me again and again to rethink those arguments.

My greatest debt of all is to Lynn Sumida Joy, not only for her particular perceptive and instructive comments on earlier drafts of this book, but for making the whole enterprise possible.

CHAPTER I

Desires, goods, and 'good'
Some philosophical issues

1.1 Desires, why they matter, what they are; what is it to have a good reason for desiring something?

Human lives can go wrong in a variety of ways and from different causes: as a result of malnutrition, illness, injury, or untimely death, from the malice, envy, or insensitivity of others, because of lack of self-knowledge or excess of self-doubt – the list is a long one. I want to focus on lives that go wrong on account of misdirected or frustrated desire. These too can be of different kinds. Someone who had set her heart on just one thing – athletic success, fame as a celebrity, preeminence as a physicist – and fails to achieve it may thereafter lead the unhappy life of a disappointed woman. Someone who wants too many different things and is recurrently diverted from his pursuit of this by the attractions of that may suddenly find that he has squandered his life away without achieving very much. Someone who wants and aspires to too little, perhaps from fear of the pain of disappointment, may never recognize that their talents and skills have never been put to adequate use. Such examples make it clear that when lives go wrong in these various ways, frustrated or misdirected or inadequate desire has played a part, even if not the only part, in making them go wrong.

The woman who had set her heart on athletic success perhaps failed to achieve it because of an injury. But it is her inability to find and pursue other objects of desire that makes her life one of disappointment. The man who wants and aspires to too little does so perhaps because of lack of self-knowledge or excess of self-doubt or both. The flibbertigibbet who pursued too many things may have had friends who encouraged him in his wasteful ways, not friends who might have given him good advice. The woman or man who invests all their hopes in a single lifelong project and is then defeated in their final attempt to complete that project will, like Gatsby in Scott Fitzgerald's novel, have "paid a high price for living too long with a single dream." If then we, thinking about such cases, are to

I

enquire about how things might go well or badly with our own desires, we will have to keep in mind the relationships between our desires and many other aspects of our lives. One question to ask about those of us who lead such flawed lives is: Did we or they desire what we or they had good reason to desire, given their or our circumstances, character, relationships, and past history?

Before we can pose this question profitably, however, we should note some other characteristics of our desires. The first is the large variety of their objects and so also, since we individuate desires by their objects, the large variety of our desires. She wants, among other things, a cup of coffee, to solve this differential equation, to join the local theatre group, never to have to return to South Bend, Indiana. He wants to lose weight, to be successful as a teacher, to visit Florence before he dies. What they want is that such and such should be the case at some point in the future. Yet what we desire for the future is sometimes that things should continue just as they now are. She is well liked and wants to go on being well liked. He is the proud owner of a Bugatti and wants to go on being the proud owner of a Bugatti. Moreover, we often desire not only that things should go well for us but also that they should go well or badly for particular others. She wants her friend to do well in her examination and the local food bank to flourish. He would be delighted if something very bad happened to the salesman who cheated him when he bought the Bugatti.

Such everyday examples draw our attention to still other relevant features of some desires. There are desires that we all share, yet may not even notice, so long as they are easily and routinely satisfied – the desire to have enough to eat, for example. But for those for whom hunger, as a result of poverty or famine, is an inescapable daily experience of felt need, this desire will be urgent and impossible to set aside. Yet we should not make the mistake of identifying the desire to eat with the felt need of hunger. Consider the case of an experimental psychologist who is studying the effects of food deprivation on a number of subjects, including herself. One of those effects is an increasingly intense felt need for food. However, the experimenter wants not to eat – and does not want to eat – for an extended period of time so that she can study the accompanying changes in herself. The felt hunger is one thing, the desire to eat another. So it might be too with a fashion model anxious to remain extraordinarily and elegantly thin. She feels hunger, but she does not want to eat.

It is of course quite otherwise with human infants, for whom the expression of desire just is the expression of felt need and the expression of frustration at not having that need met immediately. The difference between such infants and human adults is at least threefold. The adult, feeling some bodily need, is able to ask, as the infant cannot, 'Is here and now the place and time to meet this need?', and perhaps to answer as my imagined experimental psychologist and fashion model do. Such adults recognize that their needs, felt or otherwise, are one thing, what they want to do about satisfying or not satisfying them quite another. In so distinguishing needs and desires, adults differentiate themselves from infants in a second way. They look beyond the present to a series of futures, tomorrow, next month, next year, ten years later, when it will become possible to achieve some objects of present desires that are not yet attainable. And they know, although they do not always bear in mind, that how they act now may make it easier or more difficult or impossible to satisfy those desires in the future. So they sometimes have to consider whether or not they should forego satisfying some present desire for the sake of keeping open some future possibility.

A third way in which human adults differ from human infants in respect of their desires is in their awareness not only of their future but also of their past. For they know that once they were small children and now they are not and that their desires as adults are significantly different from their desires as small children. That is, they know, even if they seldom reflect upon it, that their desires have a history, a history during which objects of desire have multiplied. Some of their earlier desires have been transformed, others replaced. New and changing experiences and new and changing relationships have provided a widening range of possible objects of desire. Infantile libido has become first adolescent and then adult sexual desire, infantile hunger has become a taste for fish and chips or foie gras. And wants as various as those catalogued earlier may now find a place in their lives.

If we find reason to reflect upon the history of our own desires, we soon become aware of other aspects of that history. First, it is inseparable not only from the history of our emotions, tastes, affections, habits, and beliefs but also from that of our biochemical and neurophysiological development. Our emotions are obviously closely related to our desires. We become angry when some harm that we very much did not want to see inflicted on a friend is gratuitously inflicted on him. We grieve when someone whose wellbeing we desired falls ill or dies. So too with our tastes and our affections. I want tickets for this concert because of my liking for this kind of music; I want the radio turned off because of my aversion to that other kind of music. I want this student to do well because of my affection for her parents. With habits and beliefs the relationships to desires are again obvious. Initially I have no particular liking for this kind of music – Tudor madrigals, punk rock, whatever. Then I learn that someone whose judgment I greatly respect not only values this kind of music as a listener but is learning an instrument so as to become a performer. Impressed by this, I start listening carefully to recordings of it, I change my habits, I redirect my attention, and in time I find it rewarding to have done so. A change in belief and the development of a new habit result in changes in my desires, to what performers I want to listen, and on what occasions I want the radio turned off.

If we need convincing that the history of our desires is also inseparable from our biochemical and neurophysiological history, we need only remind ourselves of the kinds of effects that various illnesses and drugs, including alcohol, nicotine, and marijuana, can have upon our desires. But we should also notice a variety of discoveries made by neuroscientific researchers concerning what must not happen in the brain if our desires and emotions are to function as they normally do, discoveries about what happens when our lives are disordered by emotions and desires resulting from injury or other interference with the normal functioning of the brain. Why then with all these complexities should we focus especially on desires?

Consider two different types of occasion which give us good reason to reflect upon our desires. Occasions of the first type are part of the fabric of everyone's life, occasions when we cannot avoid making choices that will dictate the shape of our future lives, as when students decide for what kind of work to prepare themselves, or someone in midcareer faces alternative career paths, or someone decides to get married or not to get married, or someone decides to commit themselves to a life of religious contemplation or a life of revolutionary politics. Occasions of a second type are those when the routines of everyday life have been disrupted by, say, a serious illness or the outbreak of a war or a discovery that one has alienated one's friends, or by being unexpectedly told that one has been fired or is going to be divorced. In such situations it requires little reflection to recognize that if I am to answer the question 'What shall I do?' I had better first pause and pose the question 'What is it that I want?' Somewhat more reflection is needed to recognize that I also need to think critically about my present desires, to ask 'Is what I now want what I want myself to want?' and 'Do I have sufficiently good reasons to want what I now want?' and still further reflection to recognize that I will be likely to go astray in answering these questions if I do not also ask how I came to be the kind of person that I now am, with the desires that I now have, that is, to ask about the history of my desires.

We began by taking note of some ways in which someone's life could go wrong because there was something amiss with her or his desires. What we have now recognized is that whether a life goes well or badly may depend and often does depend on whether in the types of situation that I have identified someone thinks well or badly about their present, past, and future desires. To understand what it is to think well or badly about our desires, we need first to say more about what a desire is and about how desires relate to actions. A good place to begin is with Elizabeth Anscombe's remark that "The primitive sign of wanting is *trying to get*."[1] Here the word 'primitive' is important. What small children desire they try to get. But, as we already noticed, as they grow older they learn to delay satisfying some of their desires and develop desires that can be satisfied only at some time, even some distant time, in the future. If then it is true of some adult that she very much wants to travel to Italy next summer, it does not follow that she is doing anything to implement that desire now, but only perhaps that she is so disposed that, if and when the opportunity occurs and it is the appropriate time, she will do such things as buy tickets and make hotel reservations and that, when at the moment she entertains thoughts of Italy, she thinks such thoughts as 'I hope to be there next summer'. Yet here we are wise to say 'perhaps'. For she may indeed want very much to go to Italy next summer and yet see no possibility of doing so. In this case her dispositions are such that if the obstacles to her traveling to Italy were to be removed, which, so she firmly believes, they will not be, then she would indeed be disposed to do such things as buy tickets and make hotel reservations and to entertain the hopes of an expectant traveler.

There are then, even in such simple cases, a range of ways in which someone's desires may find expression in their thoughts and actions. At one extreme are idle wishes for states of affairs that are impossible and known to be impossible by those who wish for them. "I wish," say I, who have a voice like a corncrake and know it, "that I could sing like Dietrich Fischer-Dieskau." About such wishes there is nothing to be done, as in all those cases where we very much want something to happen, but whether it happens or not is not at all in our power. At the other extreme are desires that translate immediately into action. I want not to get wet and, as it starts to rain, I put up my umbrella. I want to quench my thirst now and I fill a glass with water and drink it. The same action can of course on different occasions express different desires, and the same desire can be expressed in different actions. Putting up my umbrella might be an expression of my

---

[1] G. E. M. Anscombe, *Intention*, Oxford: Basil Blackwell, 2nd edn., 1958, p. 67.

desire to show someone what an elegant and expensive umbrella I own. And my desire to quench my thirst might be expressed in my searching for a drinking fountain.

Between those extremes are a range of other cases. If what I want is that things should go on as they are, my desire will be expressed in my letting things be, at least until and unless something happens to disturb them. If what I want is that something – anything – should disturb the hopelessly boring routine of my life, my desire will be expressed in my openness to invitations to disturbance and disruption. If what I want is that my wants should be other than they now are, my actions will be directed, often in complex ways, to altering my habits, redirecting my attention, perhaps to conditioning myself not to respond to certain stimuli. (Whether we want to want otherwise than we now do or instead want to want just what we now do is obviously often of crucial importance at turning points in our lives. Philosophers owe their understanding of the significance of such second order desires to Harry Frankfurt's 1971 paper, "Freedom of the Will and the Concept of a Person."[2] What all such cases, as contrasted with idle wishes, have in common is that our desires are expressed both in action and in those states of mind that motivate us to act. Of course, it is not only desires that motivate; so do emotions and tastes. And so too do those attitudes that some philosophers have named pro-attitudes, attitudes of liking or approval (or anti-attitudes, dislikings, aversions). I have, let us say, an attitude of approval toward those who work to mitigate the evils of world hunger. When someone asks me to make a donation in support of this cause, it is this pro-attitude that is expressed in my immediate positive response. But notice that what the request to contribute elicits is a desire, a desire to help, a desire expressed in my handing over dollar bills. As with emotions and tastes, pro-attitudes issue in actions as they do only because of their relationships to desires and to actions expressive of desires.

Some philosophers have talked as if every action must have some particular motivation of its own, as if the question 'Why did she do that?' will always have an answer that refers us immediately to some particular desire, emotion, or the like. But this is to ignore how much of our activity is what it is because of the structures and patterns of each individual's normal day, normal week, normal year. So often enough the first answer to the 'Why?' question should be of the form 'It's a Friday afternoon and that is what she generally does on Friday afternoons.' For most of the lives of most people,

[2] Harry G. Frankfurt, "Freedom of the Will and the Concept of a Person," *Journal of Philosophy* 68 (1971): 1, reprinted in *The Importance of What We Care About*, Cambridge University Press, 1988, pp. 11–25.

there is a daily, weekly, and annual routine. This does not mean that there are not many occasions for spontaneity, for choice, and for improvisation, but these generally have as their context structures that each of us can take for granted in our interactions with others. I enter the café at 7.30 am on my way to work, knowing that someone will have made the coffee. She phones the office after 9.00, knowing that the secretary will be there to answer the phone. He arrives at the station at 10.00, since the train is due to arrive ten minutes later. And on the mornings when someone sleeps late or the coffee machine or the telephone or the train breaks down, there are standard ways of responding and coping and standard ways of responding when someone fails to cope. Let us call the dispositions to act and to react in these patterned ways – somewhat extending our everyday use of the word – habits. For the moment it is enough to note the importance of such habits and their relationship to those institutionalized routines that structure our everyday lives. But later we will have to ask questions about how our lives come to be thus structured and how in consequence our desires are transformed. For the moment I turn from habits to beliefs.

Beliefs may on occasion play a crucial part in making our desires and the actions issuing from our desires what they are. Someone may be satisfied with her present life only because she believes that there is no more pleasing alternative that is open to her. What she takes to be possible depends on her beliefs both about herself and about the relevant aspects of the social world. Imagination too has a part to play. It may never have occurred to her that she might run away and join the circus or learn to speak Japanese and take a job in Kyoto. Indeed, if someone were to suggest either of these courses of action to her, her response would be dismissive, because she would be unable to imagine herself as, say, a trapeze artist or an interpreter for tourists curious about Zen Buddhism. Her beliefs and her imagination combine to set limits to what she takes to be possible and so to her present desires. And this is not the only way in which beliefs may be related to desires.

Each of us, in acting as we do, has to take some account of the desires of others with whom we interact. Sometimes we may want to act as they desire because we love them, or because we fear them, or because we want to secure their cooperation. We may perhaps see them as dangerous competitors for scarce resources, so that, if we are to satisfy our own desires, we must prevent them from satisfying theirs. In all these cases it matters to us that our beliefs about their desires are true beliefs, just as it matters to them that their beliefs about our desires are true beliefs. Sometimes we may find it difficult to believe of certain others that they really do desire what, on the best interpretation that we can devise, they seem to desire. How, we ask, could anyone want *that*? What would be the good of acting so as to achieve *that*? These are very much the same questions that, as we noted earlier, we put to ourselves when we become reflective about our own desires. To be reflective about one's desires is to ask whether one has sufficiently good reasons for desiring whatever it is that one presently desires. To have a good reason for desiring something – when that desire is not an idle wish – is to have a good reason for acting in some particular way. So what is it to act for a good reason?

We need first to note that whether or not someone has a good reason to act in this or that particular way is one thing. Whether she or he is aware that they have a good reason so to act is another. And whether they so act just because they have a good reason so to act is a third. To act for a good reason is to act for the sake of achieving some good or preventing or avoiding some evil. The good to be achieved may be achieved simply in performing that particular action, as when someone acts generously by feeding a hungry person who would otherwise go unfed. Or it may be achieved by contributing to some shared activity, as when someone acts gracefully and beautifully by playing the cello in a performance of a Beethoven quartet. Or it may be achieved by producing some good as an effect, as when someone by eating and drinking temperately becomes healthy. To spell out the notion of acting for a good reason fully, we would have both to say more about these distinctions and to make some further distinctions, but enough has been said to make the point that we have a good reason to want some particular object of desire only if and when to act so as to achieve the object of that desire is to act so as to achieve some good.

We may of course have good reason to act in some particular way without having *sufficiently* good reason so to act, as when I have good reason to act self-interestedly by fleeing from some danger, but better reason to act courageously by standing fast in defense of innocent others who will otherwise lose their lives. So too I may have good reason to want something, but better reason to want something else. And I am able to justify acting so as to satisfy some desire, only if I can show that I had good reason for so acting and no better reason for acting otherwise. When I ask, therefore, whether I do or do not have good reason or sufficiently good reason to satisfy this or that particular desire, I am asking what good or goods are or might be at stake in my acting so as to satisfy it rather than some other desire.

To this there may be an immediate objection. Someone – anyone – may say "But surely we always have *some* reason to satisfy *any* desire. When asked to give our reasons for acting as we did, don't we often say that by acting as we did we got what we wanted? And isn't this in itself a perfectly good reason? We may perhaps have further reasons, but we don't need them." With those who make this complaint, I will at once agree that often enough in our culture 'Doing that got me what I wanted' is taken to have been a good, even a sufficient reason for some agent's having done whatever she or he did. Such an agent's claim may be no more than that it is good that this particular desire of theirs should have been satisfied. And there are of course many desires that, in particular contexts, it is good to satisfy. But the more radical claim voiced in the objection is that any desire provides not just a motive, but also some reason for acting so as to satisfy that desire. What should we say to this?

To ask what reasons I have for choosing to act in this way rather than that, in order to satisfy some desire, is to ask what would justify me as a rational agent in acting in this way rather than that. And to justify an action just is to show that the good to be achieved by so acting outweighs the good to be achieved by any alternative course of action open to the agent. Of course questions about rational justification are not the only questions that may be posed about our reasons for acting as we do. Others may on occasion find our desires and the actions that give expression to those desires not so much unjustified as unintelligible. We become intelligible to others just insofar as they can identify and understand as possible goods the goods that furnish us with reasons for desiring as we do and acting as we do. If, therefore, someone were to give as their sole reason for acting as they do that it achieves the satisfaction of some desire, without also claiming that in satisfying their desire they were achieving some good, they would have done nothing to make their action intelligible as an intended action, let alone to show that it was justified.

Yet it is of course true that considerations that have to do with our desires play a variety of parts in our practical reasoning. That I want something badly may in some circumstances give me a reason for satisfying that desire, if, for example, I will be distracted from acting as I should be acting, so long as that desire remains unsatisfied. That I want something badly may in other circumstances give me a reason for not satisfying that desire, if, for example, it is Lent and I am resisting my tendencies toward self-indulgence. But in all such cases considerations about our desires have the place that they have in our practical reasoning only because of the relationship between satisfying or failing to satisfy this or that desire and the achievement of this or that good.

A very different rejoinder to my claim that our desires are both intelligible and justifiable only if we have good reason to act so as to satisfy them would be made by someone who recognized that I have come very close to reiterating Aquinas's thesis that "Every desire is for some good" (*Summa Theologiae* I–IIae, qu. 8, art. 1, resp.) and who held that there are counterexamples that are fatal to that thesis. Aquinas's view was that every desire has as its object something taken to be good by the agent, and some critics have supposed that he cannot therefore allow for those cases where someone desires something that is on any reasonable account bad and where the agent knows that it is bad, as when the fat man with a heart condition wants to feast on profiteroles. Those critics have misunderstood Aquinas's claim. What the imprudent fat man desires is the pleasure afforded by the delicious taste of the profiteroles, and this is indeed a good. So the fat man's desire is for some good. But in that his desire is for something that will shorten his life and impoverish his family, it is also a desire for something bad. So in acting for the sake of some good, he knowingly acts from a desire for what is bad. And there is no inconsistency here. We must look elsewhere for counterexamples to Aquinas's thesis.

Walking along the street I idly kick a stone. 'What did you do that for?' 'I just felt like it.' 'But what did you want to do it for?' 'I had no particular reason for wanting to do it.' Such impulses belong to a familiar class of momentary whims, where there is indeed a species of desire, but no particular good in view. Less common are those plainly neurotic desires that are unintelligible not only to others but also to the agent whose desires they are. Someone finds herself wanting to walk only on that side of the road where the house numbers are odd rather than even. She cannot say why. Her desire, as she feels it and expresses it, is not for any good. These are genuine counterexamples not only to Aquinas's thesis but also to such contemporary versions of it as that advanced by Joseph Raz, according to which it is not desires, but intentional actions that are always directed toward something that the agent takes to be of genuine worth: "intentional actions are actions that we perform because we endorse them in light of what we believe about them, and that means that we must believe that they have features that make them attractive, or as we say, features that give them value."[3] How, then, should we respond to such counterexamples?

[3] Joseph Raz, "On the Guise of the Good," in *Desire, Practical Reason and the Good*, ed. Sergio Tenenbaum, Oxford University Press, 2010, p. 116.

We can bring out their significance by considering situations in which some desire or intention aimed at no particular good conflicts with a desire or intention to achieve some palpable good, so that, if we were to continue to act as the former desire or intention directs us, we would have to forego that good. I am, say, sitting on a bench, idly whistling a tune. If someone were to ask why I am sitting there and whistling, my answer would be "For no particular reason." I am not waiting for a friend; I did not feel a need to rest. But then I hear a child's voice calling for help. If I ignore that cry, but remain sitting there, continuing to whistle, my action or failure to act at once becomes puzzling. For anyone in such a situation has good reason to respond to such a cry, unless they have an even better reason to act otherwise. *Ex hypothesi* I have no particular reason for continuing to act as I do, yet I seem to place a value on so acting that outweighs the reason that I have for responding to the child's cry. Do such cases occur? Plainly they do and equally plainly they invite us to infer that something more is going on, perhaps that such an agent is motivated by some desire to achieve some good or to avoid some evil that she or he is not able to acknowledge, certainly to others, but perhaps also to her or himself. So, in the case of the agent who remains unmoved by the child's cry for help, the lack of response to the child's cry may be and may only be intelligible as an expression of a deep and unacknowledgable fear of getting involved.

Such situations provide further counterexamples to the theses advanced by Aquinas and Raz. But it is important that they are all of them examples of desires and intentions that the agents whose desires and intentions they are find themselves unable to make intelligible to themselves, let alone to others. So the theses advanced by Aquinas and by Raz do hold of our desires and intentions, just insofar as they satisfy two conditions. They are not momentary whims and they are intelligible. With this qualification we can reaffirm the account of desires and reasons for action that emerged from our earlier discussions, while noting the importance of the distinction between those actions where the agent is able to supply a reason for acting as she or he does and those where this is not the case. On that account we present ourselves to others, and they to us, as moved by desires for what we take to be goods. It is, insofar as the object of some particular desire really is a good, that it provides us with a good reason for acting so as to satisfy that desire. And it is always possible that on such an occasion we have an even better reason for acting in some other way, because by so acting we could achieve some significantly greater good. To be reflective about our own desires is, whenever it is appropriate, to pause before acting and to ask how good our reasons are for acting so as to satisfy that desire. To be reflective in our relations with others is to take their measure by considering both what real or supposed goods are the objects of their desires and how reflective they are with respect to those desires.

We should not, however, underestimate the extent to which we may on occasion be mistaken as to what the true object of some desire is, that is, as to what would satisfy it. And we should not ignore the importance of desires for that which we cannot as yet make it intelligible that we should desire. Desires sometimes point beyond themselves to some as yet unacknowledged, but felt lack in ourselves, something that William Desmond has made central to his treatment of desire.[4] We have to take time to learn what we do desire as well as to learn what we have good reason to desire. Nonetheless, it remains true that we need to make our desires intelligible and that to find a desire intelligible is to have identified the good or goods that would be achieved by satisfying it.

This account does of course at once raise further questions. The most important concern 'good' and good, the word 'good' and that of which we speak, when we use it. I have spoken of good reasons for actions and also of reasons that are good, but not good enough. I have distinguished objects of desire, the achievement of which would be the achievement of a good, from objects of desire of which this is not true. I have contrasted what is taken to be good by this or that agent with what is in fact good. What do we mean when we use 'good' in these various ways? A first step in answering this question is perhaps to take note of those words that we sometimes substitute for 'good', words such as 'desirable' and 'choiceworthy'. But this only takes us a very little way, since, if we are puzzled about what 'good' means, we will also be puzzled about what they mean. Why then should we be puzzled and how are such puzzles to be resolved?

First of all because of the range of disagreements and the kinds of disagreements over what is to be called good and why, that is, over what is and is not genuinely desirable and choiceworthy, and then because of the apparent inability on many occasions of those who disagree to resolve their disagreements. So we need, if we are to make further progress in our enquiries, an account of 'good' and of good which will enable us to understand these various disagreements better and to enquire how, if at all, they might be resolved, and, if not, why not. Note that what began as an enquiry into why lives go wrong because of misdirected desires then became an enquiry into what it is to have good or bad reasons for desiring what we do in fact desire, and must now become an enquiry into 'good'

---

[4] William Desmond, *Desire, Dialectic and Otherness*, New Haven, CT: Yale University Press, 1987.

and good. But the point and purpose of this further enquiry, even if it proceeds at some very considerable length and in various directions, will be in the end to return us to our original questions.

1.2   'Good', goods, and disagreements about goods

J. L. Austin[5] and G. H. von Wright[6] more recently and Aristotle and Aquinas long ago (*Nicomachean Ethics* I, 1096a19–23 and Aquinas's *Commentary on the Ethics*) emphasized the multiplicity and variety of our uses of 'good'. We speak of good knives, good jam, good poems, and good kings, but also of a good time to apply for a job or to make oneself scarce, a good place to take a vacation or to build a prison, and good qualities to look for in candidates for public office. We may say of someone that she is good with children, good at tennis, or good for nothing. And what is true of our uses of 'good' is true also and obviously of our uses of 'bad,' 'better,' and 'worse'. When 'good', 'bad', and their cognates are used as adjectives in these ways, the criteria governing their use depend upon the nouns to which they are applied.[7] What makes jam good jam is very different from what makes a poem a good poem. What makes this a bad time to apply for a job is not at all the same as what makes that a bad place to take a vacation. So what, if any, is the underlying unity in these various uses of 'good' and 'bad'? What makes them more than a series of puns?

To speak in this way of something as good or bad is to evaluate it as a member of a class or from a point of view or both. But when we attempt to go further than this, we encounter difficulties. We might think, for example, that a rough and ready characterization of what is meant should run: to say of something that it is a good something is to say that, if you want or need that something for the reasons for which things of that kind – or things viewed from that point of view – are characteristically wanted or needed, then this particular something will meet your want or need. So it certainly seems to be with good knives and good jam, with good places to take a vacation or to build a prison, but any such formulation needs to be carefully qualified. Consider the kind of difficulty posed by the word 'characteristically'. In some impoverished populations some things are characteristically wanted because, although bad of their kind, they are cheap. This type of qualification does not give us reason to

---

[5] J. L. Austin, *Philosophical Papers*, Oxford: Clarendon Press, 1961, p. 151.

[6] G. H. von Wright, *The Varieties of Goodness*, London: Routledge, 1963.

[7] See Peter Geach, "Good and Evil," *Analysis* 17 (1956): 33–42, reprinted in *Theories of Ethics*, ed. P. Foot, Oxford University Press, 1967.

abandon our original rough and ready formulation – which does indeed capture something of the first importance about such uses of 'good' – but to proceed with care in our employment of it.

What we need to do next is to note two features of such ascriptions of good. The first is the enormously varying extent to which those who use them agree or disagree as to what it is that makes this or that good of its kind or good from this particular point of view. As to what makes a good watch a good watch or good jam good jam, there is large, if not universal agreement. As to what makes good education good education, good architecture good architecture, or good government good government, there are the sharpest of disagreements. The second is that, although the *Oxford English Dictionary* says of 'good' that it is the most general adjective of commendation, to say that something is good of its kind or good from a point of view is not necessarily to commend it or to express approval. We speak not only of good violinists, but also of good thieves and forgers. We speak not only of those who are good at tennis or at making friends, but also of those who are good at cheating at cards or at corrupting the young. Any adequate account of good and 'good' will have to make these two features of our uses of 'good' intelligible.

A first step toward doing so is to take note of an at first sight quite different use of 'good' and 'bad'. It is not in the least paradoxical to assert that it is bad for someone to be good at cheating at cards, and there is no redundancy in asserting that it is good to be good at making friends. Both assertions seem to presuppose a distinction, first remarked upon by W. D. Ross, between two uses of 'good' and its cognates, one the attributive, adjectival use that we first noticed and the other the predicative use exemplified in these two assertions and in all asserted sentences of the form 'It is good to be, do, or have such and such' or 'It is good that such and such is, was, or will be the case.' It is this latter use that enables us to express not just disagreements, but complex disagreements, the kinds of disagreements that characteristically presuppose certain limited agreements.

Ferdinand and Isabella happen to agree in their evaluations of art, food, and clothes. Yet to Ferdinand's assertion that "It is good to cultivate a taste for fine art, fine food, fine clothes, so that, if you are ever able to afford them, you will know how to choose well," Isabella replies "It is bad to develop desires that you may never be able to satisfy. That way lies nagging discontent." Ferdinand retorts that it is better to be discontented as a result of having good taste than to be contented with inferior taste.

To this too Isabella registers her disagreement, a kind of disagreement that is often not resolvable. So it is also with Edward and Eleanor. Eleanor expresses her intention to recruit her coworkers to her trade union, since it would be better for them to confront their employer as union members. Edward replies that it would be better for Eleanor not to do this, since she will almost certainly be fired. Eleanor retorts that she would be worse off still if she allowed herself to be cowed by fear of her employer. Edward disagrees.

Notice first on how much Ferdinand and Isabella and Edward and Eleanor agree. In the former case they agree about what good taste is and perhaps that it is bad to be discontented, in the latter that it is bad to lose one's job and perhaps also about the benefits of trade union membership. Where they disagree is in their rank ordering of goods and in their consequent choices. Their agreements about goods and therefore about what each has good reason to desire make them and their choices unproblematically intelligible to each other. Their disagreements over the rank ordering of goods are disagreements about what provides a sufficient reason for arriving at the conclusions at which each arrives. Disagreement may, however, run much deeper than this, especially when there is little or no agreement underlying the disagreement. So, for example, there are those for whom pleasure – the pleasures of the senses, aesthetic pleasures – counts for very little, for whom it is generally a distraction from the serious business of life, and those for whom such pleasure gives life for the moment at least – and their lives are sometimes a succession of moments – its sole point and purpose. The former will renounce pleasure for what they take to be worthwhile achievement. The latter will on occasion renounce almost anything if the pleasure to be enjoyed is great enough. The judgments and actions of each may horrify the other. Indeed each may find it difficult to understand the other except in pathological terms.

Notice further that all these disagreements about goods and their rank ordering can be expressed as disagreements about what some individual or group in some particular situation have good reason or sufficiently good reason to desire. If then we are to understand what it is to have a good reason or a sufficiently good reason to desire this rather than that, we will have to be able to say just what it is that the parties to such disagreements are disagreeing about and how far, if at all, their disagreements might be resolvable. It may well turn out that we will need more than philosophy, if we are to supply adequate answers to those questions. But we certainly need whatever insights and arguments philosophy can supply. So what can moral philosophers supply, if we ask them to throw light on the nature of such disagreements?

The answer may at first seem disappointing. For what the moral philosophers of the present day supply are their own disagreements concerning the nature of such disagreements. About the meaning and use of asserted sentences of the form 'It is good to . . .' or 'It is good that . . .', they advance a number of rival and incompatible accounts. Moreover, there seems no prospect of their resolving these disagreements. What view a moral philosopher takes of how to characterize and understand those evaluative disagreements that we have been discussing will depend upon which of these rival accounts she or he accepts. I intend to consider in some detail just two such accounts, immediately inviting on the one hand the questions 'Why only two?' and 'Why these particular two?' and on the other the question 'If first rate moral philosophers with different and conflicting standpoints are unable to advance arguments that convince the adherents of rival views, why should the rest of us take their conclusions seriously?' To none of these questions can I at this stage give a satisfactory reply. It will be only after I have outlined the arguments and claims of the two rival philosophical accounts that I will be able to explain why those two deserve our attention and scrutiny in a way and to a degree that others do not. Only at that later stage will I be in a position to argue that it is only by understanding the inability of the exponents and defenders of each account to convince those who hold the rival view that the relevance of those two accounts to our enquiry will become fully clear.

Remember once again that the line of thought that I have been following in this essay began with questions about the part that desires of certain kinds have played in lives that have gone badly wrong. It became clear that if we were to find answers to those questions, we would need to distinguish between desires whose objects particular agents in their particular situations have sufficiently good reason to desire and desires of which this is not so. But there are often disagreements and sometimes unresolvable disagreements over what is and what is not a good reason to want this or that, and these sometimes give expression to larger disagreements about how it is good and best to act, both generally and in particular situations. What are those who thus disagree disagreeing about? And how should we characterize their disagreements? It is here that we cannot do without a well-grounded philosophical account of what we are doing and saying when we assert "It is good to . . ." or "It is good that . . ." and other such cognate sentences. It is in search of such an account that I first turn to the claims and arguments advanced under the title of "expressivism."

1.3   Expressivist accounts of 'good' and of disagreements about goods

Expressivism in its earlier and less philosophically sophisticated forms was known as emotivism. Both emotivists and expressivists were and are concerned with the whole range of evaluative and normative utterances. So their account of 'good' and good finds its place within a larger account, something that we should note, but can for the moment put on one side. The classic statement of emotivism is by Charles L. Stevenson in his *Ethics and Language*.[8] On Stevenson's view asserted sentences are of three kinds, those that express true or false beliefs and have what Stevenson calls descriptive meaning, those that express attitudes of approval and disapproval and have emotive meaning, and those that are both descriptive and emotive. Sentences ascribing goodness are of the latter kinds and a first rough approximation to the meaning of 'This is good' is 'I approve of this; do so as well.'[9] What this approximation may fail to suggest are the complex ways in which many sentences combine descriptive and emotive meaning. But, on Stevenson's view, what matters is that such sentences can always be analyzed so that their emotive component is distinguished from their descriptive fact-stating component.

Sentences that state purported facts are true or false. Sentences that express evaluative attitudes toward such facts are not. Disagreements in belief, disagreements, that is, over what is in fact the case, can be settled by appeal to sense experience. Disagreements in attitude cannot be settled thus, but can only be resolved if one of the parties to the disagreement is persuaded to change her or his attitude. And one of the functions of evaluative utterances is to persuade others to align their attitudes with those of the speaker. An obvious first objection to this emotivist account of 'good' and other evaluative expressions is that it is in conflict with some of our ordinary language uses of 'true' and 'fact', as when we assert that "It is a fact that it is bad to take pleasure in the misfortunes of others" or we respond to someone's assertion that rising unemployment is a bad thing by saying "What you have just said is true." How should emotivists respond to this?

They should do so and in fact do so by arguing that uses of expressions such as 'It is true that' and 'It is a fact that' function as and only as endorsements by a speaker of the asserted sentences that they govern. So a counterpart to an emotivist understanding of evaluative utterances is a

---

[8]   Charles L. Stevenson, *Ethics and Language*, New Haven, CT: Yale University Press, 1945.
[9]   Ibid., p. 21.

minimalist view of truth. What this reformulation of emotivism leaves untouched is the distinction between asserted sentences whose meaning is such that they are expressions of some evaluative (or normative) attitude, so that to endorse them is to give further expression to that same attitude, and asserted sentences whose meaning is such that they tell us how the world is, so that to endorse them is to say "That is indeed how the world is!" and to open oneself up to refutation by the facts of the matter, as determined by sense experience, being quite otherwise. This reformulation of Stevenson's account has one further advantage.

Asserted evaluative sentences at first sight function in our inferences in precisely the same way as do asserted sentences that purport to tell us how the world is. So from the premises "It is bad to take pleasure in the misfortunes of others" and "She takes pleasure in the misfortunes of others," it follows that "It is bad to take pleasure as she does." And this, it seems, would not be so, if the first of these premises could not be understood as either true or false. Yet a further consideration of the types of inference from evaluative premises that we are able to make suggests a second objection to emotivism. From the premises "If it is bad to take pleasure in the misfortunes of others, then those who do so should be condemned" and "It is bad to take pleasure in the misfortunes of others," it plainly follows that "Those who do so should be condemned." But this can be so only if and because the sentence used in the second premise is the same sentence and has the same meaning as the sentence embedded in the conditional clause of the first premise. Yet, on Stevenson's account, it seems that this cannot be so. For the sentence embedded in the conditional clause is not asserted and so cannot express the speaker's attitude, and so lacks emotive meaning, while the sentence used in the second premise is asserted, expresses the speaker's attitude, and so has emotive meaning. What has gone wrong? The notion of emotive meaning upon which Stevenson relied cannot, it seems, do the work that he tried to make it do.

What someone who wishes to rescue the core of Stevenson's theory from Stevenson in order to address this criticism has to do is to reformulate that theory in terms of some more adequate conception of the relationships between the meanings of sentences and their uses. On this revised view, the meaning of evaluative (and normative) sentences is such that to assert them is to endorse them. So someone who asserts the first premise expresses her or his endorsement of it, but, likewise, someone who asserts the second premise asserts her or his endorsement of it. And someone who endorses both premises is thereby committed to endorsing the conclusion, since inexpressive uses of normative or evaluative sentences as constituents of conditionals are to be understood as preserving their meaning in conditional sentences, the assertion of which express an endorsement of those conditionals. The argument that emotivists cannot account for the kind of inference that we have been discussing was first advanced by Peter Geach.[10] An expressivist reply to Geach that provided an interpretation of such valid inferences in terms of this richer notion of the relationships between meaning and endorsement was advanced by Simon Blackburn.[11] Was that reply adequate?

It was in fact followed by a series of replies to Blackburn's reply and then of replies to the replies to the reply by, among others, G. F. Schueler, Bob Hale, Mark van Roojen, Nicholas Unwin, Alan Thomas, and Mark Schroeder, with further interventions by Blackburn. And by now there is no reason to believe that this series of exchanges will ever arrive at a decisive end, since, although what was and is at issue was restated in philosophically more sophisticated and illuminating terms, no progress was made in resolving the basic disagreement. Everyone was given sufficient reason to refine their point of view. No one was given sufficient reason to change it.[12] Moreover, if we were to consider those other issues on which expressivists and their critics disagree, we would find that there is a story of the same kind to be told, a story of apparently ineliminable disagreement. We are entitled to conclude not only that no decisive argument, or at least no argument that an honest and philosophically sophisticated expressivist would find decisive, has as yet been mounted against expressivism, but also that there is little or no prospect of such an argument being mounted. So let us consider the expressivist case – from now on using the adjective 'emotivist' to characterize only the views of Stevenson and such immediate predecessors and contemporaries of his as A. J. Ayer – in further detail. What account have expressivists provided of good and 'good'?

Alan Gibbard has written that "Good things are desirable, and the better of two things is the one that is preferable."[13] Gibbard goes on, "the

---

[10] Peter Geach, "Assertion," *Philosophical Review* 74, 4 (1965): 449–465.

[11] Simon Blackburn, *Spreading the Word*, Oxford University Press, 1985, chapter 6, section 2.

[12] Essential reading is Mark Schroeder, *Being For: Evaluating the Semantic Program of Expressivism*, Oxford University Press, 2010, and subsequent discussions of Schroeder's version of expressivism, most recently, as I write, John Skorupski, "The Frege–Geach Objection to Expressivism: Still Unanswered," *Analysis* 72, 1 (2012): 9–18; Mark Schroeder, "Skorupski on Being For," *Analysis* 72, 4 (2012): 735–739; and Skorupski's reply to Schroeder's reply, "Reply to Schroeder on Being For," *Analysis* 73, 3 (2013): 483–487. I have not found reason here to pursue issues raised by other versions of antirealism in ethics. Some of them are discussed in *Oxford Studies in Metaethics*, vol. 6, ed. Russ Shafer-Landau, Oxford University Press, 2011.

[13] Alan Gibbard, "Preference and Preferability," in *Preferences*, ed. Christoph Fehige and Ulla Wessels, Berlin: de Gruyter, 1998, p. 241.

preferable thing is the one that it would be rational to prefer," so that our preference is warranted. "To call a preference 'warranted' is to express one's acceptance of norms that say to have the preference."[14] And "Someone who calls something 'rational' is is therefore expressing his state of mind."[15] So, when I call something good or assert that it would be good if such and such were the case, I am not only expressing preferences but also giving expression to an attitude, to my allegiance to a set of norms, norms that I may well never have made explicit. In many cases those preferences and norms will be ones that I share with others.

Gibbard is careful to do justice to the impersonal character of our judgments about what is good or bad. We are not merely giving expression to our own individual preferences and normative commitments. Those preferences and commitments and the states of mind in virtue of which they are taken to be rational may vary a good deal from individual to individual, but "Goodness is what our rational aims have in common. Goodness, in other words, is what everyone has some reason to promote if he can, whatever other rational grounds for choice apply to him in particular."[16] It is unsurprising, then, that in our judgments both about what it is for jam or watches or weather to be good or bad, and about whether it would be good or bad for this or that individual to be or do or have such and such, we find so much agreement on what the relevant criteria are. That agreement, on Gibbard's view, must give expression to an underlying agreement in attitude on what it is rational to prefer, on the norms that each of us has accepted. But what then of the cases where there are disagreements of varying extents and kinds, disagreements such as those between Ferdinand and Isabella or Edward and Eleanor? These, it seems, on Gibbard's view, must express disagreements on the norms that govern our judgments about what is good, disagreements in some cases about what the criteria for judging something to be good are, in others about the weight to be given to different criteria.

There is of course an explanatory story to be told, on Gibbard's view a naturalistic story, about the biological evolution and history of our evaluative and normative development, a story part of which Gibbard has told elsewhere.[17] It is the story of how our need to secure the cooperation

[14] Ibid., p. 243.
[15] Alan Gibbard, "A Pragmatic Justification of Morality," in *Conversations on Ethics*, Conversations with Alex Voorheve, Oxford University Press, 2009, pp. 161–162.
[16] Gibbard, "Preference and Preferability," p. 255.
[17] See Alan Gibbard, *Wise Choices, Apt Feelings: A Theory of Normative Judgement*, Cambridge, MA: Harvard University Press, 1990.

of others has issued in a responsiveness to the preferences and norms of others, to a pressure toward consensus. But any credible account of this need, this responsiveness, and these pressures must of course leave open the possibility of that range of disagreements that actually occurs. When sharp and serious disagreement does occur, disagreements as to what reasons may relevantly be adduced in support of some disputed evaluative judgment or as to what weight is to be given to different types of reason, the limits to the possibilities of resolving those disagreements will be set, on Gibbards view, perhaps by differences in the preferences of the parties to the dispute, perhaps by differences in those norms, the acceptance of which governs each of the disputants' conceptions of what it is to be rational, perhaps by both. For there is no further type of consideration to which appeal could be made.

Gibbard is then, if I have understood him correctly, committed to holding that for each of us there are limits to rational justification, so far as our judgments about good and bad are concerned, limits set by whatever fundamental cast of mind and inclination it is that finds expression in our preferences, in the norms governing our judgments, and consequently in those judgments. Our practical reasoning and our reasoned appeals to others are what they are in virtue of our underlying psychological states being what they are, and the openness of others to our reasoned appeals is what it is in virtue of the underlying psychological states of those others being what they are. An analogous point is made by Blackburn in a very different context. Those engaged in moral reflection have sometimes understood themselves as having to choose between what passion and impulse bid them do and what reason requires. Romantic thinkers have warned us against allowing passion and impulse to be stifled by the deadening influence of a calculating rationality, while those influenced by Stoics or Kantians are apt to fear that we may be seduced from the path of reason by passion and desire. And plain persons, reflecting on their moral choices, may frame them in terms of this apparent opposition between reason and passion, reason and desire. But if expressivism is true, to think in these terms is misguided. So Blackburn has insisted that "if we pose practical problems in terms of 'what I would do if I were reasonable' or 'what the reasonable person would do', we should not think we have thereby got *beyond* the subjection of the will to desire and passion. 'Reasonable' here stands a label for an admired freedom from various traits – ignorance, incapacity to understand our situation, shortsightedness, lack of concern for the common point of view." Blackburn goes on to assert that the first person use of the expression 'what I would do if I were reasonable' "signals a consideration or set of considerations that only affect me because of a contingent profile of concerns or desires or passions."[18]

This last point is of some importance. Our evaluative and normative judgments provide us with motives for action. When we utter them to others, we hope and intend to move those others to act in accordance with those judgments. But, so the expressivist asserts, merely factual judgments can never so move us. If, on seeing someone else in distress, I act so as to relieve that distress, what moves me is not the mere fact of the distress, but my attitude toward that fact, my pity or my affection or my wish to be thought compassionate. From Hume to Blackburn and Gibbard, expressivists have argued that only an expressivist account of our evaluative and normative judgments enables us to understand how those judgments motivate.

When two people disagree about what it is or would be good for someone to be, do, or have, they are then, on an expressivist view, disagreeing in their – but what shall we call them – preferences, endorsements, attitudes of approval, concerns, desires, passions, or some combination of these? For the moment it does not greatly matter how we characterize the psychological stances involved, although later it may be important to ask some questions about them. Yet it matters at once, if we are to understand such disagreements, that, on an expressivist view, they are not disagreements concerning some matter of fact, concerning something independent of the psychological stances or states of those who find themselves in disagreement. The relevant contrast remains what it was from the outset in Stevenson's formulation of emotivism. It is with disagreements about everyday matters of fact or about natural science: "It did not snow here last year before New Year" and "You are mistaken. There was nearly an inch of snow in early December"; or "Chemical chain reactions always involve free radicals" and "No, there are some exceptions." In both types of case, one party to the dispute is in the right and the other not so, in virtue of how things were or are with the weather or chemical reactions. But on an expressivist view, whether framed in Stevenson's terms or Gibbard's or Blackburn's, nothing corresponds to this in evaluative disagreements.

"It is bad to hunt foxes and to allow the hunting of foxes" and "There is nothing bad about it and therefore nothing which would justify prohibiting it." Agreement both on the relevant facts about fox hunting and on which facts are the relevant facts is perfectly compatible with this evaluative disagreement. So what is someone claiming if she not only asserts her own

[18] Simon Blackburn, *Ruling Passions*, Oxford: Clarendon Press, 1998, p. 241.

point of view but insists that she is unqualifiedly in the right and that those who disagree with her are quite mistaken? She is asserting both that fox hunting is bad and that she can envisage no consideration that might lead her to alter her judgment. Indeed, were she to change her mind, she might say, she would be mistaken. For her attitude toward the badness of fox hunting is that the badness of fox hunting does not depend upon her or anyone else's attitude toward the badness of fox hunting. And of course those who disagree with her could say the same. Nonetheless their evaluative judgments are what they are, on this expressivist view, only because their attitudes and feelings are what they are.

Were either party instead to concede that they might be in error, this would be to say only that they can envisage some possibility that further consideration might lead to a change of attitude. In both cases each party would have to recognize, if sufficiently self-aware, that what they were doing in judging as they do was giving expression to their own often complex states of mind. And this is quite different from the condition of those voicing their judgments in controversy over everyday or scientific factual questions. On such questions we justify our judgments by appeal to an authoritative standard – that of conformity to how things are – that is external to and independent of everyone's and anyone's feelings, concerns, commitments, and attitudes.

By contrast, where normative or evaluative issues are in question there is, on any expressivist view, no such authoritative standard, external to and independent of an agent's feelings, concerns, commitments, and attitudes to which appeal may be made. Or rather, if an agent does appeal to some external standard, it is only in virtue of her or his endorsement of it that it has whatever authority it has for that particular agent. In this rejection of any standard external to and independent of agents' feelings, concerns, commitments, and attitudes by appeal to which their normative and evaluative judgments might be justified, expressivists have on occasion found common ground with at least one version of existentialism. So A. J. Ayer could say of Sartre that "It is one of Sartre's merits that he sees that no system of values can be binding on someone unless he chooses to make it so,"[19] that is, unless the agent endorses it.

That evaluative and normative disagreements are not resolvable in the way that everyday factual and scientific disagreements are may be taken by expressivists to strengthen the case for expressivism. For it is a recurrent experience in our culture, as we already noted in considering the examples

---

[19] A. J. Ayer, "Jean-Paul Sartre's Doctrine of Commitment," *The Listener*, November 30, 1950.

of Ferdinand and Isobella and of Edward and Eleanor, to find ourselves in evaluative or normative disagreement with others, where disagreement is not to be resolved by any rehearsal of what both we and they take to be the relevant facts, since about these, it turns out, we agree. But such unresolvable disagreements are only to be expected, if expressivism is true. Moreover, as I remarked earlier, on those issues concerning expressivism which have elicited most philosophical debate, expressivists have been given no decisive reason – decisive from their point of view, that is – to change their minds. Do *we* then perhaps have sufficient reason to assent to expressivism? To answer 'Yes' would be premature. For we cannot say how good or bad the case for expressivism is, until and unless we have compared that case in some detail with the case in favor of alternative and incompatible philosophical accounts of good and 'good'. To the task of outlining one such account I now turn.

1.4   'Good' and goods understood in terms of human flourishing: enter Aristotle

The concept central to this rival and alternative account is that of human flourishing. Those who study the behavior of a variety of nonhuman animal species distinguish uncontroversially between individuals and groups of a given species that are flourishing and individuals and groups that are not, among them wolves and wolf packs, dolphins and herds of dolphins, gorillas and troops of gorillas. For the members of such nonhuman animal species, their flourishing requires some particular type of environment in which they can move in good health through the stages of a determinate life cycle, developing and exercising their specific powers, learning what they need to learn, protecting and bringing up their young, achieving the ends to which they are by their biological nature directed. Disease, injury, predators, including human predators, and shortages of needed food or water are bad for such animals. Their impact is to produce animals unable to develop and exercise their specific powers, animals who fail to learn, and who may as a result be bad at hunting or foraging, bad at bringing up their young. Note the indispensability of the words 'good' and 'bad' and of cognate terms in characterizing animals in this way. Note also that what it is good or bad for this particular individual or group to be, do, or have depends upon what species it is to which they belong. What is good for the members of one species – say, foxes – may be bad for the members of another – say, rabbits. Note thirdly that when we say of this wolf or wolf pack, this dolphin or herd of dolphins, that they are doing well or badly in this particular environment, our judgment is not expressive of our feelings, attitudes, or other psychological states. Its truth or falsity is determined by appeal to standards that are independent of the observer.

Just as wolves, dolphins, gorillas, foxes, and rabbits flourish or fail to flourish, so, on this rival account of 'good' and good, it is too with human animals. About human individuals and groups we may say, just as we do of members of other species, that it is or would be good or bad if they are, do, or have such and such, meaning by this that such and such conduces to their flourishing or failing to flourish qua human beings. And among such individuals and groups are of course ourselves. So, on this view, when we compare future courses of action or states of affairs as better or worse, our standard is that of how far and in what ways each will contribute to or frustrate our human flourishing. Our everyday judgments about the good and the bad, the better and the worse, at least when our evaluative language is in good order, presuppose some perhaps inchoate view of what it is that human flourishing consists in, even though it may be one that we ourselves have never spelled out. Disagreements with others on particular occasions about how it would be best to act may give expression either to disagreements about what human flourishing is in general or to disagreements about what conduces to human flourishing in this particular set of circumstances. (What do I mean when I speak of our evaluative language being in good order? That will have to emerge later.)

As with judgments about the flourishing or the failure to flourish of members of other animal species, the contrast with expressivism is obvious. Judgments about what it is good or best for me, you, or us to be, do, or have are not taken to be expressive of my, your, or our psychological states. And disagreements about what it is good or best to be, do, or have are to be settled by appeal to a standard that is independent of the feelings, concerns, commitments, and attitudes of those individuals who happen to be in contention. At once an objection will come to mind. "Is it not notorious," someone will say, "that people are often unable to resolve their disagreements about what it is to flourish as a human being? Disagreements about matters where there are genuinely independent standards of truth or falsity about, say, the weather or chemical reactions, are always resolvable. So how can they be disagreements of the same kind?" The question is very much to the point, but it poses an objection to a position that has not as yet been sketched even in outline. So for now let me remark only that, on the view that I have begun to outline, rational enquiry into and consequent disagreement about what human flourishing consists in in this or that set of circumstances is itself one of the marks of human flourishing. I postpone further consideration of possible replies to this objection, but I do need at once to say something more about the analogy between human flourishing and the flourishing of some types of nonhuman animal. Begin by considering some key differences.

For nonhuman animals their environment, whatever it is, is given. To flourish is to flourish within this or that particular environment. It is to have adapted successfully to it. Members of some species migrate seasonally from environment to environment. Members of many species interact with their environment so as to change it in this or that respect. But human beings are unique in the extent to which they have from time to time transformed environments drastically, adapting them to their needs, reshaping landscapes, harnessing and redirecting natural powers so that they serve human purposes, often with large unintended effects. In the course of changing nature, they changed themselves so that in the course of their life cycle they developed a greater range of powers than does any other animal, many of them unique to human beings. Most notable is the power of language use, a power without which their other distinctive powers could not be what they are. Four aspects of human language are crucial.

The first is its syntactic structure. It is only because sentences can be embedded within other sentences that we can ask and answer questions about the truth of our assertions, the validity of our inferences, and the justifiability of our conclusions. "Do I have reason to believe that what I saw was my father's ghost?" "Is it true that, if this well has dried up, there is no other source of water?" It is in and through asking and answering such questions that we become reflective. A second crucial aspect of language use is its enhancement of our powers of communication. We are able to formulate complex and detailed intentions, to communicate them to others, to understand their complex and detailed responses, and to respond to those responses in ways that are impossible for species without language. This makes possible kinds of cooperation and forms of association that are distinctively human. We identify not only individual but also common goods. Thirdly we are able, only because we possess languages with tenses and logical connectives of various kinds, to envisage alternative futures, long term and short term, and to set ourselves individual and shared goals that take time to accomplish. We form expectations of each other and of ourselves, and we are pleased or disappointed by how things turn out. And fourthly these same linguistic resources enable us to tell each other stories about our projects, our heroic enterprises and our tragic failures, stories that we narrate, stories that we enact, stories that we sing, stories from which we learn.

The counterpart to our possession of these capacities is the possibility for things to go wrong with our lives in a range of ways in which they cannot go wrong for nonhuman animals. We are apt to make false judgments and invalid inferences, we too often misunderstand each other and deceive each other, our thinking about the future is often wishful or fearful thinking, our stories can be distortions of and distractions from reality. It is our nature as rational animals to try to understand, but we are apt to misunderstand ourselves as well as others, and this misunderstanding sometimes extends to our and their shared uses of language. A great deal turns then on yet another distinctively human power, the ability to identify our mistakes and to learn from them. It is a notable fact about all these powers that they can be and have been developed in indefinitely many different ways – hence, the multiplicity of human cultures, each with its own way of educating its young and of understanding the human condition. Think only of the differences between ancient Sparta, ancient Corinth, and ancient Athens: a military, gymnastic, and laconic culture, a commercial and aesthetic culture, and a naval, rhetorical, theatrical, and democratic culture. Each of these rival and incompatible cultures embodied and gave its allegiance to a distinctive conception of human flourishing, expressed in its evaluative judgments.

Go further afield to, say, medieval Persia, or the Tang dynasty in China, or Mayan culture at its highest point, and it is at once evident that there are inconveniently many incompatible and rival ways in which human flourishing has been and is conceived. It may seem obvious, therefore, that there is little or no analogy between the way in which we think about the flourishing of nonhuman animals and the way in which we think about human flourishing. Human observers have little difficulty in agreeing about what it is for wolves, dolphins, and gorillas to flourish, while the prospects for arriving at agreement on what human flourishing is may seem slender, if only because it must seem that what each of us take the flourishing of human beings to consist in cannot but depend largely on what culture it is that we happen to inhabit and on what set of evaluative resources have been provided by that culture. But in fact these considerations suggest a line of thought that make an account of good and 'good' that understands them in terms of conceptions of human flourishing more rather than less credible.

First, the range of disagreements between and within cultures as to what human flourishing is is well matched by the disagreements between and within cultures as to what is to be judged good and bad, as to how goods are to be rank ordered and, more generally, as to how 'good' is to be used. And this is what we should expect, if this kind of account of good and 'good' is true. Secondly, in most cultures, perhaps in all, it is taken for granted that human flourishing is what it is taken to be in that particular culture. "In Java . . . the people quite flatly say, 'To be human is to be Javanese,'" reported Clifford Geertz, noting also that "small children, boors, simpletons, the insane, the flagrantly immoral" – that is, those who are not flourishing qua human beings – are said by the Javanese to be "not yet Javanese."[20] So in each culture, whether Javanese or that of Periclean Athens or that of NeoConfucian Imperial China, evaluative judgments express rival claims about a single subject matter, namely what it is for distinctively human powers to be exercised effectively and distinctively human ends to be achieved.

The problem is then to identify a measure for deciding between those rival claims. Is it possible for each of us to stand back from the view of human flourishing embodied in and presupposed by our own culture so that we become able to contrast that view and the rival views of other cultures with the realities of human flourishing? Enter Aristotle. It is perhaps because Aristotle's beliefs and attitudes were in so many respects, some of them highly regrettable, so characteristic of the educated Greeks of his time that we fail to emphasize sufficiently how much his conception of human flourishing put him at odds with most of his Greek contemporaries. Aristotle had drawn upon resources afforded by his culture to move beyond it, to stand back from it, and to judge its practices and institutions by standards that he was able to present as deserving the allegiance of any adequately rational enquirer. This is what made possible Aristotle's vigorous critiques of Athens, Corinth, and Sparta as inadequate political societies and his insistence that nonetheless it is only in and through the type of political society exemplified by the *polis* that human beings can flourish, an insistence that put him at odds with the Macedonian elite. What then was his core conception of human flourishing?

It has four components. First, Aristotle recognized the full range of human powers, physical, perceptual, emotional, rational, political, moral, and aesthetic. Secondly, he identified as the distinctively human powers those that I identified as powers made possible by the possession of language, notably those powers of practically and theoretically rational agents that enable us not only to reflect on what we are doing and saying

---

[20] Clifford Geertz, *New Views of the Nature of Man*, ed. John R. Platt, University of Chicago Press, 1965, p. 116.

or are about to do or to say but also to redirect our activities and our enquiries as reason prescribes. Thirdly, there are too those distinctively human abilities, the exercise of which also requires language, that enable us to associate cooperatively with others in ways not open to nonhuman animals. Human beings are by their nature both rational and political animals, and they achieve rational agency in and through their political relationships. Fourthly, our nature is such that we find ourselves directed by our upbringing, if we have been adequately educated, toward ends that we take to be goods and we have some conception, even if initially inchoate, of what it would be for someone to achieve those ends in such a way that their life would be a perfected human life, that they might justly be called *eudaimōn*.

Aristotle needs to call upon all four of these aspects of human activity, if he is to explain what it is for a human agent to flourish, to function well. For his core thought is that to flourish is to function well. Machines function well or badly. Nonhuman animals function well or badly. And, as with machines and wolves, dolphins, and gorillas, so too is it with human agents and human societies. They too function well or badly. Once again a contrast with expressivism is clear. Whether a machine, given the kind of machine that it is, functions well or badly is a matter of fact. To judge that some machine is functioning well or badly is to evaluate it and its performances, but it is not to express an attitude toward it, let alone an attitude of approval or disapproval. I may indeed, if a Luddite, have negative feelings about some well-functioning machines, but my judgment that they are functioning well is true or false, depending only on what the facts are about these particular machines. It is not in any way expressive. As with judgments about the functioning of machines, so too is it with judgments about the functioning of wolves, dolphins, and gorillas and with judgments about the functioning of particular human agents. They too are both factual and evaluative, but not expressive. They too are true or false, depending only on what the relevant facts are about those particular human agents, although, as we have noticed, the relevant facts about human agents are a good deal more complex than the relevant facts about nonhuman animals. And on the account of 'good' and good that I am now outlining, if someone judges that it would be good for some particular individual or group to be, do, or have this or that, they are judging that for them to do, be or have this or that would contribute to human flourishing. But at this point someone may protest: Are you suggesting, they may ask, or rather are the protagonists of the view that you are sketching suggesting that when we plain speakers of English or Irish or Mandarin or whatever make our everyday judgments about what it would be good to do next

Sunday or about how badly the neighbors are behaving or about what policies it would be best for the city council to implement, we are all of us speaking as covert Aristotelians? Is this not plainly preposterous? Perhaps not.

Aristotle's own claim was that in his politics and ethics he had made explicit and articulated the standards presupposed by the judgments and actions of those human beings in his own culture who themselves, as rational agents, exemplified human flourishing and in so doing had provided the grounds for an explanation of why many human beings do not flourish and why therefore there is a range of diverse and incompatible judgments about what is good and how it is good to live. My claim is that in many other cultures too the inchoate conception of human flourishing presupposed by the judgments and actions of plain persons is in important respects Aristotelian and that, when this is not so, it is because and insofar as those agents misconceive human flourishing and fail to flourish, a strong claim that may seem less preposterous once we recognize the large variety of ways in which, on a NeoAristotelian view, human beings may act well and live well.

Begin with an Aristotelian formula. Those who are or are on the way to becoming flourishing human beings have those qualities of mind and character that enable them, in the company of others and through their relationships with others, to develop their powers, so that they achieve those goods that complete and perfect their lives. What any such formula obscures is how very different in different circumstances within different cultural and social orders the lives which exemplify it must be and are. What it was to flourish qua human being was one thing for an Athenian contemporary of Aristotle, quite another for a medieval Irish farmer or an eighteenth-century Japanese merchant or a nineteenth-century English trade union organizer. And for us too, within one and the same culture, there are different ways of flourishing, given our differing abilities and circumstances. This variety of ways of flourishing Aristotle himself did not always recognize, but it is crucial for the NeoAristotelian account of 'good' and good that I am sketching that there are numerous ways in which human beings can flourish, although even more in which they can fail to flourish. So in different times and places, what is in fact the same underlying view of human flourishing may be expressed in very different and even apparently incompatible judgments about what it is good for these particular agents in these particular circumstances to be, do, and have.

Unsurprisingly, then, what it is to flourish in this or that set of particular circumstances has to be discovered and often enough rediscovered. Such discovery and rediscovery are commonly the outcome of disagreement and debate, sometimes in everyday circumstances by plain persons arguing together about what to do next for their common good, sometimes by theorists reflecting on the practical questioning of those plain persons. It is therefore equally unsurprising that from time to time disagreements about what it is to flourish multiply, and the occurrence of such disagreements provides no sort of reason for rejecting the NeoAristotelian account of human flourishing.

When I call this account NeoAristotelian, the force of the 'Neo' is intended to be this. Aristotle has had and has commentators and interpreters who disagree widely about how the relevant texts are to be construed. Into these disputes I shall not enter. The views that I am advancing I do indeed take to be derived from Aristotle's, but what matters most are the views. It matters a good deal less whether or not they are Aristotle's. Moreover, as will become evident later, they are views to the development of which a number of Aristotle's Islamic, Jewish, and Christian interpreters have notably contributed, most of all Aquinas. Yet if I were at this point to call those views Thomistic, I would find myself engaged in unnecessary controversy with rival interpreters of Aquinas. So I stay for the moment with the clumsy label 'NeoAristotelian'.

Note that this NeoAristotelian account of what we are saying and doing when we make evaluative judgments, like its expressivist rival and counterpart, does not explain 'good' and good by translating 'good' into other terms. Neither account is reductionist. The protagonists of both take it for granted that they are addressing an audience who already have at the level of ordinary language use an excellent grasp of the meaning of 'good' and who make many unhesitating judgments about goods. The members of that audience understand that 'good' is very often replaceable without change of meaning by 'desirable' or by 'choiceworthy', and they make and criticize inferences from premises containing those words. They know how to translate them into other languages. Indeed, were all this not so, they would not be able to understand the claims advanced by either expressivists or NeoAristotelian theorists. But, once they have understood those claims, it is clear to them that they are confronted by rival and incompatible accounts of what they are saying and doing in their uses of 'good' and their judgments about goods. Why should this matter to them? It should matter for a number of reasons.

1.5 What is at odds between expressivists and NeoAristotelians

If the NeoAristotelians are right, then there is a truth waiting to be discovered both about how it is good and best to act on particular occasions and about how in general it is good and best to live out our lives. When we are puzzled about how to make major decisions or when we look back with regret on our past choices, we will on the NeoAristotelian view do well not just to embark on an enquiry into those particular judgments or misjudgments, but to consider whether it may not be best to conceive of our lives as extended enquiries into how it is best to live. For if we have been or are mistaken, there is a fact of the matter about which we have been or are mistaken. By contrast on an expressivist view there is no such truth waiting to be discovered, and when we find ourselves puzzled or regretful, what we need to ask is how far and in what ways we need to reconsider and reorder our attitudes or commitments. We can bring out the nature of this contrast a little further by returning to questions that have been central to our enquiries.

Suppose that someone, a plain unphilosophical person, desires something very much but judges after prolonged consideration that she has no good reason to desire it and moreover that she has excellent reason for desiring to act in ways that would make it impossible for her to satisfy her still ardent desire. She finds herself in acute conflict and she asks herself the questions: How should I weigh my heartfelt desire against my good reasons for acting in ways that will frustrate my desire? Should I as an agent identify with my desire or with my reasons and my reasoning? If philosophers were to convince her of the truth of expressivism, it would at once occur to her that her conflict is between one part of her self and another. Her evaluative reasoning issues from and is shaped by that prerational commitment or attitude or set of feelings which finds expression in her evaluative and normative judgments. Her desires are those drives and longings within her of which she is presently aware. So now she will ask: What reasons might I have for siding with one of these parts rather than the other?

Either of two lines of thought might then occur to her. The first would begin from her noticing how little expressivists have told us about the precise psychological character of the attitudes, feelings, commitments, and endorsements which on their view find expression in evaluative and normative judgments. She might therefore open up a psychological enquiry and if, for example, she became convinced by some version of Freud's thesis that what we take to be the promptings of the norms of morality are no more than the disguised and unrecognized demands of the superego, the internalized imperatives of the paternal voice as once heard by the infant, she might well conclude that morality, as a set of constraints upon desire, was thereby discredited.

A second line of thought might begin from her noting the emphasis that Gibbard – and not only he – places upon the extent to which, on an expressivist view, our evaluative and normative attitudes have been influenced by and become what they are because of our and our ancestors' interactions with others. She has already noted in herself and is uncomfortable with what she suspects to be a disposition to be too deferential to others. At this point the author whom she comes across is not Freud, but Nietzsche, whose genealogical explanation of how she comes to have her present evaluative and normative attitudes she finds persuasive and takes to be true. She concludes that the evaluative and normative beliefs and attitudes that she has hitherto treated with great seriousness have been imposed upon her and that she herself has colluded in this imposition. She understands herself as having been the victim of a herd mentality, and she must now acknowledge in herself and in others those expressions of the will to power that she has hitherto misinterpreted. So she might now conclude, although on somewhat different grounds, that morality has been discredited.

The point that I am making here is not advanced as a hostile criticism of expressivism. What I am identifying is not a mistake, but a lacuna. Anyone who understands a conflict between what she or he in fact desires and what she or he has good reason to desire as a conflict between two parts of her or himself will be able to resolve that conflict rationally, only if she or he has a much richer understanding of the psychology of morality than any expressivist has so far provided. Freud and Nietzsche both claim to provide just such an understanding. Critics of Freud and Nietzsche have argued that their claims are unjustified. What should matter to expressivists is that, unless and until they provide an account of the moral agent's psychology which enables them, among other things, to reckon with Freud and Nietzsche, their theory is radically incomplete. And its incompleteness becomes not just theoretically, but practically important when agents find themselves in the kind of conflict that I have described.

The NeoAristotelian account, as I have so far characterized it, is incomplete in another way. Imagine once again the state of mind of someone who strongly desires something that, so she judges, she has excellent reason not to desire. In this case, however, she understands her conflict in NeoAristotelian terms and, understanding it in this way, she has already implicitly rejected either Freud's or Nietzsche's account of the origin and nature of her moral judgments. Were she to become convinced of the truth of either account, she would thereby cease to be an Aristotelian, Neo- or otherwise. So let us also suppose – for the moment at least, since we shall have to return to this issue – that she has not become thus convinced. How then

is she to understand her predicament? Her strong desire, even though it is
one that she has very good reasons not to satisfy or even pursue, will, unless
it is the kind of neurotic desire that I identified earlier, be a desire for some
good. Her predicament is one of desiring a lesser and inappropriate good
over a greater and appropriate good. So, as a NeoAristotelian, she cannot
but conclude that her desires are misdirected and in need of transformation. She has every *reason* to redirect them. But what *motive* might she
have? It is the NeoAristotelian view that, as a rational agent, she desires to
act as practical reason dictates and desires to desire only what she has good
reason to desire. That is, as a rational agent she rank orders goods and has a
higher order desire not to prefer the lesser to the greater good in particular
situations. Yet as an imperfectly rational agent she may find herself drawn
in more than one direction, and she will need to draw upon the resources
provided by her earlier moral training and education and by her present
social relationships if she is to act rightly. Aristotle provided an outline
account of her situation, partly in what he said about *akrasia* (sometimes,
but not well translated as 'weakness of will') and partly elsewhere. Later
Aristotelians, most notably Aquinas, have provided further resources, but
the NeoAristotelian account of such conflicts needs further development
and rendering into contemporary terms. Until these have been provided,
there is a psychological lacuna in NeoAristotelian theory, just as there is in
expressivist. And, as with expressivism, I see no reason to believe that what
is needed cannot be provided.

   We have then before us two rival and incompatible theories concerning
how we are to understand 'good' and good, each of them a theory that has
developed through a considerable period of time and each open to and in
need of further development. Each draws upon the insights and arguments
of an undeniably great philosopher, in the one case Hume, in the other
Aristotle. How then should we decide between them? To the posing of
this question there may well be a dismissive reaction by philosophically
well-informed readers. Why, they will object, should we be asked to decide
between *them*? After all the vast majority of contemporary academic moral
philosophers reject both, finding neither acceptable as a metaethical theory,
that is, a theory of the meaning and reference of the key expressions in our
evaluative and normative discourse, and finding no merit in the distinctive
evaluative and normative claims of NeoAristotelianism. Should this give
us pause?

   Certainly, by proceeding as I have done and shall continue to do, I am
committed to holding that academic moral philosophy at some point in
its past history took a wrong turning, marched off in the wrong direction,

set itself the task, if I may borrow a metaphor, of climbing the wrong mountain. I therefore must at some point explain and justify these large claims. But, so I shall be arguing, a necessary condition for doing this is first to understand what is at stake in deciding between the rival theses and arguments of expressivism and NeoAristotelianism. It is, however, relevant to note one striking feature of contemporary philosophy. In the course of discussing one standard criticism of expressivism, I remarked earlier that the outcome of extended debate between critics and defenders of expressivism, while it had resulted in subtler and more sophisticated statements of their disagreement, had done nothing to resolve it. But the same holds of every major disagreement in contemporary moral philosophy, whether in metaethics or normative ethics, and it holds too in a number of other areas of philosophical enquiry. Protagonists of each standpoint take themselves to have conclusive objections to every rival point of view, but deny that this is true of the protagonists of rival standpoints. And those who take themselves to have successfully resolved one or more of these disagreements find themselves embroiled in new disagreements as to whether or not they have in fact succeeded. So we can perhaps for the moment say only this, that those who are convinced of the truth of expressivism or NeoAristotelianism have as yet been given no sufficient reason to think otherwise. Yet this only makes it more pressing to decide on how the issues that divide them are to be resolved.

What is at issue is the nature or the relationship between our judgments on particular occasions about what it is good or best to be, do, or have, the attitudes or feelings expressed in those judgments, and the desires, including the higher order desires, that prompt us to act so as to satisfy them on those same occasions. One good place to begin further enquiry is with the history of those relationships in each of our lives, a history that begins in early childhood. So I return to a subject matter that I touched on briefly at the outset, the desires and frustrations of early childhood, but now with a very different set of questions.

1.6 Two rival characterizations of moral development

The thinker from whom we need first and most to learn is D. W. Winnicott, whose psychoanalytically informed advice to new mothers, in England during and after the World War II, is relevant to our present enquiry in two ways. One of Winnicott's aims was to rescue those mothers from anxiety-engendering attempts to become perfect mothers, so becoming less good mothers than they would otherwise have been. What they should aim at instead was to become good-enough mothers. The good-enough mother does what she takes to be best for the infant, knowing that, like every mother, she will act imperfectly. So we can ask what a mother has to do to be good-enough, what is meant by saying that what she does is good or best for the infant, and what the relationship between goods and desires is in each case. But first we must consider just what Winnicott told those mothers and what he tells us.

The good-enough mother has to steer a course between being overprotective of her child and thus affording her child insufficient security and being overindulgent to her child and so being too severe.[21] The infant who is not allowed sufficient freedom to explore the realities that confront her or him will be apt later to have an insufficient ability to imagine alternative possibilities. The infant whose wishes are granted too often and too easily will be apt later to become a victim of her or his wishful thinking, someone who has not learned how to draw the line between phantasy and reality. Why are those outcomes bad for the child and for the adult whom the child becomes? Such adults will frame their choices badly, in the one case unimaginatively failing to recognize the full range of possibilities open to them, in the other failing to acknowledge the constraints that reality imposes. What the good-enough mother hopes and tries to bring up are children who have the traits that, when they become adults, will issue in better choices. She functions well as a mother by enabling them to function well in their choice making. 'Good' in 'good mother' then is, so it seems, the same use of 'good' as in 'good farmer' or 'good machine' and a key mark of goodness in all three cases is that others who depend on mothers, farmers, or machines for their own functioning well, their own flourishing, are provided with what they need to flourish. So far at least the uses of 'good' are just what a NeoAristotelian would take them to be. But things are not quite as straightforward as this.

It matters that the good-enough mother wants to be a good mother and that she wants this because she wants the good of her child. Her uses of 'good', whatever else they are, are expressive of those desires and of her consequent approvals and disapprovals. And when others praise her as a good mother, they endorse those approvals and disapprovals. Our account of these uses of 'good' would therefore be misleadingly incomplete if we did not recognize the expressive aspect of these uses and their relationship to the desires that motivate and find expression in these uses. How then

---

[21] See D. W. Winnicott, *The Child, the Family and the Outside World*, Reading, MA: Addison Wesley, 1987, especially chapter 10, and Adam Phillips, *Winnicot*, Cambridge, MA: Harvard University Press, 1988, chapter 3, III.

should we understand the relationship between what is NeoAristotelian and what is expressivist in this family of uses of 'good'?

Begin with the obvious. 'Good' belongs to our practical vocabulary, and it has the place that it has in that vocabulary in part because, as we already have had occasion to emphasize, it is a recurrent feature of our human condition that we are involved in conflicts of desire, in situations in which our desires point us in too many and incompatible directions. If we were not practical reasoners, those conflicts would be resolved by the relative strengths of the warring desires, the relative attractions of the competing objects of desire. We become practical reasoners by learning how to use 'good' and its cognates in judgments that provide us with reasons for treating one object of desire as better than its rivals, and so with arguments whose conclusion is that it is or would be best if we were to be, do, or have such and such. But this transformation requires another transformation. For learning how to use good in this reason giving and argumentative way would be pointless if we did not also become motivated so that we act as the conclusions of our practical reasoning require, or rather, as Aristotle puts it, so that the conclusions of our practical reasoning *are* our actions.

We have to become, that is, agents who desire to act as reason directs, who desire to act for the sake of the good and the best, and who have a second order desire that this desire for the good and the best is a desire that we will satisfy. It is the central characteristic of human beings that they are born with the potentiality of becoming reasoning and desiring animals of this kind. And one reason that we have for gratitude to so many child psychologists and paediatricians, including such psychoanalysts as Winnicott, is that they have done so much to identify and provide the means for overcoming the obstacles to the actualization of this potentiality under the conditions of modernity. The philosophical task is to chart the different relationships that may hold between reasoning and desiring in the course of those transformations and so to throw light on how 'good' is being used, whether by mother, by child, or by psychological observer. In order to do this we need to think further about two aspects of the child's development.

As infants are transformed into children, they learn to distinguish between, on the one hand, goods and, on the other, objects of desire. "Don't eat, take, do that!" says the parent. "But I want it!" replies the child. "It will be bad for you," says the parent. Or perhaps what the parent says is "Don't eat, take, do that now. It will be better to leave it until later," to which the reply is "But I want it now!" Why should children do what their parents take to be good for them rather than what they want? Why should

a child defer the satisfaction of its wants because its parent takes it to be
better to do so? Initially, it can only be because the child desires the parent's
approval and fears its disapproval, a disapproval sometimes expressed in
punishment. But later the good-enough parent provides reasons for dis-
criminating between objects of desire and hopes that the child will come
to recognize these reasons as good reasons. How might a child do so?

One of the salient differences between young human beings and the
young of other species is that the former, unlike the latter, are at a certain
point treated as accountable for their actions. "What was/is the good of
doing that?" they are asked, not only by parents and by other adults but
also by their contemporaries, and this in a number of contexts. For as they
are initiated into a variety of practices at home, at school, in the workplace,
they learn to recognize goods internal to each practice, goods that they
and other participants can achieve only through the exercise of virtues and
skills.[22] If and when they fail in respect of these, they will commonly be
put to the question. So they find themselves having to give reasons for
their actions to others and on occasion having to advance arguments in
support of those reasons. They become rational agents when they first pose
such questions to themselves about their own failures and act upon the
answers. If they are so to act, they must of course be motivated by the
prospect of achieving those goods that have provided them with what they
take to be good reasons for acting. Their desires must to some large degree
direct them as their reasoning directs them. Insofar as this is so, they will
have begun to become accountable rational agents, accountable both to
themselves and to others.

To say this is at once to be reminded of Aristotle's characterization of
prohairesis, in Book VI of the *Nicomachean Ethics*, as desire informed by
reason or as reason informed by desire (1139b4–5). On Aristotle's account,
rational deliberation by agents who are rightly disposed by their virtues
issues in *prohairesis* – often, but misleadingly translated by 'choice' – which
in turn issues in action. *Prohairesis* is rational wanting and that idea, so
G. E. M. Anscombe suggested "should be explained in terms of what is
wanted being wanted qua conducive to or part of 'doing well,'" that is,
conducive to or part of human flourishing.[23] So this bare and skeletal
account of how the relationship between desires, feelings and attitudes,
and reason-supported judgments about what is good and desirable develops

---

[22] On the relation of virtues to practices, see Alasdair MacIntyre, *After Virtue*, 3rd edn., Notre Dame,
IN: University of Notre Dame Press, 2007, pp. 187–196.
[23] G. E. M. Anscombe, "Thought and Action in Aristotle," in *New Essays on Plato and Aristotle*, ed.
R. Bambrough, London: Routledge & Kegan Paul, 1965, p. 155.

from infancy through childhood toward adult life, an account that began from Winnicott's psychoanalytic insights, has at its outcome a portrait of the agent that is in key respects the same as Aristotle's. Does this mean that the NeoAristotelian understanding of the use and meaning of 'good' has thereby been vindicated? Not quite yet. For as any expressivist will remind us, we still have to determine how such apparently NeoAristotelian agents are using 'good', when they judge that it is good or best to be do or have such and such.

We have already taken notice of the range of disagreements both between particular agents about what it is best to be, do, or have on particular occasions and between cultures as to what it is for human beings to flourish. Whatever particular view of human flourishing is presupposed by or expressed in the actions of this individual or that set of individuals or in the prescriptions and actions of this or that culture is, so the expressivist will insist, the expression of a prerational endorsement of the evaluations and normative judgments that constitute a particular view of human flourishing and an implicit or explicit rejection of alternative and rival views. It is the voicing of whatever set of preferences or aversions has emerged from the individual's upbringing and in many cases of those preferences and aversions that are widely shared in that individual's culture. It could not be otherwise, so the expressivist will continue, since, contrary to the claims of the NeoAristotelian, there is no fact of the matter about human flourishing, independent of the various accounts of human flourishing that are in contention. And the expressivist, noting that many of our locutions about human flourishing do indeed suggest that there is such a fact of the matter, will once again find in Blackburn's quasirealism the resources for giving an expressivist account of those locutions.

To this we NeoAristotelians would do well to reply by cataloguing what we take to be the facts concerning human failures to flourish. There are failures resulting from malnutrition, injury, and ill health. There are failures of otherwise deprived and materially or culturally impoverished lives. There are failures that are a consequence of laziness or incompetence in an agent's preparing her or himself through self-discipline and the acquisition of skills for various types of rewarding activity. There are failures that result from an agent's sacrificing either the present to the future or the future to the present. There are failures that are due to an agent's inadequate relationships with others, so that there is a lack of badly needed cooperation and the agent does not learn from those others what it is of great importance for her or him to learn. And these are not all. Failures come in different sizes, some of them restricted to one particular area or aspect of an agent's activities, some affecting the agent's life as a whole, some minor and unimportant, some of great significance, some temporary and easily remediable, some more difficult to deal with or even irremediable. What they have in common, what makes them all cases of failure, is that the variety of causes that I have catalogued have in such cases prevented to some noteworthy degree an agent's realization of certain of her or his human potentialities, the development of some of her or his powers, and in consequence the achievement of some or good or goods of crucial importance for that particular agent's flourishing qua human being.

The causes of such failures are sometimes beyond an agent's control. But in other cases the failure is a matter either of agents acting against their own best judgment as to what they have good reason to desire and to do or of agents reasoning their way to false conclusions about what it is best for them to be, do, or have. In every case in which an agent survives a time of failure, what is crucial is whether or not that agent is able to learn from her or his experience. What then does such learning involve? In the former type of case, it involves an acknowledgment of the agent's deficiencies as a rational agent. In the latter type of case, it involves a recognition that either some particular judgment by the agent about what it was good and best for her or him to be, do, or have, or a series of such judgments – judgments as to how that agent should act, if her or his actions were to contribute to her or his flourishing qua human being – have been *falsified* by the outcome, so that certainly her or his conception of what it would be for her or him to flourish qua human being in her or his particular situation needs to be revised, and perhaps indeed her or his larger conception of human flourishing.

Failures then, on this NeoAristotelian view, are occasions for learning what is true and what is false, and a life in which an agent moves toward the achievement of her or his specific goods and good will characteristically be a life in which it is through constructive responses to failure that agents comes to understand what that good in fact is, an understanding commonly expressed at the level of everyday practice in particular judgments, in the directedness of desires, in intellectual and moral dispositions, and in actions, and sometimes, although much less often, as well-articulated theory. Such education in the practical life may then have as one of its outcomes a conception of the practical life as a life of enquiry whose evaluative conclusions at each stage of that life accord with or fail to accord with the facts concerning human flourishing, that is, are true or false, and this in a stronger sense than any that a quasirealist expressivist can admit.

To all this such an expresssivist has a simple and straightforward reply. It is that there can be nothing more to any declaration of either agreement or disagreement with this NeoAristotelian catalogue of alleged facts about moral failure than an act of endorsement, expressive of the particular speaker's attitudes, feelings, and commitments. For the NeoAristotelian's attempt to appeal to facts already presupposes the NeoAristotelian interpretation of those alleged facts and the NeoAristotelian's choice of a standpoint from which to interpret. What from the standpoint of the NeoAristotelian is argument and enquiry, from the standpoint of the expressivist is rhetoric. We have arrived at an argumentative impasse. Yet we have learned something. About expressivism in all its versions we can now remark that, although a metaethical rather than a first order moral theory, it is not in fact neutral between all rival first order substantive accounts of the life of practice, the moral life, since, if expressivism is true, then NeoAristotelianism is false. Expressivism is, however, compatible with and neutral between a range of other rival moral standpoints, something that becomes clear if we consider a number of different ways in which agents persuaded of the truth of expressivism might structure their practical reasoning, all of them ways that presuppose some version of the fact-value distinction, a distinction indispensable to any version of expressivism.[24]

1.7   Instructive conflicts between an agent's judgments and her desires: expressivists, Frankfurt, and Nietzsche

The extent and nature of the evaluative and normative commitments that, on an expressivist account, give expression to the attitudes and feelings of agents may vary a very good deal. They may issue in a set of utilitarian convictions or a rejection of utilitarianism. They may require that the agent gives her or his allegiance to some demanding conception of duty or to some well worked out doctrine of human rights or to a rejection of either or both of these. And we have some admirable examples of expressivist moral philosophers working their way argumentatively through alternative possibilities. So Simon Blackburn has argued that "we want our sensibilities

---

[24] That some version or other of a distinction between declarative sentences which somehow or other report or describe features of the external world and declarative sentences which afford expression to sentiments remains an ineliminable mark of expressivist theories is confirmed by the conclusion of Huw Price, "From Quasirealism to Global Expressivism – and Back Again?" in *Passions and Projections: Themes from the Philosophy of Simon Blackburn*, ed. R. Johnson and M. Smith, Oxford University Press, 2015, p. 151.

to be reliable and projectible (pulling in the direction of general rules) but also sensitive and flexible (pulling in the direction of emphasis on particular contexts). Quasi-realism, I would urge, is well placed to explain and to justify our tendency toward a mean here."[25] That is, our morality should be a judicious mix of some principles that we treat as genuinely general and universal with others about whose scope and content we are more cautious. And Blackburn appeals to a variety of reasons in arriving at this conclusion. What then is it, on an expressivist view, that determines what counts as a reason and what does not so count?

Gibbard, as we noticed while considering his account of 'good' and good in his essay "Preference and Preferability," has a straightforward answer to this question. "When a person calls something – call it R – a reason for doing X, he expresses his acceptance of norms that say to treat R as weighing in favor of doing X . . . To say that an act is rational is to say that it is supported by the preponderance of reasons."[26] Some set of norms, accepted by each agent, prescribes, that is, some rank ordering of goods and presumably also some procedure for on occasion reconsidering that rank ordering. But the acceptance of that particular set of norms is a prerational attitude or state of mind. And therefore on occasions when there is some large disagreement between what some agent, in accordance with the particular set of norms that she accepts, judges that it is good and best for her to be, do, or have and what that agent passionately and deeply desires, then she can have no further reason for identifying with her judgments rather than with her desires or vice versa. What is she to do in this predicament?

It is then that she may find further relevance in those questions posed by Freud and Nietzsche that, as I noted earlier, expressivism invites. However, while I then suggested only that expressivists had failed to pose and answer those questions, I now want to argue that Nietzsche, in particular the Nietzsche of *Beyond Good and Evil*, has arguments that, if treated with adequate seriousness, force on expressivists a significant reformulation and extension of expressivism. For what such an agent cannot avoid is a choice, an existential choice, between identifying either with that prerational attitude that finds expression in her normative and evaluative judgments or with her present passionate and deep desires. Nietzsche's invitation to such an agent is first to investigate the genealogy of her present normative and evaluative judgments and then to recognize, in the light of that genealogy, the discreditable nature of the hold that they have upon her. Where

---

[25] Blackburn, *Ruling Passions*, p. 308.   [26] Gibbard, *Wise Choices, Apt Feelings*, p. 163.

Gibbard and Blackburn speak neutrally of the influence of others upon the norms that govern our relationships to those others, Nietzsche takes those same norms to express past and present patterns of domination in which our role is either such that we share in the herdlike and resentful mentality of the vast majority or else such that we assert our independence as those who acknowledge no law but that of which we ourselves are the authors. A condition of such independence is a recognition of the various forms that the will to power can take, of the various masks that it wears, and such a recognition will discredit both the forms that past morality has taken and the forms that past moral philosophy has taken.

Morality has on this view been an oppressive expression of the *ressentiment* of the herd. As for moral philosophy – "May I be forgiven the discovery that all moral philosophy has hitherto been boring and a soporific,"[27] a complaint later to be echoed by Bernard Williams. Our deliverance from boredom is to come with Nietzsche's discovery that the philosopher who has traversed the history of past moral thought and practice, who has perhaps been "critic and sceptic and dogmatist and historian, and, in addition, poet and collector and traveler and reader of riddles and moralist and seer and free spirit and practically everything," that such a one now confronts a task which "demands something different – it demands that he *create values.*" Such philosophers have to become commanders and law-givers. "Their 'knowing' is *creating,* their creating is a law-giving, their will to truth is – *will to power.*"[28]

So our reflective agent will take from Nietzsche a set of questions about her past and present self, questions posed, if she is sensible, in a less inflated, less world historical style than Nietzsche's. Her dilemma, we recall, is whether to act as her judgments about how it is best to act dictate or as her strong desires dictate. How, she will now ask, did I come to have the judgments that I do? And how did I come to have the desires that I do? What makes them genuinely mine? Her answers will take the form of a genealogical narrative, and what is most important about that narrative is not only that it should be true but also that it should disclose what needs to be disclosed, if it is to be a source of relevant self-knowledge. What through that narrative she may become able to ask is whether and how far she identifies with her judgments, whether and how far she identifies with her desires. What she will be asking is what it is that she now most cares

---

[27] F. Nietzsche, *Beyond Good and Evil,* trans. R. J. Hollingdale, London: Penguin Books, 1973, 228, p. 138.

[28] Ibid., 211, p. 122.

about, including those attachments from her past which are still part of her present.

If this kind of reflective appraisal is successfully carried through, in what might it issue? Perhaps in a type of moral life in which the expressive commitments of the agent have been made explicit, so that they are not just expressed in but are evident to the agent in her or his first and higher order dispositions, feelings, reasonings, judgments, and actions. So what would it be to live reflectively in this way? This is a question that expressivists need to answer. Happily we already have an account of something very like this kind of life, that advanced by Harry Frankfurt, not as an account of one kind of life among others but as an account of what human life, if adequately understood, is. Frankfurt's starting point is close to my own, a conception of human agents as differing from animals of other species in our ability to stand back from our desires and other motives and to reflect upon whether or not we desire to be motivated as we presently are. (I referred earlier, in section 1.1, to the importance of Frankfurt's distinction between first and second order desires.) He notes that we identify with some of our desires and not with others, and we are, on Frankfurt's account, free agents just insofar as we are motivated by desires with which we identify and by which, therefore, we desire to be motivated. What we care about are the objects of those of our settled desires with which we identify.

The agent whom we imagined as successfully finding her way through her dilemma with the aid of Nietzsche would at once recognize in Frankfurt's account a description of her present condition, one in which she has identified with some of her desires and motivations and not with others, making it clear to herself in so doing what it is that she really cares about. "A person who cares about something is, as it were, invested in it. He identifies himself with what he cares about in the sense that he makes himself vulnerable to losses and susceptible to benefits, depending upon whether what he cares about is diminished or enhanced. Thus he concerns himself with what concerns it . . ."[29] What we care about is in part up to us, but in part not. "There are some things that we cannot help caring about" and "Among the things that we cannot help caring about are the things that we love."[30]

What we *should* care about depends entirely on what we do care about, since "it is only in virtue of what we actually care about that anything

[29] Frankfurt, *The Importance of What We Care About*, p. 83.
[30] Harry G. Frankfurt, *Taking Ourselves Seriously and Getting It Right*, Stanford, CA: Stanford University Press, 2006, p. 24.

is important to us."[31] "There can be no rationally warranted criteria for establishing anything as inherently important."[32] And so "our final ends are provided and legitimated by love."[33] Frankfurt, that is, takes a final end to be some strong affective commitment that provides a terminus for our practical reasoning but cannot itself be rationally justified.[34] Reasoning can play no part in determining our final ends, since "the lover does not depend for his loving upon reasons of any kind." Love "creates reasons."[35] What each of us treats as desirable, that is, is determined by what each of us desires. And what we desire, what we care about varies a good deal from individual to individual. It is not always the same as what we approve of.[36]

Because we are dependent on others, because we fear loneliness and being held to be of no account by others, we have a motive "to follow some general principles of good behavior which can reasonably be expected to lead to orderly, peaceful, and amicable relationships."[37] But considerations derived from such principles are only one set of considerations among others. So Frankfurt has said that he does not understand and that he sees no justification for the claim "that moral considerations are always overriding."[38] Whether they are or are not overriding for this particular individual in these particular circumstances will depend upon what that individual cares about and on her or his rank ordering of her or his cares and desires. Individuals will differ in the outcomes of their practical reasoning just as they do and because they do in their affective commitments.

Our imagined reflective expressivist will recognize that the account of practical reasoning advanced and implied by Frankfurt is in some respects different from the accounts proposed by either Blackburn or Gibbard. But my claim is not that Frankfurt is to be understood as one more expressivist moral philosopher, but rather that a reflective expressivist agent, responding to her discovery of a conflict between her evaluative judgments and her strongest desires and confronting Nietzsche's challenge to reexamine her fundamental attitudes, feelings, and other sources of motivation in the light of his type of genealogical account, might well arrive at a set of positions remarkably close to, perhaps even identical with, Frankfurt's. Frankfurt's kinship to some recent expressivists becomes clear when we consider his avowed need, like them, to dissociate himself from some

---

[31] Ibid., p. 20.　　[32] Ibid., p. 22.　　[33] Ibid., p. 26.

[34] Harry G. Frankfurt, *The Reasons of Love*, Princeton, NJ: Princeton University Press, 2004, p. 47.

[35] Frankfurt, *Taking Ourselves Seriously and Getting It Right*, p. 25.

[36] Harry G. Frankfurt, "The Necessity of Love," in *Conversations on Ethics*, Conversations with Alex Voorheve, Oxford University Press, p. 222.

[37] Ibid., p. 219.　　[38] Ibid., p. 220.

notorious aspects of Hume's original expressivism. On Hume's view our passions and, consequently, our preferences can be neither rational nor irrational, neither according with reason nor violating its canons, so that "'tis not contrary to reason to prefer the destruction of the whole world to the scratching of my finger."[39]

Since, according to Frankfurt, our preferences are determined by our final ends and reason can play no part in determining those ends, it might seem that Frankfurt would have to agree with Hume in this conclusion. But he does not. Frankfurt allows that this preference involves no purely logical mistake, but he asserts that of someone who chose to destroy the world rather than endure minor discomfort we, unlike Hume, would have to say that he "must be crazy" and that his choice is "*lunatic*" and "*inhuman.*" Frankfurt ascribes to such a one an irrationality that is not a cognitive defect, but "a defect of the will."[40] In what does such volitional irrationality consist? It is not just that the preferences of such an agent differ radically from ours. They are "incommensurate with ours."[41] We transgress the boundaries of formal reason, if we take some self-contradictory state of affairs to be possible. We transgress the boundaries of volitional rationality, if we do not find certain preferences and choices unthinkable. To be rational is not only to be careful in making judgments about matters of fact and in reasoning instrumentally. It is, according to Frankfurt, also to acknowledge constraints on our preferences and choices. Whence, on his view, do these constraints derive?

They are not and cannot be responses to some independent normative reality. "The standards of volitional rationality and of practical reason are grounded only in ourselves . . . only in what we cannot help caring about and cannot help considering important."[42] There are indeed norms of practical reason to which we cannot but assent. An example of such a norm is this: "the fact that an action would protect a person's life is universally acknowledged to be a reason for that person to perform the action,"[43] even though that person may have a better reason for doing something else. Why is this so?

"Our desire to live, and our readiness to invoke this desire as generating reasons for performing actions that contribute to that end, are not themselves based on reasons . . . They derive from and express the fact that, presumably as an outcome of natural selection, we love . . . living."[44] So it

[39] David Hume, *A Treatise of Human Nature*, ed. L. A. Selby-Bigge, Oxford University Press, 1888, ii, 3, 3, p. 416.
[40] Frankfurt, *Taking Ourselves Seriously and Getting It Right*, pp. 29–30.
[41] Ibid., p. 30.   [42] Ibid., p. 33.   [43] Ibid., p. 34.   [44] Ibid., p. 37.

is too with other reason-generating desires such as those that derive from our love of "being intact and healthy, being satisfied, and being in touch." Frankfurt concludes that these "fundamental necessities of the will" are not the outcome of social or cultural habit or of individual preferences. "They are solidly entrenched in our nature from the start."[45] How closely will our imagined postNietzschean reflective expressivist agree with Frankfurt in arriving at these conclusions?

She will have asked all the same first person questions that Frankfurt asks, but she will have her own first person answers about which of her desires it is with which *she* identifies, about what therefore *she* cares about and loves, about what therefore *she* should care about, and about what practical thoughts *she* takes to be unthinkable and what *she* discovers to be necessities of *her* will. It is from Nietzsche rather than Frankfurt that she will have learned the importance of the first person pronoun. Like both Nietzsche and Frankfurt, she will often say 'we' rather than 'I', but the import of her 'we' will be 'I and others who feel, reflect, and will as I do'. Her attitude to rival accounts of desire and of evaluative and normative judgment will be both Frankfurtian and Nietzschean in its modes of argument, Nietzschean in its scorn. What then are the answers that she will give to the questions that are central to our present enquiry?

She will understand both her own and others' uses of 'good' and its cognates in such assertions as "It is (or would be) best for me (or her, him, us, or them) in these particular circumstances to be, do, or have such and such" as expressive of her and their desires, especially of those desires with which she and they identify, and of what it is that she and they most care about. She will evaluate reasons for action as good reasons insofar as by acting on them she will attain the objects of such desires. Her ordering of reasons as better or worse will derive from her ordering of her desires, and it is by reference to those orderings that she will resolve conflicts, whether conflicts between desires or conflicts between judgments, as to how it would be best for her to act and strongly felt desires. Her practical reasoning will thus express this ordering of her desires and the coherence of her reasoning will be threatened only by incoherence in her desires. And since incoherence in one's reasoning is apt to be self-frustrating, she will value coherence in her desires and the kind of self-knowledge that is needed, if coherence is to be achieved.

That self-knowledge will take the form of a narrative, a history of her desires and judgments, which will begin with an account of the formation

[45] Ibid., p. 38.

and consequent content and ordering of her desires – and their expression in her normative and evaluative judgments – up to the point at which she became reflective about them. A second stage in her history will recount her discovery of Nietzsche's critique of evaluative and normative judgments and of desires, and her reinterpretation of her past and present self in the light afforded by that discovery, while the third stage will concern the disciplined remaking of herself into the kind of self-aware agent that she has now become. When she explains herself, whether to others or to herself, her basic appeal will therefore be to an account of the motivations of herself and others grounded in a more general account of human nature. She will, insofar as she follows Nietzsche, interpret antiexpressivist views as expressions of an inability or a lack of will on the part of those who hold them to admit to the underlying motivation of their judgments and actions, an inability to recognize who and what they are.

What those who hold antiexpressivist views cannot or will not acknowledge, on her view, is the imposition upon them, an imposition in which they cooperate, of constraints upon their thoughts and feelings which masquerade as constraints of reason. The history of these masquerades and disguises, these misrepresentations of reason, is the history of much philosophy and theology, including Aristotelianism in all its various forms. Nietzsche says little about Aristotelianism, yet enough to make it clear that, on his view, to be an Aristotelian is to be a doubly defective human being, one who both suffers from "that depression of the emotions to a harmless mean at which they may be satisfied, the Aristotelianism of morals"[46] and is a victim of "the discipline thinkers imposed on themselves to think . . . under Aristotelian presuppositions," a discipline that Nietzsche classifies with other medieval habits of mind as arbitrary and antirational, belonging to a "protracted unfreedom of spirit,"[47] one that issues in conformist and sterile habits of mind and spirit.

There is thus a double case to be made out against any NeoAristotelian point of view. Expressivists charge that it fails to recognize the truth in expressivism concerning the meaning and use of normative and evaluative sentences and the nature of moral judgment. It fails as a metaethical theory. Nietzscheans charge that it presents what is not just a false account of human flourishing, a series of philosophical mistakes, but mistakes that express both an inability and a refusal to recognize the realities of the human condition. For the expressivist NeoAristotelianism is false. For the Nietzschean it is corrupting.

---

[46] Nietzsche, *Beyond Good and Evil*, p. 198.   [47] Ibid., p. 188.

1.8   The NeoAristotelian conception of the rational agent

In the discussion of expressivism, I moved from an initial consideration of expressivism as a metaethical theory about the meaning of evaluative and normative expressions to an enquiry into what kind of evaluative and normative commitments might issue from a reflective search for practical self-knowledge by someone persuaded of the truth of expressivism. Where NeoAristotelianism is concerned, this double aspect of the theory, its combination of metaethical claims and closely related evaluative and normative claims, has been evident from the beginning. If what we mean when we say that it would be best to do such and such is that by so acting we will contribute more to human flourishing, both our own and that of others, than we would by any other course of action open to us, then we only, it seems, have to spell out what, on our view, human flourishing consists in, to identify our evaluative and normative commitments. The joke is in the word 'only'. For on any Aristotelian view we can only understand adequately what it is for human beings to flourish by developing an account of the structures of human activity and of how our uses of 'good' and its cognates find application within and to those structures. Why so?

In section 1.6 of this chapter, we took note of how young children first learn from parents and other teachers to distinguish between what they want to be, do, or have and what, so they are told, it is good for them to be, do, or have. When they are given reasons for making this distinction, they begin to learn how to make it for themselves and to make it in what are, over the years, increasingly well-defined contexts of activity. What they want may often be at variance with how it is best for them to act, but, as we also noted in section 1.6, what they want generally includes their parents' and teachers' approval. Thus, they have to learn to value and to desire what is good just because it is good, and not because it is what others whom they want to impress take to be good. So how do they – how do we – learn to distinguish what is good from what is taken to be good?

We do so, as I also noticed earlier, in the context of a variety of practices, each with its own ends internal to it, generally first by learning how to contribute to the goods of the family and household in which we find ourselves and then learning how to do better or worse in the various activities of the school, the workplace, and the sports field, activities as different as solving equations, growing vegetables, mending broken machines, playing the clarinet, reading Greek poetry, drawing cartoons, making clay pots, playing soccer. If all goes well, we develop in each area those habits, those dispositions, without which we cannot exercise the moral virtues. We also develop a habit of good practical judgment, the moral and intellectual virtue of prudence. Both types of habituation involve a transformation of desires and an increasingly sophisticated grasp of those standards, initially accepted on the authority of our teachers, by which they and hopefully we distinguish good from bad making and doing.

It is important that this kind of development of powers in and through practices is to be found in many different social and cultural contexts, many of them contexts in which the name of Aristotle, let alone his texts, is unknown. Yet the activities of those engaged in such practices are best understood in Aristotelian terms and so are their patterns of learning. Insofar as we learn successfully, on this NeoAristotelian view, we make the achievement of excellence, or at least of whatever excellence we are capable of achieving, in at least some of our activities, our own end. So in each type of activity we have a double end. We on the one hand aim to bring about that end state, the achievement of which in this particular time and place is the appropriate end of that type of activity: the statement of the elegant, significant, and difficult proof in mathematics, the harvesting of a crop of perfect vegetables and the renewal of the soil each year under unfavorable conditions in farming, the insightful performance by an orchestra of work too often taken for granted, say, Mozart's clarinet music, and so on. On the other hand, we each of us aim to become the kind of agent whose doing and whose making is informed by those skills and those qualities of mind and character that are necessary, if excellence is to be achieved. So it is with practices in general. The physician's ends are to restore to health this particular set of patients and to become or remain an excellent physician. The portrait painter's ends are to capture what is unique in this particular face and to extend her or his powers as a painter.

What such examples make clear is that some of our important ends are such that it would be a mistake to think of them as adequately specifiable by us in advance of and independently of our involvement in those activities through which we try to realize them. It is often true that it is only in and through those activities that we arrive at more adequate ideas of how to think about those ends and of how to be guided by them. So a farmer has to arrive through her or his work at a highly particular set of notions of what good farming is on this particular terrain, in this particular climate, with this kind of plough, and this kind of labor force. So a physician is concerned to learn through her or his work how to restore and sustain the health of *these* patients, with *these* particular vulnerabilities, through the use of *these* pharmacological and surgical resources. So the musician or the painter may be as surprised as anyone else when the end to which they have directed their activities emerges as *this* performance or *that* portrait.

It is not only the conception of such ends that may be unexpectedly transformed in the course of our activities. We too, while developing those skills and qualities of mind and character needed to achieve those ends, may discover that the transformation of ourselves that is involved is significantly different from what we had expected, in part perhaps because of the particularities of our circumstances, but in part because what such virtues as courage, patience, truthfulness, and justice require can never be fully specified in advance. Hence, as Aquinas emphasized, in the life of practice there are no fully adequate generalizations to guide us, no set of rules sufficient to do the work for us, something that each of us has to learn for her or himself as we move toward the achievement of the ends of our activities and the end of excellence in those activities.

To move toward these two sets of ends requires, on any Aristotelian view, Neo or otherwise, just that integration of rational judgment and desire to which, as again we noticed earlier, Aristotle gave the name *prohairesis*. Failure to move toward them, if not due to misfortune, will be evidence of bad practical or productive reasoning rooted in inadequately educated judgment or in misdirected desire or in both. It is important that – contrary to what seems to have been Aristotle's mistaken view; here he needs correction by Aquinas – progress toward good judgment and rightly directed desire is often partial and uneven, so that someone who exemplifies them admirably in some area of her or his activities may fail miserably in either or both in some other area. For even the most successful, however, there remains a problem. Granted that there are goods to be achieved and excellence to be attained in a wide range of practices, of types of activity, to which of these should I give a central place in my life, to which a marginal place, and to which no place at all?

This is a question that I cannot ask and answer entirely on my own, just by myself, and this for two reasons. First, what place I am able to give to this or that type of activity in my life and what goods I am able to achieve often depends on what place others give to these same types of activity in their lives and on how far they and I cooperate. Each of us generally relies on others in pursuing our own individual goods. And this is even more obviously the case when the goods in question are not individual, but common goods, the goods of family, of political society, of workplace, of sports teams, orchestras, and theatre companies. Such goods we can achieve and enjoy only qua family member, qua citizen, qua participant in the relevant types of activity. Deliberation as to how such common goods are to be achieved can only be shared deliberation. Moreover, it is only through such shared deliberation that we are able to overcome the partiality and one-sidedness of our own initial judgments and to correct our prejudices. Nonetheless, at certain points in our lives each of us has to make her or his own decisions as to what place this or that type of activity is to have in her or his life. So how are we, how am I to make this decision? What gives me good reason to integrate the various facets of my life in one way rather than another? (I speak in the first person to make it clear that it is I as a NeoAristotelian who am posing these questions.) In answering them several aspects of our lives need to be kept in mind.

First, there are goods central to our lives over and above the goods internal to practices: the goods of affection and friendship and the good of self-knowledge are examples, but so is the good of light conversation and joking between workmates or groups of casual acquaintances. Secondly, not only is it the case that the goods that are most important to us at one stage of life may be and characteristically are not the same as the goods that are most important at other stages, but what it is to pursue and to achieve those goods also changes over time. The friendships of the young are not the same as the friendships of the old, those friendships in which shared memories play so large a part. The self-deceptions of the young are not the same as the self-deceptions of the old, those self-deceptions in which the editing of memories plays so large a part. The jokes of the young are not the jokes of the old.

It is then with a strong sense of the heterogeneity and variety of the particularities of our lives that we should ask the question: in terms of what should we set about the task of integrating our lives, of deciding upon the due place that each good should have at each stage in my particular life? This is of course one more version of the question: How is it best for me to live qua human being rather than just qua family member or qua friend or qua student or qua farmer? We may perhaps and characteristically will already know at what ends to aim, if we are to achieve excellence in a variety of types of activity, when young as student or apprentice, later in the workplace and as spouse and parent, later still perhaps as teacher or trade union organizer, at all stages as friend, and yet may still have to learn at what end we must aim, if we are to order those other ends so that we achieve excellence as human beings. What kind of end might this final end be?

It must, given what has just been said, be an end that can be pursued by a rational agent through all the very different stages of her or his life, an end to the achievement of which all the very different activities of such a life, each with its own particular end, can be directed. That is to say, it must be the end of rational activity as such, an end to be contrasted with those various and particular ends. As the end of rational activity, its achievement must involve the attainment of some high degree of self-knowledge, of what we are, have been, and can be. Secondly, it must be an end that completes and perfects the life of the agent who achieves it. It must be such that someone who had achieved it could have no reason to want anything further or to seek anything further. It is not just that it happens to be more desirable and more choiceworthy than all other objects of desire, but that its desirability is of a different order. Thirdly, in contrasting it with other goods we are able to say a good deal about what it is not, and this is instructive. As Aquinas argues powerfully (*Summa Theologiae* Ia–IIae, qu. 2–3), life aimed at the achievement of that final good cannot be a life whose principal aim is the attainment of pleasure, power, political honor, money, or physical, intellectual, moral, aesthetic, or even spiritual excellence, although every one of these is a genuine good. For these are among the goods that have to be ordered. Fourthly, that final good must stand to all other goods in this way: that, if and insofar as other goods are given a due place in an agent's life, that agent is directed toward the achievement of this, her or his final good, and vice versa. Those other goods are all goods for this or that agent, in this or that set of circumstances, in this or that respect. Such a final good is by contrast unqualifiedly good and stands to those other goods as a measure stands to what is measured. So what does or could be such a final good?

This question, posed in this general way, may seem to demand an immediate answer, but it is too soon to ask it. Consider some general answers proposed by thinkers who have contributed strikingly to those accounts of goods and the good upon which the NeoAristotelian tradition has drawn: for Plato it is the apprehension of the Form of the Good, for Aristotle the contemplation of that which we contemplate, when, so far as we can, we view things as God views them, for Plotinus the achievement of unity with the One, for Boethius and Aquinas the vision of God. Should we assent to one of these answers or propose another such? Not until we have noted that these are answers supplied by philosophical theorists, theorists engaged in characterizing the life of practice from a standpoint external to it. But we make a mistake, if we try to characterize the life of practice in theoretical terms before we have described it in its own terms. What needs to be considered first is the place that the conception of a final end, of an ultimate human good, has in the life of practice. For it is only in making practical judgments and choices, through the exercise of the virtues, that each of us discovers in our lives a certain kind of directedness toward a final end that is our own, toward perfecting and completing the lives that are our own, by living out what in terms of our particular abilities and circumstances we judge to be the best possible life for us.

Reflective agents thus increasingly understand themselves and others in terms of a certain kind of narrative, a story in which they as agents direct themselves or fail to direct themselves toward a final end, the nature of which they initially apprehend in and through their activities as rational agents. Progress toward that final end is marked by slowly and unevenly increasing self-awareness and self-knowledge, so that agents become better able to understand what in their past has gone well and what has gone badly in their own lives and in the lives of others with whom they have interacted and why. Failure to understand is often on this view a sign that things have gone badly. And the conception of a state in which we have achieved our final end is a conception of a state in which our retrospective understanding has become such that we are able to retell the story of our lives, but now truthfully, able to take the true measure of all our failures.

It may seem paradoxical to say that it is only when we have recognized the fragile and partial character of our own present goodness, such as it is, and the realities, often the trivializing realities, of our own past badness, such as it has been, that we finally can have good reason to be satisfied with the outcomes of our lives. This is why we should resist the temptation to follow some of Aristotle's translators in giving this end state the name 'happiness'. For in contemporary English, to be happy is to be and feel satisfied with one's present state or with some aspect of it, whether one has good reason to be and feel satisfied or not. But the state to which Aristotle gave the name *eudaimonia* and Aquinas the name *beatitudo* is that state in which one is and feels satisfied with one's condition only because one has good reason to be and to feel satisfied. As both Aristotle and Aquinas point out, this is a state in which every rational agent desires to be. So our end state is to be one in which desire is finally and justifiably satisfied. It is not only an end, but – in an older sense of 'happy' – a happy ending. And to fail to attain it is to end unhappily.

Imagine now, just as we did in the case of expressivism, a reflective agent who has become persuaded of the truth of the central contentions of the NeoAristotelian position. How might this have happened? She has found herself, as we all do, pursuing a variety of goods in her life. But then she finds reason to ask: Why am I living like this? For the sake of what am I pursuing these particular goods? For their own sake or for the sake of something else? To what would each contribute in my overall life? Somehow she learns that she has been asking Aristotle's questions and she then learns from him how to pose them more sharply. Perhaps to her surprise she then finds his answers a good starting point for elaborating her own answers. She now understands her uses of 'good' in NeoAristotelian terms, and she rank orders goods as NeoAristotelians rank order them. Her life will have developed as a life of practical questioning and practical learning through which her dispositions to feel, to desire, to argue, to judge, and to act are gradually transformed. And she will increasingly order the goods between which she has to choose in a way that directs her toward her final end, so that she becomes aware of what the character of that end must be.

How, then, will she think about the relationships between her desires and her judgments when she experiences a painful conflict between what she wants most on some particular occasion and how she judges it best for her to act? She will first ask what it is about the object of her desire that attracts her and what the best case is that could be made for judging it to be genuinely desirable. She will then ask what the argument or arguments are that issue in the conclusion that she should act otherwise than as her strong desire bids her to act. So she will entertain two practical syllogisms with incompatible conclusions, a situation that Aquinas has described for us (*Summa Theologiae* Ia–IIae, qu. 77, art. 2). Her further questions to herself will be: How are the goods cited in the premises of those syllogisms to be rank ordered by a rational agent exercising the virtues of temperateness, courage, justice, and prudence? And is the way in which *she* will be rank ordering them, if she acts as her desire bids her act, be consistent with a continuing exercise of those virtues by her that will direct her toward her final good, as she now understands it? Is it at this point her judgments or her desires that are pointing her in the wrong direction, a direction defined by her relationship to that final good?

At certain points in her reflections upon herself, she may well be compelled to resort to higher order reflection upon her practical thinking. She will have to ask how she is to articulate the theoretical presuppositions of her practical stances. It is at such points that she will have to reckon with the theoretical claims of those who have most adequately spelled out those presuppositions, Aristotle and such Aristotelians as Ibn Roschd, Maimonides, and Aquinas. What their arguments will perhaps bring home to her is that her and their conception of the final end of human activity is inescapably theological, that the nature of her practical reasoning and of the practical reasoning of those in whose company she deliberates has from the outset committed her and them to a shared belief in God, to a belief that, if there is nothing beyond the finite, there is no final end, no ultimate human good, to be achieved. So she may complete her reasoning by discovering that what is at stake in her decisions in moments of conflict is the directedness of her life, if not toward God, at least beyond finitude.

It is of course only insofar as she has set herself to become a fully rational agent, only insofar as she has already developed a higher order desire, a higher order set of dispositions, to act as such an agent and to achieve the final end of such an agent, that this discovery will be motivating, rather than disturbing and disrupting. It will generally have been through decision making in the course of resolving earlier conflicts that the relevant higher order dispositions will have been developed, the relevant higher order desire strengthened. How one works through those conflicts, how one develops those dispositions depends in key part not only on one's early practical education but also on one's continuing social relationships and friendships. I already noted that many of our key decisions about how to pursue our individual goods need to be made in consultation with others, that this is always the case with respect to our pursuit of common goods, and that, as Aquinas emphasized (*Summa Theologiae* Ia–IIae, qu. 14, art. 3), our partiality and one-sidedness in deliberation need to be corrected by the judgments of competent and critical others. Our aptness to be the victims of our own fantasies, of our tendencies to engage in wishful or fearful thinking make this need even more acute. So our imagined NeoAristotelian will have recognized the indispensability of the good of friendship and will have consulted with her friends and, if some common good is in question, with others whose good that common good is, family members, fellow citizens, coworkers. How will her relationship with this range of others have to be structured if they are to share systematically in the tasks of rational deliberation?

Those who deliberate together need to ensure that no relevant voice is either excluded or ignored, that, so far as possible, what is said about both ends and means is true, and that each consideration advanced is given its due rational weight and not assigned too little or too great importance, because of who said it or how they said it or what nonrational inducements accompanied that saying. Participants in deliberation must make their decisions because of how their practical reasoning went and not from fear or as a result of fraud or because they were bribed or seduced. But this is only possible if the participants in deliberation are bound by precepts that unconditionally forbid the use of force or the threat of force against innocent individuals, precepts that prohibit the taking of innocent life or of the legitimate property of others, precepts that require truthfulness and the honoring of our commitments and obligations. Without unconditional obedience to such precepts there cannot be shared rational deliberation, and without shared rational deliberation there cannot be rational agents. So some of what Aquinas called the precepts of the natural law, that law whose authority we recognize in virtue of our nature as rational agents, are needed to structure the relationships of those who pursue their individual and common goods in the company of others. And on a NeoAristotelian and more specifically a Thomistic view, there is no other way to pursue them.

Return now to our imagined NeoAristotelian reflecting on her resolution of her conflict. It will find its place in a narrative of her life as agent, a narrative with three salient characteristics. It will, first of all, be a narrative of her life not just as an individual, but as an individual-in-relationships, of herself as family member, as student and, later on, teacher, as coworker, perhaps member of a fishing crew or an orchestra, relationships in which she is or has been dependent on others and others are or have been dependent on her. She will think primarily of how 'we' failed or succeeded at certain points, rather than only 'I', although she will have learned how to move between 'I' and 'we'. Secondly, this narrative will concern how she and those others with whom she shares common goods have learned from their failures and mistakes how to move toward the achievement of those common goods. It is of crucial importance that mistakes, even, perhaps especially, gross mistakes, come to be understood as occasions for learning and not as mere lapses in judgment or yieldings to misdirected desire. Thirdly, as we have already noted, that narrative will exhibit an increasing directedness, an increasing success in integrating her pursuits of the various individual and common goods that she values into a unified pursuit of her final good, a good that she now may or may not recognize as consisting in a relationship to God. Her narrative will thus have a teleological structure, so that, if she were to recount it to us, we would find ourselves asking 'Will she achieve her end? Will her life be completed or left unfinished?'

Whether she does conceive her final good theoretically will of course depend on what kind of a person she is, how apt to become theoretically articulate in her reflections. How she so conceives it will depend in part on the resources of the culture that she shares with those who are her partners in their pursuit of common goods, on whether she and they inhabit an ancient, a medieval or an early modern or an Enlightenment or post Enlightenment culture, on whether she and her community are pagan, Jewish, Christian, or Islamic. We have imagined her so far as both reflective and articulate, as able to tell the story of her life in an appropriate way. But many practically rational agents who are reflective about the particular situations in which they find themselves never find occasion to or may not have the resources to recount the stories of their lives. There always is a true story to recount, one which would capture the narrative structure of their lives, but rational agency does not require that agents are always able to think of themselves in terms of that story.

Whether our imagined NeoAristotelian agent does so or not, let us compare her with our imagined expressivist agent by asking how she will respond to the challenge presented by Nietzsche in *Beyond Good and Evil*. She will agree with Nietzsche that to be the kind of rational agent envisaged by Aristotle, Aquinas, and their heirs is to live and act under certain constraints, that it involves a disciplining of one's desires and one's will, but where Nietzsche views these particular constraints and that particular discipline as "unfreedom of spirit,"[48] she will understand them as enabling. What they make possible is participation in those social relationships through which she has learned how to transform her dispositions, to improve her capacity for practical judgment, and to pursue common goods. She will be impressed by the contrast between those relationships and both the relationships that Nietzsche takes to characterize the morality that he denounces, those of slave morality, and the relationships which he commends, those of master morality.[49] She will respond very differently from our imagined expressivist to Nietzsche's portrait of the philosophers of the future with their will to power.

What will strike our imagined NeoAristotelian most, perhaps, is that Nietzsche has deliberately excluded himself from and invited others to exclude themselves from just those types of practice and just those types of relationship in and through which we learn how to become practically rational agents and how to exercise those virtues without which rational deliberation is not possible. But to exclude oneself from those practices and relationships is, by impoverishing one's moral experience, to deny oneself the possibility of understanding what it is to be such a rational agent. To lead certain kinds of life is to deprive oneself of just those experiences that one most needs, if one is to know where to begin in moral and political enquiry. It is therefore to condemn oneself to misunderstanding, as Nietzsche's imagined new philosophers, whose will to truth is will to power, are condemned to misunderstanding. So the lessons that our reflective NeoAristotelian takes herself to have learned from the Nietzsche of *Beyond Good and Evil* are very different from the lessons that our reflective expressivist took herself to have learned. Yet it is not unimportant that both took

---

[48] Ibid.   [49] Ibid., p. 260.

from their reading of Nietzsche insights that it would have been difficult, perhaps impossible, for them to find elsewhere. That some of Nietzsche's texts are indispensable reading for any student of modern morality and moral philosophy – as indispensable as the writings of Hume, Kant, and Mill – is even now not as widely recognized as it should be.

1.9 Expressivists versus NeoAristotelians: a philosophical conflict in which neither party seems able to defeat the other

We have then arrived at two sets of different and incompatible answers to our initial questions. Those questions concerned how it is that someone's desires can be such as to make her or his life go well or go badly, what is involved in resolving conflicts in which either desire is pitted against desire or desire is at odds with rational judgment, and what constitutes a good reason for trying to satisfy this or that particular desire. The practical reasoning of agents whose patterns of thought and action give expression to their commitment to the truth of either of those two sets of rival and alternative philosophical answers will be significantly different from the practical reasoning of agents whose commitment is to the other. The ends set for themselves by reflective expressivists, expressivists who have learned what they need to learn from Frankfurt, will be those which give expression to what it is that they care about and they will rank order those ends in accordance with how much they care about this rather than that. It is this rank ordering of their ends that will provide them with some of the premises for their practical reasoning. They will also need premises about the situations in which they find themselves and the alternatives between which they have to choose by acting in one way rather than another. So for them as practical reasoners the immediate question will be of this form: 'Given the ends that I now have, rank ordered as they are, and given the alternative courses of action between which I have to choose, which course of action will best serve the achievement of those ends?'

Notice that this question will also be posed by NeoAristotelians. So what are the respects in which they differ? If we attend only to particular occasions of choice and action, there may well be some on which there seems to be no difference at all between the practical reasoning and the judgments of an agent who exemplifies an expressivist stance and those of a NeoAristotelian agent. However, if we look beyond such episodes to the larger histories in which each episode has its place, crucial differences are at once evident. The histories of expressivist agents are primarily histories of their affections, of what they have cared about and of how they came to

care about what they now care about. The histories of NeoAristotelians are
histories of how they succeeded or failed in becoming better judges of what
it is for a human being to flourish qua human being and to act accordingly.
They are histories of learning or failing to learn, and the standards by which
success or failure is judged are independent of the learner. The expressivist
histories are indeed also histories of judgments and reasoning, but of these
as expressive of affections. The histories of NeoAristotelians are indeed also
histories of affections and desires, but of these as according with or failing
to accord with the conclusions of sound practical reasoning.

There will be moments in both types of history in which agents put
in question some of the premises on which they have been relying in
their practical reasoning, and these will be the moments when the differences between the two types of history become most obvious. For at
such moments the expressivist agent will ask 'What is it that I really most
care about?' and 'Is the pursuit of the ends that I have been pursuing well
designed to further the well-being of that or those about which I most care?'
while the NeoAristotelian will ask 'Have I understood adequately what it is
for human beings to flourish qua human beings in this type of situation?'
and 'Is the pursuit of the ends that I have been pursuing conducive to my
human flourishing and to the human flourishing of those with whom I
interact?' The differences in the answers are from time to time likely to be
as striking as the differences in the questions.

What then happens in situations in which advocates of those rival
answers confront one another? I have already given reasons for thinking that each will find the argumentative objections posed by the other
uncompelling, so that exchanges between them are likely to be barren.
What is instructive, however, is to remind ourselves of the types of consideration that gives each confidence in her own position. The NeoAristotelian
will focus on those relationships with others without which she would be
unable to achieve either those common goods that she shares with those
others, such common goods as those of family, of political society, of the
workplace, and so on, or the individual goods made possible by participation in the projects of achieving those common goods. She will note that it
is a fact that those relationships require a high degree of mutual trust, that
it is a fact that without those relationships human powers cannot be fully
developed, and that whether a particular human being or group flourishes
or fails to flourish is to be discovered by empirical observation. Of course
on certain aspects of flourishing, there have been and will be disagreements,
but it is a mark of human flourishing to make of such disagreements matter
for further enquiry. So our imagined NeoAristotelian will reflect that her

relationships presuppose a large degree of agreement on what she and those with whom she shares common goods take to be the truths about human flourishing, truths that are what they are prior to and independently of their assent to them.

By contrast the reflective expressivist regards her relationships, like her normative and evaluative judgments, as expressing her attitudes, concerns, and feelings, more especially those attitudes, concerns, and feelings directed toward those individuals and groups, those ideals, and those causes about which she cares most. How indeed, she judges, could it be otherwise, since, if a change in what she cares about were to occur, or if she were to discover that her relationships or her normative or evaluative judgments did not in fact contribute to satisfying her desires for those individuals, groups, ideals, and causes that she most cares about, she would at once remake those relationships and revise those judgments. The NeoAristotelian's question is 'What is it that *we* presuppose?' The expresssivist's question is 'What is it to which *I* am committed?' And this difference in questions corresponds to a difference in the histories through which both we and they understand the positions that they now hold.

The expressivist's history is a history of her herself, of this particular individual interacting with and learning from other individuals, but most importantly of how *she* responded in and to those interactions and of what *she* learned or failed to learn. What her social context provides is a setting for *her* actions and reactions. What the history of her relationships provides is insight into aspects of *her* history. It is a history that begins with her birth and ends with her death. She, if she recounts it, can justly say "This is my history." By contrast the NeoAristotelian's history is a history both of her and of those groups with whom she shares common goods and within which she pursues her individual good. It is a history of how the shared project of achieving those goods, the attainment of which constitutes human flourishing, came to inform each of their lives. Her history as an individual is adequately intelligible only as a part of that history, and so she will commonly speak of *our* history rather than of her history as my history.

In both cases, as we already noticed, the content of each particular history will depend in part on which society the agent inhabits and at what period. Eighteenth-century individuals who recognized themselves in the portraits of the moral agent drawn by Hume or Adam Smith had significantly different moral histories from their twentieth-century counterparts. Thirteenth-century NeoAristotelians in Paris were engaged in very different controversies from their sixteenth-century Spanish or their twentieth-century Irish heirs. And on occasion the partisans of each stand-point will play a part in the other's history, providing a critique of the judgments and arguments of the other and sometimes a critique of the other's critique. If that critique were to be systematically carried through, it would result in each party writing a critical history of the other, a history designed to show how only from the standpoint of the writers can the errors and confusions that they ascribe to their rivals be adequately identified and explained.

We have, then, three levels of disagreement between the kind of reflective expressivist that I have described and the kind of NeoAristotelian that I have characterized. There are first order practical disagreements about how it is best to resolve this or that conflict of desires or this or that conflict between judgment and desire. There are second order philosophical disagreements about how judgments of the form 'It is in this situation good or best to feel, judge, and act thus' are to be interpreted and therefore about the form that an agent's practical reasoning with respect to such conflicts should take. And thirdly, there are disagreements about how the narratives of an agent's practical history, that history through which agents make themselves as desiring and reasoning animals intelligible to themselves and others, should be recounted.

The claim made on behalf of each of those rival histories by the protag-onists of each, explicitly or implicitly, is that it enables us to understand the conflict between those contending points of view in ways in which and to a degree in which the other does not, that it exhibits an inability on the part of the protagonist of the other party to understand their own predicaments. NeoAristotelians do not deny that there are and have been many individuals and groups, even perhaps some cultures, whose evaluative and normative attitudes and judgments are very much what expressivists take them to be. They allow that such individuals and groups speak and act on many occasions just as if expressivism were true, and, if reflective, understand themselves in expressivist terms.

What NeoAristotelians claim – and I write as such a NeoAristotelian – is that, in so understanding themselves, expressivists are unable to reckon with important aspects of themselves and that their activities over extended periods of time can only be characterized and understood adequately in Aristotelian terms. So their own histories of themselves will always be defective histories. It is with this claim and its relevance to our enquiries about desires that part of the rest of this book will be concerned. Reflective expressivists, of course, take the histories of NeoAristotelians to be histories of obfuscation and error, just as both the thinkers of the Enlightenment and Nietzsche did. And neither party has the resources to refute the other by appeal to standards that the other recognizes. So what more is there to be said?

We should first remind ourselves that a philosophical impasse is not necessarily or even usually a practical impasse. Aristotelians in ethics and politics who find that their arguments are unconvincing to expressivists have been given no reason thereby to put their Aristotelianism in question. They are after all Aristotelians not because they first arrived at a set of theoretical conclusions and then put them into practice, but rather because of the way in which they were educated into and in various practices by their elders or reeducated by others or by themselves. Their theory articulates the presuppositions of their practice in what they take to be rationally compelling arguments. Similarly, although for different reasons, expressivists, whether followers of Hume, Nietzsche, or Frankfurt, will have been given no reason for putting in question *their* attitudes and commitments. Yet there are those for whom this particular philosophical impasse may have practical import.

Remember those whose plight I described at the very beginning of this chapter, those whose lives had gone wrong, or were in danger of going wrong, because of inordinate or inadequate or distorted desire. For them, if they have become reflective, questions about the relationship of reasoning to desire and of what it is to have good or bad reasons for desiring this or that may be at once philosophical and practical and so in consequence may questions about good and 'good'. For them therefore, if they have followed the lines of argument developed so far, their discovery that there are no neutral standards by appeal to which the rival claims of NeoAristotelianism and expressivism can be adjudicated may seem to entail the frustration of an enquiry that is, for them, at once philosophical and practical. So it is not at all unimportant that the philosophical enquiry is not in fact at an end, that there are further questions to be asked.

The first of these is one that has to be put to the protagonists of both rival parties, and therefore one that I have to put to myself. It is: What conditions would have to be satisfied for you to acknowledge that the central theses of the view that you now hold are mistaken? Philosophers should have learned by now from C. S. Peirce that their claims, like those of scientists and theologians, have significant content only insofar as they are refutable, only insofar as their truth excludes certain possibilities. A statement of those possibilities is a statement of the conditions that, if satisfied, would show that particular claim or set of claims to be unjustified. This question therefore will provide a later stage of this enquiry with its subject matter.

A second question concerns how each of these types of theory functions as a mode of self-knowledge within those particular social contexts in which they are characteristically at home. If someone understands her or himself and her or his social role in terms dictated by either of the two rival standpoints that we have been discussing, are there types of misunderstanding to which she or he may be peculiarly liable? This is a type of question that theorists of ideology, such as Karl Mannheim, used to pose, but it is one that philosophers nowadays rarely, if ever, entertain. Its unfamiliarity is indeed such that it will be important to spell out the question in some detail. And this spelling out will provide another stage of this enquiry with its subject matter. But before I move on toward those later stages, I need to acknowledge what may be taken by some readers to be unjustifiable eccentricities in the way that I have proceeded so far.

1.10   Why I have put on one side not only the philosophical standpoints of most recent moral philosophers, but also their moral standpoint

What I have not yet provided is any justification for proceeding in a manner strikingly at odds with the ways of conventional academic moral philosophy. Initially, I may have seemed to be about to proceed along its well-trodden paths. For I posed questions about the meaning and uses of 'good', topics treated at length by practitioners of that discipline as part of their more extended treatments of evaluative and normative concepts and language. I have taken with great seriousness arguments and theses advanced by such notable contributors to that discipline as Stevenson, Blackburn, Gibbard, and Frankfurt. But I have proceeded as though the only two interesting and worthwhile standpoints in thinking about evaluative judgments and the nature of good reasons for wanting this or that are some version of expressivism and some version of the view that I have named NeoAristotelianism and that the debate between these is the single most important debate in this area.

To think this is from the standpoint of most of contemporary academic practitioners of contemporary moral philosophy not just mistaken but absurd. It is to neglect the work of the most influential contributors to that discipline and to leave unaddressed most of what they take to be its central problems. I therefore owe it to my readers to say something about why I have proceeded as I have, about why my approach is so different from theirs. The largest single difference between me and them is perhaps this, that they find what they identify as the subject matter of their enquiry unproblematic, while I do not. That subject matter they take to be Morality, a set of rules, ideals, and judgments concerning duties and obligations that are to be distinguished from religious, legal, political, and aesthetic rules, ideals, and judgments. I spell "Morality," as they conceive it, with a capital M, to distinguish it from "moralities" in the plural, as when anthropologists speak of the morality of the Dyaks of North Borneo or that of the Inuit peoples. Contemporary moral philosophers happily use both "Morality" and "moralities," just as philosophers of science speak both of "Science" and of sciences, the science of the ancient Greeks or the science of the medieval Arabs. The implication in both cases is the same. The moralities or sciences of other cultures are inferior versions of Morality or Science, as we now possess them in advanced modernity, and philosophers can safely take the authority of both for granted. What then is Morality, the morality of advanced modernity, thus understood?

It is presented as a set of impersonal rules, entitled to the assent of any rational agent whatsoever, enjoining obedience to such maxims as those that prohibit the taking of innocent life and theft and those that require at least some large degree of truthfulness and at least some significant measure of altruistic benevolence. Why should we obey such maxims? Here there are alternative answers. One is that obedience to such maxims by others in relation to ourselves is something that as rational agents we cannot but will, and so consistency requires that we also take those maxims to govern our actions toward those others. Another is that by obedience to such maxims we maximize well-being or happiness or utilty, variously understood. A third is that these represent the demands that it is or should be generally regarded as reasonable that we can make on others and others on us. Different versions of both rules and justificatory answers are to be found both in the discourse of everyday moral agents and in the writings of academic moral philosophers who make that discourse the subject of their enquiries. However, there is one notable difference between them.

In both there is recognition of an inescapable tension between the requirements of what are taken by some to be unconditional and exceptionless moral rules and the requirement that we maximize well-being or happiness or some aspect of these. So the injunction that we should refrain from lying is put to the question on occasion, when it is evident that only by lying can we avoid causing pain. Or the injunction never to violate someone's dignity by torturing them is put to the question when it appears highly probable that only by torturing a suspect will we make him divulge information that may save hundreds of lives. But in their response to this recognition, everyday moral agents nowadays and academic moral philosophers part company.

In everyday moral life these tensions are dealt with by indefiniteness in commitment and by oscillation. The indefiniteness is expressed in the form that many give to their moral principles: 'Always do such and such or refrain from doing so and so, except when . . . ' followed by a shorter or longer set of exceptions and ending with an 'etc.' The oscillation is between on some occasions affirming a strong, even a very strong version of some rule, as though it were exceptionless, while on others allowing maximizing and consequentialist considerations to override it. Such indefiniteness and oscillation are notable features of both the political rhetoric and the political practice of advanced societies as well as of the private lives of their citizens.

What characteristically distinguishes the academic moral philosophers of those societies from everyday language users is their insistence on resolving or at least on attempting to resolve the inconsistencies in moral discourse in such a way that both indefiniteness and oscillation disappear. Depending on how they resolve those inconsistencies, they espouse this or that particular account of the rules, maxims, and justifications of morality and reject its rivals, each claiming the support of rational argument for their particular contentious conclusions. So we find both Kantian upholders of universalizable and exceptionless moral rules and theorists who defend conceptions of inviolable human rights at odds with utilitarian consequentialists, and all of these in dispute with different versions of contractarianism. More recently the advocates of virtue ethics have added their contribution to the debates. Each party finds its own objections to the other rival standpoints compelling, and no party finds the arguments advanced against it persuasive. So it has been now for some very considerable time, during which much important philosophical work has been done. New arguments have been advanced, new distinctions drawn, new insights developed, but this in general without bringing any of the contending parties any nearer to agreement on the major issues, whether substantive or metaethical.

To this it will be objected that I am taking no account of the work of those moral philosophers who claim to have decisively resolved the major disagreements, or at least some of them, by developing theses and arguments which combine elements from various contending views in a synthesis that is argumentatively superior – at least in the eyes of its authors – to all the versions of those views that had been so far advanced. The wonderfully impressive character of these normative constructions has to be acknowledged, but the response to them has in fact been the multiplication rather than the resolution of disagreement, not at all what their authors have intended. For their syntheses have turned out to be as contestable as any other standpoint. So the protagonists of each point of view continue to represent themselves as the voice of enlightened reason, providing reason with too many conflicting voices.

Is it perhaps the case, then, that the only way to be a moral philosopher here and now is either to identify with the positions of some one of the contending parties or to construct yet one more contentious position of one's own? One can avoid having to choose between these unpalatable alternatives, I believe, only in a limited number of ways. The most interesting is that represented by expressivism. For expressivism would provide an explanation of why those who take themselves to be the voices of reason nonetheless find themselves in unresolvable disagreement. Those disagreements would be understood as giving expression to the different and incompatible prerational commitments of each party, commitments that determine which arguments each finds persuasive. But this is of course something that all those moral philosophers who take themselves to be setting out the requirements of reason are committed to denying. Hence arises the need for such moral philosophers to discover some conclusive refutation of expressivism.

This need, interestingly, is felt often enough by everyday moral agents as well as by quite a number of academic philosophers, for both take themselves to judge by a moral standard whose authority is independent of their own commitments, attitudes, concerns, and feelings. So expressions of moral conviction in our culture tend to have a peculiar character, moving between moments in which agents speak as if just such a standard were being invoked and moments apparently expressive of something quite other, of convictions prior to and stubbornly immune to argument, an ambivalence most obvious perhaps in political debates about alleged human rights. As I noticed earlier, expressivist philosophers have their own account of this double aspect of moral utterance, but it is an account that generally fails to convince those whose allegiance to Morality is paramount, that is, the large majority of the citizens of advanced modernity.

It is not of course that those citizens are able to settle their quarrels among themselves about what it is that Morality requires of them. There is more than one liberal version of Morality, more than one conservative version. And, for reasons that I already suggested, both the quarrels among liberals about what liberalism requires and among conservatives about what conservatism requires and the quarrels between liberals and conservatives are interminable. Each party speaks as if they are or are on the verge of advancing compelling reasons why their critics and opponents should concede defeat, but that point is never quite reached and no party ever finds reason to acknowledge defeat. The dominant shared culture of moral modernity is, on the one hand, one whose assertive and expressive judgments and arguments seem to be just what expressivism says that they are, yet, on the other, also one in which agents are unable to recognize or acknowledge this fact about themselves. So the recurrent rejections of expressivism, not just by academic philosophers but by everyday moral agents, may themselves be an important symptom of that culture's moral condition.

There have of course throughout Morality's history been those who have rejected its pretensions, some because they were fortunate enough to have been brought up in a culture to which its norms and values are alien – I think here of such Russian critics of Western modernity as Dostoievski and Berdyaev – others because, like Nietzsche, or our imagined follower of Harry Frankfurt, or D. H. Lawrence, they had become disillusioned. The most notable example among our contemporaries was Bernard Williams, who spoke of morality as "a special system" and a "peculiar institution," one whose requirements are at odds with any considered understanding of the ethical.[50] On Williams' account our deepest moral convictions are expressed in and through our emotions, although they are not, as on an expressivist account, expressions *of* our emotions. Early on he was impressed by Lawrence's injunction to "Find your deepest impulse and follow that" and twenty years later he could write that "I must deliberate *from* what I am. Truthfulness requires trust in that . . . "[51] How then to characterize those situations in which recognition of the demands of the ethical makes it necessary to deliberate from that starting point? Williams' rejection both of modern conceptions of morality and of the Christianity which he saw as the precursor of those conceptions led him to follow Nietzsche in an attempt to recover from the ancient Greek world – from its tragedians and historians rather than from its philosophers – alternative ways of understanding human relationships and transactions. Yet he pursued practical enquiry as he did only because from the outset he took there to be crucial objections to any version of Aristotelianism, something that he reiterated at various points in his notable intellectual career. Hence, in stating the case for an Aristotelian view of things, I have also and incidentally been stating a case against Williams. To this quarrel and indeed to the critique of Williams' views in general, I will have to return.

[50] Bernard Williams, *Ethics and the Limits of Philosophy*, Cambridge, MA: Harvard University Press, 1985, p. 174.
[51] Ibid., p. 200.

Is there then any other compelling and constructive way to respond to the condition of Morality and to the convictions and practices through which it finds expression as a distinctive and distinctively modern form of social and institutional life? No adequate answer to this question will be possible until we have identified and understood better those peculiarly modern social relationships and intellectual presuppositions from which Morality derives its character. And it might be thought that to pursue the task of identifying and understanding those relationships would be a distraction from the central questions of our present enquiry concerning desire and practical reasoning. It turns out, however, that what we need to understand is how the social and intellectual order in which Morality finds its place is one that involves the deformation of desire and the invention of new forms of practical reasoning so that this turn in our enquiry is in no way a distraction.

CHAPTER 2

Theory, practice, and their social contexts

2.1   How to respond to the type of philosophical disagreement described in Chapter 1: the social contexts of philosophical theorizing

The impasse at which we had arrived is a philosophical impasse, one in which two incompatible sets of theses and arguments confront one another and the protagonists of each are unable to identify standards shared with their opponents by appeal to which their disagreements might be resolved. It is an impasse with a double aspect, involving two sets of rival claims, one in which an expressivist account of 'good' and good is counterposed to a NeoAristotelian account and one in which something very close to Frankfurt's account of the relation of our practical reasoning to what we care about is counterposed to a NeoAristotelian account of desire and practical reasoning. In the face of it, how should we proceed? Are we simply to leave matters so that the protagonists of each party remain as satisfied with their own position as they are dismissive of that of their rivals? Is this particular philosophical enquiry, like a number of others in contemporary philosophy, either to become interminable or to terminate in unresolvable conflict?

Perhaps what we now need to think about is the nature and limitations of philosophical enquiry or rather of philosophical enquiry as nowadays characteristically conceived, since that is the type of enquiry through which I arrived at my conclusions. Does the impasse at which I arrived perhaps result from the nature and limitations of such enquiry, enquiry that is narrowly academic? As such it operates under three sets of constraints. First, it is carried on in college and university classrooms and seminars, and in journal articles and books written almost exclusively for those who teach and learn in those classrooms and seminars. So it has its own distinctive idiom, one very different from that of most plain persons, most moral agents. The question therefore arises as to whether it may be apt in some degree to misrepresent the commitments of plain persons. Secondly, it has an assigned and well-defined academic territory. Philosophy is one thing, physics another, sociology a third, history a fourth, but it is no one's province to identify the limitations of each of these types of enquiry so that questions which cannot be answered from within one discipline are always in danger of going unasked. One such question is: Does a philosophical understanding of politics and morals not require some acquaintance with the range of moral and political beliefs and concepts disclosed by historical, anthropological, and sociological studies? Thirdly, philosophical enquiry is almost exclusively the work of professionalized academic teachers whose professionalization ensures the inculcation of certain habits of thought, among them habits that ensure the stability of academic hierarchies. The prerequisites for initiation into academic professions are such that those engaged in philosophical enquiry are generally, like the members of other professions, limited in their life experience. They will rarely have been soldiers or trade union organizers, worked on farms, in fishing crews, or on construction sites, played in string quartets or been in prison. This is of course no fault of theirs. Yet what the compartmentalization of contemporary social life ensures is that those who do have these important life experiences in armies or factories, or farms, or prisons, or whatever are generally educated, just as professional philosophers are, to believe that philosophical reflection and enquiry are matter for academic specialists and not for them. Perhaps, however, at least so far as moral and political philosophy are concerned, this is a mistake. Perhaps philosophers need to begin from the everyday questions of plain persons, the plain persons that they themselves were before they took to the study of philosophy.

The narrowness of a modern philosophical training, like the narrowness of other specialized training, has undeniable advantages. It produces minds focused on certain problem sets, minds that often exhibit admirable conceptual subtlety, that are adept at producing counterexamples to a wide range of theses, that are for the most part rigorous both in theory construction and in criticism. But what is notable is the extent to which and the ways in which, by reason of the constraints that we have identified, philosophical enquiry into and discussion of moral theory is isolated from political and moral practice, both our own everyday practice and that of those who inhabit moral cultures very different from our own. Any conception of moral theory as rooted in and unintelligible apart from the particularities of moral practice is generally ignored. Any notion of moral enquiry as needing to begin from or even include anthropological and historical studies of moral practice is ruled out and with it any identification of contrasts between the moral practices of the culture that we here now inhabit and those of cultures of other times and places.

So how then should moral and political enquiry begin? We are all of us agents before we are theorists, and it is only because we are agents that we have subject matter about which to ask those questions that take us into theory. Indeed, it is as agents become reflective that they find themselves compelled to ask those questions from which philosophical enquiry begins. And when agents become philosophically enquiring, they do not cease to be agents. They cannot but bring with them to their initial theorizing commitments that they have found inescapable as rational agents, and the justification of their theoretical positions presupposes the justification of their practical commitments as agents. So how do we justify those practical commitments? It depends on who we are. For how we understand ourselves varies from culture to culture and even within particular cultures such as our own. It matters a good deal therefore that we have some degree of awareness of the idiosyncrasies of our own culture and society so that we can distinguish that in ourselves and in our practical choices and reasoning that belongs to us as rational agents from that which has resulted from our peculiar cultural and social formation.

Consider just one possibility. A shared assumption of almost all contemporary moral theorizing is that the judgments made by moral agents are singular first person judgments, answers to the question 'How am *I* to act?' Suppose, however, that, contrary to this common view, it is, as I suggested in presenting the NeoAristotelian account in section 1.8 of Chapter 1, a prerequisite for acting as an adequately reflective agent that one should recognize that in many situations the question to be answered is not 'How am *I* to act?', but 'How are *we* to act?', just because what is at stake is a common good and not just the goods of individuals. Suppose further both that those common goods are the goods of family or workplace or political society, goods to be achieved and enjoyed not by individuals qua individuals, but by individuals qua family member or qua fellow worker or qua citizen and that individuals cannot achieve their own individual goods except through achieving such common goods. Were this to be the case, moral agents could not act as such without also acting as political and social agents and the abstraction of 'the moral' from 'the political' and 'the social' would be a misleading and distorting abstraction, one whose outcome might be that moral theorists would be blind to important aspects of the life of practice, indeed to aspects of their own moral lives.

How then, I repeat, is one to understand oneself as a rational agent? It depends, I reiterate, on who we are and on whom it is with whom we interact. For to be a rational agent is not only to have reasons for acting as one does and to be able to evaluate these as better or worse reasons. It is also and inseparably to offer reasons to others for acting in one way rather than another and to be responsive to the reasons that they advance. It is therefore important not only that the moral and political question is often 'How are *we* to act?', but that the *we* in question is always a culturally and socially particular *we*, an Irish or Japanese or Brazilian *we*, a *we* identifiable in terms of occupation, social class, and education. And when the question is 'How am *I* to act?', those particularities remain important. This is why the NeoAristotelian account that I spelled out briefly in section 1.8 of Chapter 1, even though it is one that I take to be correct, as far as it goes, does not of itself provide an adequate answer to the question 'How are we to understand ourselves as rational agents?'

First, that account is a theoretical account, framed so as to clarify its differences from rival theoretical accounts. But what we now need to supply is very different from the kind of account that would be elicited from an agent reflecting – for her or his own practical reasons – on her or his particular choices and actions. And that would involve an evaluation of that agent's reasons for action. Since, as I have argued, a reason for acting in some particular way always identifies some good that would be achieved by so acting, such a one might well begin on some occasion by asking "What was the good of my – or our – doing *that*?" or "Why was I – why were we – pursuing *that* rather than some other good?" What reflection may then elicit from agents is a need to make explicit the way in which they have up till now rank ordered goods in this particular area of their lives, and perhaps more generally, so that they ask not only if they were justified in acting as they did on this occasion, but also whether they are justified in general in rank ordering goods as they do. Or such agents might instead ask, reflecting on some particular episode, what difference it has made to their achievement of the goods that they pursue that they have or have not acted under the constraints imposed by the norms of justice, contrasting perhaps those social relationships that flourish when informed by those norms with those that result from the unjust and unfair treatment of others. The movement of reflection will characteristically be at first from the particular to the general and from the concrete to the abstract, but only so as to return to the particularities of the agent's decision making.

Such agents are through reflection learning to deliberate better and what they principally learn from are their own mistakes, mistakes that have put them at odds with others or with themselves. So they may come to

understand themselves as having progressed beyond their first identifications of goods, goods internal to those particular practices to which parents
and teachers had introduced them and their first recognition of the qualities of mind and character needed to become excellent in pursuing those
goods, through a stage in which they succeeded to greater or lesser degree in
integrating the pursuit of those goods into a life which was and perhaps is
their best attempt so far to flourish as a human being, toward their present
condition, whatever that happens to be. What practices those were will, of
course, vary with the social and cultural order that they inhabit and their
place in it. Someone apprenticed to a skilled craft, whose fine singing voice
is valued by local choirs, and who is developing as a cricketer will value
different excellences and have a very different kind of life from someone
in another country, another century, and speaking another language, who
works productively on a family farm, who learns how to tell and retell artfully those stories through which a knowledge of the past is preserved, and
who has served as a soldier. Their songs will be different, but the qualities
of mind and character that they need to deliberate well will be in essentials
one and the same.

Reflective practical agents thus become self-aware in at least three ways.
They make explicit and spell out concepts and theses whose range of
application and truth they had hitherto presupposed without being aware
of it. They discover that the realities of their practical lives are captured
by narratives of failure and success as practical reasoners, of their success
or failure in exemplifying the virtue that Aristotle called 'phronēsis' and
Aquinas 'prudentia'. And they consequently become aware of more or less
of a directedness in their lives, of an uneven movement toward some end
state about which they often can say very little. I have said of such reflective
agents that they become self-aware by learning from their mistakes. On
what resources are they able to draw in correcting in correcting their
errors?

They will, as we have already noticed, have learned to take seriously
the judgments of perceptive others, especially those others who exhibit the
qualities of mind and character that they have learned to value. They will
have learned to suspect themselves in types of situation in which in the
past they have become victims of their own desires. They will have learned
to give due weight to constraints such as those that the norms of justice
impose. But of course in all this there will be a certain circularity in their
reasoning. For, unless from near the outset they had already presupposed
the truth of conclusions at which they had not yet arrived, conclusions
which initially they did not know how to formulate, they would have been

unable later on to reach those conclusions. Those who go astray from the outset, who lack the early shaping of their commitments and habits that Aristotle took to be indispensable for the political and moral life, will lack the means for identifying, let alone correcting their errors.

If this is how it is with mature rational agents who have learned to understand themselves as rational agents in their own everyday idiom, then they must have found resources for identifying and dealing with two important sources of practical error. One arises from the danger that we all confront of being led astray by our feelings and affections, likings and disliking, hopes and wishes, fears and anxieties, as these change with age and biochemistry. The other arises from the sometimes distorting and misleading influences of our own social and cultural order on our beliefs, attitudes, and choices. Just because every rational agent learns to reason in idioms informed by the particularities of her or his own culture, every rational agent is in danger of repeating and transmitting the mistakes and distortions characteristic of that culture. Those whom we initially take to be exemplars of human flourishing are likely to be those whom our elders and teachers take to be exemplars. In societies in which it matters to be rich or powerful – that is, in most societies – the lives of those who happen to be rich and powerful are often taken to be exemplary. So rational agents, if they are not to be deformed by false beliefs, must educate themselves to see through such superstitions, superstitions often a good deal more subtle and plausible than this example might suggest. Let me begin by saying something about the first of these sources of error.

Everyone needs to learn to discipline their affections, so that they do not blind us as to what is the case. Everyone needs to learn to discipline their fears and anxieties, so that they do not become disproportionate and disabling. Everyone needs to learn that if their judgments give expression to strongly felt convictions, this must be only because they have sufficient reason to assert the judgments in question as true and the truth of those judgments gives them sufficient reason for feeling as they do. It is in the course of such learning that our feelings and our dispositions to feel are transformed, so that we no longer respond as infants respond. But these tasks of disciplining and transforming our feelings have to be undertaken again and again at different stages in our lives. When we fail in them, then insofar as our judgments express our feelings, we have good reason to distrust our judgments. Insofar as we have succeeded in them, the fact that our judgments express our feelings becomes irrelevant to the question of whether or not we are justified in making those particular judgments. When, therefore, expressivist theorists give self-aware rational agents reason to believe that their evaluative judgments give expression to underlying feelings, such agents will have no reason to quarrel with this. What they in turn will urge upon expressivists is a need to distinguish the several different relationships in which feelings and judgments can stand to each other and the importance of these differences to the moral life. The expressivist's central claims, rightly understood, are, so they will argue, not in the least incompatible with their own practical understanding of their judgments and of the justification of those judgments by appeal to the facts concerning human flourishing.

They will be similarly accepting of and perhaps at first similarly unimpressed by the claims of NeoAristotelian theorists, pointing out that if those claims are true, it is only because they are an accurate representation of the stances and reasoning of self-aware rational agents. Aristotle may have argued compellingly that theoretical enquiry will be certain to go astray if its starting point is not in truths learned and only to be learned in and through practice (*Nicomachean Ethics* I, 1094b27–1095b2–8). And he may have given us good reason to hold that practice provides the test of whether we have been acting well or badly (*Nicomachean Ethics* X, 1179a18–22). But, so they may complain, it is not Aristotle's theorizing, but their own practice from which they learned this. So self-aware rational agents may take themselves to be unthreatened by the disagreements of theorists, even when those disagreements are unresolvable. They may feel in particular unthreatened by either expressivism or NeoAristotelianism, finding a place for what each has to say within their own practical reflections. So it may seem, at least for a moment, that the impasse that we were unable to move beyond in our theorizing becomes irrelevant from the standpoint of practical agency and can be put aside. However, here it is the NeoAristotelian who must demur, pointing out that even if the commitments of the rational agent do indeed provide the starting point for theoretical reflection, such reflection is indispensable to rational agents who do not break off their enquiries prematurely. Practice is apt to go seriously astray unless informed by the conclusions and insights of certain kinds of theorizing. What kinds of theorizing are those?

I remarked earlier that we are all of apt to take for granted and to adopt into our own thinking those conceptions of human flourishing and human excellence that are dominant in our own culture. But, as I also noticed, such conceptions may be and often are dangerously mistaken. And it is perhaps the principal task of the political and moral theorist to enable rational agents to learn what they need to learn from the social and cultural tradition that they inherit, while becoming able to put in question that particular tradition's distortions and errors and so, often enough, engaging in a quarrel with some dominant forms of their own political and moral culture. For much of the rest of this book, I shall be engaging in just such a quarrel with dominant modes of thought in our own culture.

Let me begin that quarrel by reiterating my claim that contemporary philosophical theorizing about morality is flawed, insofar as it concerns itself not with the range of moralities that we encounter in different cultures, but with only one of them, 'Morality', the presently dominant moral system in advanced societies, which it presents as morality as such. Central to that system, as I also remarked earlier, are certain conceptions of utility and of individual human rights, so that there are recurring debates among those who invoke these conceptions as to whether or not some violation of this or that right can be justified, if the consequences of that violation for the utility of some set of individuals are taken into account. But what if utility thus conceived and human rights thus conceived are both of them fictions and the debates which employ them charades, socially indispensable charades, but nonetheless charades?

To maximize utility was on an earlier utilitarian view to maximize pleasure and to minimize pain. More recently the thought has been that to maximize utility is to maximize preference satisfaction. Neither formulation pays regard to the fact that what we are each of us pleased or pained by and what we each of us prefer depend in key part upon our prior moral formation, upon how far we are just, courageous and temperate, and therefore disposed to act rightly. How we conceive utility thus depends on our prior formation and commitments, so that it cannot provide a standard independent of them. To propose utility maximization as such as the measure of right action must therefore be a mistake. What, then, are we in fact doing when we make decisions on the basis of cost–benefit analyses as we often do? The answer is that we are always working with some highly determinate and contestable conception of what is to count as a cost and what as a benefit in this or that type of case and with some prior determination of whose costs and whose benefits are to be counted, whose costs and benefits ignored. It is evaluations already made or presupposed that allow us to find application for the notion of utility in our decision making. The notion of utility maximization as a freestanding notion that by itself provides guidance for action is a philosophical fiction.

Another such fiction is the notion of a human right. Protagonists of this notion characteristically take it to be indispensable, if they are to be able to assert that there are some types of harm and wrong the infliction of which on others is unconditionally prohibited, prior to and independently of any particular system of positive law. My quarrel is not at all with their claim that there are such unconditional prohibitions. It is with their advancing the thesis that appeals to human rights, understood as rights attaching to each and every human individual qua human individual, provide a justification for asserting and enforcing such prohibitions. Such appeals could only function as justifications, if there were sound arguments for asserting the existence of such rights. And there are no such arguments. To show this, we would have of course to proceed argument by argument from the eighteenth-century theorists of natural rights to such twentieth-century theorists as Hillel Steiner, identifying in each case the particular argumentative failure. But this can be done. The notion of a human right is another philosophical fiction.

It is of course true that in many situations appeals to human rights thus conceived have played an important part in securing the rights of deprived and oppressed individuals and groups, just as it is true that appeals to the maximization of utility, conceived in a crude Benthamite form, have played an important part in securing benefits for those who badly needed and need them, in the field of public health, for example. In all such cases there were and are better arguments for doing what justice and the common good require than those appeals provide. But their effectiveness in such cases is at once to be welcomed and yet subjected to critical scrutiny. For debates in which claims about the maximization of utility are matched against claims about some human right are never quite what they are presented as being. Often enough there is indeed something real at issue, but something disguised by its presentation in terms of the notions of utility and rights. Later I will be arguing more generally that contemporary philosophical theorizing about morality, instead of illuminating the realities with which we have to deal as rational agents, misleads and distorts and, more than this, that it has the social function of misleading and distorting. I shall argue further that it is only when we have understood how it so functions that we will be able to characterize the theoretical impasse at which we arrived in the first part of this essay more adequately. And this will be a necessary preliminary to saying more about the questions concerning desires and reasons which were my initial and remain my central preoccupation. So what do we need to do next? We need an account of how philosophical theorizing about morality, even powerful philosophical theorizing, does on occasion function so as to disguise and conceal key aspects of social realities, of practice. Such an account best begins from an example.

I begin therefore with one particular philosophical theorist. David Hume's writings are peculiarly relevant to my overall argument, in part because the exponents of expressivism are all to some degree his heirs, and in part because he made wonderfully explicit some of the key differences between his views and those of the NeoAristotelian tradition. But Hume's moral theorizing also functioned so as to disguise and conceal from his educated contemporaries key aspects of their own social and political order and of his attachment to it. That this is so does not in the least detract from Hume's greatness, and I begin where he himself would have begun, with his moral psychology.

2.2 Hume as an example: his local and particular conception of the natural and the universal

"The chief spring or actuating principle of the human mind is pleasure or pain," so Hume asserted in introducing his discussion of what he identified as natural virtues and vices,[1] and in his treatment of particular cases it is always pleasure or pain in one of their various guises that is taken to move agents to act. Earlier in the *Treatise* Hume had straightforwardly identified good and evil with pleasure and pain, speaking of "good and evil, or in other words, pain and pleasure." "DESIRE," he had said, "arises from good consider'd simply, and AVERSION is deriv'd from evil. The WILL exerts itself, when either the good or the absence of the evil may be attain'd by any action of the mind or body."[2] Hence, Hume's account of practical reasoning: "It appears evident that the ultimate ends of human actions can never, in any case, be accounted for by *reason*, but recommend themselves entirely to the sentiments and affections of mankind, without any dependence on the intellectual faculties."[3] So if we ask someone why he acts as he does, he will answer that he desires such and such and that by so acting he brings about such and such. If then asked why he desires such and such, he will reply that he is pleased by such and such or that he is pained by its absence, so terminating his explanation. "If you demand *Why?* *It is the instrument of pleasure,* says he. And beyond this it is an absurdity to ask for a reason."

---

[1] David Hume, *A Treatise of Human Nature*, ed. L. A. Selby-Bigge, Oxford University Press, 1888, iii, 3, 1.

[2] Ibid., ii, 3, 9.

[3] David Hume, *Enquiries Concerning the Human Understanding and Concerning the Principles of Morals*, ed. L. A. Selby-Bigge, Oxford: Clarendon Press, 1902, Appendix 1, 244, p. 293.

Hume therefore has no place for a distinction between desires whose objects are such that their attainment will please us and desires whose objects are such that, whether they please us or not, their achievement will be the achievement of a genuine good. This renders the vocabulary that he employs to speak of desire very different from, for example, Aristotle's, and the contrast with Aristotle is very much to the point, if we wish to understand Hume. Aristotle too had asserted that the genesis of action is never a matter of reason alone: "Now intelligence (*nous*) does not move without desire (*orexis*). For wish (*boulēsis*) is a [species of] desire (*orexis*), and, whenever someone is moved in accordance with reasoning, he is indeed moved in accordance with wish (*boulēsis*). But desire (*orexis*) also moves contrary to reasoning, for appetite (*epithumia*) is [a species of] desire (*orexis*)" (*De Anima* 433a22–26). Terence Irwin has explained Aristotle's contrasting uses of *boulēsis*, *epithumia*, and *thumos* by saying that "Rational desire, wish, *boulēsis*, is for an object believed to be good," while "Appetite, *epithumia*, is nonrational desire for an object believed to be pleasant," and "Emotion, *thumos*, is nonrational desire for objects that appear good, not merely pleasant, because of the agent's emotions."[4]

The difference between Aristotle and Hume is that while, on Aristotle's view, desires for objects that attract only because they are pleasing to the agent who desires them are to be distinguished from desires for objects taken to be good, on Hume's there can, as I already noted, be no such distinction, just because what we take to be good and what we find to be pleasant have been identified. What follows for Hume? On Aristotle's view, as on Hume's, agreement with others in sentiments, affections, and judgments is important, but on Aristotle's view it must be agreement informed by a shared recognition of standards of practical reasoning very different from Hume's. On Hume's view agreement in sentiments is prior to and a necessary condition both for common standards and for shared practical reasoning. Individuals need to measure themselves against and to correct their judgments by appeal to those standards that express what Hume takes to be the general agreement in sentiment of humankind. So Hume is not open to the possibility that even in so measuring and correcting themselves they may be in unperceived error. Those near universal sentiments are the only measure in moral matters, and those who quarrel with those sentiments are always in the wrong.

---

4 Terence Irwin, "Annotated Glossary," in *Nicomachean Ethics*, trans. Terence Irwin, Indianapolis, IN: Hackett, 1985, p. 394.

So it is with all deviations from the normal and the natural, from those judgments that express "the *natural* and *usual* force of the passions, when we determine concerning vice and virtue,"[5] deviations due to the adoption of motivating beliefs that result in artificial lives, lives such as those of Diogenes the Cynic or Pascal the Jansenist Christian. Such individuals are eccentric in what pleases and pains them and so put themselves at odds with the generality of humankind, inviting the condemnation of all those who identify themselves with the standard that Hume takes to be natural to humankind. Hume judges that in so arguing as a philosopher he is in moral agreement with all but the eccentric. The philosopher, so Hume asserts in the first section of the *Enquiry*, can assure himself of "the true origin of morals" by cataloguing those habits, sentiments, and faculties which, if ascribed to someone, imply praise or blame. "The quick sensibility, which, on this head, is so universal among mankind, gives a philosopher sufficient assurance, that he can never be considerably mistaken in framing the catalogue, or incur any danger of misplacing the objects of his contemplation: he need only enter into his own breast for a moment, and consider whether or not he should desire to have this or that quality ascribed to him, and whether or not such an imputation would proceed from a friend or an enemy."

The philosopher, that is to say, although he may introduce his hitherto nonphilosophical readers to philosophical arguments about the place of reason and the passions or sentiments in the moral life, has no advantage over those readers in respect of the facts and judgments that have provided the philosopher with his data. Any reader who is not an eccentric can at any time confirm the philosopher's judgments by entering into his own breast for a moment. Was Hume right about this? Was there and is there in fact this broad and near universal human consensus in sentiments and in judgments? The answer to these questions is of some importance in arriving at a verdict on Hume's moral philosophy. Yet to answer them, we have to put philosophical argument on one side for the moment and consider some salient features of the social and historical setting in which and about which Hume theorized. I begin with a general point.

In the course of discussing Hume's account of justice, Stuart Hampshire remarked that "So great has been the influence within contemporary moral philosophy of Hume, Kant, and the utilitarians that it has been possible to forget that for centuries the warrior and the priest, the landowner

---

[5] Hume, *Treatise*, iii, 2, 1.

and the peasant, the merchant and the craftsman, the bishop and the monk, the clerk who lives by his learning and the musician or poet who lives by his performances have coexisted in society with sharply distinct dispositions and virtues... Varied social roles and functions, each with its typical virtues and its peculiar obligations, have been the normal situation in most societies."[6] Moreover, it was the explicit or implicit claim of each of these social orders that to live and act as its norms and values dictated is to flourish both qua warrior or peasant or monk or poet, and qua human being. It was therefore impossible for Aristotle's medieval heirs, for example, to ignore the roles and relationships, norms and values, of the societies in which they found themselves. In giving their own account of human flourishing and of the virtues required for such flourishing, they could not avoid asking whether and how far individual and common goods could be achieved through the social roles and relationships of their own time and place.

With Hume it is very different. In his moral theorizing he invites his readers to think of themselves and others only as individuals, quite apart from their social roles, motivated in their activities and relationships by what they find agreeable or useful in others and in themselves, with no standard of good beyond that provided by their agreement in sentiments with others. He explains differences between cultures in their judgments concerning personal qualities by pointing out that a quality which it is useful for individuals to possess in one set of circumstances may lack utility in another. But Hume does not for a moment entertain the possibility that some large and numerous part of the inhabitants of his own social order in Scotland and England might have sentiments and act on judgments radically at odds with those that he takes to be universal. Consider one example of such a sentiment.

In his essay "Of the Rise and Progress of the Arts and Sciences," Hume declared that "Avarice, or the desire of gain, is an universal passion, which operates at all times, in all places, and upon all persons." In the *Treatise* he had asserted that "Nothing has a greater tendency to give us an esteem for any person than his power and riches," and he had explained "the *satisfaction* we take in the riches of others, and the *esteem* we have for the possessors" by referring first to the possessions of the rich "such as houses, gardens, equipages" and the like, which "being agreeable in themselves, necessarily produce a sentiment of pleasure in every one, that considers or

---

[6] Stuart Hampshire, *Innocence and Experience*, Cambridge, MA: Harvard University Press, 1989, p. 108.

surveys them," secondly to our "expectation of advantage from the rich and powerful by our sharing their possessions," and thirdly to "sympathy, which makes us partake of the satisfaction of every one, that approaches us."[7]

It is unsurprising, then that whenever in his essays Hume alludes to the progress from less to more sophisticated agricultural economies, and beyond these to the changing forms of trade and of manufacturing that had resulted in the commercial and mercantile society of his own day, there is rarely a hint that the continuing and growing prosperity of the rich and powerful has invited anything other than the applause and approbation of the less prosperous. It is true that in the *Enquiry* Hume did for a moment entertain the possibility of replacing the inequalities of the present by an equal distribution of goods, remarking that "wherever we depart from this equality, we rob the poor of more satisfaction than we add to the rich."[8] But he at once dismissed this possibility as absurd, speaking of the seventeenth-century Levellers, who had believed in such an equal distribution of property, as "*political* fanatics" and claiming that all such egalitarian schemes are "*impracticable*; and were they not so, would be extremely pernicious to human society. Render possessions ever so equal, men's different degrees of art, care, and industry will immediately break that equality. Or if you check these virtues you reduce society to the most extreme indigence... "[9]

Hume thus identifies the standpoint of what he takes to be natural and universal sentiments, and so of what he takes to be natural and universal morality, with an uncompromising endorsement of the values of the eighteenth-century British social and economic order. Any – in Hume's terms – artificial questioning of those values, whether from the standpoint of such ascetics as Diogenes and Pascal, or from that of the egalitarian Levellers is condemned. Yet this leaves unheard the voices of those eighteenth-century English common people whom historians have described as ruled "through forms of judicial terror" and as "deferential by day and deeply insubordinate by night."[10] Indeed, they were not always deferential by day and this in respect of ideas and sentiments as well as actions. Of the crowds who engaged in food riots, E. P. Thompson wrote that the rebellious actions of "almost every eighteenth century crowd" were informed by "some legitimizing notion. By the notion of legitimation I mean that the men and women in the crowd were informed by the belief that they were

---

[7] Hume, *Treatise*, ii, 2, 5. [8] Hume, *Enquiry*, iii, 2. [9] Ibid.
[10] D. Hay, P. Linebaugh, J. G. Rule, E. P. Thompson, and C. Winslow, *Albion's Fatal Tree: Crime and Society in Eighteenth Century England*, New York: Pantheon, 1975.

defending traditional rights and customs,"[11] rights and customs excluded from recognition by Hume's moral scheme.

What Hume's account leaves wholly unconsidered are three possibilities. The first is that as a matter of fact the degree and kind of disagreement in sentiments and judgments, both in Britain and elsewhere, is such that his claims concerning what is natural to and universal in humankind are seriously undermined. I will not pass judgment here on Hume's attempt to find a place within his moral scheme for large differences in sentiments and judgments between very different cultures, but note only that attention to the class and occupational structures of Britain, Ireland, and France provides by itself sufficient evidence to discredit some of Hume's central claims. The second is that the standpoints that give rise to these disagreements are all of them, *including Hume's own*, expressive not of universal sentiments, but of the kind of motivating beliefs that Hume is compelled to characterize as artificial. What on this supposition are Hume's motivating beliefs? They are those that put him in opposition in one way to Aristotle, in another to Pascal, in a third to the insubordinate eighteenth-century laborers, his beliefs that avarice is not a corrosive vice, that humility is not a virtue, that justice may not put in question established property rights. They are, to put it in terms quite other than his, his convictions concerning what human flourishing consists in. The third possibility that Hume's account rules out is that these moral disagreements, these disagreements in motivating beliefs, are rooted in differences between and potential or actual antagonisms between those who occupy very different positions in the economic structure, differences, as the Levellers put it, between "the poorest he" and "the richest he," differences, as Hampshire put it, between landowners and peasants, merchants, craftsmen, and laborers.

What I am suggesting is not only that some of Hume's claims were mistaken, but also that one effect of his advancing them in the way that he did was to conceal and disguise from his readers the importance of certain facts about the condition of their social and economic order. (I am not imputing any such intention to Hume.) Perhaps we can go further than this. What might justify us in asserting not only that this was an effect of Hume's theorizing, but also that that theorizing *functioned* so as to produce just this effect? We may say of some set of activities or states of affairs that they function so as to sustain the ongoing workings of some institution or set of institutions, if, were it the case that the former were not what they were, the latter would be in some way and to some degree frustrated.

---

[11] E. P. Thompson, *Customs in Common*, New York: The New Press, 1991, p. 188.

So we may also say of some set of beliefs that they function so as to sustain the workings of some set of social or economic institutions, if, were it the case that those false beliefs were not held by the relevant individuals or groups, the workings of those social or economic institutions would be to some significant extent frustrated.

What I am entertaining, then, is the possibility that in eighteenth-century Britain a widely held belief in the universality of morality, conceived roughly as Hume conceived it, functioned so as to conceal from the view of many of his contemporaries the underlying moral and social conflicts of their society and by so doing sustained the workings of the agricultural, commercial, and mercantile economy to the profit of some and to the detriment of others, others who are for the most part invisible to Hume. Hume's theorizing was of course only one – and certainly far from the most influential – of the intellectual defenses of that morality, an early stage in the development of Morality. But those philosophical opponents who criticized Hume's philosophical views of morality by and large shared the substance of his moral stance.

None of this, let me reiterate, detracts from Hume's greatness as a moral philosopher. Very obviously it has no direct bearing on the truth or falsity of Hume's expressivism, let alone on those later versions of expressivism whose authors have held moral, political, and economic views quite other than Hume's. It does, however, show the bearing that historical enquiry can have on philosophical debate. Hume's claims about the universality of the moral sentiments, as he understands them, are undermined by the findings of historians and this in a way that suggests that moral theorizing may be a less innocent activity than it is usually taken to be, that philosophical theorizing about morality in some social contexts may function as a source of potentially dangerous moral and political misunderstanding.

2.3 Aristotle and his social context; Aquinas's recovery of Aristotle from that context; how Aquinas seemed to have become irrelevant

Hume is of course far from the only philosopher whose political and moral philosophy is informed by the deformations of his own social and cultural order. Aristotle is even more obviously someone whose arguments go badly astray in this way. His conception of the natural slave as one who can act in accordance with reason only as the instrument of another and his claim that women are unlike men in their inability to control their passions as reason dictates are both wrongheaded in themselves and symptoms of something more deeply wrong. Modern Aristotelians – I think, for example, of Martha Nussbaum – have not found it difficult to excise these absurdities, while remaining Aristotelian in their account of the virtues, just as later Humeans – I think especially of Annette Baier – have not found it difficult to remain Humean in their account of the virtues, while rejecting Hume's illiberal attitudes. But Aristotle's case differs from Hume's in this, that failure to reject Aristotle's social prejudices not only would have made Aristotle's whole system of political, social, and moral thought irrelevant to the vast majority of humankind but would, in fact, have condemned his system to incoherence, something too seldom noted. How so?

The irrelevance would have been a consequence of Aristotle's view that not only women and natural slaves, but also productive workers and barbarians, that is, nonGreeks, are unable to function well as human beings by developing and exercising the powers of rational agency in a political society. The incoherence arises from the tension between this negative judgment and Aristotle's account of the human *telos* and the human *ergon,* the human function. What, on his view, distinguishes human animals from other animals, what constitutes their distinctive function, is the exercise of their capacity to act as rational agents in ordering their ends and achieving that final end which is theirs by nature. But if this is the human *ergon,* it must be the *ergon* of every human being. As A. W. H. Adkins put it, "In the case of other things that have *erga,* not all of them perform those *erga* excellently: not all sculptors are as good as Phidias, not all eyes have 20/20 vision. But all [human beings] can and must perform the *ergon* to some extent," something required by the very notion of an *ergon,* as Aristotle understands it.[12] Later revisionist Aristotelians have therefore been happy to rescue Aristotle simultaneously from prejudice and from incoherence.

The importance of so rescuing Aristotle from himself in understanding his ethics and politics is a matter primarily of his questions rather than of his answers. What Aristotle articulates are questions that adequately rational and sufficiently reflective agents cannot avoid putting to themselves, since they will in any case answer those questions by the way in which they act and live: What is my good qua member of a household, qua citizen, qua human being? What qualities of mind and character do I need to identify and order these goods correctly in my everyday practice so that I may function well as a human being? How are these qualities to be acquired?

---

[12] A. W. H. Adkins, "The Connection between Aristotle's Ethics and Politics," in *A Companion to Aristotle's Politics,* ed. David Keyt and Fred D. Miller, Jr., Oxford: Blackwell, 1981, p. 90.

But Aristotle addressed those questions in the course of instructing future rulers in fourth-century Greek cities, and so some of the political and social assumptions that he shared with his students and with other members of the Macedonian elite unsurprisingly went unquestioned.[13] Yet when his formulations of those questions are detached from such assumptions, both those questions and many of his answers to them become, as I suggested earlier, resources for rational and reflective agents in any culture.

How, then, should such agents proceed? We have already noted that about each type of activity in which they engage they will need to ask: What is the good, the end, served by this type of activity and what kind of agent must I become if I am to achieve or contribute to the achievement of this end? They will also need to ask: What place does and should this type of activity have in my life? But the terms in which they ask and answer these questions will be, as we also noted, the terms of their own culture, designed to capture the particularities of activity in the social and cultural order that they inhabit. Their questions and answers will be recognizable versions of Aristotle's, but fidelity to Aristotle in later periods always involves a work of cultural translation. So it is too with Aristotle's insistence that a prerequisite for making any sort of progress as a rational agent is an initial training such that the agent becomes disposed to respond in a variety of situations as someone directed toward the achievement of her or his good. That training too has to be in terms of the particularities of the agent's time and place, if she or he is to acquire the kind of discipline needed and the kind of experience needed to grasp the point of so directing themselves. For only from such a starting point will they become sufficiently disposed to direct and transform their desires so that those desires are for the relevant set of goods in their own time and place.

There is another crucial respect in which later Aristotelians have had to supply needed resources for themselves. It concerns their justification for thinking and acting as they do. When others, or for that matter they themselves, adduce what are at first sight compelling objections to some of the premises of their practical reasoning or perhaps to the very conception of practical agency to which they are committed, how are reflective agents to proceed? When Aristotle first poses his question about the nature of the final human end in the first book of the *Nicomachean Ethics*, he considers three views that are rivals to his own, shows in what ways the arguments of each fail, and then argues from significant aspects of those failures toward

---

[13] See Richard Bodéüs, *The Political Dimension of Aristotle's Ethics*, trans. J. E. Garret, Albany, NY: SUNY Press, 1993.

the conclusion that he takes to be justified. This suggests that in general the justification of any substantive position in politics and ethics – and perhaps in the sciences in general – must proceed through stages: in the first we need to rehearse the whole range of objections to it as compellingly as possible, that is, to make the strongest possible case against it; in the second we make the best answer possible to each of these objections and only if and when all of them have been shown to fail are we able to proceed to the third stage; in that third stage we advance the arguments for the conclusion that requires justification and show that they satisfy whatever constraints have been imposed by the negative conclusions at which we had arrived in the second stage.

As those debates in which a variety of rival positions confront one another proceed through time, new concepts and insights, new arguments, new objections, and new replies to objections may always emerge. So debates in ethics and politics are in one way interminable. But this understanding of rational justification does not in the least preclude our finding the case made for certain theses by the arguments so far conclusive. What it does entail, especially in ethics and politics, is that we should always take careful account of those social and intellectual changes that may have put in question the justification of positions that we have inherited from the past. So it has been a recurrent task for Aristotelians in each historical period to confront new as well as old objections to their central affirmations.

It is then the case that both in their everyday practice and in their theorizing, later Aristotelians have had to go beyond Aristotle in finding application for Aristotle's concepts, theses, and arguments in the detail of life in their own societies and in justifying their claims for these concepts, theses, and arguments. They have done so with varying degrees of success. One necessary condition for success is that they should not endorse either Aristotle's restrictive prejudices or the restrictive prejudices of their own culture, or at least that they should not allow those prejudices to inform their constructive work in politics and ethics. A case in point is that of Aquinas. Lamentably, in his *Commentary* on the *Politics* he seems to have endorsed Aristotle's conception of the natural slave (I, 3, 7 and 10). But this excessive deference to Aristotle did not inform or deform the political and moral enquiries which enabled him to address his contemporaries. (It is indeed in tension with his treatment of the *amentes*, the mentally backward or disordered, who, he insisted, are and are to be treated as rational agents whose potentialities have been frustrated by some physical cause. *Summa Theologiae* III, qu. 68, art. 12, ad. 2.)

Happily Aquinas found contemporary application for an Aristotelian ethics and politics in a way that was exemplary both for his Dominican contemporaries and for his and their successors. In the texts of the First and Second Parts of the Second Part of the *Summa Theologiae,* his contemporaries are addressed as questioning and self-questioning rational agents and Aquinas presents, in the form of a theoretical enquiry, just those sequences of questions to which such agents, sometimes explicitly, but more often implicitly will be giving practical answers by the ways in which they judge and act. He begins with those premises about human goods and ends and their ordering which provide agents with the first premises of their practical reasoning, and he concludes at various points in the Second Part of the Second Part with discussions of how problems central to everyday life are to be resolved. At each stage the reader is compelled to engage with a full range of objections to the conclusion for which Aquinas is arguing, and that reader has to learn how to make these objections her or his own, if she or he is to make that conclusion her or his own. Who is that reader? It is clearly not in the first instance the man in the thirteenth-century field or the woman in the thirteenth-century household.

It is, however, the teacher of those who, as pastors or teachers, will advise and counsel that woman and that man in their everyday lives as rational agents. Crucial for both teachers and learners are the intermediate steps in Aquinas's overall arguments in which the implications of the first principle and premises of practical reasoning are spelled out in terms of what the virtues and obedience to the natural law require of rational agents if they are to achieve their common and their individual goods. What those virtues and that obedience require puts in question some of the social and institutional structures of their own day, structures through which established power was exercised and sustained. The precepts of the natural law are those precepts of reason conformity to which is necessary if we and others are to be able to deliberate together as rational agents and to achieve our common goods as family members, as members of political societies, and the like. The positive laws of particular societies have the character of genuine law only insofar as they are in conformity with the natural law. So plain persons, by the exercise of reason in reflecting with others on how they are to achieve their common goods, are able to put in question the actions of those with authority and power. And, insofar as such plain persons understand what at the level of everyday practice the virtues require of them, they are also able to understand what the virtues require of their rulers, especially by way of justice. The consideration of what rationality requires of rulers and ruled becomes a prologue to radical social critique.

It matters that what these texts of the *Summa* provide is instruction as to how to educate in practical reasoning. Whether the philosophical positions that Aquinas defends can be rationally vindicated against their rivals in theoretical debates is of the first importance, but much of that importance derives from the implications of those positions for the practical reasoning of plain nonphilosophical persons. What they have to learn is how to direct their questioning so that they identify correctly – at the level of practice – the ends that they are to pursue as the objects of their desires, learning also how to transform their desires so that they are rightly directed. The disciplines in which they are to be instructed by teachers who have learned from the *Summa* are the disciplines of reflective practice, disciplines which presuppose just that relationship between reason and desire which finds expression in Aristotelian accounts of action. So, for Aquinas as for Aristotle, when lives go wrong, something is always amiss in the relationship of reason to desire in those lives. Agents fail as rational agents because they desire what they lack good reason to desire.

Aquinas's identification with the concerns of plain persons as practical reasoners is evident in the range of everyday issues with which he deals: the place of manual labor in our lives, whether we are permitted to gossip, the importance of truthfulness, the importance of jokes and the role of the travelling entertainer, the moral constraints on soldiers, the limits to the rights of private property when a legalistic insistence on them would prevent us from aiding someone in urgent need, the responsibilities of parents for instructing their children. Consider how he addresses problems of the market place in his discussion of fraud as a kind of injustice (*Summa Theologia* IIa–IIae, qu. 77). That discussion is addressed to farmers, craftsmen, and merchants. It presupposes his endorsement of Aristotle's account, in Book V of the *Nicomachean Ethics*, of economic value and just exchange and of how money is a means of measuring the relative values of different kinds of goods. The value of a good, as Aquinas, following Augustine, understands it (*Summa Theologia* IIa–IIae, qu. 77, art. 2, ad. 3), consists in its usefulness to human beings in general. The value of a horse or a house or a pair of shoes is the usefulness of a horse or a house or a pair of shoes. Differences in the prices of such items should express their relative values in that particular time and place. This latter qualification is important, since the usefulness of different products may vary a good deal in different times and places.

Aquinas distinguishes two kinds of market transaction, one in which producers sell directly to consumers, the other in which merchants buy from producers and then sell to others. In the former what is generally required is simply that prices should be just, that is that the price should be equivalent to the value of the good that is sold. The price that the seller asks should be the price that he himself would think it just to pay, were he the buyer. In the latter merchants who buy and sell may increase the price at which they sell over that which they paid by no more than what is sufficient to cover the expenses incurred in their trading, except when the merchant has made what he bought into something of greater value – he trained the horse, he painted the house, he added buckles to the shoes (my examples, not Aquinas's) – or changes in social circumstances have made this particular good more valuable or the merchant had to take unusual risks in procuring the good or he had to pay some third party in order to carry through the transaction.

What these exceptions and the general rule to which they are exceptions combine to make clear is that, on Aquinas's view, it is never permissible to engage in market transactions only to make a profit or primarily to make a profit. The pursuit of profit for its own sake is unjust. The point and purpose of monetary exchanges in markets is to enable us all to benefit from each other's labor, and financial gain is to be valued only for the goods for which it can be exchanged and for the needs that it thereby enables us to meet. We are to grow wealthier by being more productive. Increasing profit is never a sufficient reason for engaging in one kind of productive activity rather than another or in one kind of market transaction rather than another. Agents need to understand that the acquisition of money is no more than a means to the achievement of and the acquisition of goods and that such achievement and acquisition is to serve common goods.

It follows that our desires have to be ordered to money only as a means of achieving our individual and common goods. Each of us needs only so much money and we have no good reason to desire riches as such and no reason at all to esteem the rich as such. This does not of course mean that greater productivity is not desirable for all sorts of reasons. It does mean that a life devoted to the acquisition of money is characteristically a life of disordered desires. The contrast with Hume is obvious. Sentiments that Hume takes to be near universal and natural among humankind Aquinas takes to be symptoms of failure as a rational agent. And in this respect Aquinas's view contrasts not only with Hume's but also with that of Hume's contemporary and friend, Adam Smith.

On Smith's account of economic activity, it is by each individual pursuing the increase of her or his own profit that productivity is increased, and that each individual benefits from the labor of others, so that the general prosperity is increased. What motivates individuals to act so as to grow as wealthy as possible is in key part, on Smith's account, a set of cheerful illusions fostered by our imaginations about the satisfactions afforded to the great and the rich by their possessions and powers, illusions that, except "in times of sickness and low spirit," set us to work. "And it is well," adds Smith, "that nature imposes on us in this manner. It is this deception which rouses and keeps in continued motion the industry of mankind."[14] It is, that is, for the general good, for the good of the large majority of individuals in the long run, that each individual should act not for the sake of that general good but so as to achieve what each individual takes, although sometimes quite mistakenly, to be her or his good. It is better that we should be victims of self-deception than that we should see things as they are. What makes this unqualified claim more surprising is that Smith himself was in no way a victim of such illusions, someone as well aware of the negative as of the positive aspects of economic and financial aspiration. It was the "disposition to admire, and almost to worship the rich and the powerful, and to despise, or, at least, to neglect persons of poor and mean condition," he had argued earlier in *The Theory of Moral Sentiments*, that was at once necessary, if the social order was to be sustained, and yet "the great and most universal cause of the corruption of our moral sentiments."[15]

What is missing from Smith's account is any conception of economic activity as capable of being cooperatively and intentionally directed toward the achievement of common goods, understood as Aristotle and Aquinas understood them, let alone any thought that it is only in and through the achievement of such goods that individuals are able to achieve their individual goods. But it should at once occur to us that that conception and that thought are not be found in Hume's writings any more than they are in Smith's. And this suggests that their absence was a matter of the general culture shared by Hume, Smith and those educated contemporaries in Scotland, England, France, and the Netherlands who were their readers and who provided the political, mercantile, commercial, and academic leadership of their societies. They shared a way of life which no longer had any place for that conception or that thought. So the sentiments that Smith and Hume catalogue and describe with such care and wit are in part not sentiments shared by all humankind, but sentiments praised and cultivated by eighteenth-century commercial and mercantile humankind and often enough by their present-day heirs.

[14] Adam Smith, *The Theory of Moral Sentiments*, Oxford: Clarendon Press, 1976, IV, i, 9–10, p. 183.
[15] Ibid., I, iii, 1, p. 61.

The question therefore arises: What happened in Europe between the thirteenth and the eighteenth centuries that could account for this state of affairs? One answer often given to questions of this kind is that Aristotle's thought, and with it Aquinas's, had been intellectually defeated in the philosophical debates of the sixteenth and seventeenth centuries. But in fact, so far as Aristotelian and Thomistic ethics and politics are concerned, there were few such systematic debates and those that did occur provide not even the beginning of an explanation for this kind of change or this degree of change. Moreover, it is not that there were that many Thomists in thirteenth- and fourteenth-century Europe. In the Middle Ages Aquinas as a moral and political thinker was an outsider, as were his Dominican followers. But what was plain at that time to theorists and plain persons alike was the immediate relevance of his thought, so that he had to be agreed with or answered, so that his questions were too often inescapable for those who were adequately reflective. The change that we need to explain therefore was not primarily a matter of episodes in the history of philosophical theorizing, but rather one of large social dimensions, one whereby the irrelevance of Aquinas's thought to the everyday life and labors of plain people came to be almost, if not quite universally, taken for granted. Plain people and theorists alike came to understand their lives in terms which seemed to rule out any possibility of conversation with Aquinas. The theorist who provides us with some of the key resources for understanding how this happened is Karl Marx.

2.4 Marx, surplus value, and the explanation of Aquinas's apparent irrelevance

The Marx to whom we need to go is not the mythological figure who was, together with Engels, the author of Marxism. 'Marxism' is the name of a system, indeed of a number of rival systems. Marx himself, although a notably systematic thinker, left us an incomplete body of work in which the bearing of one part on another often poses questions, questions generally left unrecognized by those who have projected on to his texts large and general doctrines, some of which he never held.[16] When it was suggested to Marx by Kautsky that he should publish his completed works, Marx's reply was that they would first have to be completed.

---

[16] On this see George L. Kline, "The Myth of Marx's Materialism," *Annals of Scholarship* 3, 2 (1984): 1–38.

Moreover, for a long time both sympathetic and unsympathetic philosophical commentators on Marx understandably focused on Marx's problematic and changing relationship to Hegel, so that it was only later that the
full importance of Marx's relationship to Aristotle began to be understood.[17]
And the Marx from whom we need to learn is the Marx who had learned
from Aristotle.

Had Marx achieved the university teaching appointment that he had
hoped for at Bonn in 1842, his first lectures would have been on Aristotle. In the years 1843–1845, while a radical journalist, he made a close
study of Aristotle's *Politics*. And when he refers to Aristotle in his mature
economic writings, it is always with a kind of respect that he shows to
few of his contemporaries. Indeed, he takes Aristotle to have described
accurately the forms of economic exchange of the ancient Greek world
and the history of their development. When he moves beyond Aristotle,
in order to understand the distinctive economic forms and development
of the modern world, he still employs key concepts as Aristotle used them:
essence, potentiality, goal-directedness. For Marx, as for Aristotle, to have
understood something, is to have grasped its essential properties, a prerequisite for identifying its causal relationships. For Marx, as for Aristotle,
we understand something only if we know not only what it is, but what
it has in it by its very nature to become. So he held, for example, that
"Human anatomy contains a key to the anatomy of the ape."[18] For Marx,
as for Aristotle, human agents can be understood only as goal-directed, and
we can distinguish between those goals the pursuit of which will develop
their human potentiality and those goals the pursuit of which will frustrate
their development. All these are parts of what Heinz Lubasz rightly called
Marx's "decisive debt" to Aristotle, a debt that Marx acknowledged in the
first chapter of *Capital*.

Marx is there asking how we should think about the value of the human
labor embodied in a coat and of that embodied in a quantity of linen,
so that the one becomes exchangeable for the other. Having identified
certain features of that equivalence in value, he remarks that they "will
become more intelligible if we go back to the great thinker who was the
first to analyse so many forms, whether of thought, society, or Nature,

---

[17] On this see Scott Meikle, *Essentialism in the Thought of Karl Marx*, London: Duckworth, 1985;
Jonathan E. Pike, *From Aristotle to Marx*, Aldershot: Ashgate, 1999; Heinz Lubasz "The Aristotelian
Dimension in Marx," *Times Higher Education Supplement*, April 1, 1977; and Patricia Springborg,
"Politics, Primordialism, and Orientalism: Marx, Aristotle, and the Myth of the Gemeinschaft,"
American Political Science Review 80, 1 (1986): 185–211.

[18] Karl Marx, *Grundrisse der Kritik der politischen Ökonomie*, trans. Martin Nicolaus, London: Allen
Lane, 1973, p. 105.

and amongst them also the form of value, I mean Aristotle."[19] But Aristotle's analysis of the relationships between goods and money and of the concepts of use-value and exchange-value – Marx was referring to the discussion of just exchange in Book V of the *Nicomachean Ethics* – was, on Marx's view, necessarily incomplete, because Aristotle, living in a slave society, had not grasped the equality and equivalence of all kinds of labor, something possible only in a society in which "the concept of human equality" had been widely accepted. Marx therefore found it necessary to go beyond Aristotle in order to construct an account of value and especially of surplus value that would disclose the workings of a nineteenth-century economy.

Although Marx believed that from his own nineteenth-century standpoint the workings of a capitalist economy could now at last be understood, on his view those who had in the preceding centuries by their economic activities and relationships brought that economy into being not only had not understood but could not have understood those activities and relationships, activities and relationships whose character was disguised from them by the forms under which labor was presented, by the commodification of labor. "A commodity . . . is a mysterious thing, simply because in it the social character of men's labour appears to them as an objective character stamped upon the product of that labour; because the relation of the producers to the sum total of their own labour is presented to them as a social relation, existing not between themselves, but between the products of their labour."[20] Capitalism is not only a set of economic relationships. It is also a mode of presentation of those relationships that disguises and deceives.

One consequence of this inability to understand, as Marx noted later, was that neither capitalists nor productive workers were able to recognize that capital is "unpaid labor." The contrast with capitalist modernity that Marx draws is with the activities and relationships of the immediately preceding precapitalist economy, that of the European Middle Ages, that period, although Marx did not say so, in which the relevance of Aquinas's questioning had been evident. It was a state of affairs, declared Marx, where

> we find everyone dependent, serfs and lords, vassals and suzerains, laymen and clergy. Personal dependence here characterizes the relations of production just as it does the other spheres of life organized on the basis of that production. But for the very reason that personal dependence forms

[19] Karl Marx, *Capital*, Vol. I, New York: International Publishers, 1967, pp. 59–60.
[20] Ibid., p. 72.

the ground-work of society, there is no necessity for labour and its products to assume a fantastic form different from their reality . . . Here the
particular and natural form of labour . . . is the immediate social form of
labour.[21]

Medieval people, in a setting very different from that of the capitalism that
was about to develop, saw things as they were.

It is unsurprising that Marx, although himself so willing to learn from
Aristotle, shows no awareness of any possible connection between this ability of people in the high Middle Ages to grasp the truth about their social
condition and the fact that the theorists who educated their teachers and
pastors were so often followers of Aristotle. For one thing those theorists
were philosopher theologians and Marx had learned from his Enlightenment predecessors and from Feuerbach to be dismissive of theology. For
another the scholarly historical study of the Middle Ages had only just
begun. But what was thereby concealed from Marx's view was of some
importance. What Aristotle's idiom, as employed by Aquinas and by many
others, allowed his medieval readers – and those instructed by them – to do,
as we have already noticed, was to pose political and moral questions about
the particular social roles and relationships in which they found themselves
and to construct a critique of those roles and relationships, questions that
allowed them – craftsmen, farmers, merchants, judges, teachers, soldiers,
and priests – to reflect critically upon those relationships of personal dependence of which Marx speaks. It therefore matters that the change in their
way of life that resulted in an inability to understand their economic and
social relationships was one that deprived them of that idiom and, with
it, the possibility of asking those questions. What then is it that we can
learn from Marx about that change? The Marx from whom we can learn
is the Marx of the first volume of *Capital*, and what we need to learn is
twofold.

On the one hand, his theory of surplus value is the key to understanding capitalism as an economic system, both capitalist accumulation and
capitalist exploitation. On the other, his account of how individuals must
think of themselves and of their social relationships, if they are to act as
capitalism requires them to act, is the key to understanding why in capitalist societies individuals systematically misunderstand themselves and
their social relationships. Capitalism, as Althusser emphasized, is a set of
structures that function in and through modes of dissimulation. But to be
undeceived we have to begin with surplus value.

---

[21] Ibid., p. 77.

On Marx's account, for the concept of surplus value to have application certain preconditions must be satisfied. There must first of all be a labor force of workers no longer able to meet their needs and those of their families by farming the land where they live, either as tenants of their feudal lord, or as sharing in customary rights to common land, or as farmers of their own land, so that they have no alternative but to hire themselves out for wages, for money, in markets where they may have to and often will have to compete to be hired. There must also be a class of owners of the means of production – land, tools, machines, raw materials – who as employers pay out those wages, wages that are sufficient to sustain the needed labor force in being, but that are less than the value that those workers produce. That surplus value is appropriated by the employers for their own economic purposes. It is the source of their profits and then of the investments that they are able to make in their own and other enterprises. Without the appropriation of surplus value, the value of unrecompensed labor, such investment and, springing from it, the extraordinary rates of growth in productivity that capitalism generates would never have taken place.

Yet those whose labor power had thus become a commodity did not recognize themselves as, and even now generally do not recognize themselves as having become in this respect commodities to be exchanged for money, to be bought and sold at whatever rate the relevant market dictates. They thought and think of themselves in quite other ways and understandably so. "Commodities are things and therefore without power of resistance against man . . . in order that these objects may enter into relation with each other as commodities, their guardians must place themselves into relation with one another, as persons whose will resides in those objects, and must behave in such a way that each does not appropriate the commodity of the other, and part with his own, except by means of an act done by mutual consent. They must, therefore, mutually recognize in each other the rights of private proprietors," something that finds expression in the form of a contract.[22] The relations of exchange through which those who own the means of production appropriate the unpaid labor of productive workers are disguised by their legal form as the contractual relations of free individuals, each of them seeking what she or he takes to be best for her or himself. And as capitalism becomes the dominant economic mode of production and exchange, so this way of thinking about oneself and one's relationships becomes the dominant mode of social and moral thought, both among theorists and in everyday life.

---

[22] Ibid., p. 84.

What distinguishes one mode of social and moral thought from another is the set of questions to which its precepts and arguments provide answers. So the questions to which this new, but in the sixteenth and seventeenth century rapidly maturing mode of thought had to provide answers focused on the norms needed to govern the relationship of each individual to other individuals, the norms that each individual should recognize as binding on her or himself. That is to say, the question for each individual became 'Why should I not pursue the satisfaction of my desires with unbridled egoism, resorting to force or to fraud whenever necessary?' and the case for morality became the case for altruism. Disputes among philosophical theorists become disputes as to what that case is. Hobbes gave one answer, Locke another, Hume a third, Smith a fourth, Bentham a fifth, Kant a sixth, Hegel a seventh. Their rival answers mirrored and continue to mirror the disputes of everyday life. Their originality lay in the arguments by which they supported those answers, arguments that to a remarkable extent became part of the argumentative repertoire of everyday life. So there came into being both the phenomenon that I identified in the final section of Chapter 1 of this essay as Morality (Bernard Williams' "the morality system") and its counterpart, modern moral philosophy.

It is important that what distinguishes the standpoint of Morality from that of any NeoAristotelian standpoint and most notably from that of Aquinas are the central questions that those who occupy that standpoint ask and the concepts whose unproblematic character they presuppose in asking those questions. It is important that there is no place within their conceptual scheme for such Aristotelian and Thomistic notions as those of an end, a common good, or the natural law. Their conception of happiness as a psychological state, that state in which an individual's desires have been satisfied, is very different from the Aristotelian conception of *eudaimonia* or the Thomistic conception of *beatitudo*. The result by the early eighteenth century was that when such protagonists of Aquinas as there still were put to their European contemporaries questions that Aquinas had addressed to his contemporaries, they went unheard. The presuppositions of the way of life and the mode of thought that had come into being were just too different. It was not that those whose lives were informed by a Thomist understanding of themselves and their relationships could not on occasion put the moral culture of capitalist economies to the question, but that they could do so effectively only when they presented not just an alternative body of theory, but the possibility of an alternative way of life to the capitalist way of life, that is, when they presented the NeoAristotelian tradition in its Thomistic form as an alternative set of practices informed by an alternative understanding of the relationship of theory to practice. And this was rarely so.

When – very occasionally and in exceptional conditions – it was so, it was instructive. In the sixteenth century it was Dominicans who had had a Thomistic education who argued against Renaissance Aristotelians, such as Sepúlveda, that Aristotle's texts could not be used to justify the enslavement of indigenous peoples in the Americas. In the seventeenth century it was Thomistically educated Jesuits who organized the Tupi-Guarani people and others to resist enslavement by military force and led them both in battle and on a migration at the end of which they established communities organized on the basis of a strong conception of the common good. The Indians in those communities were educated to read and write, as soldiers, farmers, craftsmen, and musicians. Their productive work was directed toward increasing and egalitarian prosperity for the entire community and the original 12,000 had grown to nearly 100,000 in the early eighteenth century.[23] The Jesuit leaders of this first modern communist society, however, not only provided, but also monopolized leadership, and as a result failed to provide for a future leadership that would have enabled that society to survive the expulsion of the Jesuits from Portuguese and Spanish territories in 1759 and 1767. So Aquinas became as irrelevant in the uplands of the Parana River as he already was almost everywhere else in the century of Smith and Bentham.

Aquinas as a NeoAristotelian theorist therefore played a very different part on the one hand as a questioner of the cultural and social order of his own time and place and on the other as someone invoked centuries later by critical questioners of the cultural and social order of an increasingly well established capitalist economy. I have argued that our ability to understand the nature of that difference adequately depends in part on our having learned from Marx just what it was about capitalism – the appropriation of surplus value – that transformed the relationships of the cultural and social order so radically and what it was that disguised the nature of those relationships. It also depends on our having learned from Marx key truths about the destructive and self-destructive aspects of capitalism. Capitalist investment combined with technological invention to produce industrial revolution after industrial revolution, developing productive capacities and

---

[23] See D. A. Brading, *The First America: The Spanish Monarchy, Creole Patriots, and the Liberal State, 1492–1867*, Cambridge University Press, 1991, pp. 172–178.

powers and raising standards of living as it did so. But it also, as Marx had observed and predicted, destroyed or marginalized traditional ways of life, created gross and sometimes grotesque inequalities of income and wealth, lurched through crisis after crisis, creating recurrent mass unemployment, and left those areas and those communities that it was not profitable to develop permanently impoverished and deprived.

It had been Marx's hope and belief that, as the industrial working class responded to their condition under capitalism by acts and institutions of resistance to what was inflicted on them, they would increasingly understand themselves and their conditions in the terms that he and Engels had provided and to some extent they did so, especially in Germany and France. Yet what Marx had not predicted was the kind of debate and the extent of debate that was to take place among working-class and other critics of capitalism. He had of course from an early stage been aware of and dismissive of the Utopian socialists and the first Christian socialists, while later he and Engels had struggled to minimize Ferdinand LaSalle's influence on the German Social Democratic Party. But there were some kinds of conflict that he had not foreseen.

These conflicts were rooted both in the changing conditions of late nineteenth- and early twentieth-century working-class life and in the need to interpret and find new applications for the teaching of Marx and Engels in those conditions. What they elicited were a set of rival Marxisms that gave expression to a range of reformist and revolutionary interpretations of Marx. The disagreements of the protagonists of these rival interpretations were various but presupposed agreement on two major issues. The working class, so it was argued, could only achieve its economic and social goals through giving its support to a Marxist political party that would provide it with leadership and direction. And the task of that party, so it was argued, was to win control of the agencies of the state and to use the power of the state to transfer the ownership of the means of production from the members of the capitalist class to the now socialist state. It would then become possible to construct a socialist society under the leadership of party and state. But those propositions were themselves of course subject matter for debate.

It mattered immensely that in Marx's later life there had already developed and was developing further a lively working-class culture in countries such as Germany, France, and England, a culture of reading and writing, of sports and games, of trade unions, mutual aid societies, and other clubs, of beer halls and bars and eating places, of music halls and circuses, of, on occasion, churches. Working-class people thought for themselves about what capitalism inflicted on them and, if their thoughts were to be Marxist thoughts, that would depend on the ability of Marxists to engage them in debate and on how that debate went. Here Marxists made notable advances within trade unions and political parties, but also encountered rival claimants for working-class allegiance. And it was not unimportant that increasingly Marxists also had to engage in quite another sort of theoretical debate, academic debate, in which their antagonists were those defenders of capitalism whose theses and arguments derived from the first emerging and then established discipline of economics. For that academic discipline presented capitalism from a perspective in which Marx's critique becomes invisible. Just because it does so, it poses the question of whether its presentation of capitalism is not one more mode of presentation well designed, although not of course intentionally, to disguise and deceive.

2.5   Academic economics as a mode of understanding and misunderstanding

Economics took on the form of an academic discipline in a number of European universities in the last decades of the nineteenth century. Its content was principally supplied by the work of equilibrium theorists in Austria, France, England, and elsewhere. The central claim advanced by those theorists and by their successors was and is that it is only through unregulated competition within free markets that scarce resources are allocated efficiently, so that prices express a matching of supply with demand and there is a movement toward a state of equilibrium in which each participant in market transactions fares as well as she or he can under conditions that are optimal for every other participant. What those theorists claimed to have achieved, and to some degree had achieved, was a representation by means of a set of equations of those relationships of exchange that determine relative prices within particular markets and so provide investors, entrepreneurs, workers, and consumers with the data that they need to make their economic decisions, if they are to act as rational maximizers. The further development of economic theory was in part the result of more or less successful attempts to accommodate within their generalizations apparent or real anomalies and to do justice to the increasing complexities of economic activity .That latter goal was achieved only by a growing sophistication in mathematics.

The history of economics in the last 150 years could be illuminatingly written as a history of its textbooks, partly because from Marshall to

Samuelson the authors of the most influential textbooks have been among its greatest theorists – something true of very few academic disciplines – and partly because those textbooks, widely taught in business schools as well as in economics departments, inculcated in those who read them just those modes of decision making that they described. The particles studied by physicists are uninfluenced by what is written in physics textbooks. But agents in economic transactions have often acted with what they learned from their textbooks in mind, something too little remarked upon by academic economists. Why does this matter? In part because what has been and still is inculcated by the textbooks as well as by the ethos of modern economic activity is an underlying conception of what it is to be a rational agent.

It took a long time for that conception to be made fully explicit, something set on foot by Pareto, but for which the final credit should go to the Chicago statistician, L. J. Savage. On this view, to be a rational agent is to make rational choices and to make rational choices is to take consistent account of one's preferences, of what one prefers to what and by how much, and of the consequences for the satisfaction of those preferences of choosing this rather than that alternative. Notice that nothing turns on how a particular agent may have arrived at her or his preferences. Those, like the preferences of other agents that may have a bearing on one's choice, are to be taken as given. To be rational is to be a consistent maximizer of preference satisfaction. This of course is a view of practical rationality deeply at odds with the accounts advanced by Aristotle and Aquinas and with the assumptions of plain persons whose self-understanding has not been shaped by a capitalist social order. Savage published his account in 1954, but what he captured was an assumption about economic agents that had been widely presupposed both in market exchanges and in economics textbooks for a very long time indeed and continues to be widely presupposed even now.

Savage arrived at his findings by considering what it would be to be an agent acting consistently under conditions of uncertainty, whatever the content and the ordering of that agent's preferences might be. He says nothing and needs to say nothing about the psychology or the social relationships of this or that particular agent. What he purports to portray is how *any* agent whatsoever must act, if she or he is, given their preferences, to make consistent choices. The agent so portrayed turns out to be a more sharply defined version of the utility maximizing agent portrayed in classical and neoclassical economic theory, types of theory very much at odds with Marx's analysis of capitalism. Unsurprisingly, academic economists by and large take a very different view and more optimistic view of the prospects of capitalism from that taken by those who have learned what Marx has to teach. For that in capitalism which tends toward crisis and destruction was relegated to the margins of study as matters of hazard and accident.

These academic protagonists of capitalism later divided into a number of contending parties. They agreed and agree that free market economies are the only engines of growth, as measured by Gross Domestic Product, the value of marketed output, and therefore of prosperity, as they understood and understand it. The crises recurrent in such economies are to be explained by the impact of external factors, on some occasions by irrationalities in human psychology, on others by imperfect information, on still others by unwise governmental interventions, all of them, we should note, factors that are objects of study by other academic disciplines, by psychology or sociology or political science. But at this point professional economists divide. For the large majority of academic economists, the gross inequalities and the recurring unemployment and regeneration of poverty that result from even the best economic policies are effects that must be accepted for the sake of the benefits of long-term growth and with it worldwide reduction in the harshest poverty in underdeveloped countries. The risks inherent in making those predictions on which economic decisions are based can be calculated and the practice of investment by those with an adequate education in economics can be justified as an art of rational risk taking. Or so they argue. What such views do not reckon with adequately or at all is fourfold.

First, even in the ordinary course of things risk taking in stock and commodities markets in everyday transactions suffers from unpredictably varying degrees of uncertainty, while characteristically and generally traders in those markets are only able to operate as they do by taking a relatively optimistic view of things, by acting as if there is rational justification for their own degree of risk taking, an attitude that for the most part serves them well until one day, in the quite ordinary course of things, it suddenly and unexpectedly doesn't. Secondly, markets function in social contexts and every few years some unforeseen event from the larger outside world – a plague, a war, a decision by a government to repudiate its debts – disrupts what had been taken for granted by those engaged in market transactions. Thirdly, the incentives for traders are designed to reward them for making profits by taking risks and for making ever greater profits by taking ever greater risks, so that they are collectively disposed to think in terms of the short rather than the long run and therefore to underrate significantly the possibilities and probabilities of failure. Fourthly and finally, what traders put at risk is not only their employers' and their investors' money, but the livelihoods of large numbers of people, unknown to them and unconsidered by them, on whom from time to time they casually and incidentally inflict great harm, something which the narrowness of their education in academic economics or in business studies helps them to put out of mind. Yet it would be unfair to ignore the fact that there are of course economists who do take such matters with great seriousness.

Characteristically, they argue that the vagaries of markets need to be and can be held in check by government action designed to limit, if not to cure, the ills of unemployment and inequality. The aim of such action is to manage aggregate demand, so that the economy will maintain a desirable rate of growth. Against this view, whose principal exponent was Keynes, monetarists have argued that this project itself distorts market relationships and that management of the money supply is what is needed. The debate between the adherents of these rival standpoints continues. One reason why some major issues posed in those debates remain unresolved is the lack of predictive power of all the major brands of theory. The stagflation of 1973–1975 was predicted by no one. The financial crisis of 2008 was predicted by very, very few academic economists and an even smaller number of observant traders, but this on empirical rather than theoretical grounds. And crises in general have been treated as unpredictable. Yet what all these contending parties have agreed upon and do agree upon is in rejecting Marx's radical diagnosis of capitalism's recurrent ills. Keynes said of Marx's thought that it was "complicated hocus-pocus" and that "My feelings about *Das Kapital* are the same as my feelings about the *Koran*."[24] Academic economists, that is, whether Keynsians or defenders of Fama's Efficient Markets hypothesis, agree in defending capitalism, unsurprisingly perhaps since so many of them at some stage in their careers act as consultants to or sit on the boards of corporations and trade associations or are employed by government to stabilize and strengthen the capitalist economic order. That is, they understand themselves and their activities in terms of their theories.

Unsurprisingly, they do not always adopt an adequately critical attitude toward their own theories. In 2013 the Nobel Prize for Economics was awarded to Eugene Fama, Lars Peter Hansen, and Robert Shiller. Fama's Efficient Markets hypothesis, first advanced in 1965 in "Random Walks in Stock Market Prices," is that asset prices are determined by

---

[24] See Robert Skidelsky, *John Maynard Keynes: 1883–1946*, London: Penguin Books, 2003, pp. 515–519.

"informationally efficient" markets, so that at any one time those prices reflect the information available to investors. It follows that market transactions can never result in irrational pricing. Yet Shiller's Nobel Prize was awarded for his explanations of episodes of irrational pricing, so-called "bubbles," and Hansen's for demonstrating that wild changes in asset prices cannot be explained by standard models. Fama recognized this incompatibility. "I don't even know what a bubble means," he has said (quoted in *The New York Times,* October 15, 2013). What that response shows, however, is a failure, shared by many of his colleagues, to recognize that his hypothesis, framed as it is to exclude the possibility of events that would falsify it, such as bubbles, is either false or unfalsifiable, something that in any other academic discipline would have led to something other than a Nobel Prize.

What misled economists and many others about the long-run tendencies of capitalism was the movement, especially in Europe, toward economic and social democratization in the period from 1945 to 1980, a period in which the destruction of inherited capital in World War II and the political acceptability of progressive taxation combined to limit and in some respects to reverse tendencies toward gross inequality inherent in capitalism. What was in fact an atypical period was not identified as such. Hence, capitalism itself was misunderstood. But the history of capitalism has also been misunderstood in another way. For economists have largely assumed that the economy can be studied in abstraction from the political and social order of which it is a part, that its history can be studied in abstraction from the political, social, and psychological factors that shape it. It cannot. What we should have learned from Marx, we have recurrently had to learn all over again.

Economists by playing their part in the legitimation of capitalism have also played a part in the legitimation of inequality and not only of economic inequality. For the power and influence of money in politics would not be what it is without economic inequality. And that power and influence are recurrently exerted to sustain capitalism.[25] The history of capitalism is thus in no insignificant part a history of economists. Academic economists have to a remarkable extent educated successive generations to think about the economic order in ways that make it difficult to resist the destructive and inegalitarian tendencies inherent in that order. It was no accident that Marx took it that any effective critique of capitalism would be impossible without an effective critique of economists.

---

[25] For recent evidence that this is so, see Martin Gilens and Benjamin I. Page, "Testing Theories of American Politics," *Perspectives on Politics* 12, 3 (2014): 564–581.

2.6   Marxists and Distributivists as rival critics of the dominant standpoint

Marxists from the late nineteenth century onwards thus found themselves in controversy both with each other and with the defenders of capitalism on a number of topics: the nature of the modern state and the part that agencies of the state might play in controlling and directing a complex modern economy, the resources that the institutions of a capitalist economy possess for living through and overcoming its crises, the question of how, if at all, economic and political power may be distributed democratically, and the question of what moral constraints should be acknowledged in a politics aimed at a radical redistribution of power. But they themselves together with the defenders of capitalism became the object of a critique which stressed how much in certain respects these two contending parties had in common. The authors of that critique had been instructed by the extraordinary reformulations of the NeoAristotelian standpoint that resulted from, on the one hand, the revival of the thought of Aquinas and, on the other, those interventions in working-class politics that gave expression to the social teaching of the Catholic Church, as restated by Pope Leo XIII.

It was of course Leo XIII who had also initiated the Thomist revival, and so unsurprisingly both the philosophy and the politics that resulted were widely thought of as Catholic philosophy and Catholic politics. Here, however, there was a misunderstanding. Thomism does indeed make theological claims, claims that involve a commitment to the truth of the Catholic faith, but the claims advanced by the early twentieth-century Thomists, and especially by those of them who understood themselves as Thomistic Aristotelians, both in philosophical argument and in the practice of politics, were secular claims addressed to their fellow citizens of any faith or none. They were claims about what it is to be and to act as a rational agent, claims of a kind long familiar in the history of Neo-Aristotelianism, but now asserted and argued for in terms of the institutions and conflicts of the late nineteenth and early twentieth century, claims concerning the nature of human goods, concerning the requirements of justice, and concerning the ordering of institutions.

About human goods what is of the first importance from this point of view is, as I have already emphasized, that individuals should understand that they can achieve their own individual goods only through achieving in the company of others those common goods that we share as family members, as collaborators in the workplace, as participants in a variety of local groups and societies, and as fellow citizens. Take away the notion of such common goods and what is left is a conception of the individual abstracted from her or his social relationships and from the norms of justice that must inform those relationships, if the individual is to flourish. It is because of the common goods served by productive work that justice is so important for the relationships of the workplace.

What elementary justice requires is that the wages paid for a week's work are sufficient to support the worker and her or his family, that the hours worked allow the worker adequate time with her or his family to pursue worthwhile activities, and that work is done in safe and secure conditions. But such elementary justice could initially be achieved under the conditions of industrial capitalism only by the organization of trade unions and by militant strike action. It is therefore significant that the first modern expressions of Catholic social teaching, as it was to be formulated by Leo XIII in the encyclical *Rerum Novarum* in 1891, anticipated that encyclical in putting its teaching into action. Notable among them was Cardinal Manning's militant support for the East London dockworkers in the great strike of 1889, and his cooperation with militant trade union leaders, some of whom were to become founding members of the Communist Party of Great Britain. Manning was unflinching both in his denunciation of the evils of capitalism and in his support for trade unions, writing to Archbishop Walsh of Dublin that "We have been under the despotism of capital. The union of labourers is their only shelter."[26] For the generation that succeeded Manning, the question that inevitably arose was that of how both to implement and to move beyond trade union action and trade union goals.

Those goals extended beyond the workplace into a politics that demanded, in time successfully, unemployment insurance and other welfare benefits, but that still left in place the larger ills of the capitalist system. So in what direction should radical critics of capitalism move? The answers developed by Marxists, whether revolutionary or reformist, were unacceptable to those who had learned from the Thomist revival and from Catholic social teaching and this for two reasons. First, what was required on the dominant Marxist view, if we were to move from capitalism to socialism, was an unprecedented concentration of both political and economic power in the hands of the agents of the state and the ruling political party. This was indeed envisaged as a prologue to a future devolution and democratization

---

[26] Shane Leslie, *Henry Edward Manning: His Life and Labour*, London: Burns, Oates and Washbourne, 1921, p. 376.

of power. But it was a central thesis of the Thomist critics of Marxism that the gross inequalities in respect of economic and political power demanded by the dominant Marxist conceptions of the transition to socialism would represent as much of a danger as the gross inequalities of the capitalist order, a thesis that became more and more persuasive as the twentieth century proceeded. There were indeed some Marxists who also recognized this danger and attempted to address it from within their Marxist perspective. But they were unable to provide a convincing account of how from their starting point they could arrive at what was, on the Distributist view that some Thomists had developed, most needed, a series of genuinely local political initiatives through which the possibilities of a grassroots distribution and sharing of power and property could be achieved. Moreover, there was a fundamental difference between Marxists and Distributists about the agents of social transformation. Marxists took it that in the end everything depended on the emergence of a revolutionary working class. Distributists held that, because there is a human interest and not just a class interest in remaking the social and economic order, needed changes can come from several quarters.

From a Distributist point of view, what is amiss with capitalism is not only what it does to the unemployed and the poor, but also what it does to the rich and to better paid workers and managers. Human beings can achieve their common and their individual goods only through concerted actions that require cooperative relationships informed by the norms of the natural law and, in order to achieve those goods, they must develop their powers as rational agents. However, the social order of capitalism not only recurrently imposes types of social relationship that violate these norms, it also miseducates and wrongly directs desires – something that Marxist critics of capitalism have also recognized – so that for many of every social class the satisfaction of their desires and the development of their powers become incompatible. What they want is too often what they have no good reason to want. Those of every class who succeed in getting what they want under capitalism are likely, therefore, just because they so often do not want what they need, to lead impoverished lives. How so?

I noted earlier that, when Savage characterized what he took to be a rational agent, the type of agent who maximizes her or his preference satisfaction in market transactions, he described that agent in terms that left entirely open the question of how that agent's preferences were formed and what their content and their objects might be. But the discipline of competition in market transactions, the costs imposed by failure, and the rewards consequent on success are themselves formative of desires and preferences and this in at least two ways. First, what agents learn from both success and failure in market transactions is the importance of increasing whatever money they have, by selling for as much as possible, by buying as cheaply as possible, by saving, and by investing, and this no matter how much money they may have already. So they learn to want more and then more and then more and become consumed by their own desires. Moreover, it is by how good they are at increasing their stock of money that others measure their success or failure, admire them or withhold their admiration. So the trait that the Greeks called *pleonexia*, acquisitiveness, a trait that both Aristotle and Aquinas took to be a vice, comes for the first time to be treated as a virtue by large numbers of people and money becomes an object of desire, not only for what it can buy, but also for its own sake. Yet this is not all.

Every economic order is an order of producers who are also consumers and what distinguishes one such order from another is in part how those who inhabit it understand the relationship between their activities as producers and their activities as consumers. The paradox of capitalism is that, while it requires that consumption should serve the ends of expanding production, it imposes on many a way of life in which their work, their productive activity, is thought of as valuable only because it serves the ends of consumption. It creates consumer societies in which its products can be successfully marketed only if the desires of consumers are directed toward whatever consumable objects the economy needs them to want. So the seductive rhetoric of advertising and the deceptions of marketing become necessary means for capitalist expansion, means that shape and elicit desires for objects that agents qua rational agents, directed toward the ends of human flourishing, have no good reason to desire. Those agents therefore who do desire what they have good reason to desire find themselves recurrently at odds with the ethos of developed capitalist societies and in conflict with those whose values are the dominant values of those societies.

It was from finding themselves at odds with that ethos and from engaging in such conflicts, quite as much as from their reading of Aquinas and Aristotle, that the English Distributists and some other Thomist critics of capitalism came to recognize that it was only in the light of a Thomist account of human agency and human ends that key aspects of the moral and political conflicts of the twentieth century could be adequately understood. Thomist moral and political theory mattered to them as a source of concepts and theses that were able to inform and direct the life of practice, so that practice became adequately reflective, adequately informed by the questioning and self-questioning of agents directed toward the achievement of their individual and common goods. So in a variety of small-scale enterprises and forms of communal life, it became possible for twentieth-century agents to make of the reading of Aquinas something close to what some of his Dominican and other contemporaries had made of it. There had of course been a variety of such readers in a number of times and places between the thirteenth and the twentieth century, but the Thomist revival and the critique of capitalism that Marx made possible opened up quite new possibilities.

Those possibilities have so far been realized in a number of ways. All of them involve commitments to making and sustaining institutions that provide for those practices through which common goods are achieved, practices of families, workplaces, schools, clinics, theatres, sports, institutions that characteristically, although not always, take the form of cooperative enterprises. What such enterprises characteristically encounter is tension and conflict with the institutions of the dominant culture, something scarcely surprising, since they put in question the morals and politics of that culture. How successful they can be in doing this is not yet decided.

2.7   What have we learned about how to proceed beyond the impasse of Chapter 1?

What can we learn from the very different examples of moral theorizing that we have examined so far, from Hume, from Aristotle, from Aquinas, from Marx, from the academic economists, from the Distributists? There are a number of morals to be drawn. First of all, the discussion of both Hume and Aristotle shows how the truth or falsity of theses in political and moral philosophy may depend upon what the historical and social facts are about human attitudes and activities. The discussion of Aquinas shows how different the task of finding application for one and the same set of evaluative and normative concepts in different social and economic orders may be. From both Aquinas and Marx we have learned how, in order to understand a particular set of theoretical claims, we may need to identify what that theorist was or is *against* as well as what that theorist was or is *for*. This lesson is reinforced by the example of the academic discipline of economics, whose presuppositions need to be put in question by anyone who has learned what Aquinas and Marx have to teach. What the example of the Distributists suggests is that the long-term importance of a school of thought may be quite other than it seemed to be to the best minds of its own time, that we may still on occasion have more to learn from, say, Chesterton than from many more distinguished thinkers. Yet over and above these particular lessons, are there any more general conclusions to be drawn?

One way in which the theorists whom we have discussed differ from one another is in how far they contribute to our understanding of the relationships between theory and practice. Earlier I argued that the initial task of theoretical enquiry is to articulate and develop further what is implicit in or presupposed by practice. And it needs to be stressed once again that agents engaged in such theoretical reflection continue to need to learn from each other, albeit not primarily as fellow students of theory, but as fellow agents engaged in achieving common goods in the practical and productive activities of everyday life, so that their moral and political education needs to be very different from that of the academic theorist. This is especially so when in some individual or communal enterprise things have gone badly wrong. The verdict of practice may initially be that our project was flawed either from lack of practical intelligence or from defective moral virtue or from circumstances beyond our control, and the reflection through which we arrive at a diagnosis of our failure will be designed to reach a conclusion as to which of these it was. We will have to ask whether the fault lay in us, in one or more of us, or in some aspect of the theory hitherto presupposed by our activity. Insofar as it was our theorizing that misled us, the verdict of practice will be a judgment on our theory as well as upon our prior deliberation.

I argued earlier that we need to distinguish the types of justification that we advance in the course of our practical self-questioning from those that we need to provide for our theoretical, our philosophical claims. But it is important to notice the close relationship between our theoretical and our practical stances, if we are adequately reflective. So, as both Aristotle and Aquinas make clear, the theorist has to be in conversation both with those agents on whose practice they are reflecting – including themselves – and with rival theorists. They have to be able to consider and respond to the full range of objections to their own positions that can be advanced from each rival theoretical standpoint in the arenas of theoretical debate. Only if they are able do so successfully, by appeal to the best standards of rational justification that they possess, are they entitled to claim that their positions remain undefeated by the advocates of those rival theoretical standpoints. Yet, as we have also just noticed, this type of theoretical justification, while necessary, is not sufficient. It is, on any justified contemporary version of their view, only by appeal to judgments grounded in the particularities of practice in our lives in the household, in the workplace, as construction workers or garbage collectors or soldiers or poets or whatever, that a final verdict is possible. Rational justification in morals and politics has these two distinct and closely related dimensions. And, as we noticed earlier, it also has a third.

From both Hume and Aristotle we have had to learn the lesson that, no matter how intellectually acute we are, we will be apt to go wrong if we allow ourselves to be the victims of prejudices that inform widely shared judgments in the culture that we inhabit, prejudices that are as apt to distort the judgments of the educated as of anyone else. We therefore have to become suspicious of ourselves, our attitudes and our feelings, and each of us has to press upon ourselves the question: What justifies my judgment that I am sufficiently independently minded to engage with integrity in the tasks of moral and political enquiry and justification? At once we encounter what may seem to be a paradox: if we are to be the kind of people who can engage in enquiry that arrives at sound conclusions concerning, for example, the place of the virtues in our lives, we must from the outset possess to some significant degree some of those same virtues. That is, as we also noticed earlier, we will only be successful in our enquiry, if the way in which we pursue that enquiry presupposes from the outset some of its conclusions. Which, then, are those virtues indispensable for successful enquiry? They are qualities of mind and character that enable agents to achieve detachment of more than one kind.

A first requirement is some degree of detachment from one's social and occupational role, so that one understands from an external point of view what it is to be whatever one is – a farmer or a musician or a banker – in this particular social order and what prejudices tend to inform the judgments of farmers or musicians or bankers. What is needed is a kind of sociological self-knowledge, in key part to be achieved by understanding how things appear from the very different perspective of those deprived and marginalized in one's society. It is in the light afforded by the stark contrast between their standpoint and that of those with well-established occupations, such as our own, that the onesidedness of each point of view appears most clearly. But to achieve this kind and degree of detachment involves also freedom from attachment to those objects of desire that bind one to one's social role, desires for success, pleasure, and reputation, a freedom that enables one to care more about seeing and understanding things as they are and about judging and acting only in ways consistent with objectivity and truthfulness than one does about pleasing those whom otherwise one most wants to please, a class that characteristically includes oneself.

What qualities of mind and character might prevent this disciplining of the desires, this asceticism? Interestingly, they turn out to be qualities not recognized as vices by either Aristotle or Hume, most notably that kind of pride, that confidence in one's own attitudes and feelings, which in different guises earns the approval of both. Correspondingly, humility, the ability to view oneself and one's achievements without either congratulatory complacency or self-denigration, is a virtue with a peculiar importance. Sociological self-knowledge may thus not always be possible for those at risk from moral self-deception and, if we are to know how far we are at risk, we characteristically need the judgment of perceptive and ruthlessly critical friends.

Rational justification in politics and morals, because it has all three dimensions, is thus a more complex matter than those who restrict themselves to the arenas of theoretical enquiry are apt to realize. But just this restriction constrained the enquiries and the disagreements of Chapter 1 of this essay. We therefore now need to move beyond the arenas of theoretical debate as usually conceived to a set of enquiries in which all three dimensions of rational justification receive their due and not only the first. We have to ask all over again what we are to make of the claims of expressivism and of cognate positions, such as those of Frankfurt's ethics, now characterizing them in terms of their social contexts and then evaluating them in the light of this enlarged conception of rational justification. There is of course an air of paradox about this enterprise. For I am inviting my readers to move beyond the limitations of theoretical enquiry in a work that itself is and remains a work of theory. Whether this is inevitably disabling, we will only discover by trying to carry the enterprise forward. A necessary first step is to situate the claims of expressivism in relationship to the claims of Morality and to understand how both Morality and expressivism function in those social contexts of modernity in which they are at home.

CHAPTER 3

Morality and modernity

3.1   Morality, the morality of modernity

Expressivism is, as we noted at the outset, a metaethical theory, a second order theory about the meaning and use of evaluative and normative
expressions. From a NeoAristotelian point of view, the key error of expressivists is not the claim that evaluative and normative judgments must be
such as to be able to motivate, that they must be expressive of desires
and passions. It is in how they draw the line between, on the one hand,
the factual and, on the other, the evaluative and the normative so that it
becomes for them an a priori truth that no judgment can be both factual and evaluative. In consequence, in their discussions of evaluation all
those empirically grounded judgments about what it is for animals of a
given species, including human animals, to flourish or to fail to flourish,
judgments about how it is best for this individual or this group to act in
these circumstances and about the norms to which she, he, or they must
conform, if it is to go well for them, judgments that observation confirms
as true or false, disappear from view. In philosophy it is never enough to
identify such a mistake as a mistake. It is also necessary to explain how
highly intelligent and perceptive thinkers could have come to make such
a mistake. As we should have learned from Marx and Nietzsche, we need
a sociology and a psychology of philosophical error. How, then, should
we NeoAristotelians characterize what we take to be this mistake made by
expressivists? It was and is, I shall suggest, the mistake of supposing that
what held and holds true of the evaluative and normative judgments of one
particular morality, embedded in one particular social and cultural order,
the order that they themselves inhabit, holds true of any and every evaluative and normative judgment in all times and al places. Which particular
morality was it and is it by which the expressivists were misled? It was
and is the morality to which I have given the name 'Morality' (Chapter 1,
section 1.10), the moral system peculiar to and characteristic of early and

late capitalist modernity. Morality, which has flourished and still flourishes in Western and Central Europe, in North America, and in other parts of the earth that their inhabitants have colonized from the early eighteenth to the twenty-first century, had and has six salient characteristics, some of which we have already noticed.

First, it is presented by its adherents as a secular doctrine and mode of practice, permitting no appeal beyond itself to real or purported divine commandments. Instead it provides standards by which the doctrines and actions of religious believers and unbelievers alike are to be evaluated. Secondly, it is held to be universally binding on all human agents, whatever the culture or social order to which they belong, and its precepts are therefore somehow or other knowable by all. Those precepts must therefore be translatable into any human language of any time or place. Thirdly, those precepts function as a set of constraints upon each individual, setting limits to the ways in which and the extent to which each may act so as to satisfy her or his desires and pursue her or his interests, and requiring her or him to take account of the needs of others. It is noteworthy that in the period in which Morality becomes the dominant morality the concepts of egoism and altruism move to a more central place in the discussions of moral philosophers and that later on, when twentieth-century biologists who identify morality with Morality try to explain the emergence of morality in evolutionary terms, they identify the problem of explaining the emergence of morality with that of explaining the emergence of altruism. It is a presupposition of the practitioners of Morality that to act for the good of others as Morality enjoins will often be to act contrary to one's own interests and desires.

Fourthly, the precepts of Morality are framed in highly abstract and general terms. They are presented as binding on individuals as such. They make no mention of occupational role or social status. Individuals too are characterized in highly general and abstract terms. Each individual is taken to aim at achieving her or his happiness by satisfying her or his desires. Each individual is presented as having or as able to acquire one and the same understanding of the key terms of Morality: 'right action', 'duty', 'utility', 'a right'. Each individual has the capacity for acting as an autonomous agent and is required so to act. It is in virtue of their possession of this capacity that individuals deserve respect. Fifthly, although the adherents of Morality include both conservative and liberal critics of whatever happen to be its present formulations, the background to their debates is a shared belief that Morality thus conceived is superior to all other moralities, the latest and highest stage in the moral history of humankind.

Sixthly and finally, Morality is such that agents from time to time cannot avoid confronting a set of problems of a highly specific character. What are they? There are, so the exponents of Morality teach, certain principles or rules that ought always or almost always to be obeyed. We ought never – or almost never – to bring about the death of an innocent other intentionally. We ought never – or almost never – to connive at the conviction of an innocent person for a crime that he did not commit. We ought never – or almost never – to inflict torture. But we ought also, according to the exponents of Morality, to act so as to maintain and increase, perhaps to maximize, the well-being of others, including those others who constitute our local or national community. Consider, then, those cases where we can only act with due regard for the well-being of some set of relevant others by violating one of those principles or rules that we ought to obey, where we can only obey one or more of those principles and rules by cooperating in causing grave harms to innocent others. Technicolor examples of such dilemmas are by now stock cases in many moral philosophy classes. Consider two such.

A terrorist knows where a bomb due to explode within twenty-four hours is concealed. We know that if it explodes, numerous innocent people will be killed or maimed. Our only means for discovering and so becoming able to disarm the bomb is to torture the terrorist. Or I am the only person in a position to prevent an out-of-control vehicle from crashing so that a large number of passengers will be killed. But my only means of doing this are such that, by acting so as to prevent the crash, I will intentionally bring about the death of an innocent bystander. In both cases we are in situations where there is obvious application for the principle that enjoins us to do everything that we can to save innocent human lives. Yet in both cases, if we act as that principle enjoins, we will violate another principle that is often treated as inviolable. Such are the dilemmas of Morality. If it is protested that these are examples of rare and highly exceptional types of case, the reply will be that much less melodramatic dilemmas of the same type recur in everyday life, as when we decide to violate the principle for-bidding lying, because of the pain to numbers of people that will be caused by telling the truth in this particular case, or we commit an injustice to a small group who are unlikely to complain in order to benefit a large and vociferous group who will make an intolerable nuisance of themselves if they do not get what they want, or we justify some infringement of the property rights of homeowners in the name of economic development.

Morality, as understood and embodied in everyday practice, provides no generally acceptable solutions to such dilemmas. Those moral philosophers

who identify morality with Morality not only exhibit imagination and ingenuity in constructing examples of them, but also often provide what they
claim to be solutions to them, each on the basis of that theory in terms of
which she or he purports to provide a rational justification for the claims
of Morality. The problem is that there are just too many such theories,
each of them incompatible with the others. So in the arenas of theoretical debate, there are Kantian, utilitarian, and contractarian exponents of
Morality and of each such view there are several versions. What appears
to be unattainable at the level of theory is agreement both on how these
types of dilemma are to be resolved and, more generally, on how particular
moral claims are to be justified. At the level of practice, there is not only
disagreement, but inconsistency and oscillation. Individuals, corporations,
and governments will on one occasion argue for the inviolability of this
or that rule or set of rights, on another for setting them aside in order to
achieve what is presented as a greater good. There is one standard rhetoric
that is well designed to be persuasive in arguing in favor of inviolability
and another equally well designed to be persuasive in arguing against it,
and contemporary moral philosophy is a storehouse of relevant arguments
for both side in each debate.

To the vast majority of those who have from early childhood been
educated into the cultures of modernity, this condition is so familiar as to
be unremarkable. Even if they have learned at some time that there are and
have been other very different moralities, from whose perspective the line
between the morally unproblematic and the morally problematic is drawn
in quite other ways, this thought has no effect on their own practical
commitments, and they remain unaware of what it is that is distinctive
in the stances of Morality. What differentiates their practical beliefs and
attitudes from those of, say, seventeenth-century Japanese Confucians or
nineteenth-century Navaho may be matter for historians or anthropologists
but has no practical relevance for them. Yet Morality *is* very different from
some other moralities, and one way to bring out what is distinctive about it
is to compare its salient features with those of an Aristotelian moral stance,
as we have already characterized it. Three contrasts will at once come to
mind.

First, for an Aristotelian the point and purpose of conformity to moral
precepts is that failure so to conform will hinder or prevent us from
achieving our goods qua human beings. By contrast, for the exponents
of Morality whether there are such goods and what they are are open
questions. The constraints of morality make it possible for each of us
to pursue the objects of our desires, no matter how conceived, provided

only that we permit others the same freedom that we enjoy. Agreement that there is a human good, let alone agreement on what it is, is not presupposed. Secondly, for an Aristotelian, individuals can achieve their own individual goods *only* in and through achieving those common goods that they share with others, qua family member, qua colleague in the workplace, qua fellow citizen, qua friend, so that care of one's family, of the ethos of one's workplace, of the justice of one's political society and of one's friends are characteristically and generally marks of a good human life. For the exponents of Morality, its requirements are sufficiently abstract and general to govern the relationships of any individual to any other individual whatsoever, and those universal requirements are framed so as to be independent of the particularities of this or that agent's relationships and circumstances. Unsurprisingly, practical intelligence – Aristotle's *phronēsis*, Aquinas's *prudentia* – the capacity to judge and act with an eye to such particularities, is on an Aristotelian view *the* key moral and intellectual virtue, while it plays no part in any of the major expositions of Morality.

Thirdly, for the exponents of Morality, as for its practitioners, 'the moral' is to be distinguished from 'the political', 'the legal', 'the aesthetic', 'the social', and 'the economic'. Each of these in the world view of modernity names a distinct aspect of human activity and, as academic disciplines emerge, each of those aspects provides a distinct discipline with its own peculiar subject matter, one that can be studied for the most part without much or any reference to the others. From an Aristotelian standpoint, by contrast, each of these aspects of activity can be adequately understood only in relation to the others, as in this or that way and in these or those circumstances it contributes to or frustrates the achievement of goods rightly ordered and so of the ultimate human good. Aristotle took ethics as an area of enquiry to be part of and subordinate to politics – understood significantly differently from modern politics – and the political life itself to be an incomplete life, since the achievement of the ultimate human good lies beyond politics. On a contemporary NeoAristotelian view, economics, sociology, and the study of law each need to be understood within a framework provided by the enquiries of politics-and-ethics so that we ask of each type of economic activity and social relationship what it contributes to sustaining or undermining those kinds of institutional, organizational, and social structures through which common and individual goods are achieved.

What this third and last contrast brings out is that the distinctive character of Morality is not only a matter of the form and content of its precepts, but also of the place that it occupies in both the everyday and the academic thought and practice of those whose lives are informed by it, relative to other aspects of their lives. An important question to ask in this respect is whence then it is that the precepts of Morality are taken to derive their peculiar authority for those for whom those precepts have authority. Laws, understood in the modern world as the positive laws of sovereign states, derive their authority from the authority and coercive power of such states. The contentions of economists, like those of other natural and social scientists, are treated as authoritative just insofar as those who advance them are able to cite compelling theoretical arguments and empirical support. But to what do the adherents of Morality appeal, if someone enquires why they should respect its precepts?

They give, as we noticed earlier, a number of different and rival answers, each of them an appeal to some standard independent of their own – or anyone else's – attitudes and feelings and each of them contested by those who advance rival answers. Because they share a conception of Morality as requiring an appeal to just such a standard, they generally understand expressivism of any kind as a threat to their convictions. But, because they are recurrently involved in ongoing disagreements and conflicts during which argument and reason giving fail to convince their rivals, so that each contending party has to fall back on assertion and counter assertion – often increasingly shrill and dogmatic assertion and counter assertion – they are apt to give the appearance of those who are doing no more than voicing prerational attitudes and commitments. They appear to be just what the emotivists said that they were.

There are, however, many moralities that lack this distinctive feature of Morality, and the attempt by both emotivists and their expressivist heirs to present their account as one that holds of evaluative and normative judgments as such, in addition to the other challenges that it has to meet, fails to take account of the idiosyncratic character of Morality. What, then, made such a morality as Morality possible? How could this particular set of judgments and ideals be presented as having, be accepted as having, authority in virtue of a standard independent of the attitudes, feelings, and concerns of those who acknowledge that authority without ever having been able to give a rationally justifiable account of what that standard is? How could a morality whose most acute theorists, utilitarian, Kantian, and contractarian, remain in permanent disagreement retain its hegemony over so many for so long? We can best approach answers to these questions by considering Morality not in isolation from other aspects of that larger culture, the culture of enlightened modernity, of which it is a part, but in its relationships to several other major aspects of that culture. Consider those desires, hopes, and fears that are distinctively modern.

3.2 The modernity in which Morality is at home

What desires agents have, how those desires are felt and expressed, and how they are related to the practical reasoning of agents vary both within and between social and cultural orders. Biological needs may be constant, but the desires that are satisfied in satisfying them can be for very different objects. Those in nineteenth-century Edo who appeased their hunger by satisfying their appetite for sashimi and those in nineteenth-century Bologna who did so by satisfying their appetite for *salsa Bolognese*, let alone those present-day eclectic Londoners who have a taste for both, had had and have had their initial desires for food educated in very different ways. Other needs and wants are similarly transformed, and in different social and cultural orders the means of satisfying them are integrated into different ways of life in which familial and occupational roles and the goals, ambitions, and hopes that attach to those roles assume distinctive forms. We noted earlier that our desires are always closely related to our affections, habits, and beliefs and that these too take different forms in different ways of life. If then we are concerned to understand what we have good reason to desire, it is of some importance to ask what parts desires play in those ways of life characteristic of the social and cultural order that we inhabit, the social and cultural order of modernity, even though in so doing we shall mostly be reminding ourselves of what is obvious. Consider some peculiarly modern forms of opportunity and hope, insecurity and poverty, regret and lament, and ambition, all of them arising from the recurrent transformations of work as economic modernity developed from the eighteenth century onwards.

Begin with opportunities and hopes. The social and cultural order of modernity in all its various forms is what it is only because of long-term – it has often seemed indefinitely long term – economic growth and technological innovation, growth sometimes slow, sometimes fast, sometimes continuous, sometimes disrupted, sometimes deliberately shaped, more generally unplanned. That growth recurrently involves the provision of new kinds of work, often enough with slowly increasing wages for workers, sometimes with new opportunities for managerial and professional careers, sometimes with extraordinary rewards for those able to set others to work and to appropriate the surplus value of their labor. And it results in new institutions and the remaking of older institutions, most notably perhaps of the schools that prepare children and adolescents for the labor force. As part of these changes, there emerge new types of inequality, new forms of class differentiation, new conflicts and struggles, and new objects of desire and aspiration. Consider just three examples of types of aspiring agent, first, nineteenth- and twentieth-century workers in more or less regular employment in mills and factories, who as workers realistically aspired to better the lot of themselves and their families, while remaining working class, secondly, those individuals of the same period who, whatever their social origin, were able to acquire the skills and had the imagination and the luck needed to make their way upwards through the class sytem toward whatever was accounted locally as social and economic success, and finally those contemporaries of unrestrained financial ambition with the initial resources to serve that ambition, for whom nothing was – and is – ever enough.

The stories of the first are characteristically stories of discoveries of the need to take collective action, stories of working-class individuals and families that became strands in the history of the trade union movement and of its politics. The stories of the second provide matter both for novelists and for those sociologists who map the changing structures of bourgeois careers through the various levels of management, or from, say, apprentice engineer or lawyer or accountant to mastery in such professions. The stories of the third are sometimes fables of the very rich, but also often case histories of an addiction, an addiction to money. But none of these stories would have the structure that they have were it not for the fact that they are stories of individuals, families, and groups moved not only by aspirations and hopes, but also by fears of frustration and failure, fears of long-term unemployment and poverty, fears of being unable to move beyond mind- and spirit-deadening forms of work, fears of the burden of debt.

It is within lives informed by these larger hopes and fears that individuals develop those likings and dislikings, those bonds and antagonisms, that take form in the multiplicity of their particular desires, tastes, affections, and habits to eat this rather than that, to spend time with these persons rather than those, in this way rather than that, to be here rather than there. And if we were to recount in adequate detail not just the three kinds of life that I have mentioned, but all those other types of life that are structured by the distinctive hopes and fears of capitalist and technological modernity, what we would have described is the range of contexts within which agents at each stage of their lives make their choices and in so doing order the various objects of their desires, treating the achievement of some only as means to the achievement of others, giving high priority to the achievement of some and low priority to others, perhaps reconsidering with pain or pleasure some of their past choices. What intellectual, moral, and social resources do such agents have, if in moments of reflection they ask how it would be best for them to order their desires and so their lives?

It turns out that too often they lack some badly needed resources, and this in part because of the modes of thought characteristic of agents in their types of situation and in part because of the nature of those situations. Begin with the latter. What those situations have in common is the degree to which they are shaped by the flow of money, initially the movements of capital, movements that may be either creative and productive or destructive or both at once. They are most obviously creative and productive when they enable the development and application of new technologies and with them new forms of work, whether in iron smelting in eighteenth-century England or in the industrial applications of chemistry in nineteenth-century Germany or in the information technologies of the twentieth-century United States. They are most obviously destructive when their effect is such that those engaged in a well-established mode of production can no longer find a market for what they produce, so that they are, often suddenly and unexpectedly, out of work, deprived of their livelihood and sometimes of their whole way of life. But, whatever their situation, what is crucial for individuals and their families in respect of their desires is the relationship between the wages and salaries that they earn and the prices of the goods and services for which they pay. They have to ask not only 'What do I or we want?' and 'What have I or we good reason to want?' but also 'What can I or we afford?'

In answering this latter question, they are constantly invited to value this or that object of desire as the market values it, as the market responds to demand. But demand is for the satisfaction of whatever may happen to be the desires and the self-identified needs of those who at this or that particular time or place happen to have enough money in their pockets, whether or not those needs are genuine needs, whether or not those desires are desires that agents have good reason to attempt to satisfy. A growing economy requires of those who do productive work that they also function as consumers and, so far as they can, those who provide goods and services to such consumers shape their tastes so that they will desire and even take themselves to need whatever it is that that economy requires them to consume. It is such producers and consumers who most need to be able to distinguish between what is or could be of genuine value for their lives and their flourishing and what the market invites them to value. But market societies make it difficult for working- and middle-class people to engage in the kind of shared reflection and deliberation which are necessary if they are so to distinguish in their everyday decision making. How so?

We get a first clue as to how to answer this question if we examine the long and tangled history of those conflicts in which resistance has been mounted to what have been presented either as means to economic growth or as necessities of the market, from the older defenses of traditional rights in the face of seventeenth- and eighteenth-century enclosures of common lands to the Luddite struggles of the handloom weavers to preserve their way of life, to militant trade union actions for the sake of decent wages and working conditions, and to the actions of urban community organizers and organizations in twentieth-century cities, such as Chicago and Boston. Among the many things that should impress us in that history is how much easier those engaged in such conflicts have found it to say clearly and articulately what they were *against* rather than what they were *for*, how incisive and to the point their various identifications of injustice have been, but how unclear the implications of those identifications for any adequate overall conception of justice. So in the face of the constructive and destructive transformations of modernity, those plain persons engaged in such conflicts have rarely been able to think through and to spell out for themselves an adequate alternative conception of the directions that social and economic change should take, one that might have enabled them to evaluate more adequately the claims that have been made for their allegiance by political movements of various kinds from the eighteenth century onwards.

The problem has been that the characteristic habits of thought of modernity are such that they make it extremely difficult to think about modernity except in its own terms, terms that exclude application for those concepts most needed for radical critique. We therefore need an account of those distinctively modern modes of institutionalized activity and of the habits of thought integral to those modes of activity that will enable us to answer two different sets of questions, one concerning the particular formations and deformations of desires that emerge in the contexts of modernity and one concerning the ways of thinking about our activities and our lives that are at once alien to modernity and indispensable for understanding it. But before I try to provide just such an account, a word of caution, especially to readers antagonized by what is negative in my view of modernity, is in place.

The history of modernity, insofar as it has been a series of social and political liberations and emancipations from arbitrary and oppressive rule, is indeed in key respects a history of genuine and admirable progress.

The history of modernity, insofar as it has been a history of artistic and scientific achievement, from Raphael to Rothko or from Palestrina to Schoenberg, and from Copernicus and Galileo to Feynman and Higgs, is indeed a history of equally genuine and admirable achievement. And nothing that I have said here or elsewhere implies otherwise. Yet it is this same modernity in which new forms of oppressive inequality, new types of material and intellectual impoverishment, and new frustrations and misdirections of desire have been recurrently generated. There are a number of very different stories to be told about modernity, all of them true. But all of these presuppose a distinctive political and economic framework.

3.3   State and market: the ethics-of-the-state and the ethics-of-the-market

The story of modern politics has at its core a narrative of the making and sustaining of the modern state, while the story of modern economies is that of the making and sustaining of modern markets, yet those stories partly fuse in the twentieth century with the emergence of a new, if often sickly, Leviathan, the state-and-the-market. The first European Leviathans, the nation states, were distinguished from the medieval forms of government that preceded them by the successful claim in each case of a single centralized secular authority to a monopoly in the use of armed force to impose order within its territory, to defend its frontiers, and to exact military service from its subjects, and in the power to issue currency and to tax its subjects. It is the state that defines and makes law and its law making powers are such that the exercise of its authority can be indefinitely extended, from the establishment or disestablishment of religion to the regulation of trade, from the founding of central banks to the inauguration of postal services, and beyond these to a wide range of educational and welfare measures. Against the verdicts of the highest legal tribunals of the state, there is generally no appeal.

As the governments of modern nation states expand the exercise of their powers, they become complex institutions, sets of agencies operating in significantly different ways, so that those ministries that direct the armed forces have one set of tasks, those that deal with financial affairs another, those that administer justice a third, those that handle welfare or educational affairs a fourth, and so on. Government is both centralized and heterogeneous, invoking a single authority, yet always liable to generate internal conflict. What is needed to unify such governments, if they are to be effective, is twofold: the enforcement of a bureaucratized, hierarchical order within and between the agencies of government and the inculcation of a code of conduct in those who direct and those who serve those agencies, the ethics-of-government. That code has to prescribe the conscientious performance of the duties of each particular role and to prohibit favoritism and corruption. Impersonality is the mark of the good bureaucrat who serves the state. It should make no difference to which Inspector of Taxes or Public Prosecutor you are referred. But now note the difference between what the ethics-of-the-state requires of such public servants and what it requires of their masters, of those who govern.

Their assigned task is to promote the good and the goods of the state, as they understand them. Those goods are public goods, goods enjoyed by individuals which characteristically serve the purposes of individuals, but that those individuals could not achieve except through some form of political organization. Such goods include the provision of roads and other means of travel and communication and the maintenance of systems of public education, but paramount among them are the goods of law and order, of a stable currency, and of national security. To achieve those goods, they must be prepared to use whatever means are necessary, while making it appear that they only use such means as are generally thought morally acceptable. This requirement is often best served by those who except on rare occasions do only use such means, but on those rare occasions show themselves adept in the arts of successful lying and of concealing their responsibility for, for example, acts of brutality, justifying what they do to themselves and their associates by appealing to what they take to be the consequences of acting otherwise. The ethics-of-the-state may seem to be potentially incoherent. For if its maxims were fully spelled out, some would seem to presuppose a consequentialist standpoint, others something more like a 'my station and its duties' point of view. However, we need to remember that its maxims have application not to individual agents as such, but to individual agents only qua occupants of well-defined roles, answerable to others whose roles confer authority. Such agents encounter those maxims as requirements in their everyday transactions and commonly few or no questions of consistency arise.

As modern states developed their extraordinary powers, it became clear to both rulers and ruled that those powers, coercive and otherwise, can only be successfully exercised in the long run if the authority of the state is recognized as legitimate by the vast majority of the ruled. So a central issue of political theory posed hard questions for political practice, and the eighteenth-century American and French revolutions became permanent reminders of this truth. Two theoretical claims were of crucial importance. The first was that the authority and the powers of the state were justified by reason of the benefits that the state provides for those over whom it rules. There is, on the best statements of this view, an implicit contract according to which the ruled agree to respect the laws enacted by their rulers and to concur in their enforcement in return for those benefits. What discredits even those statements, however, is not just skepticism about the very notion of such a contract, but the fact that, if this is how the authority and powers of the state are to be justified, then, so far as a great many of the ruled are concerned, they have lacked and now lack justification. The benefits conferred on the most exploited and oppressed are far too meager.

A second type of claim is at first sight more credible. It is that the authority and powers of the state are legitimate just insofar as government gives expression to the desires and choices of the governed. If the acts of government are what they are because this is what the governed willed them to be, then the imposition and enforcement of laws upon the governed is not imposition and enforcement by an alien power, but a form of self-rule. How is such self-rule to be achieved? By giving the governed the power to choose who will govern them, after having been able to consider which of the candidates for high political office best represents the policies and programs which the governed wish to see implemented. So acts of collective choice are institutionalized as elections, and elected governments are taken to be legitimate just insofar as every adult citizen is entitled to vote and those same adults enjoy those rights of free speech and free association that allow them to propose and to consider rival policies and programs. The struggle to achieve such liberal democratic ideals was of course a very long one, and I am here considering only its twentieth-century end product. But about that product it is important to ask: How in fact in liberal democracies is power distributed? The answer is: in grossly, even grotesquely unequal ways.

Constitutionally, liberal democratic societies enforce a certain kind of equality. Every adult individual has one vote in elections and nobody has more than one. Every adult individual is free to run for public office. But when individuals choose between candidates for public office and the policies and programs that they advance, the set of alternatives between which voters are able to choose is not determined by them. Those alternatives are determined by groups within the major political parties, those coalitions of interest groups who set the agendas for national politics. Those who play a part in setting those agendas contribute to the shaping of policies and programs in one or more of four ways. They are able to mobilize votes on some particular set of issues, they have expertise in some particular policy area, the economy, say, or defense, they are adept in the arts of political presentation through the mass media, or they are individuals or corporations who make large financial contributions to parties, to interest groups or to individual candidates for election. And, since it is money that sets to work those who contribute in the first three ways, it is money that is of the first importance in securing a hearing, directly or indirectly, for those who influence the definition of the alternatives between which voters are permitted to choose. What is never debated publicly is whether or not the alternatives that *are* debated are the alternatives that should be debated.

What I have just described, albeit much too briefly, is how in liberal democratic societies, ostensibly committed to egalitarian political ideals, gross financial and educational inequalities issue in gross political inequalities. What money and education procure is membership in one of a set of interlocking elites, political, financial, cultural, and media elites. Lack of money and lack of education result not only in exclusion from the decision-making processes, but too often in an inability to learn with and from others how to put this state of affairs in question. Yet this is of course what has to be learned by anyone who aims to construct forms of the common life in which goods may be rightly ordered and achieved, while living and acting in societies in which political power is distributed in the ways that I have described. That distribution of political power depends, as we have already noticed, on the distribution of economic and financial power, a distribution which is the work of markets. So I turn from a consideration of the state to a consideration of the market.

Market relations too are impersonal relations, relations between buyers and sellers. Their relationships are contractual relationships between individuals or corporations and corporations are constituted by contracts between individuals. Power lies with the possessors of capital, since to own capital is to be able to decide the directions that investment takes. What investment determines is how and where the labor and the skills of managers and workers are used. Markets are therefore structured by inequalities and among the qualities of mind and character that are most highly valued are those that enable some to outdo others in acquisition and in the making of profits. Acquisitiveness, *pleonexia*, is therefore a highly valued character trait, but it is important to recognize, if we are to understand the ethics-of-the-market, that acquisitiveness is not only a character trait, but also a duty. Individuals owe it to those who have invested in their enterprises to maximize the return on their investments. Moreover, acquisitiveness is not the only highly valued character trait. Contractual relationships, including market relationships, need to be sustained by a high degree of trust between the contracting parties, even when the terms of a contract can be enforced by legal sanctions. The costs of resorting to law are too high and the benefits that result from trustworthiness and reliability in promise keeping are sufficiently great for it to be impossible for law to displace the ethics-of-the-market, something regretted only by lawyers.

We find then that, just as with the ethics-of-the-state, the precepts of the ethics-of-the-market combine maximizing injunctions with injunctions to respect certain rules without regard for the consequences. As with the ethics-of-the-state, an individual who abstracted these injunctions from their contexts would have the task of rendering them consistent and would be able to do so in more than one way. But as individuals encounter them as requirements in their everyday economic and financial transactions in markets, no question of consistency commonly arises. What is important to notice at this point is that the modern state, as it has developed in the nineteenth and twentieth centuries, requires the ethics-of-the-state for its effective functioning, just as markets, national and international, could not function effectively were it not for the ethics-of-the-market. Yet both, it needs to be remarked, are in an important way parodies of ethics. Before we can understand why this is so, we need to notice two other salient features of the politics and economics of advanced modernity.

I have so far spoken as though, at least until very recently, the state were one thing, the market quite another. Yet of course they have always been related in a variety of ways, with government playing almost no role at all in economic development in some times and places, but a large and indispensable role in others. There is one kind of story to be told about Great Britain, another about Germany, yet another about Japan, and so on. Yet in the second half of the twentieth century in every major capitalist country, the complex relationships between state and market become so close that individuals in many of their transactions confront something that is not quite either, but both at once: mortgages from banks guaranteed by agencies of the state, wages paid by firms dependent on government contracts, taxes paid to provide subsidies for firms that will provide employment, schools and universities whose curricula are designed to produce a useful and amenable labor force and whose research may be supported only because its outcomes are thought to benefit economic growth – and these are only some of the simpler examples.

Individuals thus find themselves in situations in which practical questions are posed that are left unanswered by the ethics-of-the-state and the ethics-of-the-market, questions that they can only pursue as individual agents, questions that the prescriptions of their social roles, whatever they may be, leave unanswered. Given that the states whose citizens they are and the markets in which they participate are what they are, those questions will take as a crucial part of their subject matter the relationships between those precepts that enjoin the maximization of some real or supposed good and those rules that prescribe or prohibit certain types of action with little or no regard for the consequences. How are individuals who pose such questions to proceed? They will have been educated to believe that these are types of issue to be dealt with under the heading 'Morality', Morality whose precepts are distinct from, independent of, and prior to the precepts of political and economic life. Morality will not instruct them as to which goals to pursue, and so it will leave open some key questions. What it will do is to impose constraints both on their choice of goals and on the means that they may adopt in order to achieve their goals. It will do this by imposing constraints on the ways in which and the extent to which they may attempt to satisfy their desires and to further their interests. Morality is in this way indispensable for the functioning of the ethics-of-the-state and the ethics-of-the-market, since individuals can only function as modernity requires them to function, if their desires are expressed, contained, and ordered in certain ways. What then is it about modern desires that allows them to be thus expressed, contained, and ordered?

3.4   Desires, ends, and the multiplication of desires

Desires, as we have already noted, find their objects within lives structured by the needs, activities, responsibilities, and enjoyments of individuals, families, and other groups, and we will not know how to think about desires until we are also able to think rightly about needs, activities, responsibilities, enjoyments, and the relationships between these. What individuals need is that without which they will be unable in adult life to engage in those activities and to discharge those responsibilities that are the mark of a fully participant member of their society. Their needs are not only biological needs. Indeed, individuals whose needs so understood are met also need to enjoy at least some aspects of their lives and to find point and purpose in their activities. It matters therefore what attitudes, feelings, and desires are elicited in the course of their everyday routines, as they meet their needs, engage in activities, discharge responsibilities, and pursue enjoyments. Begin with needs.

Needs that are easily satisfied may go unnoticed, while an awareness of needs, especially elementary needs, that are or are in danger of being

unmet, may block out almost everything else from consciousness. So it is
with the needs of the very hungry, the cold, the desperately lonely. For those
whose needs are for the present met adequately, but for whom, say, three
weeks unemployment would be enough to make the fear of unmet needs a
realistic fear, the desire not to be out of work plays a very different part in
their lives from that which it plays, for example, in the lives of well-to-do
professionals with savings, who certainly desire not to be out of work but
are not haunted by anything like the same fears. What a desire not to be out
of work is also depends in part on what kind of work the relevant work is,
whether it is tediously repetitive and uninteresting, engaged in only because
no other work is available, or engaging and rewarding, difficult perhaps,
but providing occasions for learning. (All worthwhile work is of course
boring or unrewardingly difficult at times.) The need for companionship
resembles the need for work in generally going unfelt, so long as it is
met. The happily married, the sexually fulfilled, those with good friends,
and those who have learned how to be alone do not feel their desire for
others as a lack that can become an affliction, a lack that can through the
transformations of desire become a source of phantasies that distort and
corrupt the very relationships that they so much want.

Activities too may engage or fail to engage us in various ways. Consider
the attitudes of Japanese workers in automobile factories before and after
the reforms designed by Japanese manufacturers under the influence of the
maverick American management theorist, W. Edwards Deming. Before,
most workers were subjected to mindless routines on production lines,
just as in American factories of the same period, each worker engaged in
making one part for a whole to be assembled later, their work monitored
for quality by inspectors. After, workers became members of teams, each
team having the responsibility for making a particular car, taking it through
each stage of production, so that the excellence of the end product became
the goal of their cooperative activity and their responsibility. Before, their
work was no more than a means to a livelihood for themselves and their
families. After, their work was directed toward an end which they could
make their own. Compare with this the contrast observed by the British
sociologist Tom Burns, between the attitudes and activities of those engaged
in making television programs for the British Broadcasting Corporation in
the earlier years in which such programs were produced and their attitudes
and activities some years later.

In the earlier period, what Burns had remarked was a shared understanding of what could be achieved by talented individuals of very different
kinds, so that "engineers, scene-shifters, directors, actors, stage-managers,

porters, lighting supervisors, accountants, cameramen, secretaries" and the like were able to dovetail in with the activities of others and to treat moments of emergency or breakdown as "signals for the immediate per-formance of appropriate and complementary tasks."[1] Burns compared this mobilization of both sophisticated routines and creative improvisations in the service of a common end with that achieved by surgical teams in oper-ating theatres and by "fishing crews and ensembles of actors or acrobats or musicians," resulting in each case in work of very high quality.[2] Yet when Burns revisited the BBC a few years later, there had been a notable decline in quality and a notable change in attitude. Where previously administra-tors and managers had provided space and resources for those who shared in producing the programs to pursue the common ends that they had made their own and to devise the means for achieving those ends, administrators and managers were now imposing *their* ends and dictating the means taken by them to be appropriate. Of the activities of those at work in the earlier stage Burns said that "None of it seemed to be managed."[3] Of the activities of those at work in the later stage, it was clear that it had deteriorated in quality just because it was managed.

We thus find in two very different cultural settings, Japanese and British, with work that makes use of two very different technologies, those of automobile manufacture and of television, the same contrast between two kinds of activity, one a mode of practice in which workers are able to pursue ends that they themselves have identified as worthwhile, in the pursuit of which they hold themselves to standards of excellence that they have made their own, the other an organization of activity such that their work is directed toward ends that are the ends of administrators and managers imposed upon their activities. In the former the primary responsibility for the quality of the end products of the work lies with the workers, who in this respect are treated as agents with rational and aesthetic powers, even though their labor is still exploited. In the latter this primary responsibility is assumed by administrators and managers, and productive workers are treated as means to the ends of administration and management.

It is in and through activities of the former kind that desires are educated and transformed. Distinctions are made between real and apparent goods, between objects of desire that agents have good reason to pursue and objects of desire that need to be set aside if excellence is to be achieved. Feelings are transformed as what agents care about changes. What agents want for

---

[1] Tom Burns, *Explanation and Understanding: Selected Writings, 1944–1980*, Edinburgh University Press, 1995, p. 17.
[2] Ibid., p. 18.   [3] Ibid., p. 17.

and from themselves and for and from others is no longer what it was. More experienced workers become teachers. Managers become enablers. By contrast activities of the latter kind fail to engage such feelings. They are at best means to ends beyond work, means perhaps to a pay packet that may make life outside work, the life of a consumer, more satisfying. And as with work, so also with leisure: the key contrast is between activities in and through which desires are educated and transformed and activities in which desires are elicited by and directed toward objects in ways that conduce to the profitability of this or that enterprise. The history of advertising and of public relations is too often a history of the misdirection of desire.

Turn now from activities to responsibilities, especially the responsibilities that we have to those others who have to learn from us how to direct their own lives, most of all our children, but also our pupils, if we are teachers, our apprentices, if we are skilled workers. The question is: What do we want them to want? How we answer that question will depend in part on how enlarged or diminished our sense of possibility is, on how far we can conceive and imagine a possible way of life for those for whom we are responsible that will allow them to exercise their rational and other powers more adequately. But our ability to conceive and imagine such alternatives depends in turn on how we understand our own present situation. So it has been in all those episodes in the past history of modernity in which some imaginative vision of an alternative way of life has elicited desires for the achievement of that way of life. And it has been characteristic of modernity to generate a series of such visions, some of them ill founded and illusory, some of them well founded and realistic. This is why the theorists who provide or seem to provide warrant for those visions play such an important part in the social and political history of modernity.

What I have been emphasizing are the multifarious and heterogeneous sources of desire in the cultures of modernity and the consequent multifarious and heterogeneous desires. Nowhere is this more evident than when we pass from considering needs, activities, and responsibilities to considering enjoyments. Modernity has from early in its history been marked by both the range and the variety of enjoyments that it has made possible and the growing proportions of the population to whom it has made those enjoyments available. The enjoyments of artists, scientists, and technological inventors and makers in their activities are matched by the enjoyments of those who look at their paintings, listen to their music, and are fascinated by the ingenuity of their devices. The enjoyments of those who play games as different as soccer, cricket, and chess with great skill are matched by the enjoyments of those spectators who combine an appreciation of those skills with the devotion of fans. Theatre and music hall, Henry Irving and Marie Lloyd, Kathleen Ferrier and the Beatles, atonal compositions and hard rock extravaganzas compete for attention. Desires to excel in all these areas and desires to enjoy the works of those who excel are as multifarious and heterogeneous as any other.

It is often this cultural richness of capitalist modernity that dazzles its greatest admirers, while blinding them to its limitations and horrors, foremost among them the structures of inequality, national and global, that condemn so many to poverty, hunger, and exclusion from the cultural riches of modernity. But even those who are not thus condemned and excluded also commonly suffer from a deprivation, one of which they are equally commonly unaware. They are inadequately educated in how to make choices.

3.5 The structuring of desires by norms

The cultures of modernity are cultures in which objects of desire and with them desires are multiplied. But along with the multiplication of desires comes a need to make choices. To which desires should I give priority? Which desires should I treat as realistic and which as vain wishes? How should I respond to conflicts of desire? I happen to want this *and* this *and* this, but my pursuit of any one of these will prevent me from achieving the others. And, whichever I pursue, I may be haunted by damaging regret for my loss of the others. So how should I choose and how am I to become reflective in my choice making? Closely related questions are posed when the possibility of conflicts with others arises because, if I act so as to satisfy my desire, I will interfere with or frustrate your attempt to satisfy your desire. So how should I think about the relationships between myself and others, so that in my choices I take due account of the desires of others as well as of my own?

Here what was said earlier about childhood learning (Chapter 1, section 1.6) becomes relevant. It is a commonplace that children learn from their parents, from other adults, and from older siblings which patterns of choice making in their particular adult world are acceptable and which are not. Their own desire for acceptance by and into that world is generally such that they unreflectively reproduce what they understand to be the attitudes and choices of the inhabitants of that world. So it continues more or less when they are initiated into the roles and statuses that they will from then on occupy, in school, in the workplace, in their leisure activities, in marriage and bringing up their own children. But that 'more or less' is important and this for two reasons. The first is a truth about all cultures: roles shape individuals, but individuals also shape roles. Individuals who find that the roles that they occupy, perhaps are compelled to occupy, do not allow for the expression of, let alone for the satisfaction of, some of their desires may i   the role, they may find s   h the desire, they may :   lly, to remake the role.

Th   nodernity. It is, as those   understand it, the indiv   ssion to her or his desii   n something more and   n to be responsible for   es and can be held acco   remodern cultures. Wh   standards by which ind   nd expressing their des   acknowledgment of tha   he autonomy of the ind   hat standards, then, are   ltifarious objects of desire?

They badly need some way of rank ordering those objects, of deciding which have priority in this kind of situation and which in that, but a mark of the cultures of modernity, especially of advanced modernity, is radical disagreement as to how this is to be done. Every claim about how the objects of desire should be conceived, let alone rank ordered, is treated as contestable. The impossibility of rational agreement on whether there is any such thing as the human good, let alone as to what it is, is widely taken for granted in the politics and ethics of modernity. It is left to each individual to make her or his decisions as to how her or his way of life is to be constituted on the basis of whatever convictions she or he has arrived at. And it is a mark of liberal democratic modernity to affirm that the state should be, so far as possible, neutral between rival accounts of the human good, rival conceptions of which ways of life are best for human beings. What does concern the agencies of the state is the regulation and prevention of harmful conflict in situations where the pursuit of the satisfaction of their desires by one individual or group hinders or frustrates other individuals or groups in pursuing the satisfaction of their desires. For such conflict is always apt to generate civil disorder and even, in the worst case, civil war.

Individuals characteristically achieve success, or what is taken for success by members of the economic, financial, political, and other elites, by competing successfully with others in a number of ways: educationally, in securing appointments and promotions in the workplace, in economic and financial acquisition, and in wielding political influence or power. To be successful is to compete in such a way that it is one's own preferences that are satisfied rather than those of others. So individuals learn to deal with each other as rational agents concerned to maximize their own preference satisfaction competitively, whether in market transactions, or in the arenas of politics, or even in the relationships and activities of their private lives, and they are able to do so with some security because the law provides a stable framework within which they can engage with others, whether as winners or as the more numerous losers. What the law prohibits is the use of certain types of means, means that make use of force and fraud, to pursue the ends of competitive success. But the law does more than this. By, for example, laying down conditions to which contracts must conform and by specifying what must be done to fulfill the requirements of this or that type of contract, the law makes the behavior of preference-maximizing agents more predictable to each other than it would otherwise be.

So we have in the societies of modernity activity structured by a number of sets of norms, including those prescribed by the ethics-of-the-state, those prescribed by the ethics-of-the-market, and those imposed by the enactments of the law. Those norms shape many of our desires, attitudes, and expectations. They allow that some types of desire may or should find expression in our actions, but require that others be inhibited or repressed, or redirected. They require us to take certain types of attitude to our own desires and to the expressions of their desires by others. And, insofar as they are successful in shaping our desires and attitudes, they provide us with grounds for our expectations of others. Without those norms too many of our desires and attitudes would be on occasion disruptive in their effects, sometimes frustrating others and sometimes issuing in self-defeating or even self-destructive behavior. But by themselves those norms are insufficient, and this for two reasons.

The first is that there are too many areas of life for which the law leaves open too many possibilities for aggressively and competitively pursuing the satisfaction of our desires. The second is that even when and where the law is effective in civilizing desire to some degree, it is so only if and because conformity to the law is sustained by a moral consensus of those subject to it, a consensus grounded in a set of moral norms which agents have generally internalized, so that the limits that they set to the expression of their desires derive primarily from internal assent rather than from external sanctions. This is a truth about all settled and stable cultural and social orders and that of modernity is no exception. What is distinctive about modernity is the particular morality that plays this part in sustaining the distinctive political, economic, and social order of modernity, the morality that I have named 'Morality'. Without the institution of Morality as an instrument for setting limits to desire, modernity could not function as it does, any more than it could do so without the ethics-of-the-state and the ethics-of-the-market.

3.6   How and why Morality functions as it does

Morality can only function as it does in limiting and to some extent civilizing desire because its injunctions are held by its adherents to have definitive and overriding authority. From whence is this authority taken to derive? It is taken to be such that to fail to have due regard for Morality, to fail to feel bound to comply with the relevant injunctions, is to fail not qua citizen nor qua market participant, but qua human being. Yet it is one mark of the peculiar character of that authority that those plain persons who recognize and acknowledge it commonly cannot say in what it consists and whence its binding power derives, and, if they attempt to do so, are apt to find themselves involved in interminable debate, in this resembling Morality's philosophical theorists. Yet, as we noticed earlier, plain persons and theorists differ. Where the vast majority of plain non-philosophical persons are prepared on some occasions to judge and act as consequentialists, and even as maximizers, yet on others to judge and act as deniers of consequentialism, the moral philosophers of Morality honor an obligation to render their judgments consistent and in so doing not only revise Morality, sometimes in obvious and sometimes in subtle ways, but enter into notable disagreements with each other. What those theoretical exponents of Morality aspire but fail to provide is any conclusive reason for adopting the impersonal standpoint of Morality or, at least in certain types of situation, according an overriding importance to its claims. What the recognition of the distinctive authority of Morality by plain nonphilosophical persons involves is a conviction that there is such a conclusive reason, even if they are unable to say what it is.

Morality is only able to function as it does because in the secularizing societies of modernity, in which religion so often lacks authority, it is and is taken to be a wholly secular institution. Its claims presuppose not just a rejection of all theological claims, but a particular kind of rejection, one that was the work of certain Enlightenment thinkers. It is secular as the modern state and the modern economy are secular. When Diderot looked forward to the day when the last king would be strangled by the entrails of the last priest, he understood the power over the mind of what he took to be theological superstition as underpinned by and underpinning arbitrary political power. About the regimes against which he thought and wrote, he was by and large quite right. What had emerged in Europe from the sixteenth century onwards were a set of alliances between throne and altar in each of which some particular church was established and privileged in return for its obediently upholding the particular ruling power. There were Catholic, Lutheran, Anglican, and Presbyterian examples of this corrupting integration of church and state, and the radical Enlightenment critique of that integration not only therefore insisted upon the separation of church and state, but also upon the need to judge the misdeeds of kings and priests from an independent secular moral standpoint. But what moral standpoint was that to be?

The difficulty in answering this question was identified by Diderot with dramatic wit and psychological insight in a work written for himself and not for publication, *Le Neveu de Rameau*, a dialogue between a protagonist of conventional bourgeois virtue, *Moi*, and *Lui*, the nephew of the composer, but in fact a dialogue with himself. Both voices are the voices of Diderot. As *Moi*, he makes the case for virtue. As *Lui*, he refutes it. As *Moi*, he argues that, if each of us pursues the objects of her or his desires intelligently with the aim of faring well in the long run, we will discover that it is to our interest to be honest and truthful, to keep our promises, and to honor marital fidelity. As *Lui*, he not only argues against, but mocks *Moi*'s moral pretensions. Why, he asks, in deciding which of our desires to satisfy, should we give preference to long-term over short-term outcomes, if what the short term offers is sufficiently attractive? And does not *Moi*'s case for morality concede that if we should conform to the precepts of morality, it is only because and insofar as by so doing we will satisfy our desires? And is not this how in any case humankind is, each individual and class, so far as they can, satisfying their own desires at the expense of others?

What both *Moi* and Diderot need, but are unable to supply is twofold: a standard independent of our desires by appeal to which we can distinguish between those objects of desire which we should pursue and those which we should set aside and an argument that provides us with a conclusive reason for treating that standard as authoritative. Both standard and argument must be such as to be found compelling by all reasonable individuals, whatever their theological beliefs, not only because, on Diderot's own view, there is no good reason to believe in God, but also because in societies that are divided on theological questions there is a need for a morality that all can share. Both the resemblances and the differences between Diderot's project and what Morality supplied, as it emerged, are important. Morality is the shared morality of the religiously divided societies of modernity. The individual adherents of Morality judge and act as if its precepts are authoritative and supply conclusive reasons for adopting its impersonal standpoint and setting inviolable limits to the pursuit and satisfaction of our desires. But those individuals either cannot say why they take this to be the case or else, if they are theorists, advance arguments that are as highly contested as the theologies that they have displaced.

I have presented Morality as *the* morality of the social and cultural order of modernity, emerging as it emerged and enabling agents to act and judge as modernity needs them to act and judge. This does not mean that Morality cannot provide a basis for a critique, even sometimes an apparently radical critique of certain aspects of the modern condition. For modernity is in part constituted by ongoing debate between the more and the less liberal members of its elites, although never in such a way as to put the standing of those elites seriously in question. Yet of course, as modernity came to be in societies with very different premodern pasts through significantly different conflicts, it presented itself in different cultural guises, so that Japanese modernity is not quite English modernity and neither of these is quite American modernity. So it is too with Morality, but in all its versions Morality is *the* morality, the dominant morality, of some particular modern social and cultural order.

3.7   Morality put in question by expressivism: the limits of an expressivist critique

Given that Morality as the morality of modernity is what it is, and given that the social contexts in which it functions are what they are, what part might and does expressivism play, not in the metaethical discussions of academic philosophy, but in the thinking and conversations of reflective agents whose moral culture is that of modernity? Imagine once more such an agent – I first imagined her in Chapter 1, section 1.7 – this time someone who hitherto has unreflectively taken the injunctions of Morality with great and deferential seriousness, according them overriding authority, but who now finds herself in a dilemma. She owes a great deal to someone, a family member or a friend, who in the past at some cost to himself helped her through an otherwise unmanageable crisis. If she now acts as the impersonal injunctions of Morality dictate, by answering truthfully questions put to her by someone with the right to pose those questions – her family member or friend is competing against others for a job for which he is adequately, but not outstandingly qualified – she will have to harm that family member or friend by disclosing damaging facts. If she refuses to answer, the inference that will be drawn by the questioner will be that there are such facts. Therefore she can only serve the interests of her family member or friend either by lying or by giving an answer that, although not false, is wildly misleading and deceptive. What she must decide is whether to act out of gratitude and with respect to the ties of family or friendship or instead as Morality requires in a case where issues of both truthfulness and fairness arise. Because she regards the injunctions of Morality as binding and authoritative, as overriding other types of consideration, she initially understands herself as tempted to do wrong by her desires and inclinations. What she wants to do is to help her family member or friend. What she takes it that she Morally ought to do is to disclose the damaging facts.

Just how she thinks about her dilemma will depend, as we noticed earlier, upon both her temperament and her social situation. Her desires will have been developed in some particular kind of household, in some particular kind of workplace, through particular friendships, through frustrations and fears, through hopes and aspirations. So will her felt need to sustain certain relationships and so too her commitments and her loyalties. It is these, we are imagining, that first led her to put in question those constraints of Morality that she has hitherto accepted more or less unreflectively. But a philosophically informed friend now suggests to her that she should reconsider the nature of Morality in the light of an expressivist account of its injunctions. Her first response to the claims of expressivism is to ask herself whether there is any good reason for her to have been or to continue to be deferential to those injunctions. She consults other philosophically well informed friends and among the answers that she considers are that if she flouts those injunctions, she will be lacking in respect for herself as a rational agent, that she will be unable to universalize the maxims on which she will be acting, and that she will not be acting so as to maximize human happiness or preference satisfaction. About each of these answers, she asks whether and why she should be moved by it.

What the expressivist tells her is that whether she is or takes herself to be moved by such considerations or simply defers to the injunctions of Morality without having any such reasons for doing so, it is only because she is expressing a prerational attitude or set of feelings that moves her to judge and act as she does. What she then concludes, just like her imagined predecessor in our earlier discussion, is that, *if* expressivism is true, then her conflict must be redescribed as an internal conflict between two incompatible sets of feelings and desires. But, if that is what it is, what she now has to do is to identify reasons for judging between the rival claims of those incompatible sets of feelings and desires. She needs to identify some rationally justifiable standard independent of these and any other feelings and desires which will enable her to make a rational choice. It is at this point that, whether she recognizes it or not, NeoAristotelian claims become relevant and expressivism has to fall silent. But she still has to ask what she has learned from expressivism and what light an expressivist critique might throw on Morality.

What she should have learned from expressivism is that our evaluative and normative judgments must be such that they can motivate us to act in accordance with them and that they can only so motivate us insofar as they afford expression to our sentiments, to our feelings and attitudes. About this Hume and those expressivists who have followed him have plainly been right. Everyone who advances an account of evaluative and normative judgments has left their account incomplete until they have provided an explanation in acceptable psychological terms of how and why judgments, construed in their terms, motivate. From a NeoAristotelian standpoint, however, expressivists have failed to supply an adequate account of the range of possible motivations. They have been unable to recognize that such judgments may give expression to the attitudes and felings of morally educated agents just because they direct such agents toward and to the achievement of what they have learned to understand as their goods and good. Such judgments, asserted by such agents, are asserted as true – and not only in some weakened quasirealist construal of 'true' – and motivate as they do only because they are taken to be truths concerning matters of fact. So our imagined agent should recognize it as the truth in expressivism that our evaluative and normative judgments have a motivating power derived at least in part from the feelings and attitudes to which they give expression. What else might she have learned from expressivism? That it provides a more adequate account of Morality than the adherents of Morality themselves provide.

Consider once again the high incidence of unresolved and apparently unresolvable disagreements in judgment among the adherents of Morality and about the ways in which those disagreements are expressed. What expressivism tells us about those disagreements – and about Morality it is convincing – is that each contending party's Moral judgments give expression to underlying prerational commitments, to attitudes and sentiments that find expression in the unargued premises of their arguments. What our own observations of the utterances of agents advancing this or that claim in situations of Moral disagreement add is not only that such agents do not recognize this fact about themselves, but also that it seems that it is only because they do not recognize it that they are able to continue as they do. What appears to sustain them in their assertive Moral stances is their mistaken conviction that the injunctions to which they defer have an authority that is independent of their recognition of it, that is independent of their attitudes, sentiments, and choices. Were they to believe otherwise, so it seems, they would have to acknowledge that they have been deceived and self-deceived about the claims of Morality.

Suppose now that our imagined agent, in the course of reflecting on her dilemma, is impressed by this line of argument. She concludes that her own dilemma does indeed arise from an inner conflict between rival sets of attitudes and feelings, a conflict which she must now resolve. But how to resolve it? She needs, we recall, a standard and a standpoint independent of her own present feelings and attitudes, and she may not yet be open to considering NeoAristotelian claims. She finds no help in Frankfurt, since her problem is of the form: What should I care about most? With which of my feelings and desires should I identify? What expressivism has taught her is to be suspicious of Morality. So it would make sense for her to turn for resources to some of its most notable critics in order to consider what they can offer by way of such a standard and such a standpoint. Those include Oscar Wilde, D. H. Lawrence, and Bernard Williams, and from each of these both she and we have something to learn.

3.8 Morality put in question by Oscar Wilde

It is a commonplace in some twentieth-century writing that an artist who is deeply committed to her or his art may in following through on that commitment have to violate the requirements not just of Morality, but of morality more broadly conceived. The example most often cited is that of the Post-Impressionist painter, Paul Gauguin, about whom the story is repeatedly told that he deserted his wife and children in France in order to pursue the relentless demands of his art in Tahiti. The story serves admirably as an example. Unfortunately it is false. Gauguin for quite a number of years lived with his Danish wife and their children in Copenhagen, working as a tarpaulin salesman in order to support them, but ineffectively. It was only when his wife and her family had asked him to leave that he returned to France, and only some years after that that he left France for French Polynesia. The story as so often told is a fable. That it has so often been retold by philosophers – including me – is all the more regrettable because the same point could have been made by telling a true story, that of Oscar Wilde.

Wilde was not a supremely great artist, as Gauguin was, yet he was a not inconsiderable figure as novelist, playwright, lover of the visual arts, and, above all, wit. It matters of course in considering his quarrels with the moral and social establishment that he incurred disgraceful moralizing condemnation and legal persecution, because he was, as we now say, gay. But that can be put on one side, since it was Wilde himself, and not his homophobic critics, who first defined his own aesthetic stance in opposition to Morality, which he unreflectively identified with morality. It was from the outset a principal target for his wit, sometimes in his own voice, sometimes in the voices of characters in his plays and novels. "Conscience and cowardice are really the same thing, Basil. Conscience is the trade name of the firm. That is all" (*The Picture of Dorian Gray*). And "Morality is simply the attitude that we adopt towards people whom we personally dislike" (*An Ideal Husband*). The aphorism is Wilde's chosen genre. He does not argue. He mocks. His aim is to amuse some and to embarrass others, to amuse some by embarrassing others. What such aphorisms are designed to suggest is both that it is the feelings expressed in their judgments by the adherents of Morality that give those judgments their distinctive character and that those feelings are unacknowledged and discreditable. So Wilde's critique of Morality is an expressivist critique.

By putting his aphorisms into the mouth of fictional characters, Wilde made it possible for him, when convenient, to disown them. And sometimes he did. Yet he also made it clear that the standpoint of the artist has to be one external to Morality, indeed, on Wilde's view, to all moralities. "An artist has no ethical sympathies at all," he wrote. "Virtue and wickedness are to him simply what the colours on his palette are to the painter" (letter to the *Scots Observer*). Every artist is more than an artist, someone who needs to know not only what Wilde is happy to tell him, how not to live, but also how to live. Here in the end Wilde fails his readers, as he failed himself. He could not move, seemed to have no inclination to move, beyond his own inconsistencies. "Consistency," he said, "is the last refuge of the unimaginative." What he took to be his socialism – it was in fact anarchism – and his conversion to the Catholic faith suggest directions that he might have taken, but for his early death. But his politics was that of a

fantasy Uto   d that does
not include   Catholicism
came too l   itself is an
art, and m   ss it,"[4] but
he failed to   great artists
and that gre   e's insights
make it imp

The first concerns the due place of the arts in human life. On the view characteristic of liberal modernity, it is up to each individual to decide how it is best for her or him to live, and there are no standards by which one individual's rank ordering of goods can be shown to be superior to another's, provided that each is adequately well informed and has avoided incoherence. Yet the cultures of modernity are notable for their extraordinary achievements in various arts, in music, opera, and ballet, in painting, sculpture, and architecture, and it is common to characterize those achievements in terms that suggest that someone who has an opportunity and ability to enjoy and learn from at least some of those achievements, but fails to do so, may be a defective human being, and that someone responsible for the care of children who could provide them with that opportunity and ability, but fails to do so, does them an injustice. If we have good reason so to judge, then it seems that there are some goods constitutive of the good life for human beings that are such independently of and prior to our choices and preferences and that failure to have due regard for such goods and failure to share them with others are kinds of moral failure. If this is so, then the relationship between, on the one hand, our conception of goods and of the good and, on the other, our grasp of the requirements of morality must be other than it is commonly taken to be by the adherents of Morality. Moreover, for our imagined reflective agent it is of the first importance that these same considerations put in question what is implied by Frankfurt's account of our practical lives and especially by his claim that what we should care about must be determined for each of us by what in the end we do in fact care about, whatever it happens to be. I argued earlier (Chapter 1, section 1.7) that someone convinced of the truth of expressivism might find reason to adopt Frankfurt's account of the practical life. But Wilde now suggests a crucial objection to that account.

When for the first time, as a result of some chance encounter some particular great work of art makes a sufficiently disturbing and singular

---

[4] Oscar Wilde, *Complete Works*, New York: Harper & Row, 1985, p. 985.

impact on someone who has hitherto found nothing in art to care about, she or he will be compelled to recognize that, but for that chance event, they might have spent their whole lives not caring about what they should have been caring about. They are unable to judge the work by the standards that they have hitherto taken for granted. It is rather that the work imposes its standards on them. From then on they cannot but acknowledge, implicitly or explicitly, that there is some measure of human goods, goods that contribute to our flourishing, that is independent of their own particular concerns, cares, attitudes, and feelings, indeed independent of the concerns, cares, attitudes, and feelings of any particular agent, even if they cannot say what it is. In passing a negative judgment on the life that, but for chance, they would have led, they cannot but quarrel with Frankfurt. But this is not the only important claim that Wilde discredits.

Another question that Wilde makes inescapable is that so often posed in terms of Gauguin. If great art has the kind of value that he claims for it, may it not sometimes be the case that artists in pursuit of their ends have to violate and are justified in violating the requirements imposed by moral rules, whether the rules of Morality or of some other morality? A case in point is Graham Sutherland's portrait of Winston Churchill. The members of the House of Commons had commissioned the painting of this portrait on the occasion of Churchill's retirement from the House in gratitude for his long and impressive career as a parliamentarian. Their and his expectation had been that this gift and its ceremonial presentation would give him and them the pleasure ordinarily associated with such gifts and such occasions. They had not reckoned with the extraordinary insights and skills of the painter. What was unveiled at the presentation was a shockingly truthful portrait of Churchill as the victim of fatigue and old age, a face whose lines and planes communicated the imminent dissolution of a personality. Those who cared most for Churchill found it difficult to look at the painting. His wife first hid it and then destroyed it.

Sutherland had, I presume, not acted with the intention of hurting, yet he must have known that his painting was bound to cause pain to Churchill and to those close to him. He had spoiled an otherwise happy occasion. When I asked E. H. Gombrich what he thought of the painting, he replied "Breach of contract!" Yet the painting was a great and truthful achievement as a work of art. Was Sutherland therefore justified in painting as he did? If so, then it seems the good of artistic achievement can outweigh moral considerations, as Wilde suggests. If not, then it seems art is to be allowed to express only what morality permits, a conclusion that Wilde mocked. What are we to think? Or rather what is our imagined reflective agent to think? What part might the questions elicited by Wilde play in her thinking?

Had she read Wilde, his attitude to the injunctions of Morality might well have initially reinforced her conviction that it is only through an expressivist account of the authority imputed to them that we can understand how they function and with it her view that what she had taken to be a conflict between the claims of Morality and those of gratitude, friendship, and family ties was in fact a conflict between two sets of feelings and attitudes which it was up to her to resolve by rendering her feelings and attitudes consistent and coherent. But Wilde's story is also relevant to the tasks that confront her as she sets about that work of psychological resolution. For in trying to answer the question 'About what should I most care?' Wilde's insistence on the value of the arts should give her strong reason to pause and consider.

Suppose that she herself has become seriously committed to engaging with some art, classical music, say. Initially, she was impressed by friends who found that art rewarding but was puzzled as to why that was so. So she sets herself to learn, asking advice about concerts and moving from appreciation of music that engages easily – some Mozart, some Schubert songs – to more difficult listening, while learning the piano, initially from Bartok's *Mikrokosmos*, whose genius is to take the beginner from a standing start to the easiest Bach. As she moves forward, she becomes able to ask questions that at first she would not have understood, but only because she has become able to appreciate works that at first she would not have been able to hear, let alone appreciate. She has learned to perceive what without this kind of initiation she would never have perceived. She will also have learned to distinguish two different kinds of aesthetic judgment.

There are first the judgments of those, like herself at the outset, who listen to classical music only casually and occasionally, and who respond with uninformed enthusiasm or distaste or incomprehension to this or that work or part of a work. Their judgments express a genuine enjoyment or lack of enjoyment in a straightforward way, and an expressivist account of those judgments does them no injustice. Very different are the judgments of the musically educated listener and even more of the performer, judgments expressed in the kind and degree of attention that they give to particular passages and to the work as a whole, and to different interpretations of the score, and in their returning to this or that work again and again. Such judgments require an ability to recognize and to respond to different kinds of greatness, to Bach and to Chopin and to Schönberg. They require, too, a recognition that there are some works for which one is not yet ready,

works whose greatness one can only at present appreciate imperfectly, such
as, for perhaps almost everyone, Beethoven's op. 131.

For this second class of judgments, judgments whose formulation in
words characteristically fails to convey what needs to be communicated
(How little to the point it would be to say "What a very great work op.
131 is!"), an expressivist account is plainly inadequate. Such judgments
make the kind of claim that they do, only because and insofar as they
express the feelings and attitudes of those musically educated enough to
be entitled to pass judgment, of those who have learned how to judge. So
what do we mean when we call such musical goods goods, and how are we
to characterize the claim that they justifiably make upon our interest and
attention? What would someone be doing who recognized that such goods
can be very great goods, but decided that for him they have to be set aside,
because their pursuit would distract him from doing what he takes it to be
his moral duty to do? If our imagined reflective agent, who was enquiring
what weight she should give to moral considerations in trying to resolve
her dilemma, has followed the argument about the arts up to this point,
she may feel more perplexed than ever.

It is not that no progress has been made. Even if Wilde's characterization
of the standpoint of the artist will not do, he was clearly right in suggesting
both that something of great significance is at stake in someone's decision
to take the goods to be achieved in and through each of the arts with great
seriousness and that we will not have understood what a commitment
to morality is, unless we can give an account of the kind of weight that
we should give to moral considerations, when they conflict with aesthetic
achievement. Our imagined reflective agent cannot afford to focus only
on her own dilemma, in which moral considerations have to be weighed
against considerations of gratitude and friendship, but must take into
account a wider range of dilemmas. How is she to do this? Perhaps by
asking what kind of person she will have to become, if she is to be able
to find her way through different kinds of conflicting demands. This is
a question that philosophers have rarely asked. It is among the questions
posed by D. H. Lawrence.

3.9   Morality put in question by D. H. Lawrence

For Lawrence what makes so many of our judgments problematic is that
we are too often unable to recognize our feelings for what they are. Had
Lawrence come across the expressivist thesis that our evaluative and normative judgments express our feeling and attitudes, his response might

well have been one of alarm. For our feelings are apt to betray us and our attitudes are apt to obstruct our identifications of our feelings. "The moral instinct of the man in the street is largely the emotional defence of an old habit."[5] That habit is one of seeing oneself and identifying one's feelings in stock and conventional ways with the result that one does not see what is there to be seen and does not know what one feels. The task of the artist, of painters, poets, novelists, is to enable us to see and to feel by showing us what there is to be seen and to be felt, putting us into a new relationship to ourselves, to others, to things. "A new relationship between ourselves and the universe means a new morality."[6]

Lawrence thus, as an artist, understood himself as undermining the established morality of the social order, whatever it might be, in the name of a new and better morality. The wrongheaded attacks on his novels as immoral, and especially the banning of *The Rainbow* and of *Lady Chatterley's Lover*, only confirmed him in this stance. In fact however, as with the vicious treatment of Wilde, the longer term effect of these attacks was to liberalize the established morality. I noted earlier that there are both liberal and conservative versions of Morality. I note now that the line between what is accounted liberal and what conservative also varies with time and place. But I note, too, that Lawrence would have found himself in most ways as much at odds with the liberalized Morality of the later twentieth century as with the Morality of his own time. For every established morality, on his view, inculcates modes of perception and feeling that the artist teaches us to distrust.

Lawrence invites us now, as much as his contemporary readers, to ask which of our feelings we should trust and which distrust. There are indeed those feelings and desires that belong to us as a living animal, but generally and characteristically we are miseducated, so that our feelings are shaped by our social environment. The roles imposed upon us require that we feel as and what we are supposed to feel and desire as and what we are supposed to desire, with the result that "a man who is *emotionally* educated is as rare as a phoenix."[7] "It is cruelly sad to see men caught in the clutches of the past, working automatically in the spell of an authorized desire that is a desire no longer."[8] One central task that Lawrence set himself in his

---

[5] D. H. Lawrence, "Art and Morality," in *Phoenix: The Posthumous Papers, 1936*, Harmondsworth: Penguin Books, 1978, p. 521.

[6] Ibid., p. 526.

[7] D. H. Lawrence, "John Galsworthy," in *Phoenix*, p. 539.

[8] Letter to Catherine Carswell, quoted in her *The Savage Pilgrimage: A Narrative of D. H. Lawrence*, London: Secker & Warburg, 1951, p. 59.

novels was to show what happened to those who substitute for feelings and desires that are genuinely their own the feelings and desires authorized by the established social order. So it is with Gerald in *Women in Love*, to whom what matters is that individuals act so as to function well in their assigned role, whatever the effect on their character.

"Was a miner a good miner? Then he was complete. Was a manager a good manager? That was enough. Gerald himself, who was responsible for all this industry, was he a good director? If he were, he had fulfilled his life. The rest was by-play." When the Brangwen sisters discuss him, Ursula says "'. . . He'll have to die soon when he's made every possible improvement, and there will be nothing more to improve. He's got go, anyhow.' 'Certainly he's got go,' said Gudrun. 'In fact I've never seen a man that showed signs of so much. The unfortunate thing is, where does his *go* go to, what becomes of it?' 'Oh I know,' said 'Ursula.' It goes in applying the latest appliances.'" The same traits that betray Gerald in his relationships with both women and men – traits all too common in a technologically mesmerized culture such as our own; Gerald would nowadays be Apple's or Amazon's or Google's ideal executive – render him unable to learn what he needs to learn. So how did Lawrence think it possible to learn? It matters that he was not only a novelist, but also a poet and an essayist.

As poet he communicates both the immediacy of sense experience and emotions that are at once elicited and transformed by that which is sensed: a snake, fig trees, gentians, hummingbirds, grapes. In his poetry Lawrence uses words that not only describe, but evoke, words that express the response of the human animal to other animals, of human nature to other natures.[9] If Lawrence was right, many of us should find this poetry disturbing and unsettling. (It cannot have surprised him how much T. S. Eliot disliked it.) But, on Lawrence's account, we need to be disturbed and unsettled, if we are to be educated in how to be at one with ourselves and with others. What Lawrence's greatest novels show us is the various forms that failure to be so educated can take. One source of such failure is to be guided by reason rather than by sense and emotion. "Make any people mainly rational in their life, and their inner activity will be the activity of destruction."[10] Yet what a careful reading of those essays makes clear is that the conception of reason that led him to speak of reason in this way was itself an inadequate conception, one that failed to do justice to the fact that what he was deploying in his novels were narratives that were

---

9   On Lawrence's poetry, see Santanu Das, "Lawrence's Sense-Words," *Essays in Criticism* 62, 1 (January 2012): 58–82.
10   D. H. Lawrence, "Introduction to *Cavalleria Rusticana* by Giovanni Verga," in *Phoenix*, p. 245.

also arguments, arguments about what corrupts and undermines human relationships and what rescues and sustains them, arguments that are sound or unsound.

How far Lawrence's novels succeed as arguments does, of course, vary from novel to novel. The greatness of *Sons and Lovers*, *The Rainbow*, and *Women in Love* is not matched elsewhere. But Lawrence makes one point of the first importance for anyone who, like our imagined reflective agent, has not only found her way out of Morality through an expressivist critique of its claims, but has then entertained the possibility of making Frankfurt's account of the practical life her own, by assenting to his thesis that what she cares about provides the only defensible standard for determining her evaluative and normative judgments. Such a one has already of course encountered one difficulty in accepting Frankfurt's view as a result of reflecting on Wilde's conception of the values of the artist. For, in the arts at least, what someone cares about depends on what they have learned to value, and the value that they have come to discover is independent of their previous feelings or carings. Lawrence adds a second difficulty.

Someone who is educable in respect of their sensations, perceptions, and emotions, on Lawrence's view, is someone who is open to the possibility that what they do in fact care about is the outcome of their own inadequacies and needs to be corrected. That is, they become educable only if they have a higher order desire to care as they, given their situation and relationships, should care. But, if Lawrence is right, then there must be some standard by which we, or perhaps others who know us well, can identify our inadequacies and contrast what we do care about with what we should care about. It is one of the strengths of Frankfurt's account that attempts to say what that standard might be have so often failed. What did Lawrence take it to be? In his early polemic against Benjamin Franklin's catalogue of what Franklin took to be the virtues, Lawrence formulated a maxim that he repeated elsewhere: "Resolve to abide by your own deepest promptings . . . " That maxim badly needs spelling out further, but Lawrence takes us only part of the way. He shows us what it is to remain superficial in one's grasp of one's own feelings and in responsiveness to others. He shows us what it is to be open to overcoming that superficiality. But when he tries to go beyond this, he is notably less successful.

Lawrence's hostility to psychoanalysis deprived him of one set of resources for spelling out his maxim further. More generally, he was suspicious of what philosophical theorizing had become. "Plato's Dialogues are queer little novels. It seems to me it was the greatest pity in the world, when philosophy and fiction got split. They used to be one, right from the days of myth. Then they went and parted, like a nagging married couple, with Aristotle and Thomas Aquinas and that beastly Kant. So the novel went sloppy and philosophy went abstract-dry. The two should come together again – in the novel."[11] Yet what Lawrence the novelist shows us is how hard it is to do this and how the result of attempting it is generally a bad novel. Happily, we have philosophical resources that were unavailable to Lawrence.

It is perhaps unsurprising that the philosopher who provided them was as averse to Aristotle, Aquinas, and Kant as Lawrence was. I refer of course to Bernard Williams. Late in life, reflecting on his work in an interview, Williams remarked that "If there's one theme in all my work it's about authenticity and self-expression. It's the idea that some things are in some real sense really you, or express what you are and others aren't." He then refers to Lawrence's maxim – in Williams' version "Find your deepest impulse and follow that" – saying of Lawrence that he "is an author I always found difficult but he sure made an impression upon me with that remark." So, although Lawrence himself takes us no further, he provided Williams with a starting point for philosophical enquiry. That starting point, I shall suggest, is a good place to begin for anyone who, like the reflective agent whom we have been imagining, has drawn upon the resources of expressivism in distancing herself from the misleading claims of Morality, but who has also understood the limitations of expressivism, who has understood both why it would be a mistake to follow either Hume or Frankfurt too closely in their accounts of morality and the practical life, who has understood what Lawrence has to teach us. Let me explain further by listing some of the conditions which, on Williams' view, any adequate treatment of the subject matter of ethics and politics must satisfy.

3.10   Morality put in question by Bernard Williams

No summary can do justice to the complexity and the depth of Williams' thinking, and I am in any case concerned only with one line of thought that he developed. However, first let me pick out some characteristics of his thinking which together made not just the content of his moral and political philosophy, but also his attitude to his discipline distinctive. The first is his rejection of morality, which he came to refer to as "the peculiar institution"[12] and treated as only one among the varieties of ethical thought

---

[11] D. H. Lawrence, "Surgery for the Novel – or a Bomb," in *Phoenix*, p. 520.
[12] Bernard Williams, *Ethics and the Limits of Philosophy*, Cambridge, MA: Harvard University Press, 1985, chapter 10.

and practice. What Williams meant by 'morality' were certain features of that system of thought and practice to which I have given the name 'Morality', and his grounds for rejecting its claims were very close to my grounds for rejecting the claims of Morality. Williams takes the concept central to morality to be that of moral obligation. What moral obligation requires is impersonal and universal, binding all – "Moral obligation is inescapable"[13] – and binding everyone equally. The requirements imposed by its principles are overriding[14] and consistent, both as principles and in their application to particular cases. To violate them is to incur blame from right-minded agents.

Williams not only rejects the claims of morality. He rejects the accounts of and the defenses of morality by both utilitarians and Kantians. Neither body of theory can supply a plausible account of the psychology of the practical life, and both fail to recognize the limits and the limitations of moral theorizing. Two aspects of this failure are especially important. Neither can allow for the ineliminable messiness of our practical lives, for the heterogeneity of the considerations that we need to take into account both in making particular decisions and more generally in deciding how to live. What makes justice important is one thing, what makes truthfulness important another, what makes loyalty to our friends important a third. But it is not only such heterogeneity that moral theorizing conceals from view. There are a multiplicity of goods to be acknowledged and of evils to be avoided, and in many situations we can act consistently with one principle that we have hitherto honored only by violating another such principle. So Williams imagined a situation in which someone can save a number of lives by himself agreeing to execute an innocent man. Whatever he chooses to do, he will have done something dreadful, and neither utilitarian nor Kantian formulas allow us to recognize this adequately.

The impersonality and universality ascribed to the requirements of morality, whether in utilitarian, Kantian, or other terms, also obscure another central aspect of our lives, the place in each life of commitments and projects that matter to that individual in key part just because they are *hers* or *his*, commitments and projects not lightly to be set aside, even when allegiance to them turns out to be incompatible with satisfying the requirements of morality. Those commitments and projects provide a key part of the answer that each agent gives to the inescapable question 'How shall I live?', a question too often ignored, on Williams' view, by modern moral theorists. It matters that in answering that question we recognize our

---

[13] Ibid., p. 177.   [14] Ibid., p. 180.

historical situatedness and that the conditions of modernity leave us without the resources on which individuals were able to draw in traditional
societies. Yet nostalgia for the past is a disabling emotion and modernity
provides a range of areas in which important values are at stake: personal life, the arts, politics. In each of these areas Williams had his own
commitments. The mistake, he believed, was to try to understand such
commitments in terms of some single theoretical stance.

I have so far summarized Williams' conclusions rather than his arguments, and this for two reasons. The first is that it was those conclusions
that put him – "arguably the greatest British philosopher of his era" as the
Guardian said in its obituary notice in 2003 – at odds with every other
major figure in the discipline. Indeed, the vast majority of those now at
work in academic moral philosophy continue to write as though Williams
had never existed, although this is a more interesting fact about them than
it is about Williams. My second reason is that I am here concerned with
Williams' arguments only as they bear upon one particular line of thought
that he developed, sometimes tentatively, from 1965 onwards.

In earlier sections of this essay, I have been tracing the path that might
have been taken by a reflective agent who had, like Williams, rejected
the claims of Morality and who had, also, again like Williams, thought
her way through and beyond expressivism. The differences between our
imagined agent and Williams are of course very great. She, unlike him,
is not an academic philosopher, but someone forced into philosophical
enquiry by persistent and intelligent practical reflection. He, unlike her,
was extraordinarily gifted in a number of fields, as fighter pilot, as teacher
of philosophy, in the appreciation of opera, as administrator of a college,
and as a public servant on several commissions of enquiry in the United
Kingdom. Williams in his admirable sophistication was about as far from
the man in the street or the woman in the Clapham omnibus as it is
possible to get. Nonetheless, the path that led him to his conclusions was, I
want to suggest, a path that anyone persistently and intelligently reflective
might well have come close to following had they taken due account of
the expressivist critique of Morality, of the limitations of expressivism, of
the example of Wilde, and of the art and teaching of Lawrence. In one
particular line of thought at least, Williams spoke not just for himself but
also for others, albeit others typically innocent of the prejudices of current
academic moral philosophy. So what was that path? And to what did it
lead?

Begin with Williams' critique of expressivism (in "Morality and the
Emotions," his Inaugural Lecture at Bedford College in 1965, published in

1973).[15] His complaint is that what expressivists say about the relationship between our moral convictions and judgments and our emotions is at too high a level of generality and so fails to capture the significant relationships between particular emotions or aspects of emotions and our convictions and judgments. One such relationship is that between the strength of feeling that someone exhibits on a moral issue and the strength of that someone's convictions, a connection such that Williams takes the former to be, except in a few special cases, a *criterion* of the latter. So the issue of sincerity, of what it is not to disguise one's feelings from oneself or others, becomes central at an early stage. But this is not the only respect in which, on Williams' view, particular emotions are morally important.

Contemporary moral philosophers had, so he charges, ignored "the ways in which various emotions may be considered as destructive, mean or hateful, while others appear as creative, generous, admirable, or – merely – such as one would hope from a decent human being."[16] To direct a particular emotion toward some object is often to pass judgment on that object, and to understand what makes it appropriate to feel as we do toward this or that object is something that requires moral education. "If such education does not revolve round such issues as what to fear, what to be angry about, what – if anything – to despise, where to draw the line between kindness and a stupid sentimentality – I do not know what it is."[17] There is thus a double connection between emotion and evaluation. In judging that or presupposing that some particular expression of emotion is appropriate or inappropriate, we evaluate it. And in feeling or giving vent to our own emotions, sometimes in response to expressions of emotion by others, we characteristically treat their objects as deserving and inviting our responses to them.

Someone who acts from compassion, say, or remorse – Williams' two examples – sees the situation in which he acts in a certain light. Seen in that light, that situation provides the agent with grounds for acting as he does, compassionately or so as to repair some wrong. We cannot understand what it is for that individual to see things as he does, to reason and to act as he does "without reference to the emotional structure of his thought and action."[18] Yet there is a difference between the way in which the functioning of that emotional structure appears to others and the way in which it appears to the agent her or himself. Williams dismisses the view that someone could *decide* to adopt a set of moral principles, asserting that

---

[15] Bernard Williams, "Morality and the Emotions," in *Problems of the Self: Philosophical Papers, 1956–1972*, Cambridge University Press, 1973, pp. 207–229.
[16] Ibid., p. 207.   [17] Ibid., p. 225.   [18] Ibid., p. 223.

"We see a man's genuine convictions as coming from somewhere deeper in him than that," although "what we see as coming from deeper in him, he . . . may see as coming from outside him."[19]

The metaphor of depth is important. So is the word 'genuine' with its echoes of Lawrence. If we are to understand our moral convictions, we must not mistake the superficial for the deep or the fake for the genuine. But, even if we do not make these mistakes, there may well be that in our convictions that we do not understand or that we misunderstand. Our deliberations, so it seems, must begin from convictions for some of which we can give no further reason, convictions that, although they are not to be understood as the emotivists understood them, are expressed in emotion, so that an observer would be unable to characterize either those convictions or the relevant emotions independently of one another. Those thoughts were still with Williams when he wrote *Morality: An Introduction to Ethics*,[20] but they then found a place within Williams' overview of the discipline of moral philosophy. About this overview two things need to be remarked.

The first has to do with content. Much of *Morality* has to do with what morality is not. (Williams did not yet in 1972 use 'morality' as the name of that to which he was opposed.) And much of *Morality* has to do with the mistakes of moral philosophers. What the reader is then invited to reflect on is a small set of possibilities that remain open. But the nature of that invitation also needs to be remarked, since it is a matter not only of content, but also of style. Anyone who goes from the text of the Inaugural Lecture to that of *Morality* will be struck by the contrast between the prosaic, analytical earnestness of the former and the liveliness, wit, even gaiety of the latter. Introductory texts are commonly designed to induce a respectful regard for the discipline thus introduced. Williams, however, engages his readers by warning them against the disciplinary pieties: "most moral philosophy at most times has been empty and boring" and "Contemporary moral philosophy has found an original way of being boring."[21] Here Williams echoes Wilde. The initial problem is one of the style in which moral philosophy is to be written and spoken "in the deepest sense of 'style' in which to discover the right style is to discover what you are really trying to do."[22]

The reader is then through both argument and style invited not only to accept a set of negative conclusions, but also to pose questions about what moral stances should be taken seriously here and now, questions

---

[19] Ibid., p. 227.
[20] Bernard Williams, *Morality: An Introduction to Ethics*, New York: Harper & Row, 1972.
[21] Ibid., pp. ix and x.   [22] Ibid., p. xi.

that reopen the enquiries of the Inaugural Lecture. There, as we noted, agents were described as experiencing certain moral demands that in fact derive from some deep level of their emotions as having an external source. Williams now suggests that an agent may recognize the true source of such demands, when she or he becomes engaged by a type of moral outlook at the heart of which there is "an appeal to something *there* in human life which has to be discovered, trusted, followed, possibly in grave ignorance of the outcome."[23] It is at this point that Williams explicitly endorses Lawrence's injunction, "Find your deepest impulse and follow that," commenting that the notion "that there is something that is one's deepest impulse, that there is a discovery to be made here . . . and . . . that one trusts what is so discovered, although unclear where it will lead – these . . . are the point."[24] Williams classes this moral outlook with others that, instead of offering happiness, "demand authenticity" and briefly entertains the thought that perhaps it "rests on an illusion." In fact he was to take it with great seriousness for the next thirty years, as the quotation from the 2002 interview shows.

The problem for Williams was with the notion of authenticity. We can only be true to our deepest feelings if we are disciplined enough to be aware of them and truthful about what they are. Without such awareness and such truthfulness, deliberation will begin in the wrong place. "I must deliberate *from* what I am. Truthfulness requires trust in that . . ." The 'I' who so deliberates has, so Williams believed, the "possibility of a meaningful individual life, one that does not reject society, and indeed shares its perceptions with other people to a considerable degree, but yet is enough unlike others, in its opacities and disorder as well as in its reasoned intentions to make it *somebody's*."[25] What matters is that the deliberation through which that 'I' arrives at its reasoned intentions not only begins where it should, but then follows the right path, so that it issues in the right kind of life. "A has reason to ø only if there is a *sound deliberative route* from A's subjective motivational set . . . to A's øing."[26]

Williams emphasized that we should not think of an agent's subjective motivational set – her or his desires, dispositions of evaluation, patterns of emotional reaction, personal loyalties, projects, and commitments – "as statically given. The process of deliberation can have all sorts of effects on" it.[27] And over time it will change in various ways. But nothing can be a

---

[23] Ibid., p. 85.   [24] Ibid., p. 86.

[25] Williams, *Ethics and the Limits of Philosophy*, p. 200 and p. 202.

[26] Bernard Williams, "Postscript: Some Further Notes on Internal and External Reasons," in *Varieties of Practical Reasoning*, ed. Elijah Millgram, Cambridge, MA: MIT Press, 2001, p. 91.

[27] Bernard Williams, "Internal and External Reasons," in *Moral Luck*, Cambridge University Press, 1981, p. 105.

reason for anyone that is not actually or potentially a motivating reason. Critics of Williams have insisted that, if understood broadly enough, this formula will accommodate any view of reasons. Williams intended it, however, to exclude any alleged reason that purports to be a reason for anyone whatsoever in this or that type of situation. My reasons must be peculiarly mine, reasons grounded in my psychological history. They need not be and often will not be in the least self-interested. They must be expressions of this or that particular self.

What then is it that can give me confidence on some particular occasion that my deliberations are trustworthy? Williams had much to say that is, directly or indirectly, relevant to answering this question. There are on the one hand his arguments in support of some of his own practical conclusions on issues as various as the harm that is or is not done by pornography, the responses appropriate to this or that opera, or why we should not (Williams when young) or should (Williams when older) take Nietzsche seriously. There are on the other his philosophical reflections on what kind of liberalism is defensible and what not, and on why some of the idioms of ancient Greek tragic thought provide a more adequate vocabulary for ethical reflection than the postChristian vocabulary of modernity, and his genealogical enquiry into the indispensability of truthfulness for a certain sort of life. Yet, when all is said and done, crucial aspects of what Williams was saying to us about deliberation and about our reliance on our deepest feelings remain obscure.

Commonly, when someone says that about a philosopher, the remark is taken to be at least critical and perhaps hostile. Yet this is not at all what I mean. For perhaps what Williams was talking about is by its nature elusive, and that Williams, who cast important light on so many other areas of our thought, was unable to do better than he did is strong evidence that this is the case. Nonetheless, Williams misled himself and his readers. What I am going to argue is that Williams in pursuing the line of thought that led to his conclusions about deliberation was bound to find it difficult, perhaps impossible to say more than he said. But since I take it that this same line of thought is that which anyone in our time who had rejected the claims of Morality and who had thought their way through and beyond expressivism with sufficient intelligence and pertinacity would be likely to find themselves following, this is not just an argument about Williams. What then is it about this line of thought that it issues both in a certain kind of inarticulateness and in significant error and misunderstanding?

Williams' rejection of morality was accompanied by a recognition not only that "morality is not an invention of philosophers. It is the outlook, or, incoherently part of the outlook, of almost all of us,"[28] but also that what the philosophers of morality have tried to supply for plain nonphilosophical persons are types of argument that such persons can employ to justify their particular judgments and decisions. Such plain persons are, however, led astray by such philosophers, so that they fail to understand that "To arrive at the conclusion that one must do a certain thing is, typically, to make a discovery – a discovery which is, always minimally and sometimes substantially, a discovery about oneself."[29] Yet, if and when they do come to understand this, what are they to reply on a particular occasion to someone who suggests that, far from making a discovery, they may instead be the victims of a piece of sophisticated self-deception?

What they would have to show is that the feelings expressed in the course of arriving at their conclusions were both genuinely and deeply theirs, yet this, it seems, is, on Williams' view, something that can be discerned only from a first person point of view. "Practical thought is radically first personal."[30] At this point Lawrence provided the plain person with resources that Williams is unable to supply. For when Lawrence as a novelist shows us characters who are indeed deceived as to the depth or the genuine character of their emotions, it is only from a third person standpoint that he and his readers are able to perceive and to understand the limitations of those characters' first person standpoint. What agents need, if they are not to be the victims of deception and self-deception is, as I argued earlier, to see and understand themselves as perceptive others see and understand them. What they need is to judge and to act from a first person standpoint informed by a kind of practical self-knowledge that can only be acquired from a third person standpoint. Their confidence in the outcome of their own deliberative activities will be well founded only if it resembles in important respects the confidence that someone else might have in that outcome. But is such a thing possible?

Consider the predicament of our imagined agent, persistent and intelligent as she is, who, having found her way through and out of expressivism, and having concluded that she has no alternative but to give expression in her judgments and actions to her deepest feelings, to those feelings that are most her own, now has occasion to ask which of her feelings those are. She has been taught hitherto to think of herself in individualistic terms not only in her moral and emotional life but also in her dealings with the agencies of the state and in her transactions in labor and other markets.

---

[28] Williams, *Ethics and the Limits of Philosophy*, p. 174.   [29] Williams, *Moral Luck*, p. 130.
[30] Williams, *Ethics and the Limits of Philosophy*, p. 21.

And in turning to others for advice and assistance in identifying her deepest feelings, so that she is not deceived or self-deceived, she initially continues to think in those terms. The interesting question is: Will she be able to solve or resolve this problem about deception and self-deception without abandoning or at the least severely modifying this mode of thought? It is in and through our choices that our feelings, impulses, and desires find expression in our practical lives, and the more important the choice for the overall direction of our lives the more important it is to us to be aware of what it is that we really want and to be sure that we are not the victims of deception or self-deception. We need then to envisage some moment of choice in the life of our imagined agent when a good deal is at stake for her in the outcome of that choice.

3.11   Questions posed to and by Williams

The problem is that as we have imagined our agent so far, we have said nothing at all about most aspects of her life. Indeed this abstraction from the detail of psychological and social circumstance, so characteristic of examples discussed by moral philosophers, was necessary, if the example was to do the work that I intended it to do and hope that it has done. But, if we are to understand choices in which something of significance is at stake for an agent, we need to consider a number of dimensions of the situations in which choices are made and of the characteristics and relationships of the agents who make them, and we need to consider choices of different kinds. The agent whom we imagined having to decide which of her feelings were to govern her actions in a particular case would do well to reflect upon some of her own past choices. Consider some ways in which such an agent may look back on a past decision, one, say, in which that agent had had to choose between some more adventurous and insecure way of life, as a musician or a political organizer or a circus performer, and some more secure and predictable future, as a clerk in local government or a teacher or a garbage collector.

One possibility is that she will look back on the decision that she made without any regrets, congratulating herself for having realized that, although she had had at that time genuinely good reasons for choosing otherwise than as she did, her temperament was such that she would have always been a dissatisfied and frustrated person, if she had not chosen as she did. Another possibility is that she will have become just such a dissatisfied and frustrated person, now regretting her past choice, but now having no alternative but to live with the choice that she then made. A third possibility

is that she will now have no doubt that she then made the right choice –
and she did make the right choice – but nonetheless will recognize that she
still has hankerings for the kind of life that she renounced. And a fourth
possibility is that she will now have no doubt that she then made the right
choice, but that she did in fact make the wrong choice and her continuing
hankerings for the kind of life that is now unavailable to her are symptoms
of this. These four are far from the only possibilities, but they suggest some
initial questions that need to be posed about such choices.

Such choices are difficult insofar as agents have more or less indetermi-
nate conflicting desires for themselves or for others. So they have to become
aware of what they want and of why they want it. They have to recognize
how the consequences of choosing this or that alternative may be to alter
their present desires. They have to think about the implications of their
choices for others, especially for those close to them, and about how far and
why they do, and they should care about those implications. They need,
that is to say, self-knowledge of a kind that it is often difficult and sometimes impossible to achieve without the help of others who know them well
as a result of having interacted with them over extended periods of time.
But they need more than this kind of self-knowledge. They also need to
know whether they are describing the alternatives between which they are
choosing realistically and whether they have or will be able to acquire the
abilities and the skills that they will need in each case. Here, too, they may
need to consult with relevant others. What then is it to be well placed and
what is it to be badly placed in one's relationships with others in respect of
the acquisition of such knowledge and such self-knowledge?

About what others should we be thinking when we try to answer this
question? About family members, often of more than one generation,
about friends, about coworkers who know what goes well for them and
for us in the workplace and what goes badly, about those with whom
we share activities and responsibilities in, say, the local school, in soccer
or basketball teams, in theatre groups or in music making. At once it is
obvious that individuals may stand in very different kinds of relationships
to those with whom they interact and that the network of relationships in
which agents find themselves in their periods of decision making may be
of very different kinds, just as they themselves may differ from one another
in temperament, in inclinations, and in the history that has brought them
to this point. Consider three notably different possibilities.

The first is that the others with whom the agent interacts share to a large
extent one and the same conventional view of what the realistic possibilities
are at each stage of a human life. They are imaginatively limited. It is

not that none of them sees and feels the attractions of breaking out and breaking free from conventional pathways, but that even those who do thus see and feel have a conception of what is to break out and break free that is itself conventional, limited, and unimaginative. Worse still, among their limitations is that they do not know their limitations. Are there social milieus of this kind? That there are I do not doubt, but what is as important is that some individuals, especially but not only adolescents, may believe that this is how things are in their milieu, whether this is in fact so or not. Such individuals may recognize that they need to consult others in order to obtain information, but that otherwise they have to free themselves from the advice and influence of others so that their choice may be genuinely their own, not one that expresses the shared preconceptions and prejudices of their milieu. "What I have to ensure," says such a one to herself, although she has never heard of D. H. Lawrence or Bernard Williams, "is that my choice is really *mine*! Otherwise I am bound to regret it later."

A second possibility is that the others with whom the agent interacts and to whom the agent has become close are very different from each other in respect of their past experiences, their occupations, their hopes and expectations, their religious and irreligious views of the world. They see the choice that the agent has to make in very different lights, and this is not a matter of different information that they have. Those who have unwillingly led dangerous and precarious lives as, say, refugees see the security of life as a clerk or a garbage collector as something wonderful, only to be thought of as dull and conventional by those who do not know what the world is like. Those who have become ambitious and competitive advise that the agent should add more possibilities to her list of alternatives. And correspondingly they identify the agent's capabilities and possibilities by different measures. Where in the previous example the agent was offered too few alternatives, here she is offered too many and too many alternative standards for choosing between them. What she may well feel is that not only is the choice inescapably and burdensomely her own, but so too is her choice of how to choose.

Suppose now, however, a third case in which the relevant set of others are in many respects as diverse as in the previous case but differ in that they include some who not only are in general perceptive about the motivations of others and the outcomes of those motivations but have known our imagined agent long enough and well enough to be able to give her well-grounded advice. She in turn knows them well enough to have a justified confidence in their reasoning and their judgments. So she is able to understand how she appears and how her choice appears from a third person point of view. She is able to correct some of her previous judgments about herself and through extended discussion with some of these others to consider possibilities that she had not yet envisaged. Her choice remains inescapably her own, but the deliberations in which she engages are informed by third person as well as first person judgments and in making her final choice she is, in important respects, relying on and trusting in others. Indeed how she now reasons may be the result of her having learned from those others that she has reason to be suspicious of some of her own inclinations and tendencies.

What in these circumstances might she make of Lawrence's injunction to follow, to be true to, her deepest impulse? The metaphor of depth may point her in one or more of three directions. That in us which is taken to be deep is that which is enduring, ineliminably and importantly part of us, expressed in long-term characteristics of our desires, our commitments, and our loyalties. That in us which is taken to be deep is that which, if we ignore or suppress, will find expression in frustration or regret or resentment or all of these. And that in us which is taken to be deep is that of whose influence upon us we may even at crucial times remain unaware, perhaps because we are insufficiently enquiring, perhaps because of a need – a deep need – not to acknowledge aspects of ourselves and especially of our desires. Yet of course, when we are making choices in which much is at stake, we need to be self-aware and, that is to say, we need to see ourselves and to understand ourselves as honest, perceptive, intelligent, and insightful others see and understand us, with the objectivity that is only possible from a third person standpoint, but a third person standpoint that we have become able to make our own.

It is a grammatical and a philosophical truth that we have to learn how to use the personal pronouns as a set and not one by one. Until I know that, whenever it can be said truly of me by me that "I am doing or feeling such and such," it can be said truly by another to me that "You are doing or feeling such and such," and it can be said truly about me that "She – or he – is doing or feeling such and such," I do not understand what I am saying when I use the pronoun 'I'. It is a psychological and a philosophical truth that, where my desires and dispositions are concerned, I may often have to learn what I can say truly and truthfully about myself only by recognizing and acknowledging the truth of what others say to me and about me. Philosophers have sometimes and understandably focused on those types of sentence used by me to report what sometimes only I can report, such as 'I am in pain', where, when I am in pain and say that I am in pain, others are in no position to correct me. It makes no sense for them to ask "How do you know that you are in pain?" In this respect the first person standpoint is indeed privileged. Yet we do well to remind ourselves that the same 'I' who was once in pain may or may not remember what caused that pain, how intense it was, or how he responded to it, let alone be aware of how far memories of it are expressed in his present responses. On all these matters, he may have to depend on the trustworthiness of others for confirmation or disconfirmation of his own memories and judgments.

This, of course, Williams would not have denied. But what his account of deliberation does preclude is this: that in the end I have to arrive at the right decision not just for me, here, now, but for anyone so situated. The objectivity that dependence on others can achieve is indeed objectivity, a rescuing of the agent from imprisonment within her or his subjectivity. I am not of course maintaining that we are all equally dependent on others for the kind of self-knowledge that we so often need in making crucial decisions. I am asserting that for all of us in much of our practical deliberation, we need to have a justified confidence in the judgments of others on whom we stand in close relationships, if we are to have a justified confidence in our own first person judgments. Nor is it the case that it is only our understanding of ourselves that may be and often needs to be transformed through our interactions with such others. What we learn from them may include how to think about the objects of our desires in new and more adequate ways, so that on the one hand our desires are changed and on the other we envisage the alternatives between which we have to choose somewhat differently. And I am not maintaining – far from it – that the influence of others is always for the good. The qualities of mind and character of those on whom we come to rely matter enormously and someone whose family or friends or coworkers are unreflective or in love with money or power or celebrity may have to isolate and insulate her or himself from those others, if she is to deliberate well and to make good choices. Yet even with these necessary qualifications, a strong thesis emerges from these examples of situations of choice.

It is that whether an agent's deliberations and choices are or are not defective in various ways depends in key part on the nature of that agent's social relationships and that an agent's deliberations and choices may be most her or his own when that agent's first person standpoint is open to and informed by the third person observations, arguments, and judgments of others. So our imagined agent, confronted by her choice between alternative careers, needs to consider what her social relationships are and have been, something that would not have been suggested to her by Williams' misleading claim that "Practical thought is radically first personal." Indeed, she will now have to think in terms that will put her even further at odds with Williams. For if the strong thesis that I have proposed is true, then an agent whose motivational set – to use Williams' term – does not allow that agent to learn in appropriate ways from others will be defective as an agent. For she will be apt to be motivated by desires for objects that she has only bad reasons or insufficiently good reasons to desire.

Where, then, has the line of enquiry that we have followed led our imagined agent and where has it led us? We have distinguished that in expressivism which is true and insightful from that which is either trivial or misleading. Expressivism fails as a general account of the semantics of evaluative sentences, but it provides among other things grounds for a critique of and a rejection of the claims of Morality, a critique reinforced by other types of consideration, notably the inability of its leading theoretical voices to settle crucial issues that divide them or to respond adequately to Bernard Williams' indictment. Yet that critique compels us, as our imagined agent discovered, to go beyond expressivism, by raising questions on which it is silent, both about how our practical deliberations are related to our feelings, that is, about what it is that gives us grounds for confidence in those deliberations, and about what kinds of reason we might have for taking something – the extraordinary achievement of Gauguin's paintings, say, or the dramatic and subversive wit of Oscar Wilde or the imaginative insights of D. H. Lawrence's best novels – to be a good and for ranking it in relation to other goods. On the first of these, we have once more incurred a large debt to Bernard Williams, in part because he takes us to a point at which it becomes clear how and why his account of deliberation finally breaks down. On the second, apart from his insightful account of the good of truthfulness, Williams had remarkably little to say, and it is worth asking why this was so. It is, I believe, for two distinct, but mutually reinforcing sets of reasons. His right-minded conviction that there are radically different kinds of good – our reasons for taking justice to be a good seem to him have little or nothing in common with our reasons for taking operatic excellence to be a good – led him to endorse Isaiah Berlin's claim that it is a "deep error" to suppose that "all goods, all virtues, all ideals are compatible."[31] Williams then commented: "This is not the platitude that in an imperfect world not all the things we recognize as good are in practice compatible. It is rather that we have no coherent conception of a world without loss, that goods conflict by their very nature, and that there can be no incontestable scheme for harmonizing them."

To hold that goods conflict by their very nature is of course to put oneself at odds with Aristotle, but Williams had additional reasons for rejecting

---

[31] Bernard Williams, "Introduction" to Isiah Berlin's *Concepts and Categories*, ed. H. Hardy, New York: Viking Press, 1978, p. xvi.

Aristotle's ethics, reasons that he thought it important to advance over and over again at each stage of his work, although he modified his statement of some of them in response to criticisms by Martha Nussbaum.[32] Three of them are instructive. In *Morality* he disputes Aristotle's thesis that the distinguishing mark of human beings is their intelligence and capacity for rational thought: "To be helplessly in love is in fact as distinctively a human condition as to approve rationally of someone's moral dispositions."[33] In *Ethics and the Limits of Philosophy*, he argues that Aristotle's view of the way in which our ethical dispositions are related to our ends and our functioning well as human beings depends upon his teleological account of nature, an account which anyone who inhabits the world of modern science has to reject.[34] And in the same passage he claims that Aristotle can supply no adequate explanation of what he would take to be moral and political error, error which, on an Aristotelian view, we should note, extends to the rejection by so many agents, including Williams, of anything like an Aristotelian conception of themselves and their activities.

Nussbaum persuaded Williams that he had exaggerated the extent to which Aristotle's ethics depends upon his view of biological nature, but he remained convinced that there are concepts central to Aristotelian ethics that can function as they do only if they find application to the natural world. About this I take him to have been in some respects right. So I conclude that all four of his criticisms of Aristotle need to be answered. They have indeed already been provided with philosophical answers within the NeoAristotelian tradition, but it is important to understand how those answers find a place within any adequate statement of the overall claims and commitments in ethics and politics of a contemporary Thomistic Aristotelianism. My next task, therefore, is to deliver just such a statement, one that will give point and purpose to a response to Williams' critique of Aristotle, but that itself begins by addressing a wider set of concerns, taking account of what has been learned in our discussions so far and this in at least four ways.

First, in contrast to my way of proceeding in the first part of this essay, I will need to exhibit and communicate some awareness of the present-day social contexts of the theses and arguments that I will be advancing. It will be important to discover whether and how far NeoAristotelianism

---

[32] See Martha Nussbaum, "Aristotle on Human Nature and the Foundation of Ethics" and Williams' "Replies," in *World, Mind and Ethics: Essays on the Ethical Philosophy of Bernard Williams*, ed. J. E. J. Altham and R. Harrison, Cambridge University Press, 1995, pp. 185–224.

[33] Williams, *Morality*, p. 65.

[34] Williams, *Ethics and the Limits of Philosophy*, pp. 43–44.

can be responsive to and provide a voice for those whose desires, deprivations, concerns, and commitments are defined by their relationship to the contemporary social and economic order. Here the resources that Marx provided at an earlier stage of my argument will again be to the point. Secondly, in evaluating NeoAristotelian and, more specifically, Thomistic claims, I will have to spell out a good deal further what I said at the close of Chapter 2 about the three dimensions of rational justification. Thirdly, I will need to develop further in Aristotelian and Thomistic terms, the thesis about the connections between an agent's desires, decision making, and practical reasoning and that agent's social relationships which emerged from the discussion of Williams' account of deliberation. Fourthly, readers will have noted that I have sometimes dealt brusquely and cavalierly with objections to my point of view. How far they are troubled by this will depend in key part on what their own point of view is. But some of these objections, from my point of view, need to be taken more seriously than others, notably the four types of objection advanced by Williams, and to them I will have to respond further. Finally, through all of this it will be important to remind ourselves recurrently of the overall aim of this enquiry, to understand more adequately the part that our desires and our practical reasoning play in our lives and in their going well or badly. My arguments will lead to the conclusion that the form which gives expression to such understanding is that of narrative and of a kind of narrative which presupposes a NeoAristotelian conception of human activity. This, then, is the agenda for the next chapter of this essay.

CHAPTER 4

NeoAristotelianism developed in contemporary Thomistic terms

Issues of relevance and rational justification

4.1 Problems posed for NeoAristotelians

In the first chapter of this essay, I set out and defended, even if only up to a point, a NeoAristotelian account of 'good' and good in the course of attempting to say what we mean when, as rational agents, we speak of someone as having good reasons for desiring this or that. Now I need to develop this account further in order to address questions posed in the second and third chapters, both questions about the relevance to contemporary agents in their everyday lives of the kind of NeoAristotelian view that I have advanced and questions about how the central theses of that account are to be rationally justified in contemporary terms. It will be less misleading from now on to speak of my view as a Thomistic Aristotelianism, although always with the qualification that it is in some respects a view unacceptable to many Thomists, some because, following Gilson, they take Aristotle and Aquinas to be at odds at key points, others because they differ from me in their understanding of both Aristotle and Aquinas. What is worth noting at the outset is that issues of relevance and issues of rational justification are closely related. For the claim that a Thomistic Aristotelian politics and ethics is relevant to contemporary agents in their everyday lives would be groundless if such agents were not able to provide for themselves and others an adequate rational justification for judging and acting as such a politics and ethics dictate.

Those plain persons with whom Thomistic Aristotelians enter into conversation nowadays commonly lead double lives, something of which they are often not aware, and, even when aware, may not be able to make fully explicit. On the one hand – and here I am relying on what was said earlier about the contemporary social order – they inhabit a social world structured to some large degree by the institutions of state, market, and Morality and find themselves in social relationships shaped directly and indirectly by these. It is mostly taken for granted that what they want is what the dominant social institutions have influenced them to want and the practical thinking of those others with whom they engage is for the most part informed by the ethics-of-the-state, the ethics-of-the-market, and the norms of Morality. So they continually encounter representations of themselves as individuals envisaged as the institutions of state, market, and Morality envisage them, individuals open to being moved either by other-disregarding competitive ambition and acquisitiveness or by an at least constraining and sometimes self-disregarding care and respect for others.

On the other hand – and here again I refer back to what was said earlier – their initiation into a range of practices has enabled many of them not only to identify a variety of goods and excellences that they aspire to make their own, but also to recognize that among these goods are common goods, goods to be achieved only qua family member or qua member of this working group or this local community. Trying to give a due place to goods of these different types, they find themselves asking such questions as 'How is it best for me to live?' and 'How is it best for this community of which I am a part to live?' So they may on occasion more or less systematically try to work out answers to these questions, rank ordering in the course of their everyday activities the individual and common goods for whose achievement they hope and identifying those qualities of mind and character that they must possess and those precepts that must govern their actions and transactions if they are to achieve those goods. In all these respects they are already thinking and acting in Aristotelian and Thomistic terms, terms systematically at odds with those of the dominant culture that they inhabit, commonly without recognizing this. How far such individuals take notice of or are troubled by this fracture in their lives varies of course with their circumstances and history, with how they, their families, and their communities have fared during the changes and chances of advanced modernity. Yet without awareness of that fracture there will be a dangerous lack of the self-knowledge that rational agents need, if they are to judge rightly.

They – or rather *we*, since almost none of us escapes this condition entirely – will tend to become aware of the effect of this fracture in their lives at those moments when they experience a peculiar kind of difficulty in deciding between rival answers to urgent practical questions. Those questions often take the form of an enquiry into what, on some particular occasion when we have conflicting desires, we have good reason to desire, so that we find ourselves torn between both rival inclinations and rival arguments. What a Thomistic Aristotelian who intervenes at this point is able to provide is both a vocabulary adequate for characterizing the objects and the difficulties of such enquiries and an account of how practical reasoning arrives at sound conclusions, so enabling agents to take on the tasks of reordering their lives. To specify the commitments of a contemporary Thomistic Aristotelian politics and ethics, we therefore need to proceed by identifying each major area of political and moral conflict in contemporary lives and to ask what light such a politics and ethics can throw on the nature of those conflicts and on how they are to be resolved. I begin with issues concerning goods and more especially common goods.

4.2   Families, workplaces, and schools: common goods and conflicts

The concept of a common good, as understood by Aristotle and Aquinas, is to be contrasted with the modern concept of a public good. From Adam Smith onwards, protagonists of the free market economy have recognized that there are goods which individuals need if they are to function successfully in such an economy, but which they cannot provide for themselves. Only government can provide them. An eighteenth-century catalogue of public goods would have begun with military and naval security from external threats, law and order, and the building and maintenance of roads, and for some might have ended there. Adam Smith and his intellectual heirs understood the importance of a public system of education, to provide literate and skilled workers, and a hundred years later Bismarck and other German and Austrian conservatives were to understand the need for welfare agencies if workers and their families were not to be alienated from the political and social order. In the late nineteenth and the twentieth century the multiplication of what were taken to be indispensable functions of government – the activities of central banks, the provision of higher education, the supervision and regulation of various forms of transport and communication – became a central fact of political life and with it recurrent debate as to whether this or that is or is not a public good.

In such debate those who argue in favor of regarding this or that as a public good will often claim that by so arguing they are promoting the common good. This unfortunate rhetoric has the effect of obscuring the difference between public goods and common goods. For public goods can be understood as goods to be achieved by individuals qua individuals, albeit only in cooperation with other individuals, and to be enjoyed by individuals qua individuals, while common goods are only to be enjoyed and achieved, as I emphasized earlier, by individuals qua members of various groups or qua participants in various activities. Consider first the common goods of particular families.

What is it for the members of some family and household to act together so as to achieve their family's common good? What is it for them to fail so to act? It may be easier to supply answers to the former question, but more illuminating to consider answers to the latter. Answers to the former question may at first seem like a list of platitudes. Wives and husbands pursue their goods as family members by enabling the other through their affection and understanding to achieve her or his good. Parents pursue their goods as family members by fostering the development of the powers and virtues of their children, so that those children may emerge from adolescence as independent rational agents. Aunts and uncles pursue their goods as family members by providing their nieces and nephews with a relationship to the excitements of the adult world that is independent of their relationships to their parents. And all of them recognize, almost always implicitly rather than explicitly, that in so acting they are also acting for the good of this particular family. What is it then to fail so to act?

There are different kinds of failure. One occurs when the bonds of family and household are felt, not just occasionally, but too often, as inhibiting and frustrating constraints, rather than as enabling, or when those bonds are in fact such that they ought to be thought of as frustrating constraints. This is the case when something presented as the good of a family and household is not so, but is in fact something pursued at the expense of some members of the family for the benefit of others. Another related kind of failure is when one or more members of the family view family and household as no more than a means to the achievement of their own individual ends, when the good of that individual is pursued at the expense of the good of the family and household. Generally a flourishing family and household is one that lives through, learns from and overcomes moments of failure. Since families and households can be of very different sizes and kinds, and since the social contexts in which they flourish or fail to flourish vary a very great deal, what it is to flourish or to fail to flourish also varies. Tolstoy was wrong. Both happy and unhappy families come in very different kinds.

What it is for this or that particular family to act so as to achieve their common good in this or that particular situation is something that the members of each family must identify for themselves in the course of their shared deliberations and subsequent actions. And, if they are to avoid failure, they will need the virtues in the specific forms appropriate to their culture and their family structure: justice between parent and parent, parent and child, sibling and sibling, grandparents and grandchildren, aunts and nieces and nephews, temperateness in the expression of their desires, courage in their dealings with the outside world and with each other, prudence in their individual and shared decision making. For a family to fail in either of the ways that I have described will have involved some failure in the virtues, some failure by someone to recognize that in acting for the good of the family they are acting for their own good.

Much depends for families on what resources are available to them, resources which, especially under modern conditions, they are characteristically unable to supply for themselves. Three kinds of resource are indispensable: money, most often in the form of wages from the workplace; the education of children afforded by schools; the law, order, and other public goods provided by government. So the lives of individuals are generally structured to some large degree by the pursuit of common goods other than those of the family, some of them complementary to those of the family. What, then, are the common goods of workplaces, schools, government?

Those at work together in advanced economies are characteristically engaged in producing not only goods and services, but also wages for the labor and skills of those who produce the goods and services, and profits for those who control the means of production and the workplace. The common goods of those at work together are achieved in producing goods and services that contribute to the life of the community and in becoming excellent at producing them. But enterprises that are unprofitable are always in time eliminated and profitability may dictate the production of what is less than good, perhaps harmful or trivializing, while managerial control of the workplace may result in methods of work that are inimical to excellence. Some examples will suggest what is at stake. Begin with the effect on the Japanese automobile industry from 1951 onwards of the teaching of W. Edwards Deming, to which I referred earlier. Deming persuaded Japanese manufacturers that the type of production line in which each worker performs a single repeated operation, without any regard for the end product of those operations, and in which the quality of the end product is monitored by inspectors in fact militated against high quality. When, instead, teams of workers cooperated in taking each car through the different stages of its production, taking responsibility as a team for the quality of the end product, things went much better both for the cars and for the workers. The ends informing the workers' activity are now those of achieving through shared deliberation and decision the making of an excellent car and of becoming excellent in making such cars. It matters that they understand what they are doing and that their standards are ones that they have made their own, not standards imposed by external managerial control. They share direction toward a common good.

Deming did not use the idiom of common goods. He spoke of removing the fear of making mistakes and other barriers to pride of workmanship, of constancy of purpose, and of management as having the task of enabling workers to succeed, but he would not have quarreled, I believe, with my characterization of his findings.[1] What might have surprised him would have been the strong resemblance between his account of what productive work can be and should be with Wendell Berry's accounts of what the work of a farmer can be and should be.[2] Individuals who farm need to regard themselves as contributing to a larger project, that of making their particular farm productive while sustaining its land through generations of care. Farmers have to understand the particularities of each of their fields and of their farm animals, acting in the light of standards that they have made their own rather than responding to pressures to maximize productivity and short-run profitability. Those individuals at work on a particular farm serve the good of the farm and through so acting achieve their own goods. Deming agreed with Berry that short-term profitability is the enemy of good productive work. What makes this coincidence of views impressive is the fact that they arrived at their shared conclusions from very different premises.

Berry after all was an heir of Southern agrarianism and a major contributor to the environmentalist movement. Deming was a statistician who began by analyzing the incidence of manufacturing errors and the causes of defective products. Berry's first-hand engagement was with a 125 acre farm in Kentucky. Deming's was with manufacturing plants in Japan, Michigan, Massachusetts, New Jersey, and Pennsylvania. Yet their conclusions about work are mutually reinforcing. Note that neither ignores the need to be productive, the fact that it is the production of worthwhile goods that gives productive work its point and purpose, but both take it that such work serves a common good to which each worker contributes. Turn then to a third example, or, more accurately, to a fourth, since Tom Burns' studies of the British Broadcasting Corporation, to which I also referred earlier, already provide a third, that of the Cummins Engine Company.

[1] See Mary Walton. *The Deming Management Method,* New York: Perigee Books, 1986; for an account of the uneasy relationship between rationality of practice and technical rationality, see Joseph Dunne, "An Intricate Fabric: Understanding the Rationality of Practice," *Pedagogy, Culture and Society* 13, 3 (2005): 367–389.

[2] See, for example, Wendell Berry, *The Unsettling of America: Culture & Agriculture,* San Francisco: Sierra Club Books, 1977.

It was founded in 1919 in Columbus, Indiana, by Clessie Cummins, an automechanic with a machine shop, who had become fascinated by the potentialities of diesel engines. His business as an automechanic had been financed by a local banker, W. G. Irwin, who shared his enthusiasm for diesel engines as the key to the future of American trucking and who now invested in the company. Its first profits were not made until 1937, by which time its general manager was Irwin's great-nephew, J. Irwin Miller. The company was a research enterprise, responsive to its customers' future as well as present needs, with a remarkable record in technological innovation. Over several decades the company subordinated the need to achieve higher levels of profitability to the good of making excellent products, and individuals who worked for the company were expected to serve that common good. But of course it matters that the Cummins company, like the enterprises advised by Deming and like the farms of farmers like Berry, survived only because it did become profitable enough to survive in competitive markets and that the inexorable pressure to become, not just profitable, but more and more and more profitable does in fact result in most workplaces being quite other than those that I have just described.

Families and households prosper only through achieving the common goods of those individuals who participate in them and, when families and households fail to prosper, such individuals are generally unhappily aware of that fact. Workplaces by contrast may be organized so that the work performed by individuals is never more than a cost-effective means to ends imposed by others for the sake of high productivity and profitability. In periods of prosperity for this or that industry, such individuals may be relatively highly paid for doing work that it is not otherwise worthwhile to do. But note that in order to say this, we have to speak and judge in a way that is incompatible with the standard vocabulary of academic economics. For, as economists speak and judge, the value of work is something settled by markets and by the preferences of those who engage in market relationships, while I, in speaking of certain kinds of work as worthwhile or not worthwhile, have, like Deming and Berry, been appealing to a standard of value independent of both of these. We have therefore two distinct ways of thinking about and evaluating work, and these two modes of thought and evaluation are not restricted to the workplace. We find them again in thought about schools and about the goods of education.

Schools, in this like families and like some workplaces, are institutions where different participants may or may not contribute to the common good of this particular school. Teachers achieve their own good qua teachers and contribute to that common good by making the good of their students their overriding good, while their students contribute to the shared education of their class by their class participation, so achieving their own good. Of crucial importance is the relationship between education in skills and education in practices. Children have to make the exercise of certain linguistic, mathematical, musical, and athletic skills a matter of habit. They do so by putting those skills to a variety of uses in the different subject areas to which they are introduced. What matters is that they come to recognize that their progress in each area is both a progress in shared enquiry and a progress toward individual excellence. They learn collectively to define tasks and to propose problems, to identify difficulties to be overcome and to respond to those perceived difficulties. They make mistakes and they learn how to learn from those mistakes. If and insofar as they are being well educated, they come to understand themselves – although not probably in these words – as apprentices who are being initiated into a range of literary, mathematical, scientific, musical, and athletic practices, practices in which the achievement of common goods of performance and enquiry is also the achievement of individual excellence. But this is only true if they are being well educated. How might they be badly educated? They may of course be unfortunate enough to have incompetent teachers, teachers who themselves were either badly or incompetently educated; the highly competent may also educate badly, aiming in the wrong direction.

They do so when they focus more or less exclusively on the acquisition of skills with far less attention to the variety of uses to which those skills might be put or to the ends that they might serve. They do even worse when they concentrate on just those skills for which there is a demand in the workplace rather than on developing the powers of each child. One function of education in the school is of course to prepare students for apprenticeship in the workplace, but this is only one function among several, and students are badly prepared for the workplace when education in the school is treated as though it itself were an apprenticeship in the workplace. A good school is a place where students, in the course of developing their powers, are able to find a direction that they can make their own. An education focused too exclusively on skills, on means, leaves them without an adequate sense of the ends that should be theirs as contrasted with the ends that others for their own purposes impose upon them.

Such an exclusive focus is the expression of a will to prepare students to take their place in the workforce, so that their pursuit of their own ends may, whatever else it does, serve the ends of economic growth. What their ends are to be is ostensibly left to them as autonomous preference maximizers who bring their skills to market. The education of their preferences is taken to be no part of their schooling. So the standard by which schools are evaluated comes to be that of how high their students' test scores are. But from the standpoint of those whose care is for the common good of a school, it is one of the marks of bad schooling that ability is equated with the ability to score well in tests and that students' progress is mapped by recurrent testing. Unsurprisingly what diligent students principally learn in school systems of this kind is that they should not pursue courses of study in which they are not confident of achieving high test scores. The effect on students is the shaping of unadventurous minds, minds averse to risk taking, minds open to being victimized by conventional notions of success. The effect on teachers is an unwillingness to pursue lines of thought in the class room, no matter how interesting, which might distract from the tasks of test taking. I am not of course implying that there is no place for examinations, but they should be such that instruction does not "degenerate into preparation for the examination" and that students may approach them "with a quiet mind and without a painful preparatory effort tending to relaxation and torpor as soon as the effort is over." The quotations are from the instructions to Prussian teachers for the *Abiturientenexamen*, which so impressed Matthew Arnold during his visit to Berlin in 1865–1866.[3] It was after all the great Homeric scholar, F. A. Wolf, who had remarked – and Arnold quotes him too – that *"Perverse studet qui examinibus studet."*

Schools then resemble families and workplaces as places where common goods are identified and achieved. But, if they are as I have described them, there is much more to their resemblance than this. For in each case what we find is the same fracture, the same contrast between two kinds of social experience. There are on the one hand those who find themselves in family, school, and workplace directed toward common goods, qua family member, qua student or teacher, qua productive worker, deliberating with others as to how in this particular set of circumstances here and now to act so as to achieve the common good of this particular enterprise. There are on the other those for whom family, school, or workplace are milieus in which they have to find their own way forward as individuals under the constraints of their social relationships and of the institutionally imposed routines of family, school, and workplace. That way forward is one in which their ability to maximize the satisfaction of their preferences and their need to bargain and negotiate with others will depend in key part on

[3] Matthew Arnold, *Higher Schools and Universities in Germany*, London: Macmillan & Co., 1868, pp. 54–55.

their power, their income and wealth, and the place in the social structure in and from which their uses of power and money impact on others.

The discovery that those who pursue common goods must have made, if they are to act as they do, is that it is only through directing themselves toward the achievement of common goods that they are able to direct themselves toward the achievement of their own good qua individual. Someone who has made this discovery will find her or himself inescapably asking, in the course of decision making, how the various goods, common and individual, that they acknowledge are to be rank ordered and what place each of them should have in her or his life. If those who pursue only their own individual goods reflect on how they are to identify goals for themselves in the everyday lives of family, school, and workplace, they discover that the onus has been placed on them to find for themselves, if they can, motivating reasons for setting themselves to succeed or fail as someone of this particular age group, social class, occupation, and income. Their consequent conclusions, their choices of goods, will be and will be interpreted as expressions of their own individual preferences, no matter how arrived at. Institutions, families, schools and workplaces will be understood as sometimes obstacles to and sometimes means for achieving the satisfaction of those preferences.

The former are constituted as rational agents in and through their shared deliberations with others concerning the common goods that they share with those others and their deliberations as to how to give a due place to each good in their individual lives. The latter are constituted as rational agents by their learning first how to arrive at a coherent and relevant set of preferences and then how to implement those preferences in the social world. The former understand themselves as agents some of whose key social relationships are constitutive of their identity as agents. The latter understand themselves as individuals qua individuals whose social relationships are contingent features of their situation, to be evaluated by how far they contribute to the satisfaction of their preferences. But it would be dangerously misleading if we were to think of these two contrasting modes of being in and acting in contemporary society as characterizing two distinct populations. For many people in many societies with advanced economies, some aspects of their lives will be of the one kind, others aspects of the other.

Moreover, these two modes of living and acting are always embodied in the forms of this or that particular culture, in the particularities of kinship, occupation, religion, art, and sport. It is in and through the idioms of each culture that individuals pose questions about how they should understand and evaluate their situation and it is to individuals posing those questions in their own particular cultural terms that contemporary Thomistic Aristotelians have to justify the answers to those questions that they propose. Where then should they begin? Surely by inviting those with whom they speak to recognize and reflect upon the extent to which in their thinking and acting in families and households, in schools, and in workplaces they already presuppose the truth of some key Aristotelian and Thomistic claims concerning individual and common goods. For that recognition provides a starting point for further enquiry. Yet at once a difficulty arises. For both Aristotle and Aquinas took it that the context in which common and individual goods were ordered was that of a kind of political society that no longer exists.

4.3   The politics of local community and conflict: Danish and Brazilian examples

Political society – what Aristotle speaks of as the *polis* and Aquinas as the *civitas* – has, on their account of it, certain key features. When rightly ordered and functioning well, both ruled and rulers aim at achieving its common good. They are able to do so because it is through participation in political society that they become able to order a variety of common and individual goods in their own lives, acquiring those dispositions, the virtues, which direct them toward their final end. Withdraw political society so understood from their account, and it must seem, as it did indeed to Aristotle, that nothing of the distinctively human, including application for their conception of common goods would be left. But political society as they understood it is in key respects quite other than the modern state, whose bureaucratic institutions and liberal pluralism seem to make Aristotelianism irrelevant. And I have already advanced a parallel argument about the contemporary economic order and the irrelevance to it of Aristotelian and Thomistic concepts so that any attempt by plain persons here and now to understand themselves in Aristotelian, let alone Thomistic terms, may seem doomed to failure. What, if anything, can be said in reply?

Consider how a group of individuals who have begun to think systematically about what it is for them and theirs to flourish or to fail to flourish in various areas of their lives may find themselves inescapably committed to political and economic action, just because of their concern to achieve the common goods of family, school, and workplace. They understand that family life suffers when parents are unemployed or underpaid, have to work too long hours, or cannot find affordable housing. So the goods of the family are at stake over what happens in the workplace. They learn that children are often unable to learn when they are inadequately fed or when their parents are inadequately responsive. So the goods of the school are at stake over what happens in both the home and the workplace. A flourishing workplace requires workers with relevant skills who understand what they are doing, workers who are able to improvise in those moments of crisis that afflict all workplaces recurrently. But potentially resourceful workers are generally able to learn what they need to learn in the workplace, only if first well educated at home and school. So the goods of the workplace are at stake in both home and school.

Not everyone can be equally concerned with everything. But a concern for the common goods of the family that is not also at some times and in some ways a concern for the common goods of school and workplace will be a diminished and ineffective concern. Such caring involves concern that there is adequately paid employment and adequate housing for parents and adequate training and provision for teachers. It therefore requires strong political commitments, expressible in action through a variety of local organizations, trade union branches, community organizations, town meetings, parent teacher associations, and the like. It will often be a politics of single issues, but of issues whose importance is their bearing on the common good of the local community. So in attempting to bring into being a political society in which individuals understand their individual goods as achievable only in and through directing themselves toward their common political good, such individuals act for the sake of the goods of political society, giving contemporary form to a distinctively Aristotelian politics.

The political commitments of such individuals always may and often will involve them directly or indirectly in the politics of the modern state. But the politics of making and sustaining local forms of community, if understood as a politics of common goods, requires attitudes and procedures other than and in addition to those of the politics of the modern state, and this in two salient respects. It is first of all a politics of shared deliberation, governed by standards independent of the desires and interests of those who participate in it. It is not primarily a politics of bargaining between competing interests, although bargains may have to be made. Shared deliberation presupposes some large degree of agreement on the goods that are at stake in the decisions that have to be made. Its outcome, if successful, is agreement on what ought to be done in the interest of the local community to which particular and partial interests may have to be subordinated. When this is so, it is crucial that there is also some largely shared conception of how it is just to proceed. And an elementary requirement of justice is that every relevant voice is heard and that every relevant argument is given due weight as an argument and not because of the power or influence of whoever it was who advanced it. But this is only possible, as I noticed earlier, when there is a shared recognition of the authority of the precepts of the natural law, precepts that prohibit one from getting one's way by fraud or force.

The Aristotelian character of this kind of politics is plain in a second salient characteristic. The way in which the relationship of ethics to politics is understood in modern societies is such that morality is commonly taken to be one thing, politics another, while for Aristotle and Aristotelians, ethics is part of politics. Politics both as enquiry and as practice is concerned with the structure that government must have, if citizens are to become good human beings, good at achieving common and individual goods. Ethics both as enquiry and practice is concerned with the qualities of mind and character that agents must have if they are to be good both as citizens, ruling and being ruled, and as human beings. The political importance of those qualities and of agreement on common goods is exhibited in the histories of those communities in which a politics of the common good has achieved at least some of its goals and has been sustained in the wider political contexts of contemporary societies.

One such history has been told by Thomas Højrup in his *The Needs for Common Goods for Coastal Communities*,[4] itself a notable contribution to continuing political debate on the European Commission's Common Fisheries Policy, central to which is a system of "Individual Transferable Quotas." Højrup's is a story of the destructive effect of such privatization on fishing communities in Denmark and the successful construction of an alternative to it in one particular community, that of Thorupstrand in Northern Jutland. To understand the significance of that story, we need first to ask what someone who spends his – and now a little more often her – working life as a member of a fishing crew is doing. There are two very different kinds of fishing and two very different answers. Much deep sea fishing is financed by corporations whose return on their investment depends on the size of the catch and who, in attempting to maximize that return, compete in national and international markets. Their aim is to dominate in the most profitable fishing grounds and to compete

4 Thomas Højrup, *The Needs for Common Goods for Coastal Communities*, Fjerritslev, Denmark: Centre for Coastal Culture and Boatbuilding, 2011.

successfully in the sale of salted, canned, and frozen fish. To work for such a corporation is to be like any other worker for a typical capitalist enterprise, that is, you are serving *their* ends for the sake of the livelihood of you and yours, and there is only or principally a financial connection between your work and the ends that you have as member of a family or household or as member of a local community.

Contrast the lives of members of fishing crews in communities where share fishing is practiced, crews who are self-employed, whose fishing grounds are near at hand, and who belong to communities with long experience of this way of life. At Thorupstrand, as Højrup recounts, income from fishing was calculated, after variable costs had been paid, so that 40% was allotted for maintenance and repair of the boat and fishing gear, 20% to the skipper (usually owner of a share of the boat), and 20% each to the second and third crew members. When a loss was incurred, it was divided proportionately. Every member of a crew was therefore a partner in an enterprise, in some communities often a family enterprise, so that individuals find it difficult not to recognize three related common goods, those of family, crew, and local community, and achieve their own individual ends in and through cooperating to achieve those common goods. In the achievement of those goods, school teachers, boat builders, and pastors all have crucial roles. Such communities do of course vary in many respects. What they share, as Højrup emphasizes, is that their work is not a means to an external end but is constitutive of a way of life, the sustaining of which is itself an end.

Many European fishing crews still engage in some version of share fishing. How their communities have fared differs from country to country. Højrup's narrative begins in 2006 on the eve of legislation that prescribed the allocation of fishing quotas to individual boats, so bringing about the privatization of those quotas and the acquisition of them by investors. Those crew members with no part in the ownership of a boat lost out immediately. From now on they worked, if at all, for wages, not for shares. Those with a share in ownership could sell it for more money than they had ever envisaged having, but from then on would be permanently dependent for employment on those outside the community with even more money. A society that had valued common goods would become a society of individual preference maximizers and profit maximizers. To many in North Jutland, there appeared to be no alternative, but not so in Thorupstrand. There the possibility of retaining share fishing and with it the form of community that it sustained was explored and achieved. A cooperative company that purchased a common pool of quotas was formed.

The purchase was financed by entrance fees and by substantial loans from two local banks. Security for these loans was provided in large part by the common pool of quotas. Twenty families joined the cooperative in which decisions were made democratically, one member, one vote. The families engaged in share fishing jointly assumed responsibility for sustaining the practice of share fishing and with it their way of life. Between 2006 and 2008, years during which the price of a boat rose 1,000 percent, they watched others do strikingly well or more often badly in the market frenzy. But the crisis of 2008 had much the same consequences in North Jutland as elsewhere, one of which was a failure of one of the two local banks and with it a demand for the repayment of the loan, something that would have destroyed the cooperative. They avoided this by resorting successfully to the conventional politics of the Danish state, providing a model of political skill for others in similar situations.

Academic economists – and those who think in their terms – when they recognize that free markets can threaten certain ways of life, commonly conclude that this must be because those ways of life are inefficient and obstruct growth. What is at issue between the share fishing crews of Thorstrup and elsewhere and the protagonists of commercial fishing is how efficiency and growth are to be understood. This is not a new quarrel. It was what was at issue between Ricardo and the Luddites. It is a quarrel about ends before it is a quarrel about means, a moral and political quarrel about how economic resources and power have to be distributed, if certain ends are to be achieved. What ends we pursue and therefore what side we take in such quarrels depends upon what kind of people we are and that is a matter of the virtues and vices.

The fragile success of the *Thorupstrand Kystfiskerlaug* (Guild of Thorupstrand Coastal Fishermen) was possible only because of qualities of mind and character especially in those who provided the community with leadership and the Guild with an articulate voice: prudence increasingly informed by economic and political know how, justice in the allocation of shares and in the structure of the Guild, courage in taking the right risks in the right way, and temperateness in not being seduced by the promises of the market. Subtract any one of these and you subtract a necessary condition for the community's flourishing. It matters that the Guild is an association of families as well as of individuals, so that the relationship of the common good of the family to that of the workplace is understood. It matters too that the survival and flourishing of the community depend upon the political prudence that they bring to their continuing engagement with the economics of the market and the politics of the Danish state.

Every local community that to any degree successfully implements a politics of common goods has its own distinctive story to tell. A sharp contrast with Thorupstrand is provided by the *favela* (slum) of Monte Azul in São Paulo, Brazil, a city where impressive sustained economic growth has resulted in the characteristic inequalities of capitalism, great wealth for a few, moderate prosperity for a large number, and areas of gross poverty for the excluded. Radical change in Monte Azul had its small beginning in 1975 in the founding of a school dedicated to the principles of Rudolph Steiner by German anthroposophists. Their attention to the various needs of children and their parents – educational, artistic, health care – led to the founding in 1979 of the Associação Comunitária Monte Azul (ACOMA; see its official website: www.monteazul.org.br) whose working groups have campaigned for and achieved major improvements in sanitation and the disposal of sewage, in street lighting and safety, and in the provision of education and health care. However, the life of the community has been transformed not just by these improvements, but by the cooperative activities through which they were and are obtained.

Particular working groups and more general groups have met regularly for deliberative discussion on how to define and achieve the common goods with which they are concerned, on how to obtain the resources needed for their struggles, and how to mobilize political support, embarrassing national and municipal governments and elites that claim to be concerned for the poor, but who are strikingly unresponsive to the poor who do not organize politically (on Monte Azul see ACOMA's website and the bibliography cited there). For them the same virtues as at Thorupstrand have been important: political prudence, justice, courage, and temperateness, virtues exemplified in the most notable of the German anthroposophists in Monte Azul, Ute Craemer, but virtues without which the achievements of common goods of the 3,800 inhabitants of Monte Azul and later of their neighbors in adjoining areas would not have been possible.[5] And that achievement of common goods has enabled numerous individuals to identify and achieve individual goods.

The communities of Thorupstrand and Monte Azul are far from unique. The management of common resources for shared benefits – of water needed for irrigation, of pastures for grazing, of forests for timber – always presents problems, but across the world there are many examples of groups that have solved those problems for longer or shorter periods. What is

[5] See Ute Craemer and Renate Ignacio Keller, *Transformar e possivel*, São Paulo: Editora Peiropolis, 2010.

noteworthy is that if all human agents were the kind of practical reasoner that most economists suppose them to be, such communities would
be impossible. Individuals who seek to maximize the satisfaction of their
preferences in a predictably cost-effective way will take it to be contrary
to reason that they should refrain from securing competitive advantages
over others in a way that will destroy long-term communal ties. Hence,
economists have generally concluded that such resources will in time be
distributed through free, competitive markets, unless the state intervenes to
manage them. It was the extraordinary accomplishment of Elinor Ostrom
to show that this is false by multiplying examples of successful institutions
of communal management at different local and regional levels. She used
these examples to identify the conditions that must be satisfied, if such management is to be achieved.[6] Yet what becomes clear is that such institutions
are always at risk from the market and the state and that their survival and
their flourishing depend upon how effective their day-to-day politics is.

Neither the Danes of Thorupstrand nor the Brazilians of Monte Azul
use an Aristotelian, let alone a Thomistic vocabulary in describing their
activities and goals to themselves or to others. My claim is that both
enterprises are best understood in the terms provided by a Thomistic Aristotelianism and that such examples bring out peculiarly well how rational
agency, understood in those terms, has a necessary political dimension.
Human beings, if they act for the ends of rational agents, discover that
they are inescapably political animals, as the inhabitants of Thorupstrand
and Monte Azul did. In our society, by contrast, it is a common belief
that politics is an optional activity, one to be engaged in by those with
the time and desire to do so, but one to be put on one side, if one so
prefers. Politics, for those who so understand it, has as its central concern
the adjustment of the relationships of state and market. As such, it is an
activity in which it may or may not be to one's interest to engage. This is
therefore one more respect in which its dominant forms of thought and
action presuppose an account of human nature and agency deeply at odds
with any Thomistic Aristotelian account. So the invitation to contemporary individuals by Thomistic Aristotelians has to be significantly more
complex than I have so far suggested. It has to be an invitation to recognize
in themselves and in others both those features and concerns of which
the Thomistic Aristotelian account speaks and, alongside it, in politics as
elsewhere, a conflicting tendency to disguise and misdescribe those features
and concerns by thinking of themselves and others in the terms prescribed

[6] Elinor Ostrom, *Governing the Commons: The Evolution of Institutions for Collective Action*, Cambridge
University Press, 1990, pp. 182–192.

by the dominant contemporary culture. This conflict is perhaps most strikingly exhibited in a common enough willingness to oscillate between two different and rival conceptions of practical rationality, of each of which we have taken some note already. Each of these has its own account of how desire and practical reasoning are related.

4.4   Practical rationality from the standpoint of the dominant order

On most days most of us follow much the same established routine. It is as well that we do, since others who interact with us regularly will have formed expectations that take account both of our expected actions and of what we expect from them. What both we and they expect is a matter not only of our and their actions, but also of our and their motivating reasons. The regularities on which we and they rely include those exhibited in our and their responsiveness to reasons for doing this rather than that. So it is one obvious mark of a shared culture that its members generally have no difficulty in understanding both what others are doing *and* why. Yet even within such a culture there will often be misunderstandings, some arising when there are disagreements on how reasons for doing this or that or for wanting this or that are to be evaluated as good or bad. In extreme cases some may find it near unintelligible that others should reason as they do or be moved by the considerations that move them to action.

In a culture informed by any kind of deep-running disagreement, someone who has become able to understand both of the rival standpoints, who has an imaginative grasp of what it is to think, feel, argue, and act as those on each side of this divide do, may find it problematic to identify with either. What such a one needs are reasons for reasoning in one way rather than the other, arguments for evaluating arguments in one way rather than the other. But, so I have argued, just this is often our situation in our present culture, as we contrast what it is to think, decide, and act in terms of the common goods of family, school, workplace, and political society with what it is to think, decide, and act in the terms dictated by state, market, and Morality. We can understand what is involved in this contrast only by spelling out more fully the two rival conceptions of what it is to be practically rational that are presupposed by each of these modes of thought and action, keeping in mind that many people in our culture find themselves at some times thinking and acting in one of these two ways and at others in the other, yet are on occasion forced to choose between them. So what is practical rationality from the standpoint of the dominant economic and political order?

Begin with the type of reasoning that informs transactions in the market. Here each individual is taken by every other individual to be engaged in maximizing the benefits that she or he obtains relative to the costs of obtaining those benefits, whether selling one's labor and skills to employers or investing in a corporation or introducing new machines or buying one's food in a supermarket or growing one's own food. So, given the conditions of the market, I strike the best bargain that I can with those relevant others who are engaged in maximizing their benefits relative to their costs. What rules of reasoning do they and I follow in acting with this goal? The formal structure of that reasoning was identified by Pareto, L. J. Savage, and the other founders of decision theory and game theory, and a rough-and-ready version of the rules that they identified provides the dominant conception of rationality in the culture of advanced economies. Individuals, that is to say, are taken to be engaged in satisfying their preferences and to be a rational agent is to act so as to maximize either the probability that one will satisfy those preferences that, on reflection, one ranks highest or the probability that one will be as little dissatisfied as possible.

The preferences in question are of course one's considered preferences, those arrived at after reflection. As to how those preferences are to be rank ordered or the relevant probabilities estimated or the relevant decisions implemented under conditions of ignorance or risk, one need go only to the standard texts. Before saying something about those texts, it is worth noting two possible misunderstandings. The first is to suppose that someone who acts so as to maximize her or his preference satisfaction must be someone who acts from self-interest. This is a crude mistake. Someone's preferences may well be altruistic and even self-sacrificing, as the preferences of numerous philanthropic individuals are. The second is to believe that, if agents are often what Herbert A. Simon taught us to call satisficers, then they cannot be engaged in maximizing the satisfaction of their preferences. A satisficing strategy is one aimed at achieving not the optimal solution to some problem, the maximizer's solution, but an acceptable solution, a good enough solution. The optimal solution may be just too difficult to achieve. And evidently many agents much of the time are satisficers. To say this is to say that they are maximizers who have recognized that the costs of what may be in the abstract the optimal solution to their problem are too high for them with their limited resources. Satisficers are sophisticated maximizers.[7]

---

[7] Michael Byron, "Satisficing and Optimality," *Ethics* 109, 1 (1998): 67–93, and see the discussions in *Satisficing and Maximizing: Moral Theorists on Practical Reason*, ed. Michael Byron, Cambridge University Press, 2004.

What standard texts on decision theory and game theory supply are accounts of what it would be to be, on this view of practical rationality, an ideally rational agent.[8] But what those texts also rightly make clear is that actual agents will always fall short of this ideal and not necessarily in any damaging way. So it is with the requirement of consistency in rank ordering one's preferences, a requirement spelled out in terms of an asymmetry condition (If I prefer outcome A to outcome B, then I must not prefer B to A or be indifferent between them), a connectivity condition (For every relevant outcome, I must either prefer it to each other relevant outcome or be indifferent between them), and a transitivity condition (e.g., If I prefer A to B and B to C, then I must prefer A to C). Some large measure of consistency in their rank ordering of preferences is important for rational agents, since inconsistency is apt to result in frustration and dissatisfaction. But failures to meet the asymmetry condition or the connectivity condition or the transitivity condition in this or that respect on this or that occasion are generally unimportant. To try to be an ideally rational agent would not be rational – the costs would be too high – and this not only in respect of the requirement of consistency.

So when someone in the course of making an everyday choice estimates the probability of this outcome relative to that, a rough-and-ready calculation is commonly sufficient. Questions about how probability is to be understood, whether in Bayesian or nonBayesian terms, would be an irrelevant distraction. That does not mean that the theorists' debates on such issues are irrelevant, but that they become of practical importance only at certain sophisticated stages of the enquiry. Moreover failure to resolve certain problems at those stages gives us no grounds for rejecting this conception of what practical rationality is. Should we, for example, when choosing under conditions of ignorance, act so as to achieve that outcome which, if things turn out badly, will do most to satisfy our preferences compared with alternative outcomes, or should we instead act so that we will have least to regret? Theory provides no compelling grounds for following one rule rather than the other. But the everyday rational agent can decide as her or his temperament dictates. Nothing is at stake for her or his rationality.

As I noticed at the outset, when we reason as to what the outcome of this or that alternative action will be, much of our reasoning will depend upon our expectations of how others will behave, those same others who are in turn reasoning on the basis of their expectations of how we will behave.

[8] Excellent examples are Michael D. Resnik, *Choices: An Introduction to Decision Theory*, Minneapolis: University of Minnesota Press, 1987, and Martin Peterson *An Introduction to Decision Theory*, Cambridge University Press, 2009.

With some of those others, we will be unable to satisfy our preferences unless we successfully bargain or negotiate with them. Game theory answers the question: In any n-person game what is the best strategy for an agent to adopt, given that the other players will each adopt what is the best strategy for them? Its answers have application to all situations of bargaining and negotiation in which each party wishes to know how much she or he must concede in order to secure the best outcome for her or himself. As an axiomatized body of theory, deriving from von Neumann and most of all from Nash, it specifies precisely how economic actors must behave in market situations if they are to succeed as rational maximizers. What holds for them holds too for the rough-and-ready bargaining and negotiating know-how of many actors in noneconomic situations reckoning the costs and benefits of alternative courses of action. But to have observed this is to have reason for at least entertaining Gary S. Becker's contention that much apparently noneconomic human behavior, including many aspects of family life, is in fact explicable in economic terms, in terms, that is, of costs and benefits to agents.[9]

There are, of course, two ways to interpret Becker's claims. He himself supposed that he had discovered something about how human beings as such are, about the extent to which they are in fact rational maximizers. But his findings are equally consistent with the view that what he has shown is the extent to which, in advanced economies such as our own, many agents have been transformed, so that they are now able to think of what they had formerly taken to be noneconomic relationships and institutions in economic terms. They have thus excluded themselves from all those relationships and institutions participation in which is incompatible with thinking of oneself as or acting as a rational maximizer, all those relationships and institutions that require a kind and a degree of commitment to others that are incompatible with the commitments of anyone concerned to maximize their own preference satisfaction. It is not that such rational maximizers may not find an important place in their lives for some commitments to others. The facts of social life will generally compel them to recognize that commonly the unconstrained maximizer fares worse than maximizers who commit themselves to others and who can be relied upon to honor those commitments. And cooperation with others is possible only when those others recognize in one some concern for their good as well as one's own. Situations such as that of the Prisoner's Dilemma, where two or more people, who each act as unconstrained and uncooperating rational

---

9 Gary S. Becker, *The Economic Approach to Human Behavior*, University of Chicago Press, 1976.

maximizers, will all be worse off than if each had acted with a cooperative eye for the good of each of the others, arise wherever trust is absent. So rational maximizers have good reason to develop relationships of trust in both their economic and their noneconomic activities.

Yet they also have good reason to limit their commitments to those relationships. To those with whom they are not only in negotiating or bargaining relationships now, but they expect to be in such relationships for the long term, they have good reason to present themselves as and therefore to be reliable and trustworthy. To those on whose goodwill they have to rely because of their wealth, power, influence, skills, charm, or other advantages, they have good reason to present themselves as and therefore to be obliging and helpful. But what of those who have nothing with which to bargain or who are in no position to negotiate and who have no prospects in either regard? Here rational maximizers have no reason to take account of their interests except insofar as those interests coincide with their own. So it is notably in economic dealings.

Continuing economic growth in developing markets does in the long run benefit the world economy and in turn those in the advanced economies who benefit most from the growth of the world economy. That the proportion of the populations of the poorest countries who live in the most extreme poverty dropped from 43 percent in 1990 to 21 percent in 2010 is something that rational maximizers in advanced economies have reason to welcome. (And so do the rest of us of course.) But it is something that rational maximizers (unlike the rest of us) have reason to promote only insofar as its promotion is compatible with or required by the promotion of their own interests, the satisfaction of their own preferences. Think now on the one hand of the plight of those populations, whether in developing or in advanced economies, who lose out in the competition to benefit from investment and who have no other remedy for their poverty, and on the other of the considerations relevant to rational investors attempting to maximize the return on their investment. The latter have no reason at all to take account of, let alone to take responsibility for, the former. And characteristically they do not.

A second feature of what, on this view, economic rationality requires also deserves attention. Agents who engage in market transactions have to rely on a large and complex institutional framework, both national and international, that makes those transactions possible. Who is to pay the costs of sustaining that framework? Rational maximizers will act so as to sustain that framework at the least possible cost to themselves, so engaging in a politics whose aim is to ensure that those costs are paid indirectly by others, a politics therefore of systematically unequal distributions. Growing inequality in outcomes is not an accidental political feature of any society in which those with money and power are rational maximizers, even when those maximizers are constrained maximizers.

The constraints accepted by rational maximizers, although real, are always conditional. Changes in circumstance may always make it the case that what was in the past a set of constraints that these particular maximizers had good reason to impose on themselves are no longer such. When they do, rationality requires that they be discarded. It follows that the acceptance of genuinely unconditional commitments, the imposition upon oneself of unconditional constraints, can never, on this view, be practically rational. When therefore Becker, for example, argues that certain types of behavior are best explained in terms of cost–benefit evaluations by the agents concerned, he is arguing that those agents in those areas of their lives do not understand themselves as making – or breaking – unconditional commitments. When those areas include, as they do, their marriages, he is, as I suggested earlier, reporting a radical change in an institution.

If the practical rationality of the maximizer of preference satisfaction excludes the possibility of genuinely unconditional commitments, then it will be impossible to derive from the precepts of such rationality, that is, from the precepts of decision theory and game theory, anything approximating to, let alone coinciding with, the precepts of any morality, ancient, medieval, or modern, including Morality. All attempts to achieve such a derivation, no matter how sophisticated, are bound to fail.[10] In a society such as our own in which so much economic and political activity is expressive of the attitudes and standpoints of rational maximizers, Morality therefore continues to have a distinctive function, since its constraints extend beyond any that rational maximizers would impose and its projects are other than those that rational maximizers would undertake. It is their allegiance to Morality that enables some rational maximizers to recognize and address in the role of philanthropist just those problems of deprivation that as rational maximizers they ignore or indeed generate. It is their professed allegiance to Morality that enables Western government to make those pledges of aid that later cost–benefit evaluations give them good reason to break, as they so often do. Even therefore within those areas of social life in which the dominant conception of practical rationality is that elaborated for us by decision theory and game theory, there is a certain

[10] For the most interesting and sustained attempt at such a derivation, see David Gauthier, *Morals by Agreement*, Oxford University Press, 1986, and subsequent discussion culminating in the symposium in *Ethics* 123, 4 (July 2013).

measure of incoherence. But this is minor compared to the incoherence of lives in which there is a place not only for a conception of practical rationality defined in decision-theoretic and game-theoretic terms, but also for the radically different conception of practical rationality first identified and elaborated by Aristotle and Aquinas.

4.5   Practical rationality from a NeoAristotelian standpoint

An agent who acts as a practical reasoner need not and often enough will not at the moment of action rehearse the reasons for which she or he acts. Someone standing at the kerbside, chatting to a friend, notices that a child crossing the road will be struck by an oncoming car unless she acts instantly. She breaks off her conversation in midsentence, darts into the road, and in a single movement snatches the child up and leaps out of the way of the car. She has good reason to act as she does, and she acts as she does because and only because she has good reason. Her action in snatching up the child is intelligible as the conclusion of a piece of practical reasoning in which the premises are, first, that this child will die unless she so acts, and, secondly, that the overriding good at stake in this situation, what matters most, is the life of the child. The premises are the truthful answer that she would give to the question 'Why did you act as you did?' The action is, if we follow Aristotle, the conclusion that follows from these premises (*De Anima* 434a16–21; *De Motu Animalium* 701a7–25). At once a first difference between any Aristotelian account of practical reasoning and any decision or game-theoretic account emerges. For the latter the conclusion of a piece of practical reasoning is a decision, while for the former it is an action. The Aristotelian claim is that reasoning can issue in action. In what sort of action it issues is determined by the character of the agent, as is the nature and directedness of the reasoning in which the agent engages. How so?

If actions express the conclusions of pieces of deductive reasoning, then they must be either consistent or inconsistent with the premises asserted in that reasoning. An action is inconsistent with those premises if the end to which it is directed is other than the good identified in the premises as the overriding good at stake in this particular agent's situation. Had the adult at the kerbside, after noticing the plight of the child, continued her conversation even for a moment, while having the reasons to act that she did, her action in continuing it would have been inconsistent with those reasons. The good identified in her premises as the good at stake would have been other than the good aimed at in her action. Whether agents do or do not act for the best therefore depends upon the quality of their practical reasoning, and the quality of that reasoning depends in turn on how far they are able to distinguish genuine from merely apparent goods. Their ability so to distinguish is a matter of their moral and intellectual qualities, their virtues and vices. To be a good practical reasoner is closely related to being a good human being.

This is because the virtues are just those qualities that enable agents to identify both what goods are at stake in any particular situation and their relative importance in that situation *and* how that particular agent must act for the sake of the good and the best. "Virtue makes the *prohairesis*" – the reasoning informed desire (see Chapter 1, section 1.5) – "right" (*Nico-machean Ethics* VI, 1144a20). I began by noting that someone who acts as a practical reasoner may exhibit her or his rationality in sequences of action in which there is no opportunity for reflection. But such action requires well-formed dispositions, and reflection will have had an essential place in the formation of those dispositions, reflection both upon how in general goods are to be rank ordered and upon how they are to be ordered in particular times and places. It is then a presupposition of this kind of practical reasoning that there are standards independent of our feelings, attitudes, and choices which determine what is and what is not good and that rationality requires an acknowledgment of the authority of those stan-dards. This kind of practical reasoning is therefore that engaged in by those who understand their lives in terms of the achievement of individual and of common goods, just as the kind of practical reasoning that is identi-fied by decision theorists and game theorists is engaged in by those who understand their lives in terms of those concepts that enable them to act as maximizers of their preference satisfaction. Those who lead divided lives, at one time understanding themselves in one way, at one time in another, will oscillate between these two kinds of practical reasoning.

The premises of Aristotelian practical reasoning are of two different kinds (see once more *De Anima* 434a12–21 and *De Motu Animalium* 701a7–29). There are, on the one hand, those that identify the particular good to be achieved or the particular evil to be averted by me acting here and now in one way rather than another, the end to which I am to direct my action. There are, on the other, the facts as to how I must act, if I am to achieve that end, including the constraints under which I must act, if I am not to be the author of unfortunate unintended consequences. Practical reasoning has a different formal structure from theoretical reasoning. About the latter the logic books rightly teach us that if we conjoin to the premises of any sound argument additional true premises, the argument will remain sound. But with practical reasoning this is not so. I need to catch the next plane to Chicago. If I do not leave in the next ten minutes, I will fail to reach the airport before the time for its scheduled departure. So I prepare to leave in the next ten minutes. Then I learn that all flights have been cancelled. The effect of adding the new true premise to those that already informed my reasoning is to render the inference that I was about to make unsound.

This obvious formal point is of practical importance when someone argues that only by doing such and such will he achieve some good and is about so to act, without having asked what other goods are at stake in this particular situation, what other premises should be added to his argument. For perhaps by now doing such and such, he will make some other more important good unachievable later on. Or perhaps by delaying doing such and such, he will be able to achieve it at a lesser cost. Sound reasoning requires him to think or have thought more widely about the range of individual and common goods that it is open to him to achieve. Failure so to think is at once a failure in reasoning and a failure in the exercise of the virtues. Such failures can be of very different kinds: not only lack of imagination about the range of goods that might be achieved, but also careless or inept assessments of the harms and dangers to be confronted, insensitivity to the needs of others or to one's own needs, overrating or underrating one's own abilities or the abilities of others, and so on. Education into the virtues consists in key part in making those so educated aware in detail of the possibilities of error and of the errors to which each of them will be particularly inclined, because of temperament or social role, or whatever. Here the traditional insights of Aristotelian Thomism need to be enriched by more recent findings.

The social psychological studies of Shelley E. Taylor and Jonathon Brown, for example, confirmed Adam Smith's thesis that many of us are sustained by cheerful illusions, showing that the mildly depressed are more likely to have a realistic view of their situation than others.[11] But such illusions are among the obstacles to practical rationality. A formidable catalogue of other such obstacles has been compiled by Daniel Kahneman and Amos Tversky, who have identified types of distorting bias that are expressed in mistaken estimates of probabilities and frequencies and in a disposition to error in evaluating hypotheses and predicting outcomes. They further showed that these biases are native to the human mind and that we commonly need to be aware of them to overcome them.[12] No education

[11] Shelley E. Taylor and Jonathon Brown, "Illusion and Well-being: A Social Psychological Perspective on Mental Health," *Psychological Bulletin* 103 2 (1988): 193–210.
[12] See Daniel Kahneman, *Thinking Fast and Slow*, New York: Farrar, Strauss and Giroux, 2011.

into the virtues, into the qualities needed for practical rationality, is now complete which is not informed by their work.

When I first introduced the Thomistic Aristotelian thesis that deliberation is an activity to be conducted not by ourselves alone, but in the company of others (Chapter 1, section 1.8), my emphasis was primarily on how this is required because of the need for recurrent cooperation with others if we are to achieve our individual goods, and on the need for a common mind with those others with whom we share common goods. What Aristotle and Aquinas stress is our fallibility, our liability to error, without such shared deliberation. "In important matters we deliberate with others, not relying on ourselves for certitude" (*Nicomachean Ethics* III, 1112b10–11), wrote Aristotle, while Aquinas was more emphatic, arguing that a single individual is always liable to consider some aspects of a particular case at the expense of others, a danger that may be remedied if one consults with others (*Summa Theologiae* Ia–IIae, qu. 14, art. 3). In the light of such findings as those of Taylor and Brown and of Kahneman and Tversky, we need to be more emphatic still about our need for awareness of vulnerability to error in just those milieus in which most is at stake for the achievement of both individual and common goods, home, workplace, and family.

It matters, then, as I also noticed earlier, with whom we deliberate and how we deliberate with them. They must on the one hand be those with whom we agree for the most part in judgments about individual and common goods and about how these are to be rank ordered in particular situations, since without such agreement we will be unable to arrive at shared practical conclusions. Yet they must on the other be able on occasion to advance and accept ruthless criticism of questionable arguments and claims. The particular forms that such critical deliberation takes will be significantly different in home, school, and workplace, but there can be moments of crisis in the ongoing life of each when it is of crucial importance both for the projects of home, school, and workplace and for the individuals engaged in those projects. For individuals cannot define or redefine their place in achieving the common goods of home, school, and workplace without also defining or redefining the place in their lives of those various goods through the achievement of which they direct themselves toward that good which would complete and perfect their lives.

We go, that is, from asking 'What is my good qua family member, qua student or teacher, qua apprentice in or master of this set of working skills?' to asking 'What is my good qua human agent?' In answering this latter question, we decide how the various aspects and relationships of each role are to be integrated into a single life and how the unity of that life is to be understood in terms of the various stages through which we pass between conception and death. Of any life which has come to an ending or is about to come to an ending, whether our own or that of another, we can ask "What, if anything, makes this life, qua the life of a human being, significantly imperfect and incomplete? What is or was lacking in it which would have brought it to completion?" To answer these questions is to have found application for the concept of a final end for human beings and to have posed the problems about the relationship between our ends and our endings, about how we should tell the stories of lives that go well and lives that go badly.

When I speak of us asking and answering the questions that I have just catalogued, I do not mean to suggest that such questions or answers are always made explicit. Often enough such questions are posed and such issues resolved in the course of the decision making of everyday life. Yet if we are not to become the victims of what we too easily take for granted, we need at key moments to become more systematically reflective. So it is, for example, with regard to the conception of happiness in the dominant culture of our own society where a widespread assumption is that what perfects and completes a human life is happiness, understood in a certain way. That assumption is one that it is easy for those who reason in decision-theoretic terms and game-theoretic terms to make. For to be happy is on this contemporary view to have one's preferences satisfied. It is to be, to do, and to have, what one wants to be, to do, and to have. This conception of happiness and the understanding of practical rationality to which it is closely related, or something very like them, are already therefore presupposed at many points in the web of contemporary economic, political, and social relationships. It is unsurprising that happiness so conceived should have become an important notion in contemporary political debate.

4.6 The dominant conception of happiness

Announcements by kings of Bhutan rarely reverberate beyond the kingdom's borders. But when the then king, Jigme Singye Wanchuck, on assuming power in 1972, declared that his government would take as its goal not the maximization of the Gross National Product, but the maximization of the Gross National Happiness, he provided political rhetoric in the advanced economies with a new concept and a new theme. It is true that most of those who have made use of this concept paid scant attention to the details of what the king said, ignoring the Buddhist elements in his account of happiness. Had they not done so, they might not have found it quite so easy to announce their agreement with him. So why did they find it so easy? For two reasons.

The first is the place that a certain conception of happiness already had in much everyday thought and speech. As customers enter a local department store, a poster tells them that "Our goal is to make you happy." The king of Bhutan and the directors of J. C. Penney are joined by a host of advertisers, lovers, authors of self-help books, therapists, and politicians promising happiness, while those to whom their promises are made often believe that they have cause to feel uneasy, anxious, perhaps guilty, perhaps indignant, if they fail to be happy. For feelings of unhappiness can now be regarded as symptoms of failure, perhaps my failure, perhaps the failure of those who have not kept their promise to make me happy. Unhappiness can become a guilty secret, happiness a proud boast. Given all this it is not surprising that the proposal to make the maximization of happiness the goal of the state should have persuaded so many, but a second influential line of thought pointed in the same direction.

In 1991 Martin Seligman, a psychologist at the University of Pennsylvania justly notable for his theory of 'learned helplessness', laid the basis for the movement known as Positive Psychology by publishing *Learned Optimism: How to Change Your Mind and Your Life*.[13] One effect was a remarkable growth in studies of happiness and related topics by experimental and social psychologists with a multiplication of interesting findings. Ed Diener and his colleagues had already investigated the relationship between income and happiness.[14] Other researchers identified relationships between happiness and aging, happiness and marital status, happiness and satisfaction with work, and the like. Daniel Kahneman and Daniel Gilbert independently provided evidence of how bad we are at predicting what will make us happy. Different measures of happiness were devised and one striking outcome was the construction of the World Database of Happiness at Erasmus University in Rotterdam.

Enter the economists, who showed both how empirical happiness studies can contribute to a more sophisticated understanding of what it is to maximize preference satisfaction and what relationships might hold between certain types of institutional and social arrangements and the achievement of higher levels of happiness in a population.[15] Crucial to their findings

[13] Martin Seligman, *Learned Optimism: How to Change Your Mind and Your Life*, New York: A. A. Knopf, Inc., 1991.
[14] E. Diener, E. Sandvik, L. Seidlitz, and M. Diener, "The Relationship Between Income and Subjective Well-Being: Relative or Absolute?" *Social Indicators Research* 28 (1993): 195–223.
[15] See Bruno S. Frey and Alois Stutzer, *Happiness and Economics*, Princeton University Press, 2002, and *Happiness, Economics and Politics*, Cheltenham: Edward Elgar, 2009.

was the construction of scales that allowed measurements of happiness derived from one source to be compared with those derived from other sources. So, for example, it has been reported that in the United Kingdom an increase of one thousand pounds in someone's annual salary on average increases their happiness by 0.0007 points on a seven-point scale, while their seeing their friends somewhat more often on average increases their happiness by 0.161 points on the same scale (*Financial Times*, August 28, 2010). What is noteworthy is the extent to which the study of happiness has become a joint enterprise of psychologists, sociologists, and economists who cross-reference each other's publications. It is then of some importance that when they use the word 'happiness' and its translations and cognates, they should all mean much the same thing by them. Do they? And do they mean what the advertisers, the therapists, the politicians, and the everyday language users mean?

At first sight we may seem to have a problem. Different researchers offer different definitions, and different and rival measures of happiness have been proposed. Yet a careful reading of the literature suggests that all these are attempts to grasp one and the same notion, the very notion that is now at home in everyday thought and language. It is the notion captured by the sociologist Ruut Veenhoven, Professor of Happiness Studies at Erasmus University and Director of the World Database, when he declared that "In my fifty years of researching the subject the definition of happiness hasn't changed. It's a subjective appreciation of life" (*Irish Times,* June 5, 2009), and by Richard Layard, economic adviser to the United Kingdom's New Labour government from 1997 to 2001, when he wrote that "by happiness I mean feeling good – enjoying life and wanting the feeling to be maintained."[16] Let us spell out this notion a little further.

When they and others speak of happiness, understood in this way, they refer to a psychological state, a state of being pleased with, contented with, satisfied with some aspect of one's life – one's marital and family life, one's financial circumstances, one's work – or with one's life as a whole. It is not just that one finds one's life or this or that aspect of it agreeable, but that one finds the thoughts and feelings that one has in contemplating it agreeable. So, if one is happy, one wants to go on being happy, and, if one is unhappy, one wants to become happy. Happiness, thus understood, is taken to be something that everyone wants. Might we suppose that we are happy, when in fact we are not? Perhaps we have discontents that we refuse to acknowledge, insisting to both ourselves and others that we are perfectly

---

[16] Richard Layard, *Happiness: Lessons from a New Science*, London: Penguin Books, 2005, p. 12.

happy, so that both we and they are deceived. But by and large the best evidence that someone is happy is that they say they are without manifest insincerity and give no evidence to the contrary. It is on this assumption that the majority of our contemporaries proceed in their everyday lives and that social scientific researchers into happiness proceed in their enquiries.

To summarize: happiness, thus understood, is a state of only positive feelings. It is therefore a state of freedom from unsatisfied desires and precludes grave apprehensions and fears. It comes in degrees, as does unhappiness, and everyone on this view wants to be happy in as many aspects of their life as possible. Different individuals in avowing or ascribing happiness may give more or less importance to this or that aspect. But they agree, and on this individual agents in their everyday lives and social scientific researchers are at one, in judging happiness so understood to be a very great good, perhaps the good. From this agreement derives its political importance. Is it in fact a good? How do we answer this question from the standpoint of a Thomistic Aristotelian?

4.7   The NeoAristotelian critique of the dominant conception

Begin with the verbs that we use in avowing or ascribing happiness or a lack of it in everyday language use. We say that we are contented with, pleased by, or satisfied that such and such, or that we are pained by, displeased with, unhappy because so and so. The 'with', 'by', 'that', and 'because' are important. We use these verbs to express intentional attitudes toward something or other, and the objects of those attitudes are always such that it makes sense to ask whether they do or do not provide us with good reasons for our attitude, for being and feeling happy or unhappy in the way and to the degree that we are. "What is so pleasing about that?" we ask, or "Is that important enough to be unhappy about?" What, then, is it for someone to have a good reason for being and feeling happy?

First, the relevant object must be as that individual takes it to be. If I am happy because I passed the examination, then I have good reason to be happy only if I did pass the examination. If I am pleased because the wheat harvest is going to be unusually good, then I only have good reason to be pleased if the optimistic predictions about that harvest are warranted. Secondly, that in which I take pleasure, that about which I am happy must be such that it contributes directly or indirectly to my good or the good of others for whom I have reason to care. For someone to have good reason for being and feeling unhappy, the first of these conditions must hold and the second also, but rewritten, so that the words 'harm or loss' are substituted for the word 'good'. And of course we can have good reason for being happy or unhappy, but not *that* happy or *that* unhappy. To have reminded ourselves of these obvious truths enables us to pose the question 'Is it good to be happy?' by considering the example of a teacher with two contrasting students. One consistently does mediocre work with great cheerfulness, although capable of work of a higher standard. He views his hard-working contemporaries with contempt and prides himself on doing just enough to get by, doing only what he enjoys doing and viewing himself and his life with great satisfaction. The other student works hard and does well, but is always anxious, haunted by the thought that she could have done better. The one is a lazy, but happy wastrel, the other an unhappy perfectionist. Their teacher will serve the good of those students by making the happy student unhappy, the unhappy student happy.

This suggests a first thesis, that it is good to be happy, if one has good reason to be happy, and good to be unhappy, if and only if one has good reason to be unhappy. Why in the former case 'if', but in the latter 'if and only if'? To take account of those cases where it may be good to be happy without good reason, as when I wake up in the morning feeling unaccountably happy, not happy about this or that, just happy. And the thesis allows that, if I wake up feeling low and depressed, but having no reason for so feeling, this may be in itself bad. Is, then, the consideration of reasons irrelevant to our evaluation of those states of cheerfulness and contentment or of gloom and depression – let us call them moods – where we have no particular reason for feeling as we do? So to conclude would be a mistake. Imagine someone whose mood is one of peaceful tranquility. She has no particular reason for feeling at peace with herself and everyone else. She just does. She then receives appalling news. Someone close to her has died in distressing circumstances. She now has the best of reasons for not feeling tranquil and at peace. Were she to continue so to feel, there would be grounds for suspecting some serious psychological disorder. So it would be too with someone feeling far from cheerful who unexpectedly receives extraordinarily good news and is not in the least cheered up by it.

One generalization that is sustained by all these examples is that it is always good to be unhappy when one has good reason to be unhappy and always bad to be happy when one has good reason to be unhappy, a conclusion that seems to put us dramatically at odds with the contemporary folk belief that happiness is an unqualified good and the endorsement of that belief by so many theorists. Yet to this the reply may be that this disagreement is only apparent, not real. For, it may be said, those who take their own happiness to be a good do always in fact have reasons for their happiness. When they respond to survey questions by saying that they are happy, either with their lives as a whole or with this or that aspect of their lives, what they are telling us is that there are features of those lives which give them reason to be happy. But even if this were true, there would always be a further question, that of whether those who thus avow their happiness have a *sufficiently* good reason to be happy. Might their belief that they have a sufficiently good reason to be happy be an error, an error which, as things stand, they lack the resources to correct?

Some notable empirical research is to the point. For some three decades before 2006, Danes ranked first among Europeans in respect of self-avowed happiness, more than two-thirds of them reporting, accord to the Euro-barometer Survey, that they were very satisfied with their lives, while for most countries the proportion so reporting was less than a third. In 2006 enquiry supplied the answer to why this was so. Danes have unusually low expectations.[17] Danes, it turns out, expect less from life than do, for example, Finns or Swedes and because of this are more satisfied with their lives. Danes, we should note, have a high divorce rate and relatively low life expectancy. So the question is pertinent: Do Danes expect too little from their lives? It is a question to be asked not just about Danes but about all those who tell us that they are happy. For if they are happy only because their expectations are low or misguided, then they have no good reason to be happy.

Those who have low expectations may suffer either from a diminished sense of possibility or from a lack of hope. The former are unable to imagine large changes in their condition. The latter expect nothing positive from such changes. In either case, if they are happy with their lives, they have good reason to be happy only if they are justified in viewing the world as they do and responding to it as they do. If they are not so justified, their happiness is illusory. What matters is that they should have realistic expectations about the goods that can be achieved in the family and household, in the school, in the workplace and elsewhere, and such expectations are developed in and through a recognition of the possible and necessary transformations of their activities in shared movement toward

[17]   Kaare Christensen, Ann Maria Herskind, and James W. Vaupel, "Why Danes Are Smug: A Comparative Study of Life Satisfaction in the European Union," *British Medical Journal* (December 23 2006): 333.

the achievement of both common and individual goods. It follows that if we are to understand, let alone to evaluate avowals and ascriptions of happiness, we must be able to identify and to understand the expectations of those who take themselves to be or are taken by others to be happy.

We need too to be able to identify and to understand their desires. Ferdinand LaSalle, the nineteenth-century socialist, spoke of "the damned wantlessness of the poor," the wantlessness of those so ground down by their poverty and consequent hardships that they remained aware only of their basic everyday needs and no longer had a desire for anything beyond these. LaSalle was right in noting this as one of the effects of extreme poverty, but it is not only the very poor who suffer from lack of desire. Those who have been disappointed too often, those who have had to learn to be grateful for small satisfactions and to look for nothing more, and those suffering from fatigue or boredom or depression may all have diminished desires and therefore be too easily satisfied. Avowals of happiness may be expressions of just this kind of satisfaction.

Happiness, as currently understood, is therefore not necessarily a desirable state, and the maximization of happiness is a political ideal of which we should be suspicious. What matter are the expectations and desires of both the happy and the unhappy and to identify and interpret these is a work of some complexity. But without that work happiness studies are at best misleading. It is a work that requires attention not just to how those who are studied answer survey questions, but to the vocabularies that they employ and to the nuances in their uses of those vocabularies. Asked, for example, about their feelings about their job, someone may say that she is satisfied with it, meaning either that she is quite content with it or that she is satisfied, even if barely so. Christensen and her coauthors showed themselves admirably aware of this in their careful discussion of the Danish word *tilfreds*, which may be translated by either 'contented' or 'satisfied'. They were right to conclude that in this case nothing turns on the choice of translation, but that is not always so.

Another complexity also deserves attention. Among the states of affairs with which we may be pleased or displeased are those which consist in our being pleased or displeased. If in a moment of *Schadenfreude* we are pleased by news of the misfortune of someone we dislike, we may be pained by our being pleased by this. If we are pained by someone else's malicious remark about a third party, we may be pleased that such malice pains us. Mill asserted that it is better – and for Mill this means more pleasing – to be Socrates dissatisfied than a fool satisfied. Why does it matter that we can make and do make these higher order judgments? Consider some group who up till now had failed to recognize how bad their condition is and so had been unable to mobilize and to direct their energies to remedy it. Now that they have arrived at a true view of their situation, they are cheerfully setting about new tasks. In one respect they are a good deal less content than they were. In another they are much happier about themselves. And it would be foolish to ask if they are happier or unhappier *simpliciter*, as it would be to ask the same question about many groups in transitions that involve new moral and political awareness.

To have it as one's aim to make people happier, whether they have reason to be so or not, is therefore never justified. Unhappiness with this or that aspect of our condition is often better for us than happiness. Why then should so many of our contemporaries think otherwise? The answer surely is that they think of agents as directed toward the satisfaction of their desires and of rational agents as those who have ordered their desires, so that they are expressed as a set of preferences. Impersonal institutions are pictured as providing for such individuals opportunities for preference satisfaction under institutional and Moral constraints, in competitive markets, in competitive political systems, in the formation of personal ties, that is as opportunities for the achievement of happiness.

It is within social and cultural orders so conceived that the dominant contemporary conception of happiness has an indispensable place. To be happy is to have made those choices which have resulted in satisfying, at least for the most part, one's preferences and one's desires as expressed in those preferences. The duty of benevolence, whether conceived in quasiKantian or utilitarian terms, is to make others happy. Hence, it may seem unproblematic to those who understand themselves in this way that the aim of government should be to maximize happiness. But this is of course, as we have just argued, highly problematic. That it is so is largely concealed from the view of those who are at home in and with the dominant economic, political, and moral conceptions of the social order. Yet it remains possible to understand this social order so that what this conception conceals – and its function in concealing it – is brought to light, as it sometimes is for those who understand their activities and their lives in terms that bring them into conflict with the dominant conception and with those institutions that embody it, that is, for those who think in terms of common goods and whose practical reasoning is in the NeoAristotelian rather than the decision-theoretic mode. How then do *they* understand happiness?

Their conception of it, like their understanding of goods and their mode of practical reasoning, has an instructive history. Consider the sense of 'happy' when used to translate words from classical Latin. "Happy (*felix*) he who is able to investigate the order of things," said Lucretius. "Happy (*beatus*) he who, far from business affairs, works his family fields with his own oxen," said Horace. They were not speaking of the feelings of the scientist or the ploughman, but congratulating them on having good reason to think well of themselves. So what is it to be in that state in which one is justified in thinking well of oneself and one's life? Aristotle had answered this question and his medieval followers use the same words to name that state as Lucretius and Horace did, *felix* and *felicitas*, translated both in medieval and later English by 'happy' and 'happiness', *beatus* and *beatitudo*, translated mostly by 'blessed' and 'blessedness'. Two Aristotelian theses inform their use of these words.

First, to be happy is to engage in certain worthwhile kinds of activity, to lead a certain kind of life. What kind? One in which one's powers, physical, moral, aesthetic, and intellectual are developed and educated so that they are directed toward achieving the ends of a rational agent. To be happy then is to desire and to act as one has good reason to desire and act. 'Happiness' is not the name of a state of mind. But states of mind are not irrelevant to happiness. For a second Aristotelian thesis is this: what you enjoy, what you take pleasure in, depends upon what sort of agent you are, upon your qualities of mind and character. Insofar as those qualities are the distinctive excellences of human beings, you will enjoy just those types of activity that constitute the life of happiness for rational animals. It is because human agents are animals that the education of their biologically given feelings is important. It is because and insofar as they are rational that it matters to them whether or not they have good reasons for feeling as they do.

By calling this account of happiness 'Aristotelian', I may seem to suggest that it is no more than a philosopher's theory about happiness. But Aristotle took the philosopher's task to be primarily that of identifying and elucidating concepts embodied in and presupposed by the utterances and activities of nonphilosophical plain persons, and his medieval and postmedieval followers in their account of happiness also took themselves to be doing just that. Certainly much ordinary English – and Irish and French and Polish – usage is consistent with this claim. My claim is that, even in societies in which agents are taught to think of themselves in quite other terms, the Aristotelian understanding of happiness often continues to be expressed in and presupposed by a wide range of activities, responses, and judgments, and this because it – and the web of concepts of which it is a part – captures certain truths about human beings, truths that we acknowledge in our everyday practices even when they are inconsistent with the way in which we represent ourselves to ourselves.

If Aristotle was right about how happiness is to be understood, then unhappiness is often appropriate. To care about someone or something is to make oneself vulnerable to loss, to the unhappiness of grief. To be invulnerable to grief would be to be incapable of friendship. To make choices under conditions of uncertainty is always to be vulnerable to future regret, to the unhappiness of learning that one's choice has resulted in harm or loss to oneself or others. But to make oneself invulnerable to such regret would be to live without creative and courageous risk taking. A realistic awareness of the harms and dangers that are at hand often requires learning to live with fear, and fear is not a happy state. But a life without fears would be a life marked either by irresponsible bravado or by excessive and crippling caution. These various types of unhappiness, the unhappiness of grief, the unhappiness of regret, and the unhappiness of fear are ineliminable elements of lives informed by friendship, by courageous risk taking, and by a realistic view of how things are. But such are the lives of those who aim to achieve happiness, as Aristotle understands it. The good life, the fulfilled life, may be and often is unhappy by the standards of happiness studies. Neither Wittgenstein nor Rothko were happy by those standards, but without their unhappiness, I do not think that they could have been Wittgenstein and Rothko. It was, I take it, because he understood this that Charles de Gaulle, when asked by an imprudent enquirer if he was happy, replied "I am not stupid."

4.8   Some contemporary conflicts and incoherences

It is a characteristic of the social order that we now inhabit that many of us most of the time lead highly compartmentalized lives, moving during the normal day, the normal week, the normal year, between one social role and another, from conformity to the set of norms governing one area of our lives to the often very different set of norms governing another area. All societies exhibit some degree of such differentiation, but ours carries it to an extreme, so that we learn early in life to make these transitions easily and for the most part without noticing them. A trait that is therefore now highly valued is flexibility. So in the course of an ordinary day someone may meet with their children's teachers to discuss their progress after having cooked breakfast and chatted with those children, after having worked with colleagues on a construction site, and transacted business in a social security office, and before attending a neighborhood social occasion. Each of these milieus has its own norms governing who speaks to whom, what conversational style is appropriate, what jokes may be told, to whom deference should be shown, from whom information should be withheld, when it is permissible or obligatory to lie, and so on. But it is not only that these norms are different. They are sometimes inconsistent or would be, if they were not limited in their application. Every so often, however, issues arise which cannot be dealt with in such compartmentalized terms, issues which open up conflicts that had hitherto been partly or wholly concealed from view.

An example is the situation brought about in Chicago in 2013 by the proposal of those in authority in the Chicago Public Schools system to close down a number of schools in badly deprived neighborhoods. Their argument was that too few children now attended these schools, that the expense of maintaining them was a burden on the whole system and that efficiency, utility, and fairness required that children now attending them be transferred to other schools. Against this, parents, teachers, children, clergy, and representatives of neighborhoods and of community organizations argued not only that there would be negative effects on the children but also that those who served the common goods of those schools thereby served the common goods of the local communities and that the closing of the schools was destructive of the already fragile bonds of local community. These latter considerations were from the standpoint of those in authority intangibles. They counted for nothing in the calculus of their decision making.

By contrast those opposed to the school closings, although deeply critical of the financial conduct of the school system and of the larger financial priorities of the City of Chicago, were unable to say in any precise terms what weight should be given to the financial and other considerations that were conclusive for those in authority. Each side argued in terms that enabled them for the most part to ignore the other's arguments. So it was not argument, but power that was decisive. Those neighborhoods had little or no political influence to wield and were no source of foreseeable threats to those with established power, something always treated as relevant in the calculations of political elites. Unsurprisingly, with a very small number of exceptions the schools were closed. A sequel to those closings was the firing of a large number of teachers, also on grounds of financial exigency, resulting in a badly diminished curriculum. One conclusion is incontestable. The City of Chicago distributes costs and benefits so that the costs are paid in disproportionate measure by children, especially the children of the poor.

What matters in this example, as in others of the same kind, is first how the judgments of the two contending parties were informed by the two different and incompatible modes of political and moral thought that I have been characterizing and secondly how it was because of the need to take sides on the particular issues posed by the proposed school closings that awareness of their incompatibility and of a need to choose between them became inescapable, even if only for a time. Sometimes such awareness may be the result of a discovery by some individual of a division within herself, a discovery that she has hitherto been more or less at home with one of these modes of thought in some social contexts and with the other in other contexts, but that now she confronts issues that require an evaluation of their rival claims and a reordering of her activities in the light of her conclusions. How is she to proceed? This is a question that many of our contemporaries are liable to find themselves asking, just because so many of us lead potentially incoherent lives, lives that remain as coherent as they are only because and so long as certain questions go unasked, certain issue ignored or avoided or suppressed.

The incoherences which I have identified are, it is worth emphasizing, of two kinds. There are those internal to the dominant mode of practical thought and decision making, those that find expression, for example, in the recurrent oscillation between utilitarian and Kantian arguments. And there are those that result from the coexistence in our culture of that whole mode of practical thought and reasoning with an often inexplicit and unacknowledged commitment to reasoning in Aristotelian and even Thomistic terms about common goods. It is in key part the compartmentalization of our social life that enables us to negotiate our way through both kinds of incoherence as successfully as we do. But it is awareness of this latter kind of incoherence that, as a potential threat to the dominant economic, political, and moral order, most needs to be contained, if that order is to be sustained. It is this awareness that provides a starting point for those of us who, as Thomistic Aristotelians, are concerned to provide for our contemporaries a rational justification for our particular political and moral judgments in particular situations. What then is required for carrying through the tasks of rational justification? What *are* those tasks?

The first is that in which we have already engaged, that of identifying and understanding the relevant beliefs, attitudes, commitments, and capacities of those whom we are addressing. All justification is justification to some particular individual or set of individuals. To justify some claim, whether mathematical, scientific, theological, or political and moral, is to show to someone that their present beliefs, attitudes, and commitments are such and their capacity to recognize certain truths is such that on reflection they cannot, without some greater or lesser inconsistency, reject that claim. To which the response may be that there are surely some claims that are justified *as such*, no matter to whom they are addressed, claims, for example, that certain theorems in mathematics are provable. The standards of proof in mathematics do indeed hold for any and every rational agent. But with moral and political claims it is quite otherwise, for reasons that are already obvious.

Disagreements over the range of human goods, over how they are to be rank ordered, and over what we mean when we speak of goods to some degree divide one culture from another and often too divide one class or group or party within a culture from other such. Where underlying agreement in our practices of counting and measurement provides a basis for agreement in the application of mathematical concepts of proof, disagreement in the application of political and moral concepts arises at least in part from different modes of political and moral practice and extends to disagreement over how such disagreement is to be resolved. So when we advance political and moral claims, we need to know to what it is in the beliefs, attitudes, commitments, and capacities for recognition of those whom we are addressing that might make them open to considering our claims and perhaps to finding them rationally compelling.

In many cases and those the most interesting, we cannot learn this without entering into prolonged dialogue with them, and such dialogue requires openness on our part to the widest range of relevant objections that can be advanced by them against whatever case it is that we are making. Such dialogue is therefore a cooperative form of enquiry, which fails insofar as it becomes too adversarial. It characteristically has its starting point in some immediate practical disagreement, but a disagreement that, unlike many others, cannot be resolved without confronting at least to some extent theoretical issues. To such disagreements the contending parties will each have brought a set of beliefs, attitudes, commitments, and perplexities, unresolved problems, that issue from and are intelligible in the light of their past histories. Imagine then what is involved for contemporary Thomistic Aristotelians in entering into and sustaining such a dialogue and what is involved for self-aware and intelligent agents of opposing points of view whose judgments and presuppositions are put to the question by some Thomistic Aristotelian.

4.9 How Thomistic Aristotelians justify their claims in contemporary debate: issues of rational justification

What gives Thomistic Aristotelians rationally justified confidence in their own positions? How do they justify what they assert to themselves and to each other? That depends on whether they are answering the theoretical questions of the philosopher or the practical questions of the agent. If as philosophers they are invited to justify their account of, say, the goodness or badness of particular actions, they may initially supply an account of what a human action is and of how more generally goodness and badness are to be understood, moving from less to more fundamental theses. Such justifications will presuppose the overall Thomistic scheme of thought. But when that scheme is itself put in question, their arguments will be of a different kind. What they need to provide and can provide is an historical narrative, one that begins from Aristotle's responses to his predecessors, to the preSocratic thinkers, to Socrates, and to Plato. From Aristotle's reformulations of their questions, his criticisms of their theses and arguments, and his development of their lines of thought, there emerged a systematic set of enquiries, each with some bearing on at least some of the others. To be an Aristotelian is to participate in these enquiries, and at each stage of its subsequent history Aristotelians have had to confront multifarious problems: how to resolve incoherences internal to the system, how to accommodate new discoveries, how to respond to objections from rival schools of thought, when to abandon certain enquiries as sterile. So Aristotelians have in their commentaries recurrently revisited Aristotle's texts with new insights and resources and have reframed Aristotle's theses and arguments in the light of encounters, first with Islamic and Jewish philosophical theism, then with thirteenth-century Augustinianism, and later still with the various protagonists of modern philosophy.

What Aquinas provides is a radical restatement of Aristotelianism, one that, while theistic, returned his thirteenth-century contemporaries to the original Aristotle in a new way. After him the work of elucidation and critique continued through periods in which Thomists have had to confront objections and problems posed successively by the new understanding of law and morals that finds expression in the making of the modern state, by the new antiAristotelian natural science, by the Enlightenment, and by postKantian philosophy. What we have now is, so the Thomistic Aristotelian claim runs, the best statement of the theory so far, as judged by the best criteria of truth and rational justification to have emerged so far, one whose protagonists have been able to make an at least adequate rejoinder to the principal objections so far advanced against it. The claim is not that, is very far from being that, there are no objections yet to be met, no problems yet to be met and resolved. Thomism remains an ongoing set of enquiries and debates, in theistic metaphysics, in philosophical psychology, in politics and ethics, and in the philosophy of the sciences.

When in the course of those enquiries and debates Thomists are called upon by others who reject one or more of our theoretical theses to justify what they assert, what they need to do is to draw upon the resources afforded by this justificatory narrative. How they do this will depend upon what it is that those particular critics are questioning. But at certain points they will find it necessary, if they are to articulate their own commitments accurately, to move from theoretical to practical considerations. For their theory articulates concepts and theses that inform or are presupposed by their activity and are only fully intelligible when understood in the context of that activity. But, when so understood, it at once becomes clear that there is, as I noticed earlier, another dimension to rational justification, a second type of narrative to be told. Because the theoretical dimension requires a history of successive critical stages in the development of theoretical positions and arguments, it takes the form of a third person narrative until it reaches the present. Because the second, the practical dimension, takes the form of a particular history told by each particular agent about her or himself, its narrative is in the first person from the outset, although that first person is sometimes an 'I', often a 'we'. Each such narrative is a history of the development and exercise of that particular agent's rational powers and, since to be practically rational is to know how to rank order goods, a history of how that agent learned to rank order goods. One characteristic starting point for such learning in our own culture is, as I noticed earlier, someone's experience of a breakdown in the compartmentalization of her or his life, so that an individual who had hitherto happily lived with one set of norms in one area of her life and with different and potentially incompatible norms in some other area now and unexpectedly finds that she has a problem. Issues of truth telling provide instructive examples.

Imagine someone who has unreflectively conformed to the prevailing norms regarding truth telling and disclosure, both within her circle of friends and in her professional life. Those two sets of norms have been very different. Among the friends it is taken to be right to keep each other's secrets, even if to do so is harmful, although not unduly harmful, to others outside the circle. And on behalf of friends it is taken to be permissible and perhaps sometimes required to tell protective lies. In the agent's profession, by contrast, there are strict norms about whom it is to whom one is never allowed to lie and what it is that one must in certain circumstances disclose. (Such norms, of course, characterize many professions from medicine and the law to accountants and realtors.) Such a one may then find herself professionally required to tell a truth that from her friends' point of view, and indeed from her own point of view as a friend, will be treated as a betrayal of friendship, while to fail to tell that truth will be a serious violation of professional ethics. How should she think about her situation?

Whatever decision she makes, she will have been unable to avoid coming to some view of the relative importance of certain goods both in her own life and more generally, by asking and answering certain questions. To whom do we owe the truth and why? What do we owe our friends? About what may we speak and to whom? To whom and about what should we remain silent? What kind of respect should we give to the norms of this or that profession? What matters even more than the answers that she gives is the kind and quality of the reasoning in which she engages, practical reasoning that may at certain points involve her in theoretical reflection. Her reasoning will be defective if it does not concern both the ends that she needs to achieve as rational agent, as human individual, rather than just as family member or friend or member of a profession, and the kind of human being that she needs to become if she is to achieve those ends. This may be the beginning of an extended practical enquiry. For insofar as she becomes directed toward her end as a rational agent, her progress toward the achievement of that end will have to go through something like the stages that I described in my initial account of the NeoAristotelian view of the moral life. It will be an uneven progress in learning, one marked by a variety of mistakes and failures, and it will be a continuing progress only if she is able to learn from the mistakes and remedy the failures. That ability she will possess only insofar as she has to some degree acquired certain habits of mind and character, certain virtues, so that she is able to identify accurately what it was either in her past situation or in her past self that occasioned mistakes and failures. If then at some point she asks herself why she now has some measure of confidence in her judgments and dispositions, her answer can only be to narrate the story of her practical life as evidence of how she has become someone a good deal less prone than she was to make practical mistakes. So what this second type of narrative supplies is the best justification that the particular agent who is its narrator can now provide, by the best standards that that agent now possesses, for her or his practical judgments.

There is of course a close relationship between the two kinds of justificatory narrative. Practical reasoning and practical judgments concerning
what on particular occasions it is best for some particular agent to do,
and the actions that give expression to such reasoning and such judgments
always, on a Thomistic Aristotelian account, have theoretical presuppositions, which themselves require justification. To understand 'good' and its
cognates adequately, to treat this or that object as desirable and so good,
and to act for the sake of that good is already to be committed, at least
in outline, to a conception of agency that itself has further metaphysical
presuppositions. This is not to say that every agent is a metaphysician. It is
to say that much is at stake for every agent in whether or not the theoretical
claims of Thomism can or cannot be justified in terms of its larger narrative.
Moreover, those claims would be false if human practice, as rational agents
understand it, were not as the theory presents it.[18] Yet although rational
justification of the theoretical claims to truth advanced by Thomists in the
arenas of contemporary enquiry and debate, philosophical, theological,
and scientific, is therefore closely related to the justification by particular
agents of their practical conclusions in particular situations, each type of
narrative has its own distinctive conversational character.

   Challenged by other agents with whom they are deliberating or otherwise
interacting with the question of why it is that they act as they do in this
or that particular situation and why it is that they take the reasons for
which they act to be good reasons, agents whose actions and practical
reasoning presuppose and embody a Thomistic Aristotelian conception of
agency – most of whom are unlikely ever to have heard of Aristotle or
Aquinas – will reply not by resorting to theory, but by telling part of their
own story, whatever in it is relevant to explaining how their exercise of
practical intelligence is informed by what they learned from their previous
mistakes in identifying the kind of situation that they are now in and the
goods that are at stake in it. Their arguments will concern the particulars
of their situation and will give the grounds that they at this point have
for holding that to act otherwise than they do would be to act for the
worse. How the discussion proceeds from there will depend upon their
interlocutors' response. But they will have to acknowledge defeat only if it
can be shown either that by their own standards their reasons for acting
as they do in this situation are not good reasons or that those standards

---

[18] On the mistakes made by those who aspire to detach a Thomistic ethics from Aristotle's – and
   Aquinas's – teleology, see Ralph McInerny, "The Primacy of Theoretical Knowledge: Some Remarks
   on John Finnis," in *Aquinas on Human Action: A Theory of Practice*, Washington, DC: Catholic
   University Press, 1992, pp. 184–192.

are the wrong standards to appeal to in this situation in the light of some other considerations that they are committed to acknowledge. By contrast, when Thomistic Aristotelians are challenged by rival theorists to justify some thesis that is central to Thomistic theory, its protagonists draw not on the resources of their own histories, but on those afforded by the history of their theory to vindicate generalizations that hold of human agents as such, characteristically and for the most part.

To this it may be said that these strategies of justification, as I have characterized them so far, cannot be sufficient. For both at the level of practice and at that of theory, some philosophical objection may have been fully and conclusively answered by the standards that Thomists acknowledge and yet remain unanswered by the standards of those particular critics who advance it and who may take it to furnish, from their standpoint, a refutation of Thomism. And there are in fact quite a number of such objections. Yet in the present understanding of philosophical enquiry and debate, there often is nothing more to be said to such critics. Why this is so was admirably explained by David Lewis in his Introduction to the first volume of his *Philosophical Papers.*[19] "The reader," he wrote, "in search of knock-down arguments in favor of my theories will be disappointed," and this because philosophical theories are only rarely, if ever, refutable by knock-down arguments. What we learn from the objections advanced against our theories is the price that we will have to pay, the philosophical commitments that we will have to take on board if they are to escape refutation. The question then is "which prices are worth paying" and "On this question we may still differ." What weight we give to each of our prephilosophical beliefs and linguistic intuitions and what weight we give to each of our philosophical opinions is up to us. "Once the menu of well-worked-out theories is before us, philosophy is a matter of opinion."[20]

What matters therefore is whether or not such objections give Thomists good reason to reconsider their own theses or their own arguments. What matters most is that Thomists should be able to identify those objections which, if sustained by argument, would provide them with sufficient reason for rejecting the fundamental theses of Thomistic Aristotelianism, for taking the fundamental theses of Thomistic Aristotelianism to have been falsified, since, as we should have learned from C. S. Peirce, only those theses that are falsifiable can be true. Yet if, after due consideration, Thomists find that they have good and sufficient reason to reject the strongest

[19] David Lewis, "Introduction," *Philosophical Papers*, Vol. I, Oxford University Press, 1985.
[20] Ibid., pp. x–xi.

objections advanced by their critics, then the only remaining questions concern the nature of the mistakes made by those critics and why their objections are found compelling by those who advance them. By answering these questions, the tasks of rational justification at the level of theory, at least with regard to the particular objection in question, will have been completed. Yet it is not possible to answer those questions satisfactorily in matters concerning morals and politics without having satisfied a third set of requirements, without having recognized the third dimension of rational justification, that which involves what I called earlier sociological self-knowledge.

To have sociological self-knowledge is to know who you and those around you are in terms of your and their roles and relationships to each other, to the common goods of family, workplace, and school, and to the structures through which power and money are distributed. It is to understand what in those roles and relationships is consonant with the exercise of rational agency and what through the contingencies of an imposed set of structures inhibits or distorts that exercise. Put in those terms it may be misunderstood as a kind of theoretical knowledge. But it is in fact a kind of self-knowledge characteristically exhibited in and presupposed by the everyday reasoning of many agents wholly innocent of sociology or any other theoretical discipline, while it may be lacking in highly educated theorists. Consider some ways in which different conceptions of and attitudes to the social order may find expression in everyday judgment and action.

The first is a matter of certain concepts whose use we too often take for granted. It makes a significant difference to someone's life what she or he takes success or failure in the workplace or elsewhere to be and the place that that conception of success has in the self-ordering of her or his life. Conventional middle- and upper-class notions of success presuppose the legitimacy of established hierarchies of power and of the financial and other rewards attached to success in moving upwards in those hierarchies, whether it be in manufacturing or retail or finance or university teaching or the work of government. Since such upwards movement requires one to make oneself acceptable to one's superiors, the qualities that please those superiors become treated as virtues and the norms that define institutionalized relationships are treated as authoritative. Those diligent, conscientious, and complacent conformists who structure their activities so that their ends are the ends of a successful career may therefore never find reason to raise the question of whether their ends are compatible with the ends of a rational agent and so misconceive both what it is to be a rational agent and how their assent to the dominant social order has made them what they are, a good deal less than rational agents. Insofar as they live out these misconceptions, they lack sociological self-knowledge.

It matters too with whom one deliberates about what and the quality of those conversations. In every social order conversations are governed by norms that dictate what topics may be discussed with whom, what questions may be pursued and how far, what range of wit and satire is permissible in what circumstances. In some modern societies there are arenas of wit and satire, journals, theatre companies, and late night television programs which deliver biting and enjoyable jibes at the established order, delighting the irreverent young and outraging their respectable elders. What such young, such elders, and those who delight them commonly fail to recognize is that the established order is sustained, not undermined, by these institutions, that the role of the satirical jester has its due place in that order – kings have always needed jesters – and that what the jester provides is a harmless expression of rebellious sentiments, one that functions as a substitute for effective critique of and resistance to that order. The defenders of that order, when intelligent, understand very well that the jokes of nonconformity are one thing, effective action aimed at the redistribution of power and money quite another. To fail to understand this is to lack sociological self-knowledge.

A third set of examples has to do with the imagination of possibilities. We noticed earlier that some people are unjustifiably satisfied with their lives, because they expect too little, and that they expect too little, because they lack an adequate view of the alternatives open to them. Sometimes this is because they have too limited a view of their own abilities, but sometimes because they take the social order and their place in it as given. They have not learned first to imagine how things might be otherwise and then to ask how they might be made otherwise. They are not sufficiently open to possibilities of transformation, let alone of revolutionary transformation. Great movements of social change often have almost accidental beginnings, moments in which some group of individuals refuse to accept the treatment meted out to them and articulate together a sense of grievance and some initial mode of resistance to the status quo. But to go further they have to be able to imagine a coherent future. A French republic had to be imagined before it could exist. Trade unions had to be imagined before they could exist. And a movement for change may be defeated as a result of lack of imagination on the part of its leaders. So the student radicals of the late 1960s in both France and the United States aspired to reimagine the university and its future but were unable to do so. They asked searching questions but could supply no answers that might have provided a basis for effective long-term action rather than short-term protest and disruption. To lack this kind of imagination and so to have too limited a sense of possibility is to lack sociological self-knowledge.

To have sociological self-knowledge is, then, to have a grasp of the nature of the roles and relationships in which one is involved, of the shared assumptions of those with whom one interacts, of what in those roles, relationships, and assumptions obstructs the exercise of rational agency, and of what the possibilities are of acting so as to transform them are. Whether and how far each of us possesses such a grasp is exhibited in how we act and interact. On certain occasions it may be important that we are able to articulate and communicate what it is that we grasp, but what generally matters most is how that grasp informs our everyday practice. Lack of sociological self-knowledge is evident not only in the activities of particular individuals but in how certain types of activity and certain types of social relationship are structured so that those who participate in them are able to function as they do only because of a shared failure to understand key aspects of their social existence.

What, if anything, in this line of thought is Aristotelian? Aristotle argued both that we will go astray in politics and ethics, both in our practice and in our theoretical enquiries, if our starting point is wrong, and that whether our starting point is right depends on our early education. But what that education is generally depends upon the type of political society that we inhabit. If educated by the Spartans, we will be apt to make the errors that the Spartans make about the virtues, and, if by democrats, to misconceive freedom as they do. The critique of regimes in Book II of the *Politics* is in part a critique of different types of ruler as moral educator. What a bad civic education is apt to result in is what I have called lack of sociological self-knowledge, a sign of defective character for Aristotle as for us.

It is therefore important for all of us that we should not be open to the charge that in some respects we reason as we do, in justifying either our theoretical commitments or our practical conclusions, because of some lack of sociological self-knowledge. Here again we are dependent on those others, spouses, friends, coworkers, who are able both to identify in us attitudes and traits that we ourselves have been unable to acknowledge or have refused to acknowledge and to communicate these facts about us to us. Whether or not we can have justified confidence in our philosophical claims in politics and ethics depends in part on the quality of our relationships in the family, the school, the workplace, and elsewhere, something that goes unrecognized in the arenas of academic enquiry.

Given this account of what it is to provide – or to fail to provide – rational justifications of those theses in politics and ethics that we take to be truths of theory and of those that we rely on in practice, to whom are our justifications addressed? What should by now have become clear is that in the first instance they are addressed to ourselves and to those engaged with us in shared enquiry and shared deliberation. If we are also concerned with responding at the level of theory to those other critics whose starting points and conclusions are very different from our own, as indeed we should be, it is because and insofar as their objections contribute to our enquiry, so that we are able to correct our own earlier errors and integrate the truths in their positions into our account of the relevant subject matter. At the level of practice, however, our justifications have to be advanced not only to ourselves and those who agree with us, but also to those with whom we participate in the transactions of everyday life, in families, schools, workplaces, and elsewhere, most of them plain unphilosophical persons, able in varying degrees to articulate the commitments presupposed by their judgments and actions. Conversations with them are very different from conversations with theorists. So how are we to proceed in these two very different types of conversation? I begin with the conversations that are initiated in the contexts of everyday practice.

4.10   The relevance of the virtues understood in Aristotelian and Thomistic terms

That in our society families, schools, and workplaces must be scenes of potential and actual conflict is evident from my earlier description of the two opposing frames of mind that we bring to our common lives in those institutions. Confronted with any situation in which there are alternative possibilities for action, we may ask either 'How and under what constraints should I act in this situation, if I am to maximize the satisfaction of my preferences?' or 'How should we act in this situation in order to achieve our common good?' Those who ask the former question will find themselves on some occasions in conflict with those who ask the latter, but they may also find themselves at odds with other preference maximizers, while those who ask the latter question will sometimes disagree with others concerned about how their common goods are to be attained as well as with preference maximizers. Rational agents therefore badly need a map of those particular conflicts, open or suppressed, within or concerning families, workplaces, and schools, in which they are or ought to be involved, so that they can identify the particular goods that are at stake in each of those conflicts.

What is at stake will of course vary with local cultural, social, and economic circumstance, with what types of practice and institution structure social relationships. It will make a difference how power, income, and wealth are distributed. It matters what history different groups bring to conflicts and what their members take themselves to have learned from that history. But crucial to all of them, so runs the Aristotelian Thomistic claim, is the question of whether and how far by acting in this way rather than that the protagonists in these conflicts will open up possibilities of shared rational deliberation about the achievement of common goods or will instead frustrate and obstruct such possibilities. In claiming this, Thomistic Aristotelians are also saying to those protagonists that, insofar as they do understand their conflicts in this way, they will be understanding themselves and those with whom they are in conflict in terms that presuppose the truth of the Thomistic Aristotelian account of the human condition. How so?

Everything turns on how and to what extent agents in their everyday practice conceive of themselves and others as having the powers and potentialities of rational agents, as rank ordering goods as rational agents do, and as needing the virtues, if they are to develop and exercise those powers. Much in their cultural, social, and economic environment may stand in the way of their so understanding themselves. But insofar as they are unable or refuse to do so, they will to varying degrees be in conflict with themselves, a conflict the ongoing resolution of which is a condition of their further development as rational agents. They will have grounds for taking Thomistic Aristotelianism as a set of theses about the practical life to be justified if and only if they as rational agents, as they further develop their powers, find themselves with further grounds for assenting to this understanding of themselves and their conflicts, especially with regard to the place of the virtues in their lives. For they have to learn that it is only as they acquire the virtues that they can adequately understand their need of the virtues. How then do such agents justify their decisions and actions?

Invited to give reasons for judging and acting as they do in some particular situation, they will respond by identifying what they did or propose to do as the just or courageous or generous or truthful thing to do in that situation, given the goods and harms at stake. Invited to give reasons for taking *this* to be the just, courageous, generous or truthful thing to do, they will, depending on how articulate they are, give a more or less full account of what it is to be just or courageous or generous or truthful, citing paradigmatic examples. Invited to give reasons for being just, courageous, generous, and truthful, they will, if adequately articulate, explain how, if defective in any of these respects and above all in prudence, they will become victims of their own disordered or inadequately ordered desires, so that they will be unable to achieve those common and individual goods toward which they are directed by their nature as rational agents. How far those to whom they address these arguments find them compelling will depend on whether or not they themselves are able to assent to what has been said about justice, courage, generosity, and truthfulness as virtues and that in turn will depend on how far they themselves are just, courageous, generous, and truthful. For having these virtues is a condition of recognizing their range of application.

To have these and other virtues, even to some degree, is for one's desires to have been educated and transformed to just that degree. It is not, as the protagonists of Morality argue in respect of moral rules, to impose constraints on one's desires or rather, insofar as it does involve imposing such constraints, this is always a sign that one's desires have not yet been adequately educated, that one is still acting as one desires to desire rather than as one desires. To have the virtues is to be something quite other than a preference maximizer. We should therefore not expect preference maximizers to find compelling arguments advanced in support of the thesis that rational agents need the virtues. Does this imply that those who act as preference maximizers act are always bound to reject the kind of argumentative justifications that I have described? Certainly they will be apt to do so, since to find those arguments compelling would involve not only a radical change of mind, a withdrawal of assent from a set of theses in politics and ethics to which they have been hitherto committed, but also a change in their attitudes toward themselves and their desires, an acknowledgment of a desire to desire otherwise than as they have hitherto desired. Yet it is also true of them, on the Thomistic Aristotelian account of human nature, that in understanding themselves as preference maximizers they have misunderstood themselves, that there is that in them which has been obscured from their view by the way in which they have understood agency and agents.

Thomistic Aristotelian criticisms of their practical arguments, when well designed, are therefore advanced not only as objections to their concepts, their premises, and their inferences, but as directed to that in them which they cannot account for in their own terms. Aristotle held that those whose understanding and practice of the virtues is defective have suffered from a defective education. Aquinas held that even they have at least a minimal capacity to recognize their potentialities as rational agents, a capacity that may be elicited and even developed at any time. Certainly, however, most practical disagreements between those whose politics and ethics are a politics and ethics of common goods and those who are constrained preference maximizers will not result in a change of mind by either party. Indeed in the political arenas of the present, those who aspire to achieve common goods will often be able to argue effectively only by demonstrating to their preference maximizing critics and opponents that to act as the achievement of the relevant common goods dictates is also on this occasion, on a cost–benefit analysis, to act so as to satisfy the preferences of the relevant contending parties. How in detail such debates proceed will depend, as I have emphasized, on the particularities of the situations of the contending parties and on the argumentative and other resources that each party brings to the encounter.

The range of questions to which such agents may have to give explicit or implicit answers in the course of arriving at a decision on disputed practical questions is very large and so too therefore is the range of possible disagreements and conflicts. 'What resources of time, money skill, and/or power should I/we devote to this project?' 'What kind of risks and what degree of risk are permissible?' 'What weight should be given to long term rather than short term considerations?' 'What predictable reactions of others need to be taken into account?' 'What responsibility do I/we have for possible side-effects of our activities?' 'Is this the right time to do this?' and, prior to all of these, 'With whom do I need to deliberate about this?' Some or all of these questions are relevant, when individuals or groups face decisions as various as whether to continue working the farm or to emigrate to the city or abroad, to take time off from work for the sake of one's education or vice versa, to leave one's job or to organize a trade union branch, to stay in one's job or to borrow money to start one's own small business or to found a cooperative, decisions that are part of the fabric of a great many contemporary lives. Every one of these decisions by the way in which it delivers answers to the kinds of questions that I have catalogued is an expression of the relevant agents' stance with respect to the common goods and the virtues or the constrained maximization of preferences or perhaps in some cases both. What then is it for particular decisions to be shaped by an agent's virtues or by her or his lack of them? What goods will provide an agent with compelling reasons that would not weigh as much or at all if those decisions were not shaped by the virtues?

Of course the common goods of family, workplace, and school will have a foremost place, but only as particularized, as the particular goods needed by *this* family, workplace, or school here and now, given *these* circumstances. So a sensitivity to and a responsiveness to the particularities of both individual and institutional settings and needs will be indispensable virtues. Such sensitivity and responsiveness are aspects of prudence, but of prudence informed by those virtues – or vices – that determine which features of their situation are salient for agents in understanding their situation and deciding what to do. So someone with a strong trait of acquisitiveness, *pleonexia*, may see in a situation what he takes to be immediate opportunities and a good use for his resources, but what others view as distractions from their long-term projects. So someone may perceive the needs of others as affording him an advantage in bargaining with them, while others view those same needs as providing a basis for a future cooperative relationship.

How agents view other agents and themselves in their social settings and relationships will vary similarly. From the standpoint of the virtues, understood in Thomistic Aristotelian terms, every life has or lacks a certain kind of directedness toward that agent's end, and individual acts are to be understood either as so directed or as frustrating movement toward that end. Judgments that seem to lack any such reference to the ongoing narrative of the agent's life are certainly to the point in many contexts, as when we judge some particular action to be simply cowardly or unjust or ungenerous or some particular course of action to be self-defeating. But in such cases we are saying that *any* agent who acts thus would be going astray with regard to her or his end, while in many contexts our judgments require explicit, if often abbreviated reference to the directedness of this or that particular agent, to the relationship between her or his exercise of the virtues in particular situations and the overall direction of her or his life. As with judgments on individuals, so it is analogously with judgments on institutions. For families, schools, productive enterprises, and political societies too are directed toward the achievement of their specific goods, goods that, like those of individuals, may in their particularized forms change over time. How we evaluate them will therefore also involve reference to the relationship between the exercise of the virtues by individuals in their social roles, as family members, as students or teachers or janitors, as workers or managers or whatever, and the overall direction of the institution.

To evaluate in this way is to presuppose a narrative understanding of both individual agents and institutions, to presuppose that it is only in the contexts supplied by background narratives that particular actions and courses of action can be adequately understood and evaluated. One important source of practical disagreements therefore is between those who agree in thinking in narrative terms, but differ as to what they take the relevant form of such narrative to be. Contrast, for example, someone whose evaluative standpoint is informed by Jane Austen's or George Eliot's mode of storytelling – translated of course into contemporary terms – with someone similarly influenced by Virginia Woolf or Iris Murdoch. Another quite as important source of practical disagreement is between either of these and anyone whose evaluative and normative judgments are independent of and incompatible with any narrative presuppositions whatsoever, as is the case with judgments made from the standpoint of most modern moral philosophers, the standpoint of Morality, philosophers whose work confirms Lawrence's thesis of the loss to both the novel and philosophy when each takes no account of the other. (One test of whether a particular academic course in ethics is or is not being taught in a morally serious way is whether or not its students are taught that a close reading of certain novels is indispensable to their learning what now needs to be learned.)

I laid stress earlier on the importance of, whenever possible, treating disagreements, practical or theoretical, as opportunities for learning from one's critics. It is their positions against which one argues, not them, and the adoption of an adversarial attitude toward those with whom one is in philosophical debate is a hindrance to enquiry. But there are types of disagreement, types of conflict, that have a peculiar importance in our own cultural, social, and economic order where what the virtues require is a very different attitude, where the opponents have defined themselves as enemies of any rationally defensible conception of civil and political order. During the last thirty years, poverty has been recurrently generated and regenerated within advanced capitalism, and welcome technologically based advances in productivity have been accompanied by stagnation or near stagnation in wages. Not only, as I noticed earlier, have the costs of those measures which enable capitalism to recover from its crises been widely inflicted on children, but at the same time those who dominate the economic order have, as I also noticed, appropriated an increasing proportion of the wealth produced, especially in the United States. In the United Kingdom, as I write, the average compensation for the Chief Executive Officer of a corporation is 84 times the average compensation of a worker, while in Sweden the number is 89, in France 104, in Germany 147, and in the United States 275. These numbers are an index of how far, without any sense of their own absurdity, those with the most power and money have been able to immunize themselves from risk, while by their decisions and actions exposing the weakest and most vulnerable to risk and making them pay the costs, when those decisions and actions go astray. They have identified themselves as having an interest that can only be served and a status that can only be preserved if the common goods of family, workplace, and school are not served. Disagreement with them and with those theorists dedicated to the preservation of the economic and political order in which they flourish is therefore of a very different kind from most other theoretical and philosophical disagreements. It is and should be pursued as a prologue to prolonged social conflict.

4.11   Bernard Williams' critique of Aristotelian and Thomistic concepts and arguments: a response

At the end of Chapter 3, I listed Bernard Williams' four major reasons for rejecting Aristotle's ethics and promised to reply to them. It may well seem that the discussions in which I have engaged since then have not only delayed this reply, but have taken us in a different direction. But this is not so. By identifying what is at stake both in the disagreements between Thomistic Aristotelians and other theorists on how our contemporary social and moral condition is to be understood and in the practical disagreements of everyday life, I have already suggested how an Aristotelian reply to Williams might be spelled out. To go further, I will have to draw upon earlier expositions and arguments, and I apologize to those to whom these repetitions seem unnecessary. Begin, then, by considering Williams' charge that Aristotle lacks an adequate account of moral and political error. One initial response would be to catalogue Aristotle's diagnoses of particular types of moral and political failure in the *Nicomachean Ethics*, the *Politics*, and elsewhere, the errors of the intemperate and the akratic, of the clever, but imprudent, and of the stupid, of those good at war, but bad at enquiry, such as the Spartans, of those who care too much about money or pleasure or political success. But we could equally well or even better begin from the discussion of types of contemporary practical disagreement in which we have just engaged. If we do so, we may find ourselves characterizing the various types of practical error that we have encountered in either of two different ways, on the one hand describing them in sociological and psychological terms, on the other identifying them as due to lack of the relevant virtues.

It would be a mistake, however, to suppose that these are alternative or, worse still, rival and incompatible modes of description and identification. Aristotle's account of the virtues, when fully spelled out, is or rather presupposes a psychology and a sociology. To have and to exercise the virtues is to function well in one's social roles as citizen, as member of a household and family, and so on. A political society or a household functions well only if it educates its members in the exercise of the virtues, and political societies and households are classified and evaluated as adequate or inadequate by reference to just those social relationships – in the case of political societies the relationships of ruling or of being ruled – that are either sustained or undermined by the exercise of the virtues. So the diagnosis of moral and political error may identify the source of error either in the agent her or himself or in her or his social relationships.

To err is to act from a desire for some object that the agent has no good reason to desire. So to act, whether intemperately or akratically, is to have insufficiently disciplined passions. Is that lack of discipline the fault of the agent or of his educators? Or is it due to the established norms governing relationships in that society? Or to all of them? Is Alexander the Great's *hubris* to be blamed only on Alexander or instead or also on Aristotle and his other tutors or instead or also on the norms of the Macedonian royal household? One of the ways in which societies differ is in how the young learn to hold themselves accountable and to respond when called to account by others, and one of the ways in which a society can be defective by Aristotelian standards is in failing to educate them in accountability. The rich, Aristotle noted, do not know how to be ruled (*Politics* IV, 1295b13–16), that is, among other things they generally and characteristically have not learned to make themselves accountable, and so they will also fail as rulers.

Is Aristotle's account of moral and political error adequate? Any contemporary Aristotelian, Thomistic or otherwise, will readily allow that both Aristotle's sociology and his psychology badly need to be corrected and developed by drawing upon the extraordinary achievements of modern sociology from Weber, Durkheim, and Simmel to Garfinkel, Goffman, and Burns, of psychoanalysis, and of such psychologists as Kahneman and Tversky. But, no matter how far corrected, developed, and enriched, Aristotle's account of moral and political error would still fail to satisfy Williams. For Williams would deny, did deny, that we have any conception of what it is for a household or a political society to function well that can be legitimately put to use in the way that Aristotle and Aristotelians put such a conception to use. To judge that a household or a political society is functioning well is to judge from one particular evaluative standpoint, and there are always alternative and rival evaluative standpoints. Where Aristotle sees identifiable error, Williams sees disagreement and disagreement not to be resolved by appeal to any standard derivable from a genuinely empirical sociology or psychology. So Williams' charge that Aristotle provides no adequate account of moral and political error is closely related to his claim that Aristotle is mistaken in thinking that there is any such thing as *the* good life for human agents

Both depend on his view, shared with Isaiah Berlin and Stuart Hampshire, that the multiplicity and variety of human goods is such and the range of attitudes to those goods is such that there are indefinitely many alternative more or less well worked out conceptions of what it is to live well and no rational grounds for preferring one above the others. Like Berlin and Hampshire, Williams takes it to be of crucial importance that political institutions should be hospitable to and tolerant of a wide range of such conceptions, not identified with or designed to inculcate any one of them: hence their political liberalism and hence too their rejection both of Aristotle's account of what it is for institutions to function well and of his account of the human good. What then is there to be said for this latter? An Aristotelian account addressed to readers whose temper of mind is akin to that of Berlin, Hampshire, and Williams should perhaps proceed through four stages, noting more fully and systematically a number of points that were already sketched in Chapter 1, when Aristotle's views first received attention.

The first is a matter of identifying a set of goods whose contribution to a good life, whatever one's culture or social order, it would be difficult to deny. They are at least eightfold, beginning with good health and a standard of living – food, clothing, shelter – that frees one from destitution. Add to these good family relationships, sufficient education to make good use of opportunities to develop one's powers, work that is productive and rewarding, and good friends. Add further time beyond one's work for activities good in themselves, athletic, aesthetic, intellectual, and the ability of a rational agent to order one's life and to identify and learn from one's mistakes. Many excellent lives are so despite the absence from them of one or more of these. But the more of them that are absent the more resourceful an agent will have to be in coping with the difficulties that their absence causes. Such resourcefulness includes an ability to recognize what would have to be changed and what could be changed either in her or himself in the social and institutional order that the agent inhabits in order to achieve and enjoy the goods constitutive of the good life.

It is of course true, as Berlin in particular emphasized, that we often have to make painful choices between goods, both as individuals and as families or political communities. It may be that I can be a successful athlete or a useful medical researcher, but not both, a good husband and father or a good soldier, but not both. It may be that my community can provide good preschool education or a good theatre, but not both, better transport services or better care for the aged, but not both. But what matters for the good life is not so much which choice is made as the way in which such choices are made, the nature and quality of the deliberation that goes into the making of them. It is by their initial education as practical reasoners and by their subsequent exercise of their reasoning powers in the making of such choices that agents play their part in determining the goodness of their lives. The substance of the alternatives that they confront does of course differ from culture to culture and social order to social order and differs too depending on an agent's place in her or his social order. Family structures, kinds of productive work, distributions of authority and power take different forms. But there is one and the same need to be able to judge what kind of contribution to the achievement of the agent's individual and common goods each alternative course of action will make. So already at this first stage of the enquiry, we are able to sketch an account of the form that any good life for human beings must take, an account on which there is in fact a surprising amount of agreement.

As it is with goods, so it is also with failures and defeats and evils. About the various ways in which lives can go wrong, some of which we have already remarked, there is once again large agreement. Premature death and disabling illness, crushing poverty and the friendlessness of the excluded and persecuted can rule out the possibility of a good life. Circumstances a little less dire may provide obstacles and frustrations that can be overcome with the kind of resourcefulness that we already saw to be an important and often essential constituent of many good lives. Lack of such resourcefulness can be the result of a failure to learn or an unwillingness to take risks when risk taking is necessary. If we catalogue further the qualities of mind and character that enable agents to confront, overcome, and learn from adversity, we will find that we have constructed a list of virtues necessary for a good life in many different types of situation on which there is a large measure of agreement. But virtues are needed for other reasons too. We are apt to go wrong, as Aristotle pointed out at the very beginning of his enquiry, because we are too open to being seduced by pleasure, because of political ambition, because of the love of money. The good life, we may conclude from this second stage of our enquiry, can be characterized in terms of the exercise of the ability to make good choices between goods and the virtues required both for overcoming and moving on from adversity and for giving pleasure, the exercise of power, and the acquisition of money a due, but no more than a due place in our lives.

On this conclusion too we may expect a significant measure of agreement, but it is important not to exaggerate its extent. Those impressed by the arguments of Berlin, Hampshire, and Williams will have no difficulty in citing numerous real-life examples of disagreements, about the relative importance of certain goods in certain circumstances, about just what traits are to be included in the list of the virtues and about how they are to be characterized, about what lives are to be treated as exemplary. Such disagreements become practically as well as theoretically relevant when they have to be resolved by some individual or group in the course of their everyday decision making. How are they to be resolved? Only, as we have already noted, if the resolution is to be Aristotelian, through shared deliberation with family members or friends or coworkers or fellow citizens or as many of these as are relevant to this particular piece of decision making. But such resolution will only be possible if there is a significant degree of underlying agreement among all those involved on how goods are to be ordered and on the direction in which their community needs to move if its common and individual goods are to be achieved. The decisions that result will express a common mind as well as individual commitment.

To say this is to make it clear that, if this is a reply to Williams' objections to Aristotle, it is not one that Williams could have accepted or even entertained. For it is at odds with Williams' insistence on the first person character, a first person that is an 'I', not a 'we', of all practical deliberation that is an authentic expression of the agent. It is not after all so much the range and variety of goods between which individuals must choose, as with Berlin and Hampshire, that matters as the claim that each individual's choice among competing and conflicting goods must be authentically theirs. At this point the difference with Williams concerns the conditions that must be satisfied if rational decision making is to be possible. What I am asserting is that such decision making requires the existence of certain kinds of social relations, that individual agents are able to develop and exercise their capacity for rationality over any extended period of time only by engaging in mutual criticism with those others who share their practical concerns. So the third stage of enquiry into what the good life for human beings is concerns the kind of communities that we must inhabit, if we are to be rational. Here of course we can envisage a much wider range of possibilities than Aristotle could. Happily it is not only within the *polis* that human beings can flourish as rational animals. And it is not too difficult to rewrite Aristotle's arguments about the need for the *polis* (*Politics* I, 1253a1–39) in contemporary terms.

To do so, however, will involve confronting another of Williams' criticisms. To characterize humans as rational animals is to take an arbitrary and unfounded view of what is distinctive about human beings among animal species. Quite as distinctive, so he argues, is their capacity for falling helplessly in love. Williams here may at first seem, surprisingly, to miss the point that impresses Aristotelians. There are certainly species of nonhuman animals, gorillas, dolphins, and wolves, for example, whose members on occasion act for reasons and make practical inferences. What none of them can do is twofold. Lacking the resources of human language, they cannot reflect upon and criticize their own reasoning and that of others. And they cannot raise questions about whether or not they have good reason to believe what they do and as they do and to desire what they do and as they do. But of this, of course, Williams was well aware. What, I take it, impressed him was the distinctive affective life of human beings, the capacity to be moved by a range of fears, excitements, hates, loves, and sympathies that cannot be experienced by gorillas, dolphins, or wolves, and he saw no reason to take these phenomena to be either more or less distinctive of human beings than their rational capacities. So why should we disagree with him? Begin with the issue of distinctiveness.

Species emerge by natural selection in particular types of environment. Whether or not a given species flourishes or fails to flourish in reproductive terms depends on its environment, except in the case of human agents who have developed unique abilities to change their environments, so that natural selection no longer operates as it did and does with other species. It is not that members of some other species do not change and change with their environments.[21] And it is not of course that natural selection no longer operates with human agents, but that gradually activities emerge which engage and engross, but which no longer confer reproductive advantage, either on individuals or on groups. Hence, the need for evolutionary biologists to explain the consequent features of human life – concern with large cardinal numbers or with the history of Persian miniature painting, say, or with winning pie eating contests – as spandrels, as activities incidental to natural selection. It is, however, the number and importance of such activities in human life that make human beings biologically distinctive. But to say what such activities have in common we have to go beyond biology.

The key moment in distinctively human development occurs when someone first makes use of their linguistic powers to pose the question 'What is the good of doing this or that, of making this or that happen or allowing this or that to happen?' and is understood as inviting from others

---

[21] For two views on this, see K. Laland, T. Uller, M. Feldman, K. Sterelny, G. B. Müller, A. Moczek et al. "Does Evolutionary Theory Need a Rethink?" *Nature* (October 8, 2014): 161–164.

or from himself some statement of reasons for and against any particular answer, reasons which can then be evaluated. From then on human projects, human responses to good and bad fortune, and human relationships were taken to be intelligible in terms of the good and the bad, the rationally justifiable and the rationally unjustifiable. So there came a time when our predecessors were able to ask 'Is it a good thing or a bad thing to fall helplessly in love?' and to consider such responses as 'That depends on whom or what you fall in love with' and 'A bad thing if it happens too often'. We are of course also able to ask similar questions about members of some nonhuman species. Is this change in ocean temperature good or bad for dolphins? Are these changes in the demand for ivory good or bad for elephants? But these are questions that dolphins and elephants themselves cannot ask or answer, let alone justify their answers.

My claim is, then, that human beings have distinguished themselves from other animal species by realizing possibilities that cannot be accounted for solely in evolutionary terms and that what they have realized is a determinate form of life, participation in which requires a grasp of and an ability to find application for the concept of a good, the concept of a reason, and a number of closely related concepts. Williams was right in taking some human affective capacities to be distinctively human. Part of what makes them distinctive, however, is the ways in which they can be educated and their exercise criticized. Attention to these might have suggested that this objection to Aristotle misses the mark. It also provides a starting point for responding to Williams' charge that Aristotle's teleological account of human agency became incredible with the scientific rejection of his overall teleological account of nature. Since, unlike Nussbaum, I agree with Williams that the presuppositions of Aristotle's account of agency commit him to at least some theses about teleological explanation in the natural world, I cannot answer him as Nussbaum does. Why then do I agree with Williams?

Aristotle insists from the outset that we can understand agency adequately only if we understand it from two perspectives, that of the agent and that of the external observer. Moreover these are not two independent perspectives. As agents, we need at various points to learn from external observers, while, as observers, we need to learn from agents. As observers we initially treat human agents as we do all other animal agents, identifying the ends to which characteristically and generally their activities are directed and in terms of which those activities have to be characterized, if they are to be understood. An injured or a diseased animal is one whose functioning is such that, although nothing in the environment prevents them from functioning well, their activities fall short of achieving their characteristic ends. Injured cheetahs fail to hunt successfully. Young male dolphins, infected by disease, cease to engage in play. Notice that it is for the tasks of identifying and describing animal activity that teleology is indispensable. How that activity is to be explained remains at this point an open question.

As with nonhuman animals, so it is too with human agents. We observe the ends to which characteristically and generally their activities are directed. We note how with them too disease and injury prevent them from attaining their ends. We also note, still as external observers, two important differences from nonhuman animals, the length of time after weaning during which their young remain dependent on their parents and other elders and the amount and kind of education that they have to receive from those parents and other elders, if they are to function well as adults. Without that education or, if they have been badly educated, they will be unable to achieve their ends, since as agents they will not know how to rank order goods correctly and to identify their final end. But at this point we are inescapably aware that they are we, that as agents we are engaged, if we have been rightly educated, whether by ourselves or by others, in discovering what our end is, so that in our practice we may be directed toward its attainment. For, on Aristotle's view, human agents, as participants in the form of life that is distinctively human, have a final end and what it is is a matter of fact. They can only be understood, they can only understand themselves teleologically. It was Williams' recognition that this conception of teleological understanding is integral to Aristotle's morals and politics that furnished him with perhaps the most important of all his reasons for rejecting Aristotle. What then is to be said in defense of Aristotle's thesis?

Aristotle was deciding between rival answers to the question 'How is it best for me to act qua human being?' The contrast is with such questions as 'How is it best for me to act qua aunt or qua student or qua farmer or qua physician?' In these latter cases what it is to be a good aunt or student or farmer or physician, and whether it is good to be an aunt, student, farmer, or physician, may be relatively unproblematic given that we have a clear enough conception of the role and place of aunts, students, farmers, or physicians in the social order that we inhabit. In each role we are to aim at the ends of that role. Aunts aim at supplying what is needed for the well-being of their nieces and nephews that parents or other family members are unable or unwilling to supply, while students aim to complete the current stage of their education. The end of farming is to produce food and to sustain land and farm animals, while the end of medical practice is to restore and maintain the health of patients. But how are we to integrate those various activities in which we engage in each of our roles, so that we act as it is best to act qua human being? What are we to aim at, what is our end, qua human being?

Here we have to revisit the arguments of the NeoAristotelian whom I imagined in Chapter 1, section 1.8, noting that these are questions about all our activities, including those activities in which we engage in our various roles. The final human end must be such that we are to aim at it in the course of aiming at the achievement of our other ends. It is at once clear that there are two obvious ways in which we may fail as human beings. We may on the one hand lead compartmentalized lives, failing to integrate our different roles, so that in effect we lead a number of different lives, something that it is all too easy to do in a culture such as our own. What compartmentalization is apt to obscure is the extent to which decisions in one part of our lives impact upon our other activities and relationships. How we allocate our time is a more accurate indicator of what we care about and how much than are our subjective feelings, and the more time that we expend in any one area of our lives the less time that there is for other areas. So it may be a very important fact about someone, even if quite unnoticed by that someone, that he never finds time to listen to Bach or never sits alone in silence. One alternative to living compartmentalized lives is to live somewhat haphazardly, to lead lives in which we recurrently allow activities in one area to disrupt or frustrate or defer activities in other areas. Such lives are themselves arguments for introducing order.

Suppose then that someone, recognizing the need to integrate their activities, but being fearful and cautious, adopts as a principle to act so as to minimize their exposure to situations that can get out of hand, that might take them into unfamiliar and unpredictable territory. To that principle there are two major objections. The first is that those who adopt it exclude from their lives in advance goods that it may at some later stage be important for them to achieve. The second is that to live by this principle is, although it may not look like it, to live as a hedonist. Why do I say this and what is wrong with being a hedonist? Hedonists act so as to ensure that, so far as possible, what they do and what happens to them gives pleasure and avoids pain. Our imagined fearful and cautious agent makes the avoidance of what pains him his overriding objective, so making the hedonist mistake of supposing that agents should take their appetites and aversions as given and choose their goods accordingly rather than working to transform their appetites and aversions, so that they may achieve goods which otherwise they will have to renounce. What pleases and pains us depends on what kind of person we are, as Aristotle and Aquinas both stress, and what matters is to become someone open to achieving the goods of a good life. Whatever the final end of human activity may be, it cannot be the achievement of pleasure or the avoidance of pain. What else can it not be?

In putting the question in this negative way, I am following the example of Aquinas, whose name for the state in which someone who had achieved her or his final end qua human being would be was *beatitudo*, his translation of Aristotle's *eudaimonia*. At the beginning of the Second Part of the *Summa Theologiae* (Ia–IIae, qu. 2, art. 1–8), he proceeds negatively by showing what beatitude cannot consist in, at each stage providing grounds for his argument as to what it must consist in. So he argues that it cannot consist in the acquisition or possession of money, political honors, reputation, power, health, or pleasure, all of them goods in their due place, but none of them our final good. From his reasons for these and other rejections, he arrives at three conclusions. Whatever that good in attaining which we have completed our lives by arriving at our final end is, it cannot be a means to something else, since that something else would be that for the sake of which we engaged in it and so would have a better title to be our final end. Moreover, it cannot be a particular good of the same order as other particular goods, although greater and exceedingly greater than any of them, for, if so, it too would have its due place in our lives, presumably the greatest place in our lives, but it would not provide the measure of what the due place of each type of good and each particular good is in our lives, while any good that completes our lives must provide just such a measure.

The good that is our final end does not compete with other goods. We value other goods both for their own sake and for what they contribute to our lives as a whole, as a unity. The good that is our final end constitutes our lives as wholes, as unities. So in acting for the sake of achieving some particular good, we also act for the sake of achieving our final end, and it is this that, if we act rightly, gives our lives a directedness toward that end. It is for this reason – and here of course I am moving beyond (some Thomists would say away from) Aquinas – that our lives have the narrative structure that they have and that we can only make ourselves adequately intelligible in narrative terms. As throughout our lives we move toward our final end, we are each of us enacting a story that has, on Aristotle's view, a number of different possible types of ending. When I die, it seems at first from Aristotle's initial formulations that I may be either *eudaimōn*, yet not *makarios*, or *eudaimōn* and *makarios*, or not *eudaimōn* and therefore *athlios* (*Nicomachean Ethics* I, 1100b8–1101a8). For to be *eudaimōn* is to have become an agent whose activity is in accordance with the best and most complete of the virtues in a complete life (1098a 16–18), while to be *makarios* is to enjoy the goods of good outcomes, of rewarded achievement and good fortune. (To be *athlios* is to be wretched, struggling, unhappy.) So what then of the possibility of an agent who is *eudaimōn*, yet not *makarios*? Aristotle in the end rules it out. Without the goods of achievement and good fortune, he concludes, one cannot be *eudaimōn*. Was Aristotle right?

What Aristotle excludes, but Aquinas does not, is the possibility that there are situations in which defeat in achieving particular finite goals, no matter how great, is not a mark of failure. Consider the common enough case of someone who has treated some finite and particular good as if its achievement were not just a very great good, but her or his final end. They care about the well-being of their child or spouse or friend, or they aspire to some extraordinary athletic or intellectual feat in such a way and to such an extent that, were that child, spouse, or friend to die or were they to fail to attain their athletic or intellectual goal, their life, so they believe, would no longer have point or purpose. They might as well be dead and there would be, they take it, no good reason for them not to commit suicide. It is Aquinas's contention that this is never true of anyone and that rational agents find themselves committed to believing that it is not true of themselves, insofar as they are reflectively aware of the directedness of their lives toward an end that cannot be identified with any finite and particular end.

What could such an end beyond all finite ends be? In our practical lives we learn how to characterize it as we move toward it, the final and supreme object of desire, through a series of denials. It is not this, not that, not that other. For anyone educated into the NeoPlatonic tradition, as Aquinas had been by his reading of PseudoDionysius, the obvious parallel is with how through the disciplines of the contemplative life we come to characterize God, the final and supreme object of devotion, in a similarly negative way. It therefore matters to Aquinas as a philosophical theorist whether he does or does not have appropriate grounds for affirming that God, characterized as He is in our practical and contemplative lives, exists. It is Aquinas's conviction that he does have such grounds. What *we* have to ask is whether or not Aquinas's philosophical theses on God's existence are able to withstand not only the objections that he entertained, but the strongest contemporary objections. But of crucial importance as that question is, it may distract us from giving due weight to Aquinas's central insight about the final end of human beings.

It may seem paradoxical, but is not, to express that insight by saying that on his view we complete and perfect our lives by allowing them to remain incomplete. A good life is one in which an agent, although continuing to rank order particular and finite goods, treats none of these goods as necessary for the completion of her or his life, so leaving her or himself open to a final good beyond all such goods, as good desirable beyond all such goods. Defective lives are those in which agents either mistakenly identify some particular finite good that they have achieved or will achieve as their final good or suppose that failure or defeat in achieving such goods is failure to achieve their final good. Does one have to be a theist to understand one's life in these terms? Of course not. Whether Aquinas is right about the presuppositions of such a life is one thing. What the character of such a life is is quite another. Note that on this view lives cut short by inopportune and untimely deaths are not thereby imperfect. What matters is what the agent was open to at the time of her or his death, not the perhaps great, but finite goods of which the agent was deprived by that death.

This discussion and defense of a Thomistic Aristotelian account of the human good began as a response to the criticisms of Berlin, Hampshire, and especially Williams. Would they, could they, have judged it adequate? Quite certainly not! Indeed the theistic elements in that account would have given all three sufficient reason for rejecting it quite apart from any other consideration. And this is a mark of how systematic the disagreements are between anyone who in their everyday practical activities and choices presupposes something close to a Thomistic Aristotelian account and someone whose presuppositions are closer to those of Berlin, Hampshire, or Williams. Consider now a further implication of the Thomistic Aristotelian account.

4.12 Narratives

In evaluating a life what kind of unity are we ascribing to it? It is the unity of a narrative, often a complex narrative, of which the agent who enacts it is at once subject and author, or rather coauthor. What kind of a narrative it is and the ways in which we become aware of it are both best understood by considering what it is for each of us to be accountable. Accountability is one more distinctively human characteristic. For, unlike dolphins, gorillas, and wolves, each of us may at any time be asked to give an account of ourselves, to say just what it is that we did, are now doing, or plan to do, to make our actions intelligible by explaining what motives and reasons we have or had for acting, and to justify our actions by showing that those reasons were sufficiently good reasons. Others with whom we interact need to identify just what we did, are doing, or will do and why we so act and take ourselves to be justified in so acting, if they are to be able to respond to us, and so such questions are recurrently put to us by such others. But, since how we respond will determine our future relationships to them, we need to be reflectively aware of our past, present, and proposed actions and of their explanation and justification. So these are questions that we pose to ourselves. What each of us draws upon in answering them is the narrative of each of our particular lives, so far as we are aware of it. Compare two examples.

I may be called to account for something that, allegedly or in fact, I did, a very long time ago. What matters is twofold: whether or not in fact I did it and why I should now be called to account for it by this particular individual or group. What do I owe to this particular individual or group by way of accountability for what I then did? This is a question that others may put to us or that we may put to ourselves, as some have recently had to do in Eastern Europe when accused of having, in the era of Soviet and proSoviet regimes, collaborated with the secret police. In reply they have had to tell the story of their lives at the relevant time, leaving out none of the relevant aspects. Or someone may have become something of an enigma to her or himself, puzzled perhaps as to how they could have done or thought or felt certain things that they did or thought or felt, or as to whether they now need to make amends to others or even to themselves for having been so ruthless and unforgiving or so careless and unreliable a person. Once again the only possible reply is by telling a story, a story that will provide an answer by being intelligently selective. In both cases what is selected from is the larger narrative of the storyteller's life. It matters of course that the story told is true, that the selection is not a work of art designed to conceal and obscure what the storyteller was and is. We are all of us, as we have learned both from Augustine and from psychoanalysis, too often in the grip of fantasies and so apt, even when we think ourselves truthful, to deceive ourselves first and then others. But it is not, as Sartre held, that the narrative structure of the story itself falsifies. There are no true stories, says Antoine Roquentin, the character who is Sartre's mouthpiece in *La Nausée*.[22] Living is one thing, telling stories another. When we tell a story, we begin as we do because we already have in mind the ending, the outcome. In life we never know the outcome in advance, and so there

---

[22] Jean-Paul Sartre, *La Nausée*, Paris: Gallimard, 1938, trans. Robert Baldick as *Nausea*, Harmondsworth: Penguin Books, 1965, pp. 60–62.

are no such endings and no such beginnings. Things just happen. Hence
Sartre's conclusion that there are no plots, no true stories. But this is a
mistake. Why so?

The enacted narrative of our lives begins at conception. It finds its
ending at the point at which we have achieved or failed to achieve our
ends as rational agents, when we have or have not completed our lives
appropriately. So the argument that Sartre is mistaken is as weak or as
strong as the argument that our lives can be completed, that there is indeed
a final human end, Aristotle's and Aquinas's contention that we have just
rehearsed. This was of course something of which Sartre was well aware,
responding silently to his Thomistic contemporaries. But it is of some
importance that Aristotle's and Aquinas's argument is grounded in the
practical experience and awareness of agents, the directedness of whose
lives begins with their initial education into the virtues. Such agents know
very well some of what Sartre would tell them, that they never know in
advance the outcomes of their actions. They also know, however, even if
at the beginning inchoately, what it would be for those outcomes to turn
out well or badly, and in knowing this they have from their beginnings
some sense of an ending and that they are enacting a narrative. To this the
Sartre of *La Nausée* will respond that this is just not how things in fact
are, and Antoine Roquentin shows us what it is to have a life lived without
narrative illusions. To which the Thomistic Aristotelian response must be
first that Roquentin is a splendid example of an intelligent agent who has
never been educated into the virtues and so fails to understand his own life,
and secondly that the narrative of Roquentin's doings and sufferings that
Sartre provides has the interest that it has only because it depicts a certain
kind of life as it actually is, that is,that it is a truthful story of a kind that
would be impossible if what Roquentin is made to say about storytelling
were true.

What traditionally gives significance to the story told in a novel, a play, or
an epic poem is that something is at stake for one or more of the characters
with regard to their relationship to their final end. Generally, of course,
little or nothing is said explicitly about that relationship. The *Divina
Commedia,* that great theological epic, is the obvious exception. What is
immediately at stake is characteristically some good on the achievement of
which so much turns for the characters that its loss will put the direction
that they have tried to give to their lives in question.[23] But so it is implicitly
in the vast majority of stories from Homer through authors as various as

---

[23] Here I am drawing on Francis Slade, "On the Ontological Priority of Ends and Its Relevance to the
Narrative Arts," in *Beauty, Art, and the Polis,* ed. Alice Ramos, Washington, DC: American Maritain
Association, 2004.

Euripides, Ovid, Shakespeare, Sterne, Flaubert, and Henry James, stories in which the qualities of mind, heart, and character of the protagonists are revealed through struggles and conflicts that issue in success or failure to achieve some end and sometimes also in the discovery that success and failure are quite other than they were originally taken to be. With the twentieth century new kinds of storyteller and story emerge, storytellers, such as Sartre, who take the concept of such goods and such ends to be a metaphysical illusion, and stories of characters who inhabit worlds constructed so as to put in question that concept. Francis Slade considers two contrasting examples, the screenplays of Quentin Tarantino and the novels and short stories of Kafka.

Tarantino's characters, so Slade points out, inhabit a fictional world in which ends, whether ultimate or subordinate, have been erased, so that there are only rival and conflicting desires and purposes directed toward achieving the satisfaction of those desires, among them the desires of some characters to give aesthetic form and grace to the exercise of their skills and the violence of their encounters. The outcomes of those encounters are artfully imposed by Tarantino so that we are presented with an aesthetically disturbing world which is not our world. Kafka, by contrast, shows us – in an even more aesthetically disturbing way – our world as we sometimes fear it to be, a world in which the possibility that we have ends and not just desires and desire serving purposes, the possibility that there is a point and purpose to our lives, is never quite foreclosed, but in which we cannot but continue in a protracted state of suspicion that at most "There is a goal, but no way; what we call way is only wavering."[24] What Tarantino and Kafka as storytellers put in question is the possibility of there being any such thing as a directedness in human life toward goods on the achievement of which everything might turn for an agent. Is there a story to be told that goes one step further, portraying a world recognizable as our world, but devoid of goods and ends? It might seem that there could be no such story, since in it nothing of genuine significance could happen. But there is indeed such a story, one of the great novels of the twentieth century, unrecognized as such up till now only because written in Irish, a wonderfully impressive Irish whose translation presents unusual difficulties.

I refer to *Cré na Cille* by Máirtín Ó Cadhain (1906–70), published in 1949, made into a splendid film with English subtitles as *Graveyard Clay* (2007), and only recently translated into English.[25]

---

[24] Franz Kafka, *The Great Wall of China*, trans. W. and E. Muir, New York: Schocken Books, 1946.
[25] Máirtín Ó Cadhain, *Cré na Cille*, Dublin: Sáirséal and Dill; trans. Alan Titley as *The Dirty Dust*, New Haven, CN: Yale University Press, 2015, and trans. Liam Mac Con Iomaire and Tim Robinson as *Graveyard Clay*, New Haven, CN: Yale University Press, 2016.

Cré na Cille is a novel of many voices, voices of the dead in a graveyard on Ireland's Western seaboard, speaking sometimes to each other, sometimes to themselves, expressing feelings and concerns that they brought with them to the grave, enmities, resentments, anxieties, pleasure in the misfortunes of others, obsessions, pretensions, wishes to puncture the pretensions of others. The dead are endlessly what they were when alive.

Caitriona Pháidin, Ó Cadhain's central character, nurses several grievances, against her still living sister, against her son's mother-in-law, another inhabitant of the graveyard, and against her son for having had her buried in a fifteen shilling plot rather than in a more expensive one pound plot. When from time to time the newly dead and buried bring news of events among the living, Caitriona anxiously enquires whether her son has as yet arranged for the green basalt headstone for her grave on which her heart is set. Like the dreadful Caitriona, the other characters are moved by what they care about, by what they cannot help caring about, mocking others for what *they* care about, not because they appeal to some standard with regard to what is genuinely worth caring about, what is genuinely a good, but because mocking is among the few things that they enjoy. So Caitriona's son's mother-in-law, Nóra Sheáinín, complains that the schoolmaster is consumed by his interest in gossip that his widow, immediately after his death, had taken up with Bileachaí an Phosta, the mailman, instead of, as an educated man should, cultivating his mind. So Caitriona in turn mocks Nora's pretensions to culture. It is not that in this world of the dead nothing happens. There is even an election with candidates from the one pound plots, the fifteen shilling plots, and the half guinea (ten shillings and sixpence) plots, during which the half guinea candidate advances a Marxist analysis of the class structure of the graveyard, parodying Ó Cadhain's own political views. But his, like all the rhetoric, is nothing but self-serving self-expression, talk leading to nothing but more talk, so that on the novel's last pages there are still voices competing with more voices, but no finality and no prospect of finality.

What Ó Cadhain portrays is a world marked as much by its absences as by its presences. There are desires and objects of desire, there are purposeful activities, but there are no goods that the characters might have good reason to desire, no ends to pursue that would give their activities point and purpose and their lives a directedness toward and beyond those ends. This is a horrifyingly deprived world in which the narratives of the characters' lives have lost their structure, so that their stories no longer have endings, while that this is how they endlessly are is the ending of the tale that Ó Cadhain tells. *Cré na Cille* is a work of great linguistic art, not only giving expression to his purposes as an artist, but vindicating those purposes just because it is a novel in which the writer achieves the end of the novelist's art in exemplary fashion. The voices in the novel speak only through Ó Cadhain's book, but he in making those voices heard, speaks as they cannot speak, acts as they cannot act, achieving just that finality in completing and perfecting his art which is wholly absent from his characters' afterlives. The author's ends and the ends of his art are what is left out of his book.

That this is so might suggest that *Cré na Cille* can be read as a striking confirmation of the philosophical theses about how human activities and lives are structured that I have been advancing and defending. But to say this would be misleading. For it would suggest that such theses can be adequately spelled out and understood independently of and prior to telling those stories that provide examples of how and why those theses find application in our practical lives, and this would be a mistake. Stories and theses, stories and theses about rule-following and rule-breaking, about achieving and failing to achieve goods, have to be understood together or not at all. There is therefore of course a danger in treating stories as in themselves, without reference to rules or maxims, sources of practical guidance. We may, for example, too easily cast ourselves imaginatively in roles that provide pretexts for indulging desire for objects that we have no good reason to desire. Yet if we are to understand adequately why we do so, not just in general, but in particular instances, we will only be able to do so by both finding application for the relevant theses and discovering the true story to be told about those segments of our lives in which we became storytelling self-deceivers.

This, however, is a task whose nature and whose difficulty varies from culture to culture, since cultures themselves vary in their storytelling practices, as to who it is that tells stories to whom and as to what stories they tell. It is through listening to and reading stories of different kinds that children and young adults learn how to tell themselves stories in the course of answering such questions as 'What did I do today and what happened to me?' 'How did today's doings and happenings relate to those of past days, weeks, years?' and 'How do they point forward to tomorrow's doings and happenings?' So the young learn, or fail to learn, to imagine themselves as they were, as they are, and as they might become and the limits of their imagination set limits to their desires and to their practical reasoning. They learn to hope for the best that they can imagine, and they despair when they can imagine no good future. Because this is so, the storytelling resources of each culture are of great political and moral importance. Some cultures are rich in myth, others not. Some recapture their shared past more adequately than others. Some develop theatrical and other literary genres that educate in storytelling, some genres that entertain by trivializing.

So it is that children and adults come to see themselves and episodes in their lives in comic, tragic, or even epic terms and to recognize differences between comedy and farce, tragedy and meaningless disaster, epic and romantic exaggeration masquerading as epic. So it is that they are rescued from illusion by satire, parody, and caricature. It is no accident that those philosophers who have thrown most light on the political and moral life, Aristotle, Aquinas, and Marx have each provided ways of understanding ourselves that require a retelling of the stories of our lives, the replacement of a less by a more adequate narrative. Yet it can happen, and it has happened in the culture of advanced modernity, that the practices of storytelling become such that they no longer provide resources for individuals struggling to narrate the story of their own lives, and this both because of what has happened to storytelling and what has happened to those lives. Begin with the shaping and structure of those lives.

I noted earlier that one large difference between every culture of advanced modernity and other cultures is the degree and nature of its compartmentalizations. What then happens to storytelling in such a culture? It too is assigned to various compartments in each of which which it functions very differently. So there are stories to be told to children, stories read in school and college literature classes as academic assignments, stories presented on television or cinema or theatre as entertainment, stories recounted in the news media for political significance or human interest ('Woman keeps zebra in back yard', 'Forty-seven die in fire of unknown origin'), all of them stories about others. What is too often missing is any conception of listening to stories and telling stories as activities of crucial importance to each of us in understanding ourselves and others, any sense of how much we need to learn first to listen and then to narrate.

Yet this is after all just one more aspect of the dominant culture that is inimical to those relationships that sustain and are sustained by the exercise of the virtues, a counterpart to other such aspects that we had already identified. The exploitative structures of both free market and state capitalism make it often difficult and sometimes impossible to achieve the goods of the workplace through excellent work. The political structures of modern states that exclude most citizens from participation in extended and informed deliberation on issues of crucial importance to their lives make it often difficult and sometimes impossible to achieve the goods of local community. The influence of Morality in normative and evaluative thinking makes it often difficult and sometimes impossible for the claims of the virtues to be understood, let alone acknowledged in our common lives. So too the culture that entertains and distracts makes it often difficult and sometimes impossible to develop those imaginative powers that are of the first importance for living the life of the virtues. We therefore have to live *against* the cultural grain, just as we have to learn to act as economic, political, and moral antagonists of the dominant order. We can only learn how so to act, not from abstract theorizing, but in key part from the stories of those who in various very different modern social contexts have discovered what had to be done, if essential human goods were to be achieved, and what the virtues therefore required of them, so making themselves into critics and antagonists of the established order. I therefore need to proceed beyond my theoretical conclusions to give accounts of some exemplary lives. Before I can do this, I have to confront the objection that by so doing I am myself surrendering to illusion. I have already responded to the arguments against any narrative understanding of human life advanced by Sartre. But more powerful philosophical arguments tending to the same conclusion have been advanced more recently from within both the phenomenological and the analytic tradition.

4.13   Continuing disagreements concerning narrative

Those from within the phenomenological tradition were the work of László Tengelyi in his *The Wild Region in Life-History*.[26] Tengelyi draws upon both Husserl and Merleau-Ponty in constructing a view of the self which leads him to reject my account of narrative. Husserl had observed uncontroversially that there is that given in the present otherness of the other which is never appropriable by me, a thought developed in more striking and controversial terms by Levinas. Merleau-Ponty had moved beyond this thought of Husserl in another direction. In encountering the bodily other, we encounter what is "beyond the objective body as the sense of the painting is beyond the canvas,"[27] something that we cannot always reckon with in our own terms because it has a strangeness that has not yet been and sometimes cannot be culturally domesticated within our familiar forms. Reflecting on what he had learned from Mauss and Lévi-Strauss, Merleau-Ponty had gone on to write of a "wild region" in human life beyond all

---

[26] László Tengelyi, *The Wild Region in Life-History*, trans. G. Kállay with the author, Evanston, IL: Northwestern University Press, 2004.

[27] Maurice Merleau-Ponty, *Le visible et l'invisible*, Paris: Gallimard, 1964, p. 167, quoted by Tengelyi, p. 104.

particular cultures, the region from which those cultures originate. Tengelyi follows Merleau-Ponty in speaking of what he calls the wild as that
in our lived experience without which we could not live and think as we
do, without which our lives would lack the meanings and forms that they
have, but which itself remains beyond all culturally determinate forms.
How does this bear upon his rejection of my understanding of lives as
"enacted dramatic narratives" in *After Virtue* and elsewhere?

Tengelyi argues that "the ground of selfhood is to be sought not in
the unity of a narrated life story, or in life as a complex of told stories,
but in life as a totality of lived experiences,"[28] and that there is that in
those experiences which cannot find expression in narrative. There are key
moments in our lives, moments when something radically new begins,
something with "ingredients that do not lend themselves to the retroactive
constitution of such a sequence" in a narrative.[29] In the stories that we tell
subsequently, these "recalcitrant shreds of sense" may be ignored, dismissed,
or repressed, but they leave significant traces in our lives and may reemerge
in striking ways. To understand life in narrative terms is to confer upon it a
coherence that it does not possess and to disguise that in it which belongs
to the wild.

Tengelyi is of course right in holding that there are in every life experiences whose significance we do not know how to spell out, let alone
to reckon with, experiences that threaten the coherence of our lives. He is
right too in stressing our tendency to disguise from ourselves our awareness
of their significance and in pointing out that one way in which we do this
is by telling stories that conceal their place in our lives. Yet none of this
is incompatible with my central contention. For how we reckon or fail to
reckon with such experiences is a central issue for all of us, and there is
always a story to be told about it. We can acknowledge the incoherence
and unintelligibility of this or that aspect of our lives in a coherent and
intelligible narrative without disguising or misrepresenting the incoherence
and unintelligibility. Indeed there is no other way of acknowledging them
adequately.

A very different criticism of my use of the notion of narrative has
been made by Galen Strawson in his essay "Against Narrativity,"[30] where
his arguments are principally directed against positions taken by Charles
Taylor and Paul Ricoeur –Ricoeur is also discussed by Tengelyi – and by the
psychiatrist Oliver Sacks, and the psychologist Jerome Bruner, but where

[28] Tengelyi, *The Wild Region in Life-History*, p. xix.   [29] Ibid., p. xxxi.
[30] Galen Strawson, "Against Narrativity," in *The Self?*, ed. Galen Strawson, Oxford: Blackwell, 2005,
pp. 63–86.

I am identified as "the founding figure in the modern Narrativity camp." This latter is a little misleading, since I was and am very much indebted to Taylor, Ricoeur, Sacks, and Bruner. Strawson rejects two theses which he takes it that some or all of us endorse. The first is what he calls the psychological Narrativity thesis, "that human beings typically see or live or experience their lives as a narrative or story of some sort, or at least as a collection of stories." The second is the ethical Narrativity thesis "that experiencing or conceiving one's life as a narrative is a good thing; a richly Narrative outlook is essential to a well-lived life."[31]

Strawson's rejection of both theses is stated in terms of two distinctions. The first is between "one's experience of oneself when one is considering oneself principally as a human being taken as a whole, and one's experience of oneself when one is considering oneself principally as an inner mental entity or 'self' of some sort – I'll call this one's self-experience."[32] The second is between two forms of self-experience, the Diachronic in which one "figures oneself, considered as a self, as something that was there in the (further) past and will be there in the (further) future" and the Episodic in which "one has little or no sense that the self that one is was there in the (further) past and will be there in the future." Those whose self-experience is or is mostly Episodic, for whom the self that they once were is not the self that they are now and for whom neither is the self that they may become – Henry James and Proust are among those cited as providing examples – "are likely to have no particular tendency to see their lives in Narrative terms."[33] Strawson counts himself among the latter and concludes that, as a generalization about human beings, the psychological thesis is false. For those for whom it does not hold, it makes no sense to evaluate their lives in narrative terms and in fact a life thought of and evaluated in this way is inferior to certain other kinds of life. By contrast "the truly happy-go-lucky, see-what-comes-along-lives are among the best there are, vivid, blessed, profound . . . a gift for friendship is shown in how one is in the present."[34] He therefore rejects among other versions of the narrative view my claim that to ask "What is the good for me?" is to ask how my life, understood as having the unity that is disclosed in its narrative, might best be brought to completion.[35]

The disagreements that Strawson and I have with each other's conception of the self are rooted in fundamental differences in the philosophy of mind on issues that require further philosophical attention – personal

---

[31] Ibid., p. 63.   [32] Ibid., p. 64.   [33] Ibid., p. 65.   [34] Ibid., pp. 84–85.
[35] Ibid., pp. 71–72.

identity, self-knowledge, intention – and these I cannot pursue here. However, Strawson's remarks on narrativity reveal some misunderstanding of
my position. It is not at all my view that human beings most of the time
experience their lives as narratives, something that would involve a remarkable and unfortunate degree of self-dramatization. But happily most of us
are not such self-dramatizers. We generally become aware of the narrative
structure of our lives infrequently and in either of two ways, when we
reflect upon how to make ourselves intelligible to others by telling them
the relevant parts of our story or when we have some particular reason to
ask 'How has my life gone so far?' and 'How must I act if it is to go well in
future?' It is in answering these sometimes harsh practical questions that
the question 'What is the good for me?' with its narrative presuppositions
is also answered. What occasions the asking of these questions is a need
to make critical choices at points in our lives in which alternative futures
open up, and here I once again have to reiterate what I said earlier.

For all of us, when we become adults or even before that, we have to
decide on how to earn our living: Do I stay to work on the farm or become
an apprentice carpenter or emigrate to another country? For some, the
unexpected loss of a job in middle age or a life-threatening illness or the
death of someone on whom we have depended gives reason to ask equally
searching questions. For some, either the discovery of new possibilities, of
what might be achieved by organizing a trade union branch or by learning
to paint, may elicit them. It is in attempting to answer them that we draw
upon our history, upon our knowledge of what we have hitherto done and
been, of what we have learned about our capacities and our limitations,
about the errors to which we are prone and the resources that we possess.
Agents do of course vary a great deal in the way in which they pose and
answer these questions. There are different modes of intelligent reflection,
and for many how they reflect is as much a matter of what they do as
of what they say, of what they leave unexpressed as of what they express.
Someone, however, who on such occasions of crisis and choice failed to
ask these questions, and to draw upon the narrative of her or his life in
relevant ways, would be lacking in practical intelligence.

What Strawson takes to be at issue in asking whether and how far
someone thinks of or experiences her or his life in narrative terms is
therefore significantly different from what I take to be at issue. What then of
Strawson's praise for "truly happy-go-lucky, see-what-comes-along-lives"?
If Strawson were to justify that praise, he would have to give us examples
of such lives spelled out in some detail, that is, he would have to provide
us with narratives on which he could draw to respond to key objections to

his thesis. Even a life lived episodically has a history and can be evaluated as a life. About the kind of life that Strawson praises, it is to the point to remark that those who live them characteristically are able to do so only because others who are not leading happy-go-lucky lives are sustaining the relationships and institutions that make their lives possible. Families, schools, workplaces, clinics, theatres, and sports teams only thrive if there are not too many happy-go-lucky lives. So the questions arise: What are the happy-go-lucky able to say in explaining and justifying their lives, when they are called to account by those others? What has Strawson to say on their behalf?

I do not doubt that Tengelyi and Strawson will have telling replies to my responses to their responses to my theses about narratives. Here once again there is ongoing enquiry. But where narrative is concerned, we need not only more arguments, but also more narratives. For if it is true, as I have claimed, that we understand both the vicissitudes of our desires and the course and outcomes of our practical reasoning in narrative terms, then this is best demonstrated, not by philosophical arguments, necessary as those are, but by illuminating examples of narratives of the relevant kind, narratives that make the actions of particular agents intelligible and show them to be justified or unjustified.

CHAPTER 5

Four narratives

5.1   Introductory

A single, if complex, theoretical conclusion emerged from the first four chapters of this essay. It is that agents do well only if and when they act to satisfy only those desires whose objects they have good reason to desire, that only agents who are sound and effective practical reasoners so act, that such agents must be disposed to act as the virtues require, and that such agents will be directed in their actions toward the achievement of their final end. This sounds like a complex platitude, until it is spelled out. But these are not four independent sets of conditions that agents must satisfy if they are to act rightly and well. Spell out any one of them adequately and in so doing you will also have to spell out the other three. Moreover, like all theoretical conclusions in politics and ethics, this one can be understood adequately only by attention to the detail of particular cases that in significant ways exemplify it, not imaginary examples, but real examples. Understanding such conclusions is inseparable from knowing how they find application. Yet such examples will be of agents who are, like the rest of us, not yet fully rational, who are still learning how to act rightly and well, and who therefore are more or less imperfect in all four respects. That they are so makes it possible for them on occasion to serve another purpose, that of exhibiting the relevance of the generalizations of theory to reflection by particular agents on the singularities of their own lives. And this is of peculiar interest when those agents are ones from whom we ourselves need to learn.

The four individuals whose stories I am going to recount, at least in part, were just such agents. Each had a singular history, yet one that throws light on other lives lived out in in very different circumstances. For each there is an adequate record of the relevant episodes in their history. All four are neither too close to us that our view of them is distorted by our own concerns, nor too distant that the relationship of their lives to ours is problematic. All four led untypical lives, confronting issues that many of us never confront. But each by their choices throws light on the everyday choices of everyday modern life. There is, of course, a certain arbitrariness in my picking out these four, but my aim is no more than to illustrate the part that narratives of others play in our understanding of practice. So what I am presenting is too selective to be adequate as biography, and the focus of my attention is very different from that of most biographers. But I am of course deeply indebted to their various biographers, both for the facts of their lives and for their illuminating perspectives. I begin with Vasily Grossman, born in Berdichev in Ukraine in 1905, continue with Sandra Day O'Connor, born in El Paso, Texas, in 1930, and with C. L. R. James, born in Trinidad in 1901, and end with Denis Faul, born in Louth in Ireland in 1932.

5.2 Vasily Grossman

Berdichev had been a center of Jewish culture for centuries, home to notable rabbis and home too to an educated class of secularized Jews. Grossman's parents belonged to that class, spoke Russian, not Yiddish, and gave their son a secular upbringing. His father was a chemical engineer, his mother a teacher of French. At some early point his parents separated and from 1910 to 1912 his mother took him to live in Switzerland. Like his mother he became a fluent French speaker. He was not yet twelve years old when the October revolution occurred and only fifteen at the close of the Civil War. From 1923 until the end of 1929, Grossman was a student of chemistry at Moscow State University, a period in which the Soviet leadership struggled over issues of agricultural collectivization and industrialization. The political history of those struggles was also the history of Stalin's rise to supreme dictatorial power. Some aspects of that rise to power and of Stalin's subsequent exercise of that power are notable. The first is the exclusion of any dissenting voices not only from the Central Committee of the Communist Party, but from all the leadership positions in both party and state. To what was assent required? To every detail of Stalin's policies on industrialization and on the measures needed to remake Soviet farming, so that it served the goals of industrialization, and to every detail of Stalin's claim that by following those policies a socialist order would be constructed, so that the Soviet Union was in the vanguard of human progress. Secondly, the ruthless use of terror against Stalin's rivals extended into a wider system of purges and punishments, institutionalized in the OGPU and the Gulag. But if we are impressed by this ruthlessness and by the scale of Stalin's crimes, as we certainly should be, we may fail to notice that Stalin's Russia could not have functioned as it did if it had been a society only of the terrified and of self-serving cynics. An immense number of Soviet citizens came to understand themselves and their everyday tasks, at least for the most part, just as Stalin intended them to understand them, among them the young Grossman. What did this entail? The claim made by the party leadership was that the path to future human flourishing was that taken by the Soviet Union, that human goods were to be ordered as the party ordered them. It was because and insofar as Soviet citizens assented to this, because and insofar as their practical reasoning conformed to the norms laid down by the party, that Stalin's Russia became to a remarkable extent Stalinist Russia.

Thirdly, because Stalin presented himself as the legitimate heir of Marx, Engels, and Lenin, the rhetoric through which he and his apologists presented their theoretical stances, the policies that embodied those stances, and the effects on Soviet daily life of those policies had to employ the same terms by which Marx, Engels, and Lenin had defined their commitments. But because Stalinism was in crucial respects at odds with the Marxism of Lenin, let alone with that of Marx and Engels, its rhetoric functioned so as to conceal the gap between Soviet realities and any truthful Marxist account of them, such as that supplied by Trotsky. Hence, the need for recurrent and obsessive denunciations of Trotskyism. Hence also some of the peculiar problems that confronted Soviet writers. Writers had been assigned the task of shaping the Soviet imagination, so that their readers would come to understand themselves in Stalinist terms. "The production of souls is more important than the production of tanks," declared Stalin in 1932, proposing a toast to writers as "the engineers of human souls." Grossman was to become just such a writer.

During his studies he had decided that it was not his vocation to become a chemical engineer. Already married when he graduated – the marriage lasted only until 1932 – and with a daughter born in 1930, a daughter at first brought up by his mother, he took a series of jobs, in a soap factory, as an inspector of mines, as a teacher of chemistry in a medical school in the Donbass region, and in the Sacco and Vanzetti Factory in Moscow. But already, before he graduated, he had been publishing articles in magazines and newspapers and his reading and thinking now became a counterpart to his writing. In 1929 he had read Tolstoy's *Death of Ivan Ilyich*, and the questions that Tolstoy asks about the relationship of death to everyday life became Grossman's questions. They are posed in the short story that first made Grossman well known, "V gorode Berdicheve" ("In the Town of Berdichev"), published in *Literaturnaya gazeta* in April 1934.

The setting for the story is Yatki, home of the poorest Jews in Berdichev, during the war between the Bolsheviks and the Poles. It has two heroines, the political commissar of a Red Army cavalry unit, whose pregnancy by a fellow soldier is too advanced for an abortion, and the Jewish wife and mother in whose home she gives birth. The political commissar is no longer the one who gives the orders, the one on whose skill and steadfastness others depend. She and her child are now dependent on the skills and steadfastness of the mother and the midwife. So how is she to be both good mother and good soldier? When her child is one week old, the Red Army unit has to move out of Berdichev, because the Poles are advancing, and she finds that she cannot refuse to go with them, even though it means abandoning her child. The Jewish wife and mother is at once dismayed and baffled: how could any mother act like this? Her husband sees and admires the political commissar's resoluteness. But neither has the last word. That is voiced in the crying of the child.

So Grossman leaves his readers with two unanswered questions. More generally, when they have to choose between goods of such very different kinds, how are they to do it? And, more particularly, when the choice is between the goods of children and family on the one hand and the good of the Soviet state on the other, what regrets and griefs must they put behind them? These were questions to which many of Grossman's readers must have had to give answers by choosing as they did in the course of their everyday lives, by the weight which they had given to various conflicting considerations in making those choices. What Grossman's story suggests is that those choices were sometimes deeply problematic, that some dilemmas of practical reasoning always remained unresolved. Yet it was a presupposition of Stalinist thinking that the good Soviet citizen's choices in ordering goods were unproblematic. What Stalin's leadership had provided was a way to think about oneself and one's choices as serving the goals set by that leadership, so that hard moral and metaphysical questions did not arise.

The year 1934 also saw the publication of Grossman's *Glyukauf*, a short novel about hardships endured by coal miners under the leadership of a Communist Party official who drives them to exhaustion and himself to death. It was published in the quarterly review, *Almanakh*, edited by Maxim Gorky, then the chief ornament of Stalin's cultural policies. Gorky's positive view of Grossman's writing was qualified by his criticism of what he took to be Grossman's naturalism. The naturalist supposes that by telling the truth about how things are, about present reality, she or he tells the truth *simpliciter*. But what matters is not so much this as the truth about what things are becoming, about the reality that will be, but is not yet. So Gorky, enunciating the doctrine of Socialist Realism, complained that "in *Glyukauf* the material governs the author and not the other way round." Grossman should, on Gorky's view, have asked "Which truth am I confirming? Which truth do I wish to triumph?"[1] The truth about Soviet realities to be confirmed by artists in general and writers in particular is that affirmed by the Central Committee of the Communist Party, that of the not yet. So Grossman still had to prove himself by showing that what he presented in imaginative terms gave expression to the Stalinist understanding of Russian social life. That he had done so became clear when in September 1937 he was admitted to membership in the Union of Soviet writers, which carried with it material rewards, including a large apartment in Moscow.

It would be a bad mistake to suppose that Grossman could only have achieved this by sacrificing his integrity. The genuine achievements of the Soviet regime and the worldview inculcated by Soviet journalism provided him and his contemporaries with a number of ways of justifying and excusing what were from any external point of view, among them of course that of Trotsky, moral crimes and irrationalities. Indeed this is how accusations of 'Trotskyism' in that period should be understood. To judge Soviet realities from any standpoint external to that defined by Stalin was in the Soviet Union in the 1930s to invite accusations of Trotskyism. As to what was involved in accusations of Trotskyism Grossman was well aware. In March 1933 his cousin, Nadya Almaz, who had worked in Moscow as assistant to the head of Profitern, the international Communist trade union organization, had been arrested by the OGPU and charged with Trotskyism, probably because she was in touch with Victor Serge, custodian of the ideals of 1917, who was arrested in 1933, sentenced to three years in exile, and then allowed to leave the Soviet Union. Nadya Almaz was similarly expelled from the Party and exiled for three years to Astrakhan. A few years later both would have been sent to the Gulag or executed. Grossman was among those questioned by an OGPU agent dealing with his

---

[1] Report of October 7, 1932, in the Gorky Archive, quoted in John Garrard and Carol Garrard, *The Bones of Berdichev: The Life and Fate of Vasily Grossman*, New York: The Free Press, 1996, pp. 105–107. I am deeply indebted both to the Garrards' biography and to Frank Ellis' *Vasiliyi Grossman: The Genesis and Evolution of a Russian Heretic*, Oxford/Providence, RI: Berg, 1994, for my understanding of the facts of Grossman's life.

cousin's case, so he could not have been unaware of the travesties that were being perpetrated. But what writers such as Grossman characteristically argued – how Grossman himself argued we do not know – was that great and rapid social change always involves some errors and injustices, that what matters overridingly is the end to which that change is directed, and that, if she or he contributes to that end by imaginative writing informed by the truth as she or he sees it, then she or he will contribute both to the achievement of that end and to overcoming error and injustice.

For some writers whose art and insight was such that they could only see Soviet realities as they in fact were, that argument was never compelling. And for every writer who for a time found that argument genuinely compelling there would come some moment at which it became impossible any longer both to tell the truth with imaginative power and integrity and to remain in good standing with the Writers' Union and indeed with Stalin, some moment of radical choice. In 1936 that moment had not yet arrived for Grossman. His practical reasoning proceeded from premises that were answers to questions of the form: 'By doing such and such will I develop my literary powers?' 'By doing such and such will I further my career as a writer?' 'By doing such and such will I further the good of my family members and friends?' 'By doing such and such will I contribute to achieving the goals of Soviet society, as the Party defines them?' and 'By doing such and such will I act as a good human being would act?' but questions posed not in these general and abstract terms, but in terms of the concrete detail of his own everyday life and circumstances. What always matters, both about individuals and about social orders, are the resources that they have within themselves for resolving dilemmas or for living with unresolved dilemmas, when considerations of these various kinds conflict. What Stalinist society imposed on those of its writers who over considerable periods of time attempted both to express their own imaginative vision and to secure the approval of the bureaucrats of the Writers' Union, the Party, and Stalin, was a double life, a life of oscillation, a life sometimes of dangerous risk taking, sometimes of self-serving silences, sometimes of self-serving speech. Such was Grossman's life.

How different from us, we may think. But in one respect this type of life is not unfamiliar. I noted earlier how in the contemporary social order our lives are compartmentalized, so that in one area of our lives, the workplace, say, we may allow ourselves to be governed by a very different set of norms from those to which we conform in another. Sometimes indeed those norms may be incompatible, but even in those cases we often move with remarkable ease between one area and another, without any loss of sincerity. So it seems to have been with those writers who were at once creative and Stalinist, such as Grossman.

Some of his friends among former members of the literary and philosophical group *Pereval* began reading more widely in philosophy. That group had been forced to dissolve in 1932, because of the challenge that it had mounted to Gorky-style Socialist Realism. The key ideas of *Pereval* were those of Alexander Voronsky. Gorky and Voronsky had once been literary allies in founding the journal *Krasnaya Nov'* in 1921. Unlike Gorky, a latecomer to the revolution, Voronsky had been a Bolshevik since 1904 and had suffered imprisonment and exile before taking part in the insurrection in Odessa in 1917. Unlike Gorky, he followed Trotsky and Lunacharsky rather than Stalin and took his own distinctive stance in the literary conflicts of the 1920s. It was Voronsky's claim that the arts are independent sources of knowledge and that theorists have to be open to learning from artists. He advanced this claim as a Marxist, taking it that what the arts disclose about the ugliness and the beauty of human realities and what Marx's theory discloses complement and reinforce one another. "The artist does not invent the beautiful, he finds it in reality with his special sensitivity."[2]

The criteria by which the artist judges intuitively, the criteria that guide the artist in creating, are objective. "The beautiful is anything that gives us joy through its life, its abundance, unruliness, growth, and development."[3] The implication was clear. The party needs on occasion to learn from the artist and always to respect the artist's independence and integrity. Voronsky was expelled from the party in 1928, recanted, and was readmitted, later was expelled again, and was then executed in 1937. His achievement was to make it impossible for writers and other artists to ignore his challenge. They were at least for a time unable to define their commitments without reference to his as well as to Stalin's and Gorky's. So Voronsky played a key part both in defining the double life of the Soviet writer and in keeping writers aware of their duplicity. Grossman's duplicity was especially notable when in 1937, at the time of the trials of the old Bolshevik leaders, he signed a letter, published in *Literaturnaya gazeta*, denouncing the "Trotsky-Bukharin conspiracy" and calling for the death penalty for those on trial.

In February 1938 at the height of the Stalinist terror, Grossman's wife – his second wife – was arrested by the NKVD. Her former husband, Boris Guber, had been a member of *Pereval* and a number of *Perevaltsy* were either executed, as Guber was, or sent to the Gulag. Grossman's silence in

---

[2] Alexander Voronsky, *Art as the Cognition of Life: Selected Writings 1911–1936*, trans. and ed. F. S. Choate, Oak Park, MI: Mehring Books, 1998, p. 368.
[3] Ibid.

the case of his *Perevaltsy* friends contrasted with his courage in the case of his wife. He not only went to the NKVD offices to argue for her innocence and her release, but appealed by letter directly to Yezhov, the head of the NKVD, actions that could well have led to his own arrest. In fact he was successful and Olga Mikhailovna was set free in the late summer of 1938 so that they could resume their privileged lives as members of the Stalinist literary elite.

I spoke earlier of Grossman – and others – as leading a double life. It is now possible to characterize that duplicity a little further. For much of the time he lives, thinks, and acts *as if* a wholly convinced Stalinist, not someone on whom Stalinism has been imposed. Yet for some of the time he thinks, acts, and writes *as if* Voronsky's teaching were true, *as if* his own perceptive vision of how things are enabled him to recognize aspects of social reality that were deeply incompatible with Stalinism's claims. Something turns on how that 'as if' is to be understood. Was Grossman, even while apparently an undoubting Stalinist, troubled by aesthetically grounded doubts? Or did he move easily between his two standpoints, for most of the time an undoubting Stalinist, for some of the time something very different, yet able to fend off awareness of his duplicity?

Those leading such a double life argue to practical conclusions at this or that particular time from premises incompatible with those from which they argue at certain other times. The goods that provide them with their reasons for concluding as they do at this or that particular time are at other times dismissed as apparent, but not real goods, as desired, but not genuinely desirable. Such agents may be consistent, even inflexibly consistent rational agents in each part of their divided lives. It is in respect of those lives as a whole that they fail in practical rationality, something that they may disguise from themselves over long periods. But they are always liable to encounter situations in which the compartmentalization of their lives breaks down, moments when choices between incompatible goods become inescapable. Responses to such situations may be of at least three kinds.

They may simply choose that alternative, if there is one, that will allow them to continue as comfortably as possible in their duplicity, although no longer able to disguise their incoherence from themselves. From now on they are cynical hypocrites. Or they may instead choose between the alternatives in such a way as to render their lives coherent, although only in this particular area in which choice has become inescapable. Or they may, perhaps with difficulty, in pondering this particular choice, recognize the overall duplicity of their lives and by the choice that they make put an end to their duplicity. There were Stalinists of all three kinds alongside the self-deceived Stalinist faithful. It was Grossman's fate to survive the years of terror in the late 1930s and to discover such moments of existential choice only during his war service from 1941 onwards and in the aftermath of the war.

During those years of terror, writers, like composers and painters, were peculiarly vulnerable because of the strong personal interest that Stalin took in their work. Akhmatova, the greatest Russian poet of the century, lived unpublished and in poverty under Stalin's regime, until Stalin approved the publication of *From Six Books* in a small edition in 1939. In 1938 her son had been sentenced to a five-year prison term and an arrest order for her was about to be issued when Stalin countermanded it. Pasternak, who had refused to accept the doctrines of Socialist Realism, to his very great credit refused to sign a letter from the Writers' Union demanding the death penalty for General Yakir and Marshal Tukhachevsky in 1937. He feared terrible consequences for himself and his family, but none ensued. When Stalin found Pasternak's name on a list of those to be executed, he ordered that it be taken off, saying," Let that inhabitant of the clouds live!" Mandelstam, who had defied Stalin in 1934 by circulating a poem that ridiculed him, was by contrast imprisoned and died as a prisoner late in 1938. When Grossman's novel *Stepan Kol'chugin*, a portrayal of revolutionary life in Russia from 1905–1916, was widely praised and selected as a finalist for the Stalin Prize in 1940, Stalin intervened to veto any award to Grossman, calling his standpoint Menshevik.

What Grossman cared about during the 1930s, what gave him reasons for choosing and acting as he did, was at least fourfold. There were his personal ties: to his second wife and his stepson, to his mother who, though far from well-to-do, had brought up his daughter, to his daughter, to his father, to his cousin Nadya, who returned embittered from her exile in 1939, and to a variety of friends. Secondly, there was his genuine devotion to the Soviet project of building socialism, a devotion shared by the huge majority of Soviet citizens, even when sharply critical or cynical about this or that aspect of their lives. Thirdly, there was his commitment to his career as a writer and his deep reluctance to act so as to hinder that career. And, finally, there was his commitment to his art, the art of the short story writer and the novelist. What would happen if he had to choose between any one of these and one or more of the others? This he was to find out in stages.

One notable failure was in prudence. Soon after Nazi Germany invaded the Soviet Union on June 22, 1941, Grossman must have realized that Berdichev, where his mother lived, would soon be occupied, and he had the resources to move her and her mentally disabled niece to a place of safety. His wife had argued that there was no room for anyone else in their tiny Moscow apartment and, perhaps because of this, Grossman failed to act before the Germans occupied Berdichev. His mother, her niece, and all his relatives there suffered the common fate of the 30,000 Jews of Berdichev in September 1941. For this Grossman never forgave himself, and it was immediately after the occupation of Berdichev that he volunteered as a private soldier. What the military made of him was a journalist, a war correspondent for *Krasnaya zvezda, Red Star*, moving with frontline troops from battle to battle. It was to *Red Star* that millions of Russians, both civilian readers and the troops themselves, went for their daily war news, and Grossman was notable among those journalists who acquired avid readers. As both journalist and soldier, he consistently acted with great courage and was decorated both for his journalistic achievements and for his actions in combat.

Stalin had refused to believe that Hitler was about to invade the Soviet Union and had left his armed forces unprepared. His insistence on the control of the military by the party had further hindered the military response to the invasion. In the weeks that it took to overcome confusion and panic, before a unified and effective military leadership took charge and military and civilian resistance was mobilized in every sector, the *Wehrmacht* occupied much of the Ukraine and advanced steadily toward Moscow. What Grossman observed and reported in this first period was not only panic and confusion, but the emergence of a remarkable and shared will to resist. What he observed and reported as the war progressed through two epic battles, those of Stalingrad and Kursk, and hundreds of lesser engagements were example after example of the exercise of the virtues, of resourcefulness and judgment in the face of the unexpected, of courage and self-sacrifice as everyday virtues, of justice and friendship in conditions of great difficulty and hazard, and of these as exercised toward a common overriding end, while at the same time brutality, ruthlessness, self-serving avoidance of danger, and bureaucratic stupidity were also part of the fabric of life. Notably, he recorded the crimes of Soviet troops against German civilians in the closing phases of the war as faithfully as he had the crimes of German troops against Russian civilians. All this Grossman communicated without moralism through his reports from the frontline – some later published as *Stalingrad Sketches* – and in a novel, *The People are Immortal*, published in installments in *Red Star*.[4]

[4] For Grossman's wartime writings, see *A Writer at War: Vasily Grossman with the Red Army 1941–1945*, ed. and trans. A. Beevor and L. Vinogradova, London: Harvill Press, 2005.

It was as the Red Army recovered the lost territories that Grossman discovered the facts of the Holocaust, of the systematic mass murder of Jews, first when he returned to Berdichev, later when he reported on Treblinka. That report, "The Hell of Treblinka," first published in *Znamya* in 1944, was introduced as evidence at the Nuremburg trials. Stalin had allowed the creation of a Jewish Anti-Fascist Committee in 1941 for propaganda purposes. Grossman had contributed to its Yiddish newspaper, *Einigkeit*, and in 1943, as a member of its Literary Commission, joined with Ilya Ehrenburg in compiling a record of the Holocaust on Russian territory, which they planned to publish as *The Black Book*. Grossman's Jewish identity now found expression in a deeply felt responsibility to all the Jewish dead. He later expressed a desire to be buried in a Jewish cemetery.

It is one of the paradoxes of war that, at least for those fighting in wars that they take to be just, the disciplines and constraints of war can be felt as liberating. There is a shared overriding good to which all other goods have to be subordinated. The role and the responsibilities of each member of a unit are well defined. What each owes to others and can expect from others is generally not matter for debate. So, given the final goal and the set of constraints that are shared, individuals act as rational agents and do so in solidarity not only with those close to them in action, but with all those engaged in the same enterprise. It is when wars end and the tasks imposed by victory or defeat are confronted that some individuals find themselves with questions that, to their surprise, they are no longer sure how to answer. So it was in a number of countries in 1945. So it was notably in the Soviet Union and not only because the war had ended.

It was among Stalin's central concerns that the history of the war should be written so as to disguise some key realities of that war. Any memory of Stalin's own military bungling or of those episodes in the war which had put in question Stalin's actions or the role of the Party was to be erased, so far as possible, from Soviet consciousness. The policies which gave expression to Stalin's postwar concerns had an effect on Grossman in three ways. First, the doctrines of Socialist Realism in their crudest form were reasserted and imposed on writers, composers, and painters by A. A. Zhdanov, to whom, until his death in 1948, Stalin entrusted the implementation of his cultural policies. Here Grossman was not made an object of public humiliation, as were Akhmatova and Zoschenko, now denied publication altogether, but he had to negotiate his way carefully toward publication, exposed to the criticism of Stalinist hacks. Secondly, the publication of *The Black Book* was first delayed and then prohibited. All attempts to commemorate the fate of Soviet Jews were met by declarations that no group in Russia deserved distinctive commemoration, declarations that were a mask for Stalin's

anti-Semitism and the growing anti-Semitism of the Party. Members of
the Jewish Anti-Fascist Committee were arrested or killed and the Committee itself dissolved. Yiddish books were no longer published and the
Writers' Union disowned its Yiddish writers. Jews increasingly became victims, most notably and finally in the prosecution of Jewish physicians for
the so-called Doctors' Plot in the months before Stalin's death in March
1953. Had Stalin not died, Grossman too might have become such a victim,
something that he no doubt had in mind when he allowed his name to be
added to a letter calling for the severest punishment of the falsely accused
physicians. In spite of his awareness of his Jewish identity, conformism to
the Stalinist norms was a price for survival that he was still prepared to pay.

   At stake was not only his life, but also the publication of his novel,
For a Just Cause, at first titled *Stalingrad*, now retitled at the suggestion of
Alexander Fadeyev, head of the Writers' Union. For a third area in which
Grossman encountered the negative effects of Stalin's determination to
control Soviet memory was as a chronicler of the battle of Stalingrad. Parts
of his novel had already been published in *Novy Mir* in 1946, 1948, and
1949, when he submitted the novel as a whole for publication. Rewriting
after rewriting was demanded. And rewriting after rewriting took place.
At one point Grossman was telephoned by General Rodimtsev, who had
commanded the 13th Guards at Stalingrad, the unit to which Grossman
had been attached, to warn him that Mikhail Suslov had invited him to
comment on the manuscript,[5] evidence that the scrutiny of Grossman's
narrative was from the highest level. But when the final section of *For a
Just Cause* was published, an initially favorable response was followed by
denunciations. Fadeyev reversed himself and the consequences for Grossman appeared grim. But at this point Stalin died. and although attacks on
Grossman continued – Fadeyev now accused him, among other things, of
having underestimated the part played by the Party at Stalingrad and of
identifying with the antiMarxist views of two of his characters – Grossman
was able to continue with his career.

   How then should *For a Just Cause* in its final version be read? Both
Russian and Western readers have been divided in their verdicts, some
dismissing it as no more than a conventional Soviet novel, some seeing
in it an anticipation of the radical critique of Soviet society delivered
in *Life and Fate*. Who is right? The answer is that both are right in
some measure, that the novel, like Grossman himself up to this point, is
ambiguous. Grossman had been and was both a conformist and a rebel,

---

   [5] Garrard and Garrard, *The Bones of Berdichev*, p. 223.

oscillating and compromising. But as he began to write *Life and Fate,* he disambiguated both his work and himself. I do not mean by this that he now deliberately set himself at odds with the regime – far from it. For one thing the regime changed after Stalin's death, from a brief period of collective leadership to Khrushchev's ascendancy, marked dramatically by his 1956 speech denouncing Stalin, to the rehabilitations and releases of many thousands from the Gulag and the resultant hopes for cultural openness, to the reaction against Khrushchev in the Party leadership and the death of those hopes. So too in the Writers' Union there was corresponding change, marked dramatically at the outset by Fadeyev's apology for the wrongs that he had done to other writers, including Grossman, and by subsequent reflections of the changing attitudes of the Party leadership. Through all this Grossman continued to live and work in a way that deferred to the limitations imposed by the regime, except, from now on, in one crucial respect.

He had now committed himself unconditionally to writing a novel about the war that would be truthful from beginning to end. What then is it for an historical novelist to be truthful? It is first of all to be careful that her or his narrative is not merely consistent with, but informed by the best historical knowledge available as to how things were at the relevant times and places. It is, secondly, to be imaginatively faithful in communicating how things were variously seen and felt by those inhabiting that particular past, so that characters who are fictions, who are imagined, enable the reader to understand what it would have been to be just such an actual inhabitant of that past. It is, thirdly, to avoid sentimentality, to refuse to allow irrelevant feeling to romanticize or to vulgarize or to domesticate the past. Such novels give expression both to the feelings of the characters portrayed and to the novelist's own feelings. Those feelings cannot but embody or presuppose judgments about what it is most important to care about and why it is important so to care. Given these requirements, the truthful historical novelist will always do more than merely describe, or rather her or his descriptions will be such that, once they have been grasped, there is no further task of evaluation. His descriptions are evaluations. The realism of the truthful historical novelist is more and other than naturalism.

In saying this, I am of course so far concurring with the proponents of socialist realism. Writing in 1955, Lukács argued that what the natural-ist lacks is a sense of perspective. It is the perspective of the writer that determines "the course and content" of her or his narrative, "the direc-tion in which characters develop, the possibilities that are realized or left unrealized."[6] What Lukács did not say and perhaps could not have said is that such a perspective requires commitment to an evaluative standpoint, an ability to distinguish not only the good and the better from the bad and the worse, but also the various kinds and degrees of badness, deceit, and self-deceit, incompetence and thoughtlessness, deliberate evil and weakness in collaborating with evil, and the masks which each of these on occasion wears. For Lukács had in his time carefully averted his eyes from a great many evils. Grossman no longer averted his eyes.

So what is the relevance of all this to his practical reasoning? Grossman could not be truthful in his novel without becoming truthful about the narrative of his own life. Too many episodes in that life coincided with episodes in his novel. What the novel put on record was how he had learned to order goods in particular situations during his war service, something learned often enough from failures and mistakes. He had learned what he had good reason to desire and to do, and this knowledge informed his choices and his activities during the years when he was writing his novel. His practical arguments and decisions as a writer reproduce and reiterate the practical arguments and decisions of those from whom he had learned most as journalist and soldier. So all else became subordinated to a single aim. If and insofar as he now compromises with the regime, it is no longer because he is a divided self, but because he has accepted one overriding responsibility, that of completing his novel in the service of the good of truthfulness.

I have spoken of Grossman's novel as an historical novel and such it was and is. But it could not escape also being a novel about the Soviet present. For in spite of their repudiation of Stalin, the leadership of the USSR legitimated itself by appeal to an often fictitious history of how things had developed after Lenin's death and of the Party's role throughout. So although the regime was anxious not to appear repressive, there were strongly enforced limits to cultural openness. It became part of Soviet academic and literary culture to know how far one could go, not just in respect of what was said, but with regard to those to whom one spoke or within whose hearing one spoke. The smuggling of the text of Pasternak's *Doctor Zhivago* out of Russia, its publication in Italy, its translations, and the Nobel Prize that was awarded to Pasternak both alarmed and outraged the regime's ideological caretakers. *Life and Fate* was well designed to alarm them even more. Why so?

[6] Georg Lukács, "The Ideology of Modernism," in *Realism in Our Time*, New York: Harper & Row, 1964, trans. J. Mander and N. Mander from *Probleme der Realismus*, Berlin: Aufbau Verlag, 1955, and reprinted in *The Lukács Reader*, ed. A. Kadarkay, Oxford: Blackwell, 1995, pp. 200 and 192.

First and most obviously because it catalogues fully the crimes and defects of the Soviet regime, the monstrous mass murders and cruelties of Stalinism, the dishonesties, indeed the bureaucratization of dishonesty, the crippling of the Red Army by Stalin's purge of the officer corps, the ineptitude of Stalin and of the Party in the first months of the war, the viciousness of Russian and especially Ukrainian anti-Semitism, the viciousness of Russian and especially Ukrainian collaboration with the Germans. Nothing is omitted, and all these evils are presented in memorably vivid terms and through telling examples. Grossman goes very much further than Khrushchev had done. It might therefore seem that *Life and Fate* is a straightforwardly anti-Soviet novel. But to reads it as such would also be to make a serious mistake. This was not what Grossman intended and indeed this is not how the authorities read his novel. Grossman had looked forward to its publication and was surprised and disappointed by the response of the regime. So what did elicit that response?

What the authorities could not allow was the publication of *Life and Fate* at that particular time or in any future foreseeable by them. For while Khrushchev's revisionism had unleashed a new kind of questioning and an openness to rethinking a wide range of social and cultural issues, those in authority were at best ambivalent about this, recognizing some measure of questioning as inevitable and even welcome, but only insofar as it remained under their control and within the increasingly narrow limits that they imposed. *Life and Fate* by contrast invited its readers to engage in open and radical questioning of the whole Soviet enterprise. It did not and does not prescribe any particular set of answers – proSoviet or antiSoviet – to its questions and it leaves open the possibility of a newly critical form of Soviet life and thought still inspired by and directed toward some version of the goals of the October revolution. But what *Life and Fate* would have undermined was anything close to the official Khrushchevite version of Soviet life and Soviet history. Its remarkable imaginative power was therefore an immediate danger to the regime.

Critics have compared its overall scope and ambition to Tolstoy's in *War and Peace* and Grossman's art in portraying character to Chekhov's. But the readers whom he addressed were very different from Tolstoy's or Chekhov's, scarred by experiences unknown to their readers, and invited by Grossman to see themselves in his characters while asking his, Grossman's, questions. The novel begins in a Nazi concentration camp, where Russian prisoners of war are held alongside political prisoners and common criminals. That camp, where things are so contrived by the SS that it is the prisoners themselves who administer the camp and cooperate in sustaining the evil, is an image of the power of evil. When, later on, Liss, the camp commandant, argues compellingly to the still faithful old Bolshevik, Mostovskoy, who had been captured at Stalingrad, that Stalin's Russia is the mirror image of Hitler's Germany, that each values what the other values, the case that has to be answered has been made. But Mostovskoy also has to respond to the arguments of other Russian prisoners, of Chernetsov, the former Menshevik, and of Ikonnikov, the disillusioned Tolstoyan, whose pursuit of the questions "What is 'good'? 'Good' for whom? Is there a common good – the same for all . . . ? Or is my good your evil?" had led him to dismiss all philosophical and religious answers, while discovering that when evil is defeated it can only be by "the powerlessness of kindness, of senseless kindness."[7]

Life and Fate is not a work of philosophy, of abstraction. The reader moves through many different kinds of scene, responds to many different kinds of character, in the street by street fighting of Stalingrad, in the discussions of staff officers behind the lines, in the theoretical and experimental enquiries of physicists, in the political intrigues of Soviet science, in a discussion of the merits of Chekhov, in love affairs that go well and love affairs that go badly, in police interrogations that go badly and walks in the countryside that go well, in jokes and sneers and memories and griefs and deaths. Remember that the reader is to engage in questioning, not to assent to conclusions, but some conclusions are inescapable. "Let's begin with respect, compassion and love for the individual," says the mathematician, Sokolov, in the course of his praise of Chekhov.

Alexandra Vladimirovna, whom we first meet early in Part One, we last encounter nearly eight hundred pages later (in the English translation), as an old woman "wondering why the future of those she loved was so obscure and the past so full of mistakes, not realizing that this very obscurity and unhappiness concealed a strange hope and clarity, not realizing that in the depths of her soul she already knew the meaning of both her own life and the lives of her nearest and dearest."[8] What she already knew was that it is in living and dying as human beings that we achieve an "eternal and bitter victory" over the destructive forces of history. But what, then, are the qualities that enable us to live and die as human beings? They are certainly not just "respect, compassion and love for the individual." For one thing it matters enormously who won the battle of Stalingrad. "Stalingrad was to determine future social systems and philosophies of history." It matters

---

[7]   Vasily Grossman, *Life and Fate*, trans. Robert Chandler, New York: New York Review Books, 2006, Part One, 1–4, 67, Part Two, 14–15.

[8]   Grossman, *Life and Fate*, trans. Chandler, Part Three, 60.

too how the battle was won and that the story should be told truthfully. So the virtues of the soldier's life and the virtues of the writer's life must be among those qualities. But, given this, what then is the Russian reader to make of the social system and the philosophy of history that had in fact resulted from Stalingrad eighteen years later?

Grossman had already published extracts from *Life and Fate*, when he submitted it for publication to the editor of *Znamya* – he already had a contract with *Znamya* – in October, 1960. In January, 1961, he finally learned not only that it had been rejected, but that the editorial board had unanimously characterized it as "anti-Soviet." In February three KGB officers came to Grossman's apartment with a warrant authorizing them to seize every copy of his novel, together with rough drafts, typewriters, and carbons. Grossman himself was left at liberty. He appealed first to the Writers' Union and then to Khrushchev himself. It is a mark of the importance that the ideological guardians of the Soviet Union attached to Grossman's novel that he was summoned to meet with Mikhail Suslov, member of the Politburo and soon to become, after Khrushchev's fall in 1964, Second Secretary of the Communist Party. Suslov, admitting that he had not read the book, but only reports of it, told Grossman that publication of his book would do only serious harm to the Soviet state and that it must go unpublished.[9] Grossman was devastated and remained deeply unhappy until his death from cancer in 1964. He was not to know that a copy left with a friend would much later be smuggled out of Russia and later still be published in Switzerland.

This unhappiness did not prevent him from continuing to write. In late 1961 he visited Armenia and left a lively record of his visit – and of reflections on himself as a visitor – in *I Wish you Well*, to be published only after his death and then in a version in which what he had had to say about Soviet anti-Semitism had been deleted. But his greatest achievement was to continue working on his final novel, *Everything Flows*, begun as long ago as 1955 and unfinished at Grossman's death.[10] It is the story of the return to Soviet society of Ivan Grigoryevich after thirty years in the Gulag and of his reckoning with both the past and the present. He encounters the informer responsible for his own imprisonment and, in a play within the novel, four informers of different types tell their stories. Grigoryevich's landlady turned

---

[9] For Grossman's notes of the conversation, see Garrard and Garrard, *The Bones of Berdichev*, pp. 357–360.

[10] Vasily Grossman, *Everything Flows*, trans. R. Chandler and E. Chandler with A. Aslanyan, New York: New York Review Books, 2009.

lover confesses to her part in inflicting deadly famine on her Ukrainian neighbors. But it is not only a novel of confessions, but also of extended reflections, reflections on Stalin, on Lenin, and on their relationship to the prerevolutionary Russian past. Confessions and reflections serve a single unifying purpose, that of presenting an unqualifiedly negative verdict on Soviet society. *Everything Flows* is the straightforwardly antiSoviet novel that Suslov had supposed *Life and Fate* to be. What then is its central thesis?

That Stalin was indeed Lenin's true heir, that Stalin gave expression to "what was most essential in Lenin,"[11] and that Lenin was the true heir of a Russian tradition, exemplified by Peter the Great, in which "Russian progress and Russian slavery were shackled together."[12] In the nineteenth century the emancipation of the serfs and the struggles of revolutionary thinkers had opened up the possibility of freedom, of progress without slavery. But that possibility was foreclosed in 1917. It was not that Lenin willed the continuation of Russian slavery." It is, indeed, tragic that a man who so sincerely loved Tolstoy and Beethoven should have furthered a new enslavement of the peasants and workers."[13] However, the reimposition of slavery to the state was the inevitable result of his love of power and his "frenzied, unyielding strength of will."[14] That state still lives. The state founded by Lenin and constructed by Stalin has now entered upon a third stage. So in these last years Grossman finally avows himself an enemy of the regime, finally becomes what Suslov had taken him to be, but to an extent unimagined even by Suslov.

The contrast with *Life and Fate* is important. There Grossman had put in question all philosophies of history. Here he advances his own philosophy of Russian history. There he invites his readers to question. Here he invites their assent. There nothing turns on his own philosophical commitments. Here a great deal of his argument invokes a never spelled out conception of freedom, one that seems closely akin to Isaiah Berlin's conception of negative liberty. The theses that he now advances require a great deal more argument than he supplies. Indeed, he nowhere recognizes adequately that there is a case to be made against him. (For that case see, for example, the first-hand testimony of Victor Serge, Grossman's cousin Nadya's alleged coconspirator, who agreed that Bolshevism had Stalinist tendencies from the beginning, but also insisted that it could have developed very differently, that there was no inevitability in the move from

---

[11] Ibid., p. 187.   [12] Ibid., p. 180.   [13] Ibid., pp. 181–182.   [14] Ibid., p. 172.

Lenin to Stalin.[15] So his rhetorically powerful, but argumentatively weak book expresses his final stance. Yet it is important to remember that he was already writing *Everything Flows* while he was writing *Life and Fate*, and, insofar as they express very different attitudes, they express once again a divided self. What, then, are we to say in conclusion about Grossman as a practical reasoner?

I have said almost nothing about the fabric of his everyday life both before and after the war, his relationships with his wives, his daughter, other family members, his friends – and he had some very good friends – and his collaborators. And I have said nothing at all about the structure of his everyday life as a writer, of the routines that governed his day, his week, his month. For Grossman, as for everyone else, most of his practical reasoning would have concerned the ways in which he lived out those routines and sustained or failed to sustain those relationships. And for Grossman, as for everyone else, others would have formed fixed expectations about his actions and his reactions and formed beliefs about what it was that he cared for. It is, however, when everyday routines are interrupted and familial and other relationships disturbed, especially by unexpected events, that individuals have to reflect and to identify what they take to be good reasons for acting in one way rather than another, so that they discover, perhaps for the first time, to what course of action they are committed by their rank ordering of goods, and then have to decide whether that rank ordering stands in need of revision. It is on such occasions that an agent's practical reasoning becomes evident and open to evaluation by that agent or by others. Some very different occasions or sets of occasions were crucial in determining the course of Grossman's life.

The first were all those episodes in which Grossman was invited to and agreed to endorse and collaborate with the agencies of the Stalinist state, beginning with his interrogation by an OGPU agent after his cousin's arrest in 1933, continuing with his call, as a member of the Writer's Union, for the infliction of the death penalty on Bukharin and others in the monstrous show trial of 1938, and still continuing in 1953 when he once again endorsed a call for the infliction of the death penalty, this time on the physicians accused in the so-called Doctors' Plot. What motivated Grossman? Doubtless to some extent fear of the consequences of acting otherwise. But for most of his life at least, it also mattered to him that he

---

[15] See Victor Serge, *Memoirs of a Revolutionary*, trans. P. Sedgwick with G. Paizis, New York: New York Review of Books Classics, 2012. See also Marcel Liebman, *Leninism under Lenin*, trans. B. Pearce, London: Jonathan Cape, 1975.

should act as a good Soviet citizen, and he believed that the goods which he chiefly valued, excellence in his writing and success as a writer, were goods recognized by and sustained by the Soviet state. Hence his acceptance of the tasks of rewriting so as to achieve publication, and hence his apparent lack of any concern for the treatment of Akhmatova and Pasternak. He structures his life as on the one hand his career requires, and on the other as the Stalinist state requires and, like millions of others, he finds no good reason to do otherwise. But this necessarily involved him, like them, in not raising certain questions, in closing their minds, so far as possible, to certain dreadful possibilities. And this necessarily involved him, like them, in not caring too much about the truth, in not letting a concern for the truth interfere with his life.

This is the stance from which Grossman begins as a practical reasoner. We all of us, whatever the time and place that we inhabit, begin as practical reasoners from some received view of things into which we have been initiated and educated, adopt some stance that provides us with a starting point. What differentiates us is whether or not and how we move forward from it. June 22 and July 7, 1941, were dates that marked a first radical change in Grossman. Those are the dates on which Hitler's Germany invaded Russia and the 11th Panzer Division reached Berdichev, making it impossible for Grossman to rescue his mother. What he then recognized was the relative insignificance of the reasons that he had had for not moving his mother and his niece to Moscow. It was not that they carried no weight as reasons. Like the vast majority of Muscovites, his living space was small and cramped, there was little privacy, his wife was understandably unwilling to have things made worse. But his failure to respond immediately to the German threat had fatal consequences, and he at once understood it as a failure in his responsibility for his mother and his family, a responsibility which became in time a responsibility to all those Jewish dead at the hands of the Nazis and then to all those Jews who had suffered as a consequence of anti-Semitism, whether, German or Russian, Polish or Ukrainian. This commitment became so central and so consistent that his lapses from it during the hysteria before Stalin's death can only be understood as expressions of a fear that he and his could not otherwise survive, a fear that was fully justified. So from then on Grossman was committed to discharging his responsibility to the Jewish dead as soon as possible, for acting on the reasons that he already had for providing a truthful account of the war.

I spoke earlier of Grossman as having disambiguated his work and himself as he began to write *Life and Fate*. But this disambiguation began earlier with those experiences of war that were seminal for the later writing of the novel. It was in the war that he had discovered what it was to live a life with an overriding goal, to which all else had to be subordinated, that of victory. But of victory over what enemy? Much Soviet wartime rhetoric, that of Ilya Ehrenburg, for example, took the enemy to be Germany and the Germans. But increasingly the enemy was identified as National Socialism. What Grossman came to understand was that the enemy had indeed been National Socialism, but National Socialism as one of the forms taken by human evil and that truthfulness about what it is that you are against, if evil in some of its various forms is what you are against, is a condition of discovering what it is that you are for. So the achievement of truthfulness became Grossman's overriding goal, providing major premises for his practical reasoning. The obstacles to the achievement of truthfulness in the years in which he was writing *Life and Fate* were considerable.

The repudiation of Stalin and Stalinism by Khrushchev and his colleagues had been, as we already noted, only partial. And it took some time for Soviet thinkers and writers, let alone for ordinary citizens, to find out how the line between what it was now permissible to say and what remained impermissible was now drawn. The young philosopher Ewald Ilyenkov had published his dissertation on the abstract and the concrete in Marx's *Capital* in 1956, a dissertation whose originality and insight had earned him a well-deserved reputation. But when he and a colleague questioned Stalin's conception of dialectical materialism, they at once lost their jobs at Moscow State University. This did not mean an end to their academic careers. It, like other incidents of the same kind, was sufficient as a warning to their colleagues, who learned what could be said to whom and when, what truths might be told, what truths must be told, and what truths were never to be told.

Someone may remark that this is something that children learn in all societies, and this is true. What distinguished Khrushchevite and postKrushchevite Russia from, say, California or Sweden either then or now is that conformity in respect of the norms of truthtelling and lying was politically enforced, that one's and one's family's livelihood was at stake, and that enforcing as well as observing such conformity was required. So dissembling became a widely valued quality and unconditional regard for truthfulness dangerous. But this led to other moral deformations. Because successful dissembling was rewarded, those who were prepared to dissemble on behalf of others – their superiors in the workplace, those who allocated housing and other benefits, those who controlled the outcomes of bureaucratic processes – looked for rewards from those others. So in many

areas of Soviet life patronage, corruption, and cynicism, those marks of
the later Brezhnev era, increasingly flourished alongside continuing Soviet
patriotism and devotion to ideals.

Grossman's concern for truthfulness was far from unique among Soviet
citizens. But his vocation as a writer, especially a writer with a well-
established reputation, gave it a peculiar importance. His aim was no
less than to elicit from as wide a range of readers as possible the kind of
questioning, about their own forms of social life, about how the virtues and
the vices, including the virtue of truthfulness, flourish or fail to flourish,
that can be satisfied by nothing less than the truth. Was this a task in which
he could have succeeded? The answer is clearly 'No', and this for two very
different kinds of reason. The political condition of Soviet society in the
1960s made it certain that Grossman would be defeated. Yet, had that
condition been very different, Grossman would still have been unlikely to
succeed, except in as limited way. For the condition of life in every modern
society is inimical to the kind of ruthlessly truthful self-questioning that
Grossman attempted to elicit. So his task was one that could not have been
completed. Yet it was a task that completed Grossman's own life.

I do not mean by this that Grossman understood his life to have been
thus completed. He died a dissatisfied and unhappy man. Nonetheless,
what was crucial was his now unwavering commitment to a task that
gave point and purpose to everything in his life that had, after so many
vicissitudes and uncertainties, issued in that commitment. It was insofar as
his practical reasoning directed his actions toward the ends mandated by
his task that he showed himself a rational agent. It was the pursuit of those
ends that gave finality to his life, so making it unhappy in the modern
sense, but in fact *eudaimōn*.

5.3   Sandra Day O'Connor

Sandra Day O'Connor's judicial argument and decision making will provide most of the subject matter for my account of her as a practical reasoner.
But my concern with them will be very different from that of a legal theorist. For I am concerned to ask what patterns of practical reasoning were
exemplified in her choices to think and act as she did in arriving at her
decisions on the United States Supreme Court, what it was about her as
a rational agent that made her the judge that she was. I need therefore to
begin by remarking on two of her notable characteristics as a rational agent.
The first is that in at least some contexts the goods that she was able to
achieve as a judge were placed lower in her rank ordering of the goods that

she set herself to achieve than some others. I refer especially to her decision to retire from the Supreme Court in 2006 at the age of seventy-five. This was something that she had planned well in advance, in order that she and her husband could resume a shared life in which outdoors activities would once again have a central place. As it happened, soon after her retirement her husband's sad affliction by Alzheimer's made him instead the object of her devoted care. What both intention and action confirmed was that the goods of family and married life had always been assigned what she took to be their due place, and sometimes an overriding place, in her decision making. Secondly, as everyone who has written about her has emphasized, certain traits of character have persisted throughout her life. And she had early on developed a set of skills which she has recurrently put to good use.

O'Connor's childhood on a cattle ranch made her at once self-reliant, cooperative, and tough-minded, someone who faced with a well-defined problem would set about solving it efficiently. She had the support of an affectionate family and was brought up as an Episcopalian, although often attending a local Methodist church. Her Episcopalian commitments seem to have been unwavering throughout her life. She came at an early age to care about becoming excellent in her activities, something evident later in her golf and her bridge as well as in her practice of law. She has a first-rate mind and her Stanford degrees in economics and law gave her an unusual ability to confront what to others might seem large and intractable issues as well-defined problems. She had a gift, when unable to pursue some goal, of finding a way to move forward, so that in the longer run her further goals were achieved. Unable to find any position with a law firm when she graduated, because of entrenched prejudice against hiring women, she learned the trade of a deputy county attorney in San Mateo County, Arizona, and then, after the birth of her first child, joined with another young lawyer in founding a law practice. Unable to continue with that law practice, if she was to bring up her children as she wanted to, she undertook volunteer work with civic organizations, which led in time to her becoming in turn president of the Junior League of Phoenix, a precinct worker for the Republican Party, a state assistant attorney general, a member of and then the majority leader of the Arizona State Senate, and finally a judge, first on the Maricopa County Superior Court and then on the Arizona Court of Appeals. The combination of patience, intelligence, a respect for others, and a certain quiet, but sometimes abrasive relentlessness in the advancement of her legal career and in her life in general is notable. She has more than most wanted what she has had good reason to want and has acted as she had good reason to act, if she were to get what she wanted.

It matters therefore that O'Connor pursued each of her goals in a way that was consistent with pursuit of the others. It matters too that she had to overcome and knew how to overcome prejudice against women at different stages of her career. And it matters also that her conception of what it would be for her to excel in any of her roles, whether as lawyer, or as wife and mother, or as politician, or as judge, was always by and large an established and conventional conception, one shared with many Americans of her social class, educational background, and income group. Her admirable and obdurate insistence that women should not be discriminated against and her equally admirable repudiation of any kind of racial discrimination, expressed in her admiration for Thurgood Marshall's patient courage in resisting it,[16] are for her not only deeply felt, but required by the fundamental shared values of the social order that she inhabits. The history of the United States is on this view a history of uneven, but continuing progress toward democracy, liberty, and equality, and in the world at large the United States is both a role model and an agent for the realization of those ideals. Of course there are setbacks and conflicts, but "Discord is a sign that progress is afoot; unease is an indication that a society has let go of what it knows and is working out something better and new."[17] That history has provided the background narrative in which the narrative of O'Connor's own life, as she understands it, has been embedded. It is a narrative one of whose presuppositions is that, whether or not a particular human being flourishes is up to them, but the social conditions required for human flourishing are those supplied by the American social order.

It may be asked: How could anyone become a Justice of the United States Supreme Court and believe otherwise? Yet it also matters that such belief makes it impossible to entertain, let alone to assent to, certain thoughts: that the United States is in fact governed by economic, financial, political, and media elites who determine the peculiarly limited set of alternatives between which voters are allowed to choose in state and federal elections, that money functions in American political life, so that the United States is in some respects not a democracy, but a plutocracy, and that the United States in recent decades has been a too often destructive force in world affairs. I put aside the question of *why* an inability to entertain such thoughts matters and note only the inability.

The American system of justice, like the American social order, is then on the view shared by O'Connor and the vast majority of Americans, an

---

[16] See especially Sandra Day O'Connor, *The Majesty of the Law: Reflections of a Supreme Court Justice,* New York: Random House, 2003, chapter 15.
[17] Ibid., p. 276.

expression of a set of what are treated as if incontestable values, something generally presupposed by what they take to be sound practical as well as judicial reasoning. However, the goods that are to be pursued by individual or corporate agents on particular occasions do indeed vary with time, place, and circumstance and, since they are of very different kinds, may be such that the pursuit of one turns out to be incompatible with the pursuit of one or more others. Hence conflicts arise and, when they do, the relevant fundamental principles have to be brought to bear, so that each appropriate consideration can be given its due weight. So it is with judicial reasoning and so it is with practical reasoning in general. It is in answering the question of how this is to be achieved that O'Connor's own distinctive mode of practical and judicial reasoning becomes evident. But, before I consider that mode, it is important to remark on two characteristics of O'Connor so obvious that we might be tempted to take them for granted.

The first is that she is reflective, but not at all a theorist. Her conservatism, unlike that of most American protagonists of conservatism and that of some other Supreme Court Justices, is a matter of attitudes, not theories, and theories do not provide the premises for her judicial reasoning or more generally for her practical reasoning. The second is that, as I already suggested, her commitment to her basic beliefs is unquestioning, so that in the making of particular decisions a great deal is often taken for granted, is left inexplicit, something that some of her more ideologically minded critics have found irritating. Consider how these traits are illustrated in her dissenting opinion in *Akron v. Akron Center for Reproductive Health*, her earliest judicial statement on abortion. In *Roe v. Wade* the justices had concluded that in the first trimester of a pregnancy the woman had an unqualified right to decide to have an abortion, but that, as the pregnancy progressed, the right of the state to regulate what is or is not permitted might take precedence over that right of the woman. O'Connor had two quarrels with *Roe v. Wade*. The first was that its distinction between trimesters reflected the state of medical science at the time of that judgment, but that increases in medical knowledge and skills needed to be taken into account if the relevant principles were to find justifiable application to particular cases. What were those principles? Here O'Connor made explicit her second quarrel with *Roe v. Wade*. What is required is not a decision between the claims of two rival principles, one upholding the reproductive rights of women, the other protecting the life of the unborn child, but a balancing of two sets of interests, of two sets of considerations. Women have a legitimate interest in safeguarding their right to make reproductive decisions. The state has a legitimate interest in protecting both the life of the foetus and the health of the mother. What weight should be given to each set of considerations varies from case to case and must be decided with reference to the particular context and circumstances of each case.

O'Connor's judicial reasoning follows consistent patterns. When faced with dilemmas or conflicts, there is commonly more than one principle, more than one set of considerations, to be invoked. Each principle identifies one good or set of goods that is at stake in making this particular decision. It is of peculiar importance to identify correctly the characteristics of the situation in which the dilemma or conflict arises, since without such identification we will not know how to apply any of the relevant principles. But, having done so, our task is to give its due weight to each of the sets of considerations and to strike a balance. The ability to do this is what constitutes good judgment. Note at once that what I have just described is not only a mode of judicial, but also a mode of practical reasoning, and everything that we know about O'Connor suggests that this is her mode of practical reasoning. Both when O'Connor speaks in public and when she publishes books and articles, she always has in mind some particular audience or set of readers and knows how to address them: children in her books for children, students, political opponents and political colleagues, those with shared concerns of various kinds. For each she has a voice and knows how to take their concerns into account in framing what she has to say. It is to the point that she makes excellent jokes.

Both as judicial and as practical reasoning, this mode of discourse and argument contrasts sharply with some other modes of judicial and practical reasoning, most obviously with reasoning that appeals for its major premises to principles which are treated as indefeasible, which are treated as such that if they have application to a particular case, that alone determines how the case is to be decided. Appeal to no other principle can give grounds for holding that the case should be determined otherwise. For O'Connor the notion that there are any such bedrock principles is to be rejected. In her concurring decision in *Rosenberger v. Rector and Visitors of the University of Virginia*, she wrote that "When bedrock principles collide, they test the limits of categorical obstinacy and expose the flaws and dangers of a Grand Unified Theory that may turn out to be neither grand nor unified." So she repudiated not only a type of view held both by some liberal and some conservative colleagues on the Supreme Court, but a mode of practical reasoning that is to be found at work in many areas of our political and moral lives.

It matters to O'Connor not only that our reasoning should have the structure that I have described, but also that, when engaged in argument, we should exhibit certain virtues. Lawyers should not envision argument as battle, but as discourse, discourse aimed at forwarding an investigation whose aim is to arrive at the truth and at a just outcome. To achieve these, civility is crucial.[18] And it is evident that what she holds of lawyers she holds of everyone engaged in argumentative discourse. What makes it possible for her to view judicial reasoning and practical reasoning in this way is her conviction that both presuppose a certain underlying agreement, what she has called "American reliance upon considered change to preserve enduring values."[19] Adequately considered change, whether in the courts or in individual lives, proceeds through decision making in particular situations. If things go wrong, it must then be because either some feature of the situation had not been taken into account or some consideration or set of considerations had not been given its due weight in arriving at a balanced view. The metaphors of weight and balance are of the first importance here.

At the beginning of Chapter 3 of this essay, I characterized the dominant morality of modernity as one in which heterogeneous types of consideration provide reasons for choice and action. So principles assigning rights either to some class of individuals or to human beings as such are apt on occasion to conflict with precepts enjoining the maximization of happiness or the promotion of economic progress or of national security, and I remarked that often enough the result is inconsistency in deciding to which type of consideration to give priority, so that sometimes individuals act as if consequentialists, while at other times they act as if believers in inviolable rights. But, when they are reflective, how do they make those choices and how do they think of themselves as making those choices? Sometimes at least and perhaps commonly, they do so in terms very close to O'Connor's. They think of themselves as giving more or less weight to each type of consideration, as balancing each against the others. But then two questions arise. The first is: How do they decide which considerations are relevant and which not? The second is: What are the scales which determine weight and balance, what, moving beyond the metaphor, is the standard to which appeal is being made in arriving at their practical conclusions? These are questions both for them and for O'Connor.

It seems to be both for them and for O'Connor a question of fact which principles, which kinds of consideration, are relevant in any given problematic situation. They are all and only those principles to which rival

---

[18] O'Connor, *The Majesty of the Law*, pp. 226–228.   [19] Ibid., p. 70.

disputants in a conflict do in fact appeal in order to justify their contentions.
So a group of individuals have to decide what is to become of a particular
piece of property, a large plot of land. Members of the local neighborhood
association wish to purchase it for use as a public park. Of the three siblings
who jointly own it, one believes that it should be sold to the neighborhood
association, one that it should be sold to the highest bidder, whoever that is,
to pay for the education of the owners' children, and one that it should not
be sold, but preserved as family property for future generations. So there are
conflicting principles to which appeal is made, considerations that point
in different directions: the good of the local community, the good of the
children, perhaps the rights of the children, the good of future generations
of the family, of future generations of the local community. Plainly, if the
contending parties each insist on the achievement of one of those goods at
the expense of the others, there will be irresolvable conflict. In the United
States this will very possibly lead to a law suit. (Eighty percent of the world's
lawyers live in the United States.) What O'Connor's mode of reasoning
provides is a way through such disagreements to a resolution, whether in the
courts or before they reach the courts. Two aspects of the reasoning are to the
point.

The first, as I noted earlier, is her insistence on careful attention to the
facts of the particular case. So in the case that I have imagined she would
find it indispensable to consider the size of the plot of land, its suitability
for various purposes, and its present and future market value, the number
and ages of the children and the various ways in which provision might
be made for their education, and so on. Those facts impose a first set of
constraints on what can be accounted a reasonable resolution. Secondly,
as I also noted earlier, O'Connor will look for a solution that gives some
weight, if possible, to what each of the contending parties values, looking
for a limited consensus. If giving some weight to this consideration, while
more or less to that other consideration, can secure the agreement, even
if the reluctant agreement, of the contending parties, then that is itself a
reason for holding that due weight has been given to each consideration.
Consensus is a great good.

What I have presented as a way of resolving conflicts between two or
more individuals is also a way in which agents whose principles are such
that in particular situations they are confronted by dilemmas, one principle
requiring or favoring a course of action ruled out by another, can resolve
their conflicts. Given that they have identified the facts of their situation
adequately, what they have to ask themselves is what resolution of their

conflict they will find it easiest to live with both now and in the future. They look, as it were for inner consensus. In saying this. I am of course going beyond anything that O'Connor says and it would be quite wrong to impute to her what I have taken to be the implications of the stances that she has taken. But what she shows of herself in her autobiographical writings is at least not inconsistent with this characterization of her mode of practical reasoning and decision making. Those who reason and choose in this manner negotiate their way through life, doing what they understand as weighing reasons, both those reasons advanced by others with whom they have to come to terms and those which they themselves independently find compelling. It is not difficult among our contemporaries to recognize individuals whose style of practical reasoning this is. What then is or might be questionable about that style?

What is notable is what and how much is taken as given and unquestioned: the shared background beliefs concerning not only fundamental values, but the institutions that are taken to embody those values, the confidence in the principles that one and one's contemporaries bring to problematic situations, the value attached to consensus, the assumption that there is indeed a standard, a set of scales, that enables one to assign due weight to each set of considerations, in spite of the fact that this standard is never made explicit. There seems to be for this scheme of thought no way of standing back from these commitments and questioning them from some external standpoint by appeal to some independent standard. Those whose scheme of thought it is may therefore seem to be imprisoned within their own culture. Is this in fact so?

The reply may be that what we have here is in O'Connor's case not at all imprisonment within a culture, but rather membership in a particular tradition, a type of tradition familiar from the longer history of political conservatism. It is tradition informed not only by a regard for the past and for the present-day established institutions that have emerged from that past, but also by a deep distrust of abstract reasoning and a reliance on shared prejudice, on judgments that are prior to and presupposed by our reasoning. And, if this is the reply, it may suggest that O'Connor's stance is that of a certain version, a peculiarly American version, of Burkean conservatism, one adopted not through reading Burke – for to value one's own tradition as a result of reading Burke, that is for theoretical reasons, would be not at all Burkean – but because of the way that she had been brought up and the influence of her mentors. If this is so, and I take it to be so, it explains the antagonisms that developed between O'Connor and other self-identified conservatives. Most contemporary American conservatives, including some of her colleagues on the Supreme Court, are committed theorists, adherents of some body of principles to which they give unconditional allegiance. Her disagreements with them derive from what Nancy Maveety has called her "aversion to rigid ideological principles."[20] But now the question arises: Is this reply sufficient to rescue O'Connor from the charge that she is imprisoned within her own political culture?

Of any tradition we may ask what resources it provides for critical scrutiny of its own beliefs and practices, when these are put in question ? Lack of such resources inevitably leads to significant failures, to an inability to renew the tradition by rethinking and reformulating its commitments in the face of inescapable questions. The history of many types of tradition is marked by periods of such failure. Examples can be drawn from religious history, from the history of architectural and other craft traditions, from the history of labor movements and other political movements, indeed even from the history of traditions of enquiry, of philosophical and scientific traditions. But there is a type of tradition that is peculiarly and unsurprisingly prone to such failure, that which counts among its deepest commitments a rejection of the possibility of radical self-criticism by educating its adherents into thinking in terms of a false opposition between abstract reasoning on the one hand and reckoning with the particularities of social life on the other. And just this opposition is presupposed by O'Connor's modes of practical reasoning.

Yet it may be replied that in the case of O'Connor the charge that she is imprisoned within her own political culture is palpably false. For, unlike some of her colleagues, she thinks it important to learn from foreign jurisdictions. She has emphasized the origins of United States law in English law and reminded us of the earlier American practice of citing English precedents. "We should keep our eyes open for innovations in foreign jurisdictions that, with some grafting and pruning, might be transplanted to our own legal system."[21] And she argues that attention to foreign law is necessary if American courts are going to be able to deal adequately with international disputes. But this admirable openness to learning from elsewhere is itself exercised only in a limited way.

It never provides an occasion for putting in question O'Connor's basic assumptions either about the principles that make the premises of her

---

[20] Nancy Maveety, *Justice Sandra Day O'Connor: Strategist on the Supreme Court*, Lanham, MD: Rowman & Littlefield, 1996, p. 40; my discussion of O'Connor's judicial opinions is indebted to Maveety's insightful analysis. For a different perspective on O'Connor, see Joan Biskupic, *Sandra Day O'Connor: How the First Woman on the Supreme Court Became Its Most Influential Justice*, New York: Ecco, 2005.

[21] O'Connor, *The Majesty of the Law*, p. 235.

judicial and practical reasoning what they are or concerning the form that her judicial and practical reasoning takes. And hers is in no way an openness to any thoughts, whatever their provenance, that might be subversive of the established order. What is absent throughout her discussions of the historical and social context of the American judicial system is any sense of the relevance of the facts of radical inequality, the financial, educational, political, and legal inequalities that find political expression in rule by elites, facts that are what they are, because the capitalist economic order is what it is. It is this awareness from which she is insulated by her Burkean presuppositions. This is not to deny that she has been one of the more admirable members of the recent Supreme Court and that many of her decisions were much to be welcomed by any rational agent. It is to say that her limitations both as judicial and as practical reasoner had an inescapable political dimension. As had so many of her activities.

5.4 C. L. R. James

No life, viewed from the standpoint of rational agency, is without errors and limitations. This trite thought, even though a cliché, has to be borne in mind when evaluating particular lives. I have told Grossman's story in a way that has emphasized the errors that can arise from large theoretical commitments, O'Connor's in a way that has emphasized the limitations of a focus on particularities. Both are nonetheless stories of unusual professional success, success due to excellence in their exercise of professional skills. Both were able to integrate into a single life the pursuit and achievement of various and heterogeneous goods, both individual goods and common goods, and did so by learning how to rank order different goods on particular occasions of choice. So the questions arise: To what standard, to what measure of goods, did each appeal when engaged in such ordering, in arguing from premises to practical conclusions? And what directedness emerged in each life as a result of that ordering, to what end did the activity of each become directed?

Neither ever spells out explicitly their particular answers to those questions, and this is unsurprising, since such explicitness characterizes very few lives, even among those otherwise highly articulate, like Grossman and O'Connor. Grossman became increasingly and angrily suspicious not just of Soviet Marxism, but of anything purporting to yield a theoretical account of the human good. O'Connor systematically resisted attempts to move beyond a case-by-case treatment of dilemmas. Neither therefore was prepared to understand her or himself from a theoretical standpoint, but both of course were reflective. Yet just because neither was able to articulate the directedness toward and beyond particular finite goals that informed their lives, neither was able to put her or his mode of reflection in question. Are these two aspects of their practical thinking related? Are their limitations to be explained by their aversion to theory? It may at first seem that this cannot be so, that the last thing that those who are puzzled as to what turn to take in their everyday lives need is a theory. We do not need to be followers of Burke to recognize how often theoretical reflection has led those who indulge in it astray in their practical lives. But perhaps this was because the theory that was to blame for their errors was defective theory. Perhaps those who have made the case against theory so compelling were able to do so only because of their choice of examples. It is this possibility that I want to bear in mind while telling the story of a third life, that of C. L. R. James.

James had the benefit of two educations. His first was from his teachers at the Queen's Royal College in Port of Spain, the capital of Trinidad, then a British Crown colony, who transmitted to their pupils the ethos and tradition of the English public school and who nurtured in James his already developing passions for English literature and for cricket. The second was from those Marxists who had followed Trotsky's lead and who were to found the Fourth International. Both educations were indispensable to James' development and both informed his later mode of practical reasoning. Neither would have had the effect that it did, were it not for his early upbringing. James was born in Tunapuna, a small town eight miles from Port of Spain. His ancestors were African slaves and his grandfather's elderly cousin Nancy told stories of her life as a house slave before emancipation in 1834. His father's family were Anglican, his mother's Wesleyan. His mother was an avid, if undiscriminating reader, but her reading included Dickens, Scott, Thackeray, and Shakespeare, and what she passed on to him was her intense pleasure in reading. His father, a school teacher, bought him books. At the same time, like almost every other Trinidadian small boy, James' heroes were those local young men who excelled at cricket. He wanted to be like them. When he won a scholarship to the Queen's Royal College, the youngest boy ever to do so, he began to learn not only the part that literature and cricket can play in enriching our lives, but something of the relationship between them. What, as he recognized later, made that possible was the self-discipline inculcated by his family, by his teachers in the classroom, and by those with whom he played cricket.

The ethos of his family he later identified as Puritanism, exemplified above all by his Aunt Judith, an enmity to carelessness and self-indulgence, an insistence on both self-respect and care for others. What his teachers inculcated was the ethos of the English public school, as Thomas Arnold had understood it, and in literary studies the primacy of great literature, as Mathew Arnold had understood it. What initiation into cricket required was a passion for excellence and a shared respect for the rules of the game. All three outlawed cheating and dishonorable behavior. Sixty years later James was to ask: "What was it that so linked my Aunt Judith with cricket as I, a colonial, experienced it? The answer is in one word: Puritanism; more specifically, restraint, and restraint in a personal sense," restraint learned not only from his mother and his aunt, from his school teachers and on the cricket field, but also from his reading of English literature.[22] What matters about restraint as a character trait is the kind of practical reasoning in which it issues.

To be restrained is necessary, if one is to have the ability to be reflective about one's desires, so that one takes the time to ask of any particular object of desire: How good a reason do I have to desire *that*? What was remarkable about James' childhood and adolescence was its twofold character: on the one hand the encouragement to desire and enjoy a range of very different goods, those of family life, those of academic excellence, that of excellence as a cricketer, together with an enlarged sense of possibility, and on the other the inculcation of the virtues of restraint and discrimination. Desire and enjoyment without restraint undermine the virtues. So does joyless self-restraint. James' family and his teachers provided an upbringing as good as any ever.

"I, a colonial," wrote James. Trinidadians of African descent made up something like two-fifths of the population of Trinidad, those of Indian descent – East Indian, the descendants of indentured laborers – about a third, those of mixed race most of the rest, with a very small prosperous and privileged white minority. But although James would recurrently find himself in struggles against racial barriers and racial prejudice, he does not seem to have experienced racial discrimination either as a student or later as a teacher at the Queen's Royal College. What he did acquire was a sense of himself as an unusually articulate member of that vast class, the exploited of the Third World, and this long before he thought of that class in those terms. In order to do so, he had to become a Marxist.

When he was thirty-one, he left Trinidad for England, hoping to become a novelist. (He had already published two novels.) He had been invited to stay at the home of his friend, the Trinidadian cricketer, Learie Constantine,

---

[22] C. L. R. James, *Beyond a Boundary*, London: Hutchinson, 1963, p. 47.

who lived in the mill town of Nelson in Lancashire. Constantine, who had played for the West Indies against England in the Test Match series of 1928, had stayed on in England as a professional cricketer, playing for Nelson in the Lancashire League. The players of the teams of that League – founded in 1892 – each team representing a small to middle-sized Lancashire town, were and are ordinary working men, but each team employed one professional, often a cricketer of some distinction. So James found himself at home in English working-class society, participating in its social and political life, meeting political militants, witnessing the Great Lancashire Cotton Strike of 1932, and, perhaps as a result, reading Marx. But all this he did while still devoted to Trinidad, publishing, while in Nelson, *The Life of Captain Cipriani: An Account of British Government in the West Indies*, three chapters of which he later reissued as a pamphlet, *The Case for West-Indian Self-Government*, published by Leonard and Virginia Woolf's Hogarth Press. (Arthur Andrew Cipriani, former army officer, trade unionist, and socialist mayor of Port of Spain, had been the most effective opponent of British colonial rule in Trinidad.)

What Constantine had wanted from James was help in writing his auto-biography. What Constantine helped James to get was a much desired job, that of reporting on cricket for the *Manchester Guardian* on those occasions on which its principal cricket correspondent, Neville Cardus, was unable to cover an important game. Cardus, eleven years older than James, was to be in one way a model, in another his antithesis. For Cardus, like James, had two passions, one for cricket and, in Cardus's case, one for classical music. About both he wrote excellently for the *Manchester Guardian*. But, unlike James, he compartmentalized his life and his passions. James understood both cricket and literature as forms of high art and was to argue that those who fail to understand this fail to understand art. Cardus thought cricket a mere recreation for the masses, music a fine art for an educated elite. For James, although he admired Cardus's writing, this involved severe limita-tions in Cardus's understanding of cricket, of music, and of the capabilities and sensibilities of ordinary working people.

With his new job James had decided to move to London. He lived in Bloomsbury, went to lectures and meetings at Student Movement House, home and meeting place for students from many parts of the world, and frequented Lahr's radical bookstore. He encountered literary Bloomsbury in the person of both the Woolfs and Edith Sitwell and political London in all its variety. His response to the former was to reaffirm his identi-fication with the English literary tradition, to the latter to acknowledge that he had become a Marxist and one identified with Trotsky. So what was it to be a Trotskyist in London in 1934? It was first of all to have a particular diagnosis of the worldwide crisis that had become evident in the stock market crash of 1929 and the subsequent depression. This crisis had economic, political, and cultural dimensions, and it was crucial to understand the relationship between them. The potentially revolutionary working class had undergone a series of defeats in various countries and the reactionary forces of Fascism, Nazism, and Japanese militarism were growing in strength. What was now needed was to forge principled alliances with progressive movements in order to resist those forces and to create or recreate a self-consciously revolutionary working class and a vanguard party to guide and lead it. In the Soviet Union Stalin had betrayed the cause of socialism both at home and internationally. The Soviet Union was still a workers' state, but a deformed workers' state, ruled by a bureaucratic elite. The Communist Parties of the Third International had become agents of Stalin's unprincipled maneuvering.

To be a Trotskyist, however, was not merely to agree with Trotsky in these political conclusions. It was to have learned that only Marxism provided the key to understanding the contemporary world and with it a rational justification for arriving at these conclusions. So Trotskyist groups aspired to provide for their fellow workers an education into the Marxist view of things, and James found himself involved not only in day-to-day political activity, but also in reading, thinking, and arguing about the relationship between his earlier passions and commitments and the version of Marxism to which he now gave his allegiance. Yet in fact that he was able to learn from Marx and what he was able to learn depended in key part on what he had already learned from his earlier teachers. Later he was to write that "Thackeray, not Marx, bears the heaviest responsibility for me."[23] For it was from Thackeray and other nineteenth-century novelists that he had first learned those facts about social class and economic dependence which Marx's theory captured and illuminated. And, as he developed his own thought, he understood that the insights of the novelist and the analyses of the theorist complement one another. Both informed his activities from the outset. And what a range of activities those were!

The Trotskyist group to which James initially belonged worked within the Independent Labour Party (ILP), and so the day-to-day political activity in which James found himself included the mundane political tasks of both his Marxist group and the ILP: attending meetings regularly, selling newspapers and pamphlets, writing articles for the ILP's *New Leader*, canvassing,

---

[23] Ibid.

supporting local strike actions, constantly arguing and debating. His cooperation with others of African descent to mobilize support for Ethiopia,
when it was invaded by Mussolini in 1935, led to a growing involvement
with PanAfrican causes, so that he became editor of the newsletter of the
International African Service Bureau, headed by his friend, George Padmore. Add to these his continuing work for the *Manchester Guardian*.
James had finally abandoned any thought of a career as a cricketer when
he turned down an opportunity to play as a professional in the Lancashire
League shortly before he left Nelson for London in 1934, but this made
his writing about cricket all the more important to him. In 1934 he published forty-nine reports of cricket matches in the *Manchester Guardian*,
in 1935 fifty-two. And when he no longer worked for the *Guardian*, he
wrote about cricket in the *Glasgow Herald*. Add still further that he had a
complex personal life in which his attractiveness to intelligent women led
him into relationships in which those women were recurrently baffled and
irritated by his self-sufficiency. (His first marriage had broken up when he
left Trinidad.)

In 1936 he published *Minty Alley*, the last of the novels that he had
written in Trinidad, in 1937 his political indictment of Stalinism, *World
Revolution 1917–1936: The Rise and Fall of the Communist International*, and
in 1938 *A History of Negro Revolt*, a short monograph that was to have a long
life. Among the conversations that were seminal for James in this period
were those with George Padmore, who had been a childhood friend in
Trinidad and whom he encountered again at Student Movement House.
Padmore had joined the Communist Party and had worked for Profitern
in Moscow before breaking with Stalinism in 1935. It was Padmore who
was to become the chief theorist of PanAfricanism and he founded an
African Bureau in London as a place of contact for all those engaged
in struggles of liberation, whether in Africa itself or in the PanAfrican
Diaspora. James edited its journal. But he did not allow this to distract
him from completing his major and splendid historical work, *The Black
Jacobins: Toussaint L'Ouverture and the San Domingo Revolution*.[24] James
had first written this as a three act play and, when it was produced in
London in 1936, Paul Robeson played the leading part.

The story that James told with impressive clarity was a complex one with
three narrative strands: that of the revolts by the African slaves in the French
colony of San Domingo in the 1790s, slaves who claimed those same rights

---

[24] C. L. R. James, *The Black Jacobins: Toussaint L'Ouverture and the San Domingo Revolution*, London:
Secker & Warburg, 1938; New York: Dial Press, 1938.

that the French revolutionaries were claiming for themselves; that of the failure of those revolutionaries – for the most part – to recognize the justice of the claims made by the slaves, because of the extent to which their respect for the rights of property nullified their respect for the rights of man; and that of the emergence of Toussaint L'Ouverture as military and more than military leader, someone who enabled his fellow Africans to act together as free and self-liberating human beings, until his betrayal, imprisonment, and death at the hands of Napoleon. What is central to James' story is his stress on the richness of the culture that the slaves had brought with them from Africa and on how the struggle to be free actualized potentialities that neither they nor others had recognized. By acting as they did, they became more and other than they had been. James' story is also one of failure, of the destructive character of self-serving ambition, and of the roots of these in the economic and social conditions of the time. It was written both with historical care and with an eye to the lesson that it held for those engaged with him in the political struggles of the 1930s, that Africa and Africans, whether in Africa or in the West Indies, would only realize their potentialities for living as free and creative peoples by engaging in those struggles in their own way and under their own leadership.

The view of the past that James expressed in *The Black Jacobins* was one that was partially to define his own future. So it is important to ask what the relationship was between James' everyday practical reasoning in this period and his historical enquiries. The form that his activities took was largely, although not wholly. imposed by his political commitments. James had left behind the Independent Labour Party and joined with those Trotskyists who had formed the Revolutionary Socialist League, which understood itself as the nucleus of a Leninist vanguard party of disciplined activists. What his role as a party member demanded of James seems to have involved little or no conflict with his personal life. His first marriage had ended when he left Trinidad and he was unable or unwilling to sustain relationships that he formed in England. So the claims upon him that he recognized were primarily three: on the one hand to earn his living as a writer and historian, to excel in these activities, and to advance the cause of socialist revolution, as his Trotskyist party defined it and as it instructed him. And for quite some time he did not take these three to be in tension, let alone incompatible. What he wrote to earn a living was by and large what he needed to write, if he was to excel, and what he valued as a writer were just those human qualities and achievements that would, so he believed, be exemplified in the societies that would result from a socialist revolution.

Much of his reasoning then was, like that of many Marxists, a type of means–end reasoning. Some of his activities had point and purpose only if and insofar as they were a means to the end of socialist revolution. Others were worthwhile in themselves and also because they contributed to the cause of socialist revolution. Others again were worthwhile because they earned him a living and so enabled him to function well as a writer and as a revolutionary socialist. So the theory-informed rank ordering of goods that directed his activities was on the surface a simple one, disguising the complexity both of his cultural inheritance and of his character. But the theory that informed that rank ordering was defective in two ways. It was, as James was soon to discover, defective by the standards of Marxist theory rightly understood. And it was, like other versions of Marxist theory, defective in its conception of human goods.

The discovery that the Trotskyism of the 1930s was defective as a version of Marxist theory was one that James made in stages. In 1938 he accepted an invitation from the Socialist Workers' Party (SWP) in the United States to tour the country, speaking to and helping to organize black workers. He was able to visit Mexico and to meet with Trotsky. When he returned from Mexico, he stayed on in the United States until he was deported in 1953. During those almost fifteen years he played a notable part in the disputes within the SWP and in groups that had separated themselves from it, and it was in the course of those debates that his conception of what it was to be a Marxist was transformed. James' first major disagreement with Trotsky, one that they had discussed when they met in 1940, was over the relationship of black liberation groups to the vanguard party. Where Trotsky saw black workers as one more segment of a potentially revolutionary working class, who needed the leadership of that party, if such potentiality was to be actualized, James argued that there had to be an independent black movement, PanAfrican in its understanding of itself, with its own forms of leadership. But this was not all.

When James returned to the United States, he found himself in agreement with a minority in the SWP who had rejected Trotsky's characterization of the Soviet Union as still a workers' state, even if, under Stalin, a deformed one, and with it any obligation to defend the Soviet Union. On their view the Soviet Union had become a state capitalist society, one more imperialist power. A major protagonist of this view was Trotsky's former secretary, Raya Dunevskaya, and James and she formed an alliance. Since within the party, James used the pseudonym 'Johnson' and Dunayevskaya the pseudonym 'Forest' – the use of pseudonyms was to deceive FBI informers who had infiltrated the party – those who took their part became known as 'the Johnson–Forest tendency'. Discussion among them led to an even more radical disagreement with Trotsky's political stance, one that resulted in the end in both Dunayevskaya and James separating themselves from the Trotskyist movement. What they now rejected was the whole conception of the vanguard party as leader and teacher of the exploited, providing them with a voice and a definition of goals that they were unable to provide for themselves. What they now insisted was that the exploited had to speak for themselves with their own voices, voices in the plural, out of their various cultural traditions, and to define their own goals. The task of a Marxist was to become a participant in those conversations and to work toward the achievement of those goals.

Surprisingly, neither Dunayevskaya nor James took themselves to be rejecting Leninism in making this turn. For they had identified a strand in Lenin's thought which subsequent Leninism, even Trotsky's Leninism, had suppressed. No party, on the view that Lenin had expressed both in *State and Revolution* and in the debates after the Soviet revolution, could bring about revolutionary change unless it gave a central place to the spontaneous self-organization of workers themselves and was prepared to learn from the experience of those workers and other oppressed peoples.[25] So political activity had to be grassroots activity, entering into conversation with all those who were struggling against their exploitation, whether in American or African or West Indian factories, mines and farms, and helping them to reflect and to set their own goals. This required not just a knowledge of, but an imaginative identification with the particular and often rich cultural inheritances of those whose voices had too often gone unheard in the elite cultures of the world. It required too a better account of capitalism as it was now developing, of a capitalism in which the relationships of government agencies to private capital were being transformed. This was the perspective that informed James' political agenda from then on.

He remained of course a committed Marxist and the structure of his practical reasoning was unchanged. But, as I noted earlier, Marxism had from the outset a defective understanding of human goods. What Marx had identified were those barriers to human flourishing, to the achievement of human goods, that are presented by capitalist economies. What Marxists had added to this was an identification of the barriers to such flourishing that were characteristic of nineteenth- and twentieth-century imperialism. That those who were exploited and denied freedom would in consequence struggle against capitalism and imperialism not only followed

---

[25] See Raya Dunayevskaya, *Marxism and Freedom*, New York: Bookman Associates, 1958.

from their theory, but was confirmed by the history of class struggle in all its multifarious forms. But if someone who was well able to make a satisfactory life for her or himself and for her or his family within the social order of capitalism and imperialism were to ask "Why should I identify with the struggle against capitalism or imperialism? Why should I pursue the aims of that struggle rather than a range of other goods?" Marxists often found themselves falling back on a tired rhetoric, just because they had no adequate answers. Appeals to benevolence or generosity were ruled out by Marx's condemnation of abstract moralism. Appeals to the self-interest of the questioner were clearly not to the point. So Marxism often seemed to presuppose some crude variant of Benthamite utilitarianism, according to which agents will secure their own well-being by acting so as to bring about the greatest happiness of the greatest .number. But Marx had rejected Bentham's philosophy. Here Marxists tended to fall silent or to change the question.

There was another set of closely related questions that they also did not ask. What kind of human being do I need to become, if in struggling for the replacement of capitalism and imperialism by a more humane order I am to achieve my own good? What virtues do I need, if I am not to be open to corruption at certain points? The importance of these questions for those who had followed Trotsky should have been obvious and this for two reasons. First, the dramatic history of the prelude to the October revolution, of that revolution itself, and of its subsequent betrayal was in key part a history of conflicts between individuals with strikingly different characters, each with their own virtues and vices: Lenin against Martov, Lenin against Trotsky, Shlyapnikov against both Lenin and Trotsky, Stalin against Lenin's other heirs. The history that had generated Trotskyism was a moral history. Secondly, life within the Troskyist movement presented its own temptations to distortion and corruption. On the one hand it demanded self sacrifice, self discipline, courage, generous cooperativeness, patience, a certain kind of practical intelligence. On the other it could elicit in some of its members a narrow intolerance of other views, an inflated sense of self-importance and of self-congratulation on being right-minded, a corrupting pleasure in the exercise of power within the group over the group.

Those were not James' flaws. He was fortunate enough to have been able so far to pursue his various goals without ever asking what sort of a human being he would have to become, if he were to continue to integrate the pursuit of those goods into a single life. That question was posed by episodes of very different kinds. Soon after he arrived in the United States he had met a young actress, Constance Webb, herself a committed and active socialist. She was eighteen, he thirty-seven. In 1945 they met again, when they were both in New York. Between 1938 and 1945 James and she exchanged more than two hundred letters, an extraordinary prologue to their marriage in 1946. Webb, during the period in which they corresponded, had enjoyed striking success as an actress, had modeled for Salvador Dali, had continued to engage in socialist politics, and had lived through an unsuccessful first marriage. It was she who in a letter in 1943 posed the question of what shape her life should take. James' reply is instructive. He says to her that what she called her monomaniac devotion to acting is an expression of powerful feelings within her that must be given expression: "the thing that matters is to live your life, to express yourself, so long as it is not ignoble or mean."[26]

To her uncertainty about what she should be doing, he responds: "Some pseudo-Marxist has been getting at you, telling you that what you should do is join a party and work in a factory. Just tell them to go to hell, that's all." And James then goes on to say that he himself had made his own way as a writer and that "thank Heaven, I find that I am still making my own way while so many others are floundering around." What is remarkable here is what James adds: an injunction to give expression to powerful feelings that surge within us, to a life that for many is "stifled by capitalism," but that in some, such as he and Webb, breaks through. This insistence by James that one should trust one's own feelings may suggest that he had learned from D. H. Lawrence – he was in fact no follower of Lawrence – and it invites the same question that Lawrence invites: Which are the feelings that one should trust and which are the feelings of which one should beware? This question James does not ask and his confidence in his own practical judgments as expressive of the life within him gives us reason to revise our account of James as a practical reasoner.

I remarked earlier upon the pattern of reasoning that had appeared to govern his choices. What he made clear to Webb was that he took himself to reason as he did only because so to reason did give expression to his own feelings and attitudes. James presented himself to Webb as someone whose apparently impersonal practical reasoning – if anyone with my characteristics in my situation acts in this way, he will become excellent as a writer or he will further the cause of the socialist revolution, so this is how I should act – was the expression of an underlying trust in his own feelings

---

[26] Letter of September 1, 1943, *The C. L. R. James Reader*, ed. Anna Grimshaw, Oxford: Blackwell, 1992, p. 128; anyone writing about James owes an immense debt to Anna Grimshaw.

and of first person reasoning of the form: This is how I feel, therefore this is how I should act. A further question therefore arises: Had James at this point really understood himself? Was he in fact what he now took himself to be? The further course of his life points toward an answer.

His marriage to Webb had ended after five years, perhaps because of James' affairs with other women, but perhaps because of his insistence on dictating the terms of their relationship, an insistence evident in other relationships. In other respects his political and literary activities remained very much as they had been until in 1953 he was detained and served with a deportation order, ostensibly on the ground that he had not renewed his visa. That he had stayed beyond the date on his visa was true. But James and others understood his arrest as one more example of the persecution of Communists of all kinds, Stalinist, Trotskyist, postTrotskyist, that had developed as the United States pursued its Cold War against the Soviet Union. That the Soviet government had no more principled and determined enemies than James and his political allies counted for nothing. But this was not the ground on which James contested his deportation.

During what was to be the last year that he spent in the United States, James had written a study of Herman Melville, *Mariners, Renegades and Castaways: The Story of Herman Melville and the World We Live In*. It was privately published in New York and, while James was detained on Ellis Island, he arranged for a copy to be sent to every member of the Senate. Why? James judged it important to present himself as he now was, that is, as someone deeply engaged by American culture and American history. Three key moments in the history of that culture were represented by Whitman, Melville, and the great filmmakers of the twentieth century. Whitman was the poet of a democratic individualism that is at once peculiarly American and of significance for everyone. In "a land of equality and heroic individual achievement," he struck the pose of a rebel but had nothing to rebel against. He never understood the limitations and potential dangers of individualism, and so his was a limited, but real poetic achievement, real because of his "conviction of the worth of the individual as an individual in work and play and all aspects of life, and the recognition that this individual could only find his fullest expression with other individuals equal to himself,"[27] but limited by his failure to recognize that the economic, social, and political forms taken by that individualism were deeply inimical to those values. What Whitman had

[27] Quoted from an early 1949–1950 draft of James' *Notes on American Civilization*, of which James made use in writing *Mariners, Renegades and Castaways*, chapter 12 in *The C. L. R. James Reader*, pp. 203 and 208.

failed to understand, Melville, or at least the Melville of *Moby Dick* had understood.

Unlike Whitman, Melville was able to describe accurately "individuals in their social setting, the work they did, their relationships with other men."[28] What as a result he understood and portrayed though the forms of the novel was the socially destructive threat presented by rampant individualism, a threat to the relationships between human beings and to their relationship to the natural world. In his so characterizing Melville, the expression "through the forms of the novel" is important. James valued Melville as a great artist and he took artists to communicate more and other than do, say, sociologists or economists. Moreover to understand individualism adequately, we need the novelist quite as much as the sociologist or the economist, and novelists speak to those unable to hear what sociologists and economists say, although by mid twentieth century those artists who speak most compellingly about the human condition are no longer novelists: "artistic creation in the great tradition of Aeschylus and Shakespeare finds its continuation today in films by D. W. Griffith, Charlie Chaplin and Eisenstein."[29] This was the line of thought that James was developing in the period immediately before and after his departure from the United States.

Why then did he send his book on Melville to the members of the Senate? James was not given to empty dramatic gestures, and he must have known that this mass mailing would do nothing to prevent his deportation. What he did was to affirm his right to be heard, a right that he had earned as a major contributor to ongoing political conversation about the significance of America and American culture, both for Americans and for others. It was his final political action before he returned to Britain, a Britain remarkably changed from the time that he had left it. With a number of these changes he was going to have to reckon, but at first he found himself at a loss, unsure how to proceed. Grace Lee, who had been a political ally in the United States, visited him in London and found him "at loose ends, trying to find his way."[30] So did George Padmore. This was an unfamiliar experience for James and he had to come to terms both with the situation in which he found himself and with himself. The latter took longer than the former.

Two social and political changes were of the first importance both in themselves and for James. In 1948 what was to turn into a mass migration of West Indians from the Caribbean to Britain had begun. By 1962

[28] *C. L. R. James Reader*, p. 209.
[29] James, "Popular Art and the Cultural Tradition," in ibid., p. 247.
[30] Grace Lee, *Living for Change*, Minneapolis: University of Minnesota Press, 1998, p. 69.

it would amount to about a quarter of a million people. Areas in some cities, including London, became West Indian communities, confronting economic difficulties and hostile discrimination, but also enjoying a rich cultural life. The BBC broadcast a radio program, *Caribbean Voices*, presented at one stage by the Trinidadian, V. S. Naipaul. Beginning in 1950 London publishers regularly published novels by authors from the West Indies.[31] The Caribbean had become a new kind of presence in Britain. And political change in the Caribbean itself was impending.

In most of the various British colonies, there were powerful movements demanding democratic self-government and it had become in the interest of the United Kingdom government to negotiate orderly transfers of power. The question was: What form should the new political order take? Both the United Kingdom government and James strongly favored a West Indies Federation and in January 1958 such a federation came into being, including Trinidad and Tobago, Jamaica, Barbados, and a number of other islands. James returned to Trinidad and became editor of *The Nation*, newspaper of the newly ruling People's National Movement (PNM). But it was not long before he quarreled with the Movement's leadership. For James what mattered was not just independence from colonial rule or even the immediate reforms that independence made possible, but the direction then to be taken. In his thinking about this direction, James was influenced in part by the example of George Padmore.

It was James who much earlier had put Kwame Nkrumah in touch with Padmore, whose conception of PanAfricanism was to inspire Nkrumah's politics. When Nkrumah achieved power in Ghana, Padmore was at his side as his closest adviser. James visited Ghana in 1957 and took both the achievements and the limitations of the Ghanaian enterprise to be exemplary for political thinking about the Caribbean. What the inhabitants of the Caribbean needed was to be educated into a strong and shared sense of what was distinctive about their cultural inheritance, so that they could contribute in an equally distinctive way to the revolutionary transformation of the world order. Independence from imperialist rule was a necessary step toward such a transformation, but one that had to issue in a new kind of politics. And neither in Ghana nor in Trinidad did this happen. The immediate issue over which James quarreled with Eric Williams and the other leaders of the PNM was that posed by their opposition to the West Indies Federation, which broke up in 1962, so that Trinidad and Tobago

---

[31] See Dillon Brown, *Migrant Modernism: Postwar London and the West Indian novel*, Charlottesville, VA: University of Virginia Press, 2012.

became an independent state. James resigned from his position with *The Nation* and returned to Britain. But his conflict with Williams was much more than disagreement over a single issue.

In both Ghana and Trinidad, as elsewhere, the form taken by state power after independence was achieved faithfully reproduced the structures of colonial government. New black elites replaced their colonial predecessors and a new political rhetoric replaced the old imperialist and paternalist rhetoric, but the relationships of rulers to ruled were remarkably unchanged. And the new rulers in Trinidad had little concern for providing the workers and small farmers of Trinidad with the cultural and political education that they needed, if they were to transform their lives. Padmore and Williams had been prepared to take power in whatever form it was open to them to do so, and James admired their devotion, their persistence, and their skills. But for him, unlike them, political independence from imperialist powers mattered only insofar as it enabled continuing social transformation of a radically new kind. Both Padmore and Williams admired James as an historian, but took him to be politically disabled by his theoretical cast of mind. Padmore had spoken scornfully of James as "making his paper revolution."[32] Williams by now valued James only as he contributed to the advancement of the PNM.

When James returned to England in 1962, he was sixty-one years old. He had discovered painfully that there was no longer any role for him within what was now conventional West Indian politics, and it might have seemed that, back in London, he would find himself once more at a loss, just as he had when he returned to England from the United States eight years earlier. But it was not so. For during those eight years, James had reidentified and rediscovered that in his life which gave him and it point and purpose. How had he done this? He had been rescued by cricket. His rediscovery of cricket had begun as he reestablished himself as a journalist, when he first returned to England from the Unitede States. Neville Cardus by then contributed only occasional articles to the *Manchester Guardian*, and between May and July 1954 James had provided forty-two reports of county matches. From then on, he took cricket with great seriousness, reflecting both on the contemporary game, on its history, and on its notable aesthetic qualities. Later in Trinidad, as editor of *The Nation*, he campaigned successfully to have Frank Worrell named as captain of the West Indies team for the test series with Australia in 1960–1961, the first black player to be so named. He

---

[32] Carol Polsgrove, *Ending British Rule in Africa: Writers in a Common Cause*, Manchester University Press, 2009, p. 130.

did so not because Frank Worrell was black, but because he was uniquely
well qualified for the position, a paradigm of cricketing excellence and of
good judgment. But James' preoccupation was not just with cricket, but
with the part that cricket had played in his own moral formation.

One starting point for such reflection had been as early as 1950 in the
United States, when James had been deeply shocked by newspaper reports
that college basketball players had accepted bribes from bookmakers to fix
the results of games. Such a thing, he told his American friends, could never
have happened with cricketers, whether in Trinidad or in Britain. He was
quite as shocked to discover that the young Americans whom he knew best,
college graduates whose principled support for socialist political causes had
often been at considerable cost to their careers, saw nothing wrong in such
bribe taking. The concept of loyalty to the school for which you played
and of such loyalty as precluding cheating meant nothing to them. James
continued to discuss this difference in attitude with his contemporaries
and "we have arrived at some conclusions. These young people had no
loyalties to school because they had no loyalties to anything. They had a
universal distrust of their elders and praeceptors . . . Each had had to work
out his own individual code."[33] James' American friends were surprised
by James' reaction and at first "had looked at me a little strangely," but
quite soon, James reported, "I was looking at myself a little strangely."[34] He
had discovered something of high importance about himself which he had
failed to recognize for quite some time. His practical reasoning and his
practical judgments were other than he had thought them to be.

It was in the period in which James, together with Dunayevskaya and
others, was rethinking and reformulating his Marxism that he became, as
he reported later, "increasingly aware of large areas of human existence"
about which even that sophisticated Marxism had little or nothing to say.
"What did men live by? What did they want?" Were their desires now
what they had been in the past? What part did art and culture play in their
lives? A first response to these questions was to take note that "when the
common people were not at work, one thing they wanted was organized
sports and games," and this greedily and passionately.[35]

James proceeded to revisit the narrative of his own life and to do so
by considering what it was about cricket that had helped to make him
what he had become. The outcome was a book that was both a history
of cricket and a history of James, *Beyond a Boundary*, published in 1963.
In it he records four discoveries. The first concerned cricket, that it is

---

[33] James, *Beyond a Boundary*, p. 53.   [34] Ibid., p. 54.   [35] Ibid., p. 150.

an art, just as literature and music are. To say that it is an art is to say that there are standards of excellence internal to it and that the good of achieving such excellence is what gives cricket its point and purpose. And just because cricket is an art, there is an art in writing well about it. The second concerned himself, that he had only been educable, so that he could discriminate in his choices of goods to be pursued, because of the qualities of character that his parents and other family members had inculcated and that his schoolmasters had strengthened. A third discovery was that the social relationships in the family, at school, on the cricket field, and elsewhere that make the appreciation and the achievement of genuine excellence possible have to be informed by a shared allegiance to a code whose prohibitions – against cheating and taking bribes, for example – make certain types of action unconditionally unacceptable. Fourthly and finally, James recognized that he was able to understand himself in this way, both in the world of cricket and more generally, only because he inherited from his family, his schoolmasters, and the great names in the history of cricket a tradition of thought, judgment, and action which it was now for him to transmit to others.

About each of these discoveries more needs to be said. I begin with the fourth. The tradition into which James had been educated had a number of strands, each with its own starting point. Games and sports had become an important part of the everyday life of plain people in the modern world in the same decades – the 1860s and 1870s – in which the labour movement and democratic reform became important to those same plain people and the same ways of thinking about sports and games and about popular democracy had come to inform much of West Indian life. Thomas Arnold, who reformed Rugby School between 1828 and 1842, so that the inculcation of moral character and good manners, of self-discipline and trustworthiness, became its educational goal, had himself no interest in games. But some of those who had learned from Arnold, among them Thomas Hughes, the author of *Tom Brown's Schooldays*, soon realized that it is in and through such games as Rugby football and cricket that self-discipline and trustworthiness may be developed, along with an ability to recognize and value excellence, and not only excellence at games, but also in literary studies. So the attitudes, codes, and loyalties of the English public schools were transmitted to the Queen's Royal College in Port of Spain.

To understand oneself in terms of some tradition is not only to understand one's present in terms of one's past, but also to find in one's past a

key to the conflicts of the present. It was in the context of those conflicts
that James discovered the justification for his moral stances. In 1932 the
cricketing community had been torn apart by controversy over the body-
line bowling of Harold Larwood and others, fast bowling in which the
bowler aimed not at the wicket, but at the batsman. Nothing in the rules
of cricket prohibited this, but it was plainly incompatible with the spirit of
the game, with a self-imposed moral restraint that had not hitherto required
explicit defense. Body-line bowling was in the end outlawed, but James in
retrospect took this episode to be a symptom of something more general,
"the violence and ferocity of our age expressing itself in cricket," the same
violence and ferocity that in the same period found expression in a variety
of assaults on democracy.[36] So James makes it clear that the justification
for upholding unconditional moral rules and for developing qualities of
character is that without these rules and qualities, goods indispensable to
human flourishing cannot be achieved.

What James also acknowledged was that the fabric of social life is such
that the necessary moral commitments and qualities of character have to be
transmitted through families and schools, if they are to find expression in
workplaces, in games and sports, and in political struggle. Political struggle
for the radical democratization of social life is necessary, because "The end
of democracy is a more complete existence,"[37] an existence enriched by
the arts. And among the fine arts are various games, including cricket. On
cricket as an art, James was still following Cardus,[38] although perhaps now
unaware of this. He looked to Bernard Berenson and Adrian Stokes for
his characterization of aesthetic values and drew striking and illuminating analogies between what it is that gives grace and elegance to a great
painting and what it is that gives grace and elegance to a great cricketer's
performances. *Beyond a Boundary* ends with a eulogy of Frank Worrell's
achievements in the Test series against Australia in 1960–1961, both as cricketer and as a captain who knew how to bring out the best in the members
of his team, presenting Worrell as the finest contemporary representative
of a tradition now, as always, under threat from commercialization and the
loss of values. "Thomas Arnold, Thomas Hughes and the Old Master himself" – W. G. Grace – "would have recognized Frank Worrell as their boy."

Beyond a Boundary is as remarkable a book as *The Black Jacobins*, and
no summary, let alone one as bare and skeletal as this, can be a substitute

---

[36] Ibid., p. 186.   [37] Ibid., p. 206.
[38] See Neville Cardus, *Autobiography*, London: Collins, 1975, pp. 32–33.

for reading it. Toward its close James records his return to his family in Trinidad and with it his recognition of the relationship between the values practiced by his aunts and the values that sustained excellence in cricket, excellence in literature, and excellence in politics. Comparing his early to his present – 1963 – life, he says of himself "I have changed little. I know that more than ever now."[39] But how far was that in fact so?

Was it the case that James had now discovered what it was that he had always been, but for long periods without recognizing it, as he now did? Or was it rather the case that he had moved away from the evaluative and normative commitments of his upbringing, to some extent while in England, but even more while in the United States, and had now moved back, imputing a continuity to his life that was in fact a fiction? Was his Trotskyist and postTrotskyist practical reasoning an expression, even if perhaps an unrecognized expression, of those earlier commitments, or had it displaced them? Was the confidence in himself, in his own feelings and attitudes, just because they were his own, that he had expressed to Constance Webb, yet another disguised expression of those same commitments or a substitute for them? If we are to answer these questions, we need to characterize a little further the view of himself and of the world which had informed James' upbringing and education, the view finally spelled out in *Beyond a Boundary*, but even then not fully.

Right action has several characteristics. Right action aims at and contributes to the defeat of injustice and so to liberating agents from the limiting and distorting relationships imposed by systems of enslavement, exploitation, and arbitrary rule. And, since such liberation can only be achieved through action together with many others, action informed by social relationships of trust, right action is characteristically the outcome of deliberation with others. Secondly, right action aims at achieving those goods which make the life of a free human being worthwhile, the goods of family life, the goods of education and of intellectual enquiry and of artistic achievement. And, since such achievement is only possible through action together with many others, action informed by social relationships of trust, once again right action is characteristically the outcome of deliberation with others. Thirdly, what those who deliberate together share, what binds them, is a common acceptance of certain norms and a recognition of certain common goods, but this always in forms that derive from and are defined in terms of the particularities of a shared cultural inheritance. So in their practical reasoning at any particular time and place, there will

[39] James, *Beyond a Boundary*, p. 246.

always be some measure of rough-and-ready agreement on how goods are to be ordered.

Fourthly, they will also have to be aware not only of the strength of those forces to which they find themselves opposed in particular conflicts, but also of the various ways in which they themselves are apt to go wrong in their practical reasoning. Consider just three of these, as noted by James. The public school tradition had been transmitted to him through men whose attitudes to black Trinidadians, formed by British imperialism, were at best paternalist. Cricketers, because of their huge crowd-pleasing value, have often been seen as presenting investors with opportunities for money-making, and cricketers themselves have on occasion been prepared to restructure the game for the sake of money. Cricket, like other games, affords, especially to the highly skilled, ample means for self-aggrandizing self-expression. The arenas of left-wing politics are often the scene of competition for power and influence. Revolutionary zeal can be and has too often been a mask for the love of power. Those, like James, who are deeply indebted to all three, have in each case a peculiar responsibility for identifying and resisting these forms of radical moral failure. As James notably did.

If this is a true, even though highly abstract account of the fundamental moral stance to which James expressed his allegiance in *Beyond a Boundary*, what answer should we give to the questions that I posed earlier? Had these same attitudes and commitments been James' throughout his adult life or had he in fact varied a good deal at different periods, something that he now failed to recognize? Begin by noticing the key part that shared deliberation has in this account of the moral life and of the practical reasoning that informs it, and notice further the very remarkable differences in the various groups in which and with which James argued and arrived at decisions at different stages in his career: in the class and ethnically divided Trinidad of his upbringing and education, in the working-class solidarity of a Lancashire devoted to the Labour Party and to cricket, in the literary and political milieus of his life in London, in his relationships with political organizers and with the workers with whom they engaged in different cities in the United States, in the England and the Trinidad of the 1950s and 1960s when he returned to them. What a great many of those with whom he worked and discussed and argued brought with them to those discussions and arguments, by way of cultural and moral assumptions, would not have been at all what James brought to them. So it would have been surprising if James' progress in each of these milieus and in his transitions from one to another had been entirely straightforward. Clearly at different periods, deliberating with and interacting with this group rather than that, he rank ordered both the goods that he valued and the qualities that he valued in others in significantly different ways, and this in ways that he himself did not always recognize. Hence derived his naive surprise at finding that his American political allies did not share his abhorrence of cheating.

James had of course been aware that in giving priority to some particular goods and goals in this particular period of his life and to some other set of goods and goals in some earlier or later period, he was making choices, choices that gave expression to something fundamental in himself. But to what? The answer that he gave, when he asked this question, changed over time. In the 1940s, as we noted in his correspondence with Constance Webb, he took his choices to express a confidence in his own judgments, a trust in his own feelings, and nothing more. Their explanation terminated with him. By the 1960s this individualist conception of himself had been displaced. He now understood those same choices as an expression of his formation by and his allegiance to a complex tradition or set of traditions. He recognized himself for what he was. It seems true, then, both that James had at some points in his life understood himself in terms that were alien to his upbringing – the Trotskyist terms of his 1930s, the individualism of his 1940s – but also that there had always been an underlying continuity. The story that James tells in *Beyond a Boundary* is by and large a true story, and one that allows us to arrive at a further conclusion about James as a practical reasoner.

It is that to some degree he led a double life until about 1960; not that he was duplicitous, but in some periods of his life one set of goods was dominant, those to be achieved only by emancipatory political action, in others quite another set of goods, those to be achieved only through devotion to the art of cricket and participation in the life of the cricketing community. In the pursuit of both sets of goods, it was always important that he was a writer, learning from his great literary predecessors from Aeschylus to Thackeray. And *Beyond a Boundary* was in part his attempt as a writer to give an account of the relationships between these two sets of goods, most notably in his ambitious and much too brief history of the place of athletic contests in the life of ancient Greece and of the relationship of the art of tragic drama to the Athenian democracy. But compare with *Beyond a Boundary* a short book that James published in 1958, *Facing Reality*.[40] *Facing Reality* is perhaps the best statement that we

[40] C. L. R. James, *Facing Reality*. Chicago, IL: Charles H. Kerr Publishing Company, 2005; Grace Lee had collaborated with him in writing it and the French theorist, Cornelius Castoriadis, contributed a chapter.

possess of the political positions at which James finally arrived. It is a systematic critique of both the state-and-market capitalism of the West and of the state capitalism of the Soviet Union. It is an attempt to define the possibilities for social and political change that have opened up and the responses needed from both workers and intellectuals, if they are to understand those possibilities. But no reader of *Facing Reality* would learn anything about the relevance of sports and games to the life of those for whom it was written or more generally about the relationships between the arts and politics. It might indeed seem that *Facing Reality* and *Beyond a Boundary* had been written by two different authors.

We can only conclude that the attempt that James made in *Beyond a Boundary* to integrate the two sides of his life expressed what had been up till that point for the most part aspiration rather than achievement. What had been lacking? In *Beyond a Boundary* James spoke of "a more complete existence" as the "end of democracy" and of the Greek audience for the *Oresteia* and those who watch modern Test Matches as both grasping "at a more complete human existence,"[41] but he never spelled out what it would be to attain completeness in a human life, let alone in the kind of double life that he had lived out so impressively. Yet from about 1960 onwards, James acts so that his two devotions complement one another. He had never lacked integrity. Now he achieved some measure of integration. But there was a limit to that integration.

Writing to Maxwell Geismar in 1961, James had reflected on the lack in American life of any sense of the tragic, which he defined as "a sense of the inability of man in society to overcome the evil which seems inseparable from social and political organization."[42] The American character is one which in its pursuit of happiness refuses to accept the place of evil in human life and therefore to acknowledge its tragic character. James himself of course believed that a radical transformation of the forms of social and political organization was possible, so that evils could be overcome and human life cease to be tragic. But if one was to be the kind of human being who could engage constructively in social and political conflict, it was of crucial importance to acknowledge the tragic character of human existence so far and in our own time and to learn from the great masters of tragic drama. And what has to be learned is not only that we need to strive for completeness in our lives, but that completeness is not to be attained. So James lived out what he took to be a necessarily incomplete life.

---

[41] James, *Beyond a Boundary*, p. 206.   [42] *C. L. R. James Reader*, p. 278.

He was able to return to the United States in the late 1960s, where he taught courses at the University of the District of Columbia and later on at Northwestern University. Later still he returned to London, living in Brixton, by that time home to quite a number of AfroCaribbean enterprises. He was recognized as a much needed teacher by younger political activists, who recurrently brought him their questions, questions to which he characteristically gave patient attention. In 1989, not long before James' death, Steve Pyke published a volume of photographic portraits of contemporary and recent philosophers, each face accompanied by a short philosophical statement. Almost all are of academic philosophers, almost all at work in the analytic tradition. But among these academic faces appears that of James, gaunt and handsome, seldom before identified as a philosopher, even in the period nearly forty-years earlier when he was working through Lenin's *Philosophical Notebooks* with Dunayevskaya. What was it that Pyke had now discerned? Was Pyke right to identify him as a philosopher? James' philosophical statement is a quotation from *Beyond a Boundary* on how long it had taken him to discover "that it is not quality of goods or utility which matter, but movement; not where or what you have, but where you have come from, where you are going, and the rate at which you are getting there."[43]

Put this statement back into the autobiographical context in which James uttered it, and it may seem to lack – it does lack – the abstract and argumentative character of most philosophical claims. Yet, if the discovery that it records was a genuine discovery, then a number of well-known theses in moral and political philosophy must be false. For, on James' view, human lives do have a teleological structure, one which each of us has to discover for her or himself through the pursuit of particular goods, so that we become aware of the directedness in our lives. A retrospective justification of our earlier actions is that they enabled us to become the kind of self-aware agent who can tell the story of his life, so that its point and purpose emerges in that telling. The practical reasoning that issued in those actions took as its premises a set of theses about particular goods and about how they are to be achieved and contributed to deliberation with like-minded others. The discovery in which, if things go well, they result is of a conception of human flourishing, always articulated in the agent's own particular cultural terms.

So James' account of what he had learned has both some notably Aristotelian features and some features that put him very much at odds with

[43] James, *Beyond a Boundary.* pp. 116–117.

Aristotle. It is not a Platonic nor a Stoic nor a Kantian nor a Benthamite nor an Hegelian account. And it puts all those rival accounts in question. Steve Pyke was right. James was a philosopher. He died on May 18, 1989.

5.5   Denis Faul

The three case histories of practical reasoners that I have described so far are drawn from very different social environments. Yet they share some notable characteristics which make them atypical of practical reasoners – that is, of people – in general and this may be thought to lessen their value as examples. Two out of the three were novelists. Two out of the three published autobiographical works. All three have a kind and degree of articulateness that most others lack. In one way this makes them excellent examples for study. They provide just the kind of evidence that we need. And they are untypical in the way that every reader of this book will be untypical. For most of the human race never read books like this. So in attempting to learn from such examples we may be in danger of confusing what it is to be a practical reasoner with what it is to be the kind of practical reasoner that we – Grossman, O'Connor, James, you, the reader, and I, the author – are. Can we avoid this danger?

First, we should note that in enquiring about practical reasoners we do well to begin with the articulate, with those who have already answered at least some of our questions before we even asked them. For from them we will perhaps be able to learn which questions to ask and how best to formulate those questions. We may also learn that those who are most articulate about themselves are those most likely to deceive us and indeed themselves. So I take my project to be no more than a pilot project.

Yet it is also worth remarking that the belief that there is a sharp contrast between those who are articulate and capable of spelling out those patterns of reasoning that issue in and find expression in their actions and the inarticulate, because unschooled, many is a characteristic folk belief of those who have enjoyed some large degree of formal education. Those who mix only with others of the same kind, who have never had extended conversations with small farmers or factory workers or those who cope with unemployment and homelessness, tend to ascribe inarticulateness to those whose opportunities for conversation and modes of conversation differ from their own. As I write, large numbers of working-class Americans, especially black Americans, have been demonstrating in the streets against the arbitrary, brutal, and sometimes lethal mistreatment of black young men by white police officers. Those of them interviewed on television as to their reasons for acting as they did were highly articulate, made important distinctions between good and bad reasons for various kinds of response, and showed themselves to be in varying degrees both responsible and reflective. I conclude that sharp distinctions between kinds of agent who are articulate and self-aware in respect of their practical reasoning and kinds of agent who are not may themselves be dangerously misleading.

Yet this last example suggests another respect in which Grossman, O'Connor, and James are atypical practical reasoners. Like everyone else their practical reasoning presupposes a set of attitudes toward the established order of the society in which they find themselves and with it a political dimension to their lives. But, unlike many, they found themselves at key points in their lives compelled to spell out those attitudes and to do so systematically, so that their rank ordering of goods in their everyday practical reasoning becomes other than it would otherwise have been. Here again they make explicit assumptions and attitudes informed by those assumptions that are often left implicit. And here again what makes their reasoning atypical is what makes their example instructive. So it is with a fourth case, one as different from those of Grossman, O'Connor, and James as they are different from each other, that of Denis Faul.

Denis O'Beirne Faul was born in the village of Louth in Ireland in 1932, ten years after Ireland had been partitioned into the twenty-six counties of the newly independent Irish Free State, including the County Louth, which took its name from the village, and the six counties of Northern Ireland, which remained under British rule, although having their own provincial government at Stormont. The border between the two divided the County Louth from the County Down in Northern Ireland. Not only were over 90% of the inhabitants of the Free State Catholics, but Catholicism was that state's official religion, while Lord Craigavon, as Prime Minister of Northern Ireland, was to speak of his as "a Protestant government for a Protestant people." Within the Free State, which in 1949 became the Republic of Ireland, there was a small Protestant minority, respected and not always without influence, but constrained by the imposed norms of a Catholic culture. In Northern Ireland there was a substantial Catholic minority, regarded as a continuing threat to their hegemony by the Protestant majority, and systematically discriminated against in a variety of ways.

Denis Faul's father was a physician in general practice. Denis, one of seven children, enjoyed an affectionate family life, one typical of the prospering professional class in the new Ireland. Its values were those of a conservative Catholic culture, one that saw nothing amiss in the activities of the Censorship of Publications Board or the ban on Catholics attending Trinity College, but that placed a high value on education. Faul was only nine years old when he decided that he had a vocation for the priesthood, and in this intention he never wavered. From his schooling in Dundalk and Armagh, he went on to undergraduate studies at St. Patrick's College, Maynooth, and the work as a seminarian that preceded his ordination to the priesthood in 1956. About Maynooth he was to say: "Up at six to say our prayers. We ate bread, butter and mutton every day and we played Gaelic football, which kept the mind clear. We were not allowed to ask questions. But it was the days of Pius XII and everything was very straightforward."[44] After two years of graduate study, first at Maynooth and then in Rome at the Gregorian University, he was appointed to a teaching position at St. Patrick's Academy in Dungannon in the County Tyrone. Here he remained, first as a school master and later as the Principal, for nearly forty years.

Father Faul brought with him to his work as priest and teacher a range of strong interests and concerns. He continued to play Gaelic football in Dungannon. He was fluent in and cared about the Irish language. Later, for quite a number of years he acted as Chaplain to the Summer School in Irish in Teelin, Co. Donegal. He was a lifelong Pioneer, a member of the Irish temperance movement founded by Father James Cullen at the end of the nineteenth century. And the subjects that he taught, initially Latin and religion, also engrossed him. He was a lifelong learner.

His students sometimes found him demanding, just because he cared very much that things should go well for them and not only academically. In late 1956 the Irish Republican Army, dedicated to reuniting the six counties of Northern Ireland with the rest of Ireland, resumed its armed struggle against British rule. Raids against police stations and military installations in the North were mounted from the counties south of the border by the Volunteers of the IRA, and support for its campaign was at first significant. The campaign continued until 1962 and idealistic young Catholic Republicans, brought up to admire the heroism of those who had died for the Republican cause, were often tempted to become Volunteers, among them some of Father Faul's pupils. He saw clearly, as they often did not, not only that the campaign was doomed to failure, but also that the then leadership of the IRA was making use of those recruited to it for political purposes that they themselves had not thought through. Father

---

[44] Quoted by Anne McHardy in her obituary notice, *The Guardian*, June 21, 2006.

Faul did all that he could to persuade his students not to be seduced by this political temptation.

That the border campaign was not sustainable became increasingly clear to the IRA's then leadership, and in the same period a number of them became persuaded by a Marxist analysis of the Irish situation. The conflicts between Catholic nationalists and Republicans on the one hand and Protestant Unionists on the other had been distracting attention from and disguising the conflicts between the working class, both Catholic and Protestant, and the capitalist class and its allies. What was needed was to persuade the Irish working class on both sides of the border of their common interests, and this could not be achieved by military action. So its members turned to a socialist politics aimed at achieving working-class unity. But the most significant developments in Northern Ireland were to come from elsewhere and were to mark the beginning of Father Faul's political transformation.

Until he was in his early thirties, his modes of practical reasoning were those characteristic of an Irish priest and teacher. He would have led a highly structured life as both, saying mass and performing his other priestly duties in accordance with the daily, weekly, and annual routines of the church's life, teaching his classes and performing his other scholastic duties in accordance with the daily, weekly, and annual routines of the school's life. So that a first answer to the question 'Why is he doing *that now* ?' would often have been 'This is a Thursday in March and it is two o'clock in the afternoon.' A second answer would have been that he was acting for the most part as any tolerably conscientious and cheerful priest and school teacher in his circumstances would have had good reason to act. The reasoning that found expression in his everyday life took its beginning from premises about what both natural and divine law prescribed and permitted for someone such as himself, including the Aristotelian and Thomistic teaching about the importance of enjoying whatever it is that you do. But more was to be required of him than he had anticipated.

From 1964 onwards, there was an increasingly strong movement for civil rights in Northern Ireland, leading to the founding of the Northern Ireland Civil Rights Association in July 1967. The civil rights demanded were the elementary rights of modern democracy. Where such democracy requires that the vote of each individual has the same weight as that of every other individual, in Northern Ireland in local elections only ratepayers – property owners – could vote and in parliamentary elections constituency boundaries were gerrymandered, so that in each case Protestant Unionist votes counted for more than Catholic votes, ensuring underrepresentation

of Catholic nationalists and republicans. Where such democracy requires
that government jobs be awarded on merit and public housing allocated
according to need, in Northern Ireland preference was given to Protestant
and Unionist applicants, irrespective of merit or need. Where such democracy requires that the police treat all citizens equally and humanely, the
nearly 100 percent Protestant Royal Ulster Constabulary (RUC) were generally dedicated to inculcating fear in Catholics, especially young Catholics.
The B-Specials, a Protestant police reserve force, behaved worse than the
RUC. The Special Powers Act allowed the police to arrest and to detain
without having to charge those arrested and detained with any crime.

In 1968 a series of marches across Northern Ireland were organized by
the Civil Rights Association, the first of them from Coalisland to Dungannon. By then there had developed a strong negative and violent response
to the civil rights movement among Protestants, especially working-class
Protestants. Paramilitary organizations had formed and a Free Presbyterian minister, Ian Paisley, had emerged as a demagogic political leader.
Marchers were systematically harassed. In October 1968 the Northern Irish
government banned a civil rights march in Derry. When in defiance of the
ban it was held, the RUC assaulted the marchers and beat many of them
savagely. In January 1969 the People's Democracy, the student branch of
the civil rights movement, marched from Belfast to Derry. The marchers
were recurrently attacked, at one point by some two hundred loyalists, as
they styled themselves, including off-duty police officers, armed with iron
bars and throwing bricks. When the marchers arrived at Derry, they were
once more attacked and that night RUC officers launched an attack on
the Bogside area of Derry. The attack was successfully repelled and the
inhabitants of the Bogside established themselves as 'Free Derry', a place
which the RUC could not enter. What had been a civil rights conflict was
on the verge of becoming a war.

Father Faul had identified with the civil rights movement from the
outset. He took part in several marches and he soon became known for his
well-articulated protests, always carefully backed up by evidence, of acts of
injustice perpetrated against the marchers. He was not the only priest so
to act. Father (later Monsignor) Raymond Murray of Armagh played quite
as notable a part in this respect, and there were others. So it is natural to
ask: Were these priests acting as they did only because as Catholic priests
they identified with the Catholic community and abhorred wrongs done
to it? The answer has to be that in part they certainly saw themselves
as having pastoral concerns for the members of their own community.
But what was overridingly important to them was their shared underlying

commitment to a generally Thomistic conception of justice that could be justified in secular terms and that required impartiality. When they protested, they appealed to standards of justice that they believed were accorded recognition in much of British law, standards of justice that they took to be binding on any rational agent. By 1972 Father Faul had become a spokesperson for the Association for Legal Justice, a largely left-wing group that targeted the wrongs committed by the police and by the British Army.

The British Army had become a major actor in Northern Ireland as early as 1969. In July of that year, there had been clashes between the RUC and Catholic demonstrators in which Catholics had been physically assaulted and two of them – both innocent bystanders – died from their injuries. Tensions were therefore already high when a march by the loyalist Apprentice Boys in Derry turned into an assault on the Bogside. Fighting broke out in a number of areas, especially in Belfast, with similar assaults on Catholic areas by loyalist paramilitaries and by the RUC. RUC units fired on unarmed rioters in Dungannon, Armagh, and Coalisland. IRA units were often badly prepared and fought back with varying success. The United Kingdom government, compelled at last to face the fact that the RUC, far from being a guardian of law and order, was a major source of violence and disorder, brought in troops in considerable numbers. But before the August fighting was over, there were eight dead, over 750 injured, over 1,500 Catholic families – and over 300 Protestant families – driven out of their homes and over 400 homes and business premises, the vast majority belonging to Catholics, burnt down or otherwise destroyed.

The arrival of British troops was at first largely welcomed by Catholics. But, as it became clear that they were in fact working with the RUC and on occasion the loyalist paramilitaries, this changed. At the same time the so-called Provisional IRA had emerged as more than a defense force for Catholic areas. The moment of decisive political definition occurred on Bloody Sunday, January 30, 1972. The Civil Rights Association, defying a ban on civil rights marches, had organized a march in Derry from the Bogside to Guildhall Square to protest against the internments that had been taking place. Soldiers of the First Parachute Regiment were dispatched to Derry to prevent the march from reaching the Square. They did so by opening fire on the unarmed marchers and bystanders, killing fourteen. Although there were many eyewitnesses to what had happened, the British government systematically lied about this atrocity and contrived that the investigation by the Widgery Tribunal should find that the actions of the soldiers were justified. It took over forty years for that government to acknowledge the truth.

Mass internment without charge of those who were suspected of supporting the Republican cause had begun in August, 1971, with the rounding up of over 350 men aged nineteen and over, many of them married and with families. That number later rose to nearly 2,000. Care not only for those interned and for those sentenced to prison terms for their actions, but also for their families, therefore became an urgent concern and so was the treatment of those interned and imprisoned.

Fourteen of those detained in August 1971 were taken to the RAF station at Ballykelly. There their heads were covered by hoods so that they had difficulty breathing and could not see or identify their captors. They were isolated, beaten and kicked, subjected to extended sleep deprivation, denied food and water for periods, made to believe that they were about to be executed. When, later on, some of them were able to report what had been done to them, it became urgently necessary to call those responsible to account. This became one of the responsibilities assumed by Father Faul. But it was only one among a number.

Immediately after the announcement of the internments he put an advertisement with his telephone number in the Belfast newspaper, the *Irish News*, inviting anyone who needed advice to call him. He, like a number of other priests, became a crucial resource for many families of those interned. "Where people needed his assistance and advice, time and distance meant nothing to him," wrote his former colleague at St. Patrick's, Mgr. McEntegart. "I often saw him setting out for Belfast or Derry or perhaps both, after a day's teaching in class to help to allay the pain and anxiety of a family in distress due to army or police intervention."[45] Where the so-called "Hooded Men," the victims of extreme interrogation techniques at Ballykelly, were concerned, the Association for Legal Justice took on the task of calling those responsible to account. The evidence was gathered and in 1974 a small book documenting the accusations of torture was published.[46] The case made in the book was then in 1978 brought to the European Court of Human Rights. At the same time Faul continued to identify gross injustices of various other kinds outspokenly, including some perpetrated in the courts of Northern Ireland. It was his outspokenness that offended some Irish bishops.

The British government labelled Father Faul "an IRA priest." His response was always the same: "I want to see Ireland United, but I am

---

[45] "Tribute to Mgr. Denis Faul," *Pioneer*, July, 2006.
[46] Denis Faul and Raymond Murray, *The Hooded Men*, Association for Legal Justice, Northern Ireland, 1974.

not going to kill anybody for it. I am not an IRA man. I am a real republican. I love the British people, but they have no business in my country."[47] The partition of Ireland was itself an injustice over and above the injustices committed in the course of defending that partition. So what then are we to say at this stage about Father Faul's practical reasoning? We need to look at his priorities, at those with whom he found himself deliberating, and at the principles that provided the premises for his moral and political reasoning.

His priorities were pastoral, first as priest and schoolmaster in Dungannon, then ministering to the needs of those families who had lost husbands, fathers, sons, occasionally daughters, to internment or imprisonment, later as an assistant to the Catholic Chaplain in the Maze Prison. Protest and political action was secondary to pastoral care. Where protest and political action were involved, his commitment to principles of nonviolence was crucial. In the Association for Legal Justice, he worked closely with former members of the IRA whose political organization from 1972, Sinn Fein the Workers' Party – in 1982 it became the Workers' Party – was informed by the insight that the violence of the Provisional IRA's armed struggle rendered Unionist hostility to the republican cause more and more implacable, so making any prospect of a genuinely united Ireland more and more remote. Violence as a means not only generated further wrongs, but was self-defeating for any genuine republican. This was also Father Faul's view.

The principles that he shared with other members of the Association for Legal Justice were the same Thomistic principles that he had made his own during his education from his own schooldays and from his studies first at Maynooth and later in Rome. If one were to spell them out, they would be almost tediously familiar to anyone with a similar education from that period: in the rote learning of the Catechism, in the encyclicals that are definitive for the Church's social teaching, in the classical theological and philosophical texts of his graduate studies. Yet, if this conception of justice was a shared possession of so many, why did Father Faul emerge as so singular a figure? His critics took it to be in part a matter of his imprudence, his obstinate persistence in speaking forcefully in public on occasions when more could, on their view, have been achieved by a less offensive approach to the authorities. This seems to have been the attitude of Cardinal Conway. Was there substance to this criticism? Later we will see that he could on occasion become the prisoner of his own rhetoric. Yet what was much more important was how he developed his stance through time.

[47] Anne McHardy, "Monsignor Denis Faul," Obituary notice, *The Guardian*, June 22, 2006.

His initial condemnations of Unionist and British injustices established his credibility in the republican community. His responses to the needs of the families of those interned and imprisoned only had the effect that it had because he turned out to be resourceful, truthful, and dependable. So initially his evenhandedness in condemning sectarian killings, no matter by whom committed, and particular wrongs perpetrated by particular Provisional IRA units was not viewed as putting him seriously at odds with the Provisional leadership. This was to change.

During a ceasefire that began in December 1974 and ended early in 1976, the Provisional Leadership concluded – and, given the failure of the Sunningdale Agreement, understandably – that there was no prospect of achieving their goals through negotiation. They embarked on "a long war," one of indefinite duration, in which the British would finally have to recognize that the price to be paid by them economically, politically, and in loss of human life for keeping Ireland disunited was just too high. But such a war did not satisfy the criteria for a just war, as understood within the Catholic and Thomistic tradition. A war can be justified as a just war only if its just aims are determinate and achievable within a limited time, those aims cannot be achieved peacefully, and in which the cost in human lives is not disproportionate to those aims. So by 1977 Father Faul was committed not only to exposing particular injustices, but to opposing the IRA's campaign. Yet he was able to do so while still being regarded as trustworthy by the IRA leadership, as someone whom they could use as an intermediary when they wished to communicate privately and secretly with the United Kingdom government. This too was to change.

From 1976 that government had insisted on treating imprisoned IRA members as criminals, not as prisoners of war, and over 500 of those in the H-blocks of the Maze Prison responded by refusing to wear prison uniforms, having only their blankets as cover. They were restricted to their cells and denied the right to have visits from their families. In April 1978, when a prisoner was savagely beaten by the prison officers and the imprisoned men protested by smashing the furniture in their cells, they were deprived of anything in their cells except for a mattress and a blanket. Unable to leave their cells to empty chamber pots, they moved from the blanket protest to the dirty protest, smearing excrement on the cell walls. The appalling squalor can be imagined. In 1980 six members of the IRA and one member of a left-wing schism from the IRA, the Irish National Liberation Army, began a fifty-three day hunger strike, demanding that prisoners be permitted not to wear uniforms, to associate freely with other prisoners outside their cells, to receive visitors and mail, and more generally to be restored to a humane form of imprisonment. This first hunger strike ended only when one of the hunger strikers was at the point of death, and it ended only because the hunger strikers were informed that the United Kingdom government was about to agree to their demands. But this was in fact not so.

At the time of the first strike, Bobby Sands had replaced Brendan Hughes as the Officer Commanding the IRA H-block prisoners. On the basis of their vote, he began the second hunger strike on March 1, 1981. He insisted that two weeks elapse before a second prisoner joined him, in the hope that the strikers' demands would be met before there was any loss of life. Others joined in the strike one by one, and before it came to an end ten men were dead. It became an urgent task for Cardinal Tomás O' Fiaich and for his priests at work in the prison to save as many lives as possible. Father Faul accompanied the Cardinal to meetings at which they tried to persuade the United Kingdom government to make genuine concessions to the hunger strikers. But Margaret Thatcher was implacable. Father Faul, like other priests, argued with individual hunger strikers, but unsuccessfully. He reported of his last conversation with Bobby Sands that "He finished by saying to me, 'Greater love hath no man than this, that a man lay down his life for his friends', and that he, Father Faul, replied 'I won't argue with you after that.'"[48]

After the strike had begun, the independent Republican member of parliament for South Tyrone and Fermanagh died and a by-election had to be held. Bobby Sands was nominated as the Anti H-Block/Armagh Political Prisoner and on April 9 was elected to parliament, receiving over 30,000 votes. This demonstration of public support for the hunger strikers gave them additional reason for continuing the strike, and on May 5 Bobby Sands died, aged twenty-seven. But the distress of the families of the dying men was intense and Father Faul, in order to save lives, persuaded some families to intervene so that the dying strikers were fed and brought back to life against their will. This had the effect of ending the strike, and the government's response was at last to concede the strikers' demands. The view of the IRA leadership and of the strikers themselves was and is that they had been betrayed by Father Faul. Lawrence McKeown, who was close to death when the strike ended, twenty-five years later remembered Father Faul's earlier visits to the prisoners, his smuggling in cigarettes, tobacco, and pens, his bringing news from the outside world, with gratitude, but added "I do think that the steps that he took to intervene in the hunger strike

---

[48] "Monsignor Denis Faul," Online obituary, *The Times*, June 22, 2006.

were totally reprehensible in the extent to which he went to manipulate the families of those on the fast."[49]

This was a good deal less harsh than the Republican Press at the time. Father Faul, said a writer in *Iris*, was "a conniving, treacherous man" who was guilty of "emotional and moral exploitation, distortion of truth, vilification, and downright political hostility to the hunger strike."[50] There were two charges. One was of moral arrogance, of failure to respect the well thought through position of such strikers as Bobby Sands, Bik McFarlane, and Lawrence McKeown, the other McKeown's accusation that he not only "manipulated the grief of families" but "attempted to drive a wedge between them and the Republican Movement."[51] Are these accusations justified? Consider first the moral perspective of the strikers. Their experience had been one in which from an early age they had seen their parents and neighbors gravely wronged, physically assaulted, driven from their homes, deprived of their jobs. Resorting to armed resistance as Volunteers in the IRA – and they had no other resort – they had been treated as criminals, but subjected to mistreatment far worse than criminals receive. Continuing their resistance in what they now took to be the only way possible, they took themselves to have a right to the support of every Republican. The Republican leadership outside the prison shared Father Faul's doubts, both about the effectiveness of the strike as a tactic and about the loss of lives, but did not believe that they had a right to overrule the decision of the strikers. To do so would have been a flagrant breach of the moral and political solidarity necessary to achieve their goals. For them Father Faul's intervention constituted just such a breach. He could no longer be regarded as a well-intentioned, if trenchant critic, or as any sort of ally.

Reflection on the second accusation, that he had exploited the grief of the families, brings out very well what put Father Faul at odds with the hunger strikers. For them there was a single overriding good to be achieved, that of victory for the Republican cause, and to this all other goods were to be subordinated. But for Father Faul there were a number of different goods to be taken into account, and his care for the hunger strikers' families would not allow him to let their good be sacrificed to the Republican cause. In truth he had never been a reliable ally.

In the days and weeks after the hunger strike ended, he too showed some of the negative effects of his deeply felt engagement with the dying prisoners

---

[49] *Irish Republican News*, June 22, 2006.
[50] Quoted in Padraig O'Malley, *Biting at the Grave: The Irish Hunger Strikes and the Politics of Despair*, Boston: Beacon Press, 1990, pp. 127–128.
[51] *An Phoblacht*, July 27, 2006.

and their families. He did not always speak prudently. McKeown in his 2006 recollections showed himself peculiarly offended by Father Faul's talk of having "defeated the IRA" and of having the ability to defeat them in the future. And this was not just imprudent speech, but an overconfident misreading of the situation, with the result that his voice was no longer heard by many with Republican sympathies, a tragic outcome since what he would have to say about the IRA's leadership and their misuses and abuses of power during the next fifteen years badly needed to be heard and acted on. One effect of the hunger strike and of the massive public support for the strikers shown in the South Tyrone and Fermanagh by-election was that the IRA and its political counterpart, Sinn Fein, embarked on the long and tortuous military and political path toward the political solution of the Northern Irish conflicts that was embodied in the Good Friday Agreement of 1998. But the pursuit of this goal involved a brutal exercise of authority in some of the areas that the IRA controlled, abductions and executions of those believed to be British informers or sympathizers, sometimes on wildly inadequate evidence, punishment by crippling of those accused of various criminal offences, and the manipulative and deceitful use of power to secure support for the leadership's policies.

There were always strong Republican critics of such leadership within the IRA and Sinn Fein, and they have put us in their debt by their truthfulness and by their setting the complex historical record straight. (One notable debt is to Anthony McIntyre, H-block prisoner and later historian, for his oral history project, his *Good Friday: The Death of Irish Republicanism*, and his blog, *The Pensive Quill*.) But no one was more constant in his critique of the IRA and Sinn Fein on all these particular counts than Father Faul, who was now prepared to characterize the IRA leadership as 'Fascist'. At the same time he continued to devote himself to the needs of Republican prisoners and especially of their families, while still working to expose some long-standing injustices that he had denounced from the beginning. In 1975 six Irishmen had been sentenced to life imprisonment for planting bombs in two Birmingham pubs in 1974 and causing twenty-one deaths. In the same year three Irishmen and one English woman had been sentenced to life imprisonment for a pub bombing in Guildford, while six Irishmen and one Irish woman received long prison terms for supplying the explosives. All were in fact innocent, convicted on the basis of manufactured evidence and of confessions elicited by torture. All of them, the Birmingham Six, the Guildford Four, and the Maguire Seven, finally had their convictions overturned by the Court of Appeals between 1989 and 1991, as the result of a campaign initiated and sustained to the end by Father Faul and his colleagues. So he remained quite as much at odds with the United Kingdom government as he now was with the IRA.

Yet, if he had critics and enemies – from time to time he received death threats, some of which had to be taken very seriously – his persistence in going to the aid of those most in need with quiet kindness and generosity often won over harsh critics. When in 1998 he retired from St. Patrick's Academy and became Parish Priest of nearby Carrickmore, a local group of IRA supporters objected noisily to his appointment, and, when he met with members of the Police Service of Northern Ireland, some parishioners asked for his appointment to be rescinded. But it was not long before his personal qualities won over all but his harshest critics. The church had raised him to the rank of Monsignor in 1995, a recognition that he was an exemplar of the priestly life. And he had great political hopes of what might flow from the Good Friday Agreement, but without illusions about how long genuine reconciliation would take to achieve. He was happy that Northern Ireland, by remaining British, continued to enjoy those health and welfare benefits that made the life of the poor less hard. But he took it that what was now needed was a patience with and a tolerance of those with whom one had been for so long in conflict, difficult virtues, although no more difficult than the virtue of justice, the virtue which he had exemplified for so many years.

The changes in both Northern Ireland and Denis Faul between 1956 and 2006 were remarkable. Equally remarkable were three constants in Monsignor Faul's life. The first was the warmth of his relationships to siblings, other family members, and friends. I am tempted to speak of the energy that he expended in sustaining them, but this would be misleading, since they sustained him. The second was his continuing passion for Gaelic football. While he was Principal of St. Patrick's Academy, their team won the Hogan Cup, for which secondary school teams throughout Ireland compete. Nothing could have given him more pleasure. The third was his appetite for learning, for understanding what the live issues were in contemporary theological and philosophical debate and coming to terms with them. Here he read widely, as critically engrossed by the Protestant Stanley Hauerwas as by the Catholic Jean Porter. Toward the end of his life he set himself to learn Hebrew. (These reports of Monsignor Faul's interests and attitudes derive from conversations and correspondence during the last fifteen years of his life.)

It was others who characterized his theological commitments as conservative. They were in particular angered by his resistance to proposals that Catholic children in Northern Ireland should no longer be educated in Catholic schools, but that Catholic and Protestant children should be educated together in state schools. The liberal proponents of this change were well intentioned. They believed that only thus would the members of the Unionist and Republican communities be freed from their traditional and deadly antagonisms. It was Monsignor Faul's view by contrast that the members of the two communities had to be reconciled without losing their identities, an immensely difficult, but worthwhile task. A distinctively Catholic education was essential for the formation of educated Catholics able to take on this task, but the task itself was political. At the end of his life, he said that the only party that he could now have voted for was the Workers' Party, the Marxist heirs to his old associates in the Association for Legal Justice.

Monsignor Faul died of cancer on June 21, 2006. There was a very large gathering indeed at his funeral Mass, not only family, friends, and parishioners, but grateful former prisoners and their families, hunger strikers, and leading members of Sinn Fein, the latter anxiously insisting in interviews with the press that they were only there because of Monsignor Faul's earlier role in the conflicts of Northern Ireland. It would have amused him greatly to see a congregation of so many genuinely good people together with a handful of rampant scoundrels.

5.6   So what?

These then are four examples of agents whose lives exemplified virtues, the kind of lives that we need to understand, if we are to understand what the virtues are. Those lives went well and this not only in respect of desire and practical reasoning. Theirs, like every other life, could have gone badly, and this from no fault of their own, if they had been afflicted with too much or too extreme bad fortune. But those same lives could also have gone badly because of the agent's misdirected desires and flawed practical reasoning. And of course in each of these particular lives, as in every other, there were occasions when desires were in fact misdirected and practical reasoning flawed. What turns out to have been important for all of them is a relationship between the agent's identification of her or his own goals and the agent's understanding of the obstacles to achieving those goals. It matters that in all four cases some of those obstacles came to be understood not merely as inconvenient obstructions to that agent's getting her or his own way, but as wrongs or evils to be confronted as wrongs or evils.

The obstacles in each case were notably different from those in the other three. The lethal anti-Semitism encountered by Grossman was prejudice of an altogether different kind and order from the mindless prejudice against women in the American legal profession that O'Connor had to overcome. The ethnic and class injustices against which James contended had a very different character from the religious and class injustices identified by Faul. But for all four the agent's conception of her or his own good and of what would be involved in achieving it, even when still relatively immature and inchoate, set her or him in opposition to what were taken to be intolerable wrongs and evils. So that we should perhaps take seriously the thought that, had it been otherwise, they would not have been conceiving of their own good as a genuine good. To set oneself to achieve one's good as a good always may be and often is inseparable from setting oneself against those particular wrongs and evils that stand in the way of achieving it and not just because they stand in the way of achieving it. But, if this is so, then this will be reflected in the objects of the agent's desires and in her or his practical reasoning.

Consider first how it is with objects of desire. Those who have learned to discriminate between objects of desire that they have good reason to pursue from those that it is better to put on one side will already in so doing have identified goals that it would be good for them to pursue. They know by now how to rank order goods and they will reason accordingly, but at some point they may find themselves frustrated by often unanticipated barriers to their achieving their goals. How they respond involves them in answering the question: Are these particular barriers something for them to find their way around or through with as little cost as possible or do they instead represent some type of wrong or evil so intolerable that, even if they can avoid being frustrated by them on this occasion, their response cannot but be one of strong emotion, of intense desire that an end should be put to those barriers and not only for them? Of someone not so moved, someone lacking such an intense desire, it is highly probable that their desire to achieve their own good qua good is defective. They do not care enough about that good as good to be outraged, even if quietly outraged, by the bad and the evil.

If they do care enough, they will from now on reason in some significantly different ways. For they will have an additional goal or set of goals and on particular occasions they will have to consider how the achievement of their own immediate particular good in these particular circumstances is related to their commitment to struggle against this or that evil that they have identified. So it was on many occasions for both Grossman and James. But their examples may be misleading. For a great many agents much of the time, evils that they encounter in their everyday lives as barriers to their goals, evils such as petty greed, selfishness, callousness, and heedlessness, sometimes institutionalized, do not present themselves in anything like the large, world historical terms of the Stalinism of Grossman's youth or the imperialism of James'. Yet the relationship between such agents' genuinely caring about their own good as good and not merely as theirs and their being moved to struggle against those evils as evils and not merely as barriers to the achievement of their own particular goals is one and the same, as it was in the case of Grossman and James. And as with desires, so is it too with practical reasoning. Such agents in the routines of their everyday lives will have not only goals that are peculiarly their own, but also, if they care about their own good qua good, commitments to struggle against certain types of evil, something that has to find a place in their practical reasoning.

With this in mind we can now ask what it is about these four lives that make them instructive about what it is to live well, to desire and to act so that one has good reasons for desiring and acting as one does. But here we need to be careful. I maintained earlier that we can only understand political and moral generalizations and the concepts to which they give expression if we know how to apply them to some range of particular cases. Hence the need for the turn to narrative. Now, after narrating these four lives, it should also be clear that we can understand such narratives adequately only if we also understand the relevant generalizations and concepts. Theoretical understanding and narrative understanding turn out to be inseparable. Yet it is also true that what each narrative shows is the singularity of each life, the degree to which its particularities resist capture by generalizations. This is why such narratives are, if true to the facts, not edifying in any simple way, not a source of easy moral examples, even although exemplary narratives of admirable lives. Those who do not recognize their complexity may make the mistake of supposing that we can formulate some set of generalizations sufficient for practical use in advance of decision and action, generalizations that might function as prescriptions for anyone and everyone. If this were so, one moral life could be in its salient aspects a mere repetition of another, something that the singularity of each life precludes. Nonetheless, the four lives that we have examined do have important common features, especially in their early stages.

There are first those features that belong to the initial formation of character. Different as the early childhoods and education of O'Connor, James, and Faul were – about Grosssman's childhood we know too little – it is evident that, as all three well recognized, it was family and school that made them able to and anxious to learn and to develop beyond family and school. So here generalizations are certainly to the point and the empirical studies of psychologists relevant. Three qualities are crucial at this early stage, since where they are lacking the further development of key virtues will be difficult, perhaps impossible. One is that reliability, that dependability, which justifies others in forming expectations about how and to what one will respond. A second closely related quality is that of truthfulness, so that others can rely upon what one asserts. Without these two qualities, certain types of relationship, including certain types of friendship are impossible, just the types of relationship that are characteristically and generally needed for the further development of character. A third badly needed quality is of a different kind. It is that of being able to imagine alternative courses of action to those in which one is presently engaged, different goals, different ways of achieving one's present goals, so that one is compelled to ask what reasons one has for continuing as one does and how those reasons compare with the reasons for acting otherwise. Without such an imagination and without good judgment as to when to exercise it, one will inevitably be a defective practical reasoner. All three qualities are generally marks of a good upbringing.

To say this is to supplement and extend what was said earlier about the nature of such an upbringing. And a consideration of the large differences between the four lives similarly supplements and extends what was said earlier still about how very different lives that give expression to one and the same conception of human flourishing can be. What I emphasized then were differences that result from the particularities of the different cultures in which those lives are lived out. Yet while the differences between the lives of Grossman, O'Connor, James, and Faul are partly a matter of the culture that each inhabited, what are as notable are differences that are marks of the distinctive individuality of each agent's desires and practical reasoning. For it is one of the characteristics of a good practical reasoner to be able to identify the relevant particularities of her or his situation, what it is on occasion about that situation that makes it difficult to apply generalizations and dangerous to rely on precedents. The negative prohibitions of the precepts of the natural law, as I stressed earlier, by telling us only what not to do, characteristically leave open a range of possibilities.

Which particularities in an agent's situation are relevant to her or his decision making is a matter of which goods are at stake in that particular situation and of their relative importance in that situation. How clearly agents perceive what is at stake and how adequately they judge often depends on how far they are able to take into account not just how that situation appears to them, but also how it appears to those others who are involved in that situation, especially those others with whom they cooperate in the achievement of common goods. And that ability is acquired only through deliberating with perceptive and truthful others, so that one becomes able to transcend what would otherwise be the limitations of one's own particular standpoint, as I already noticed. It matters then what common goods one acknowledges and what kinds of friend one has, something that makes it all the more important that children should develop those qualities of character without which they cannot hope both to care about relevant common goods and to have good friends of very different kinds. Such care for common goods and such a capacity for friendship are salient characteristics of each of the four lives that I have narrated.

Some of Grossman's key relationships were forged in his earlier life, some during his wartime and postwar experiences, some in the Soviet literary world. O'Connor developed close ties to a wide range of different types of American, among them family members, farm workers, law clerks. James was as at home with cricketers as novelists, with Lancashire trade unionists as Detroit auto workers, not to speak of his family ties. Faul had the same close family ties, continuing friendships with school colleagues, with some priests and some members of the Workers' Party, and with all those of us in whom he inspired lasting affection. Take away their friendships and you would also take away what was crucial to their desires and to their practical reasoning. It is an insufficiently appreciated Aristotelian and Thomistic thought that one of the marks of a fully rational agent is that she or he characteristically and generally has a variety of good friends.

To have good friends one must be a good friend and to be a good friend requires that one have not only the qualities of reliability and dependability and the virtue of truthfulness, but also the two virtues of integrity and constancy, integrity, so that one's commitments do not vary from situation to situation, constancy, so that those commitments endure over time. Bad character may sometimes in these respects be a mirror image of good character, an unvarying and enduring commitment, for example, to getting one's own way. But such an unvarying and enduring commitment makes continuing friendships, as contrasted with temporary alliances, impossible. It matters then how an agent's integrity and constancy are perceived by relevant others. It is characteristically their judgments about the agent's character, not the agent's judgments about her or himself, that are to the point. And it is those relevant others who are generally best able to judge of the overall directedness or lack of directedness in a particular agent's life. In what does this overall directedness consist?

It has two aspects, one of which we noted earlier, both of which are exemplified in all four lives. The first is a pattern of development in the ordering of goods on particular occasions, so that some good or goods emerge as having overriding importance. a good or goods that cannot be finally and perfectly achieved by achieving this or that on some particular occasion. So it was with Grossman's self set task of representing Russia to Russians as it is, a goal not to be finally achieved by writing this or that particular book, no matter how great his literary achievement. So it was with O'Connor's conception of what it is to live a life of public service, a goal not to be finally achieved by serving well in this or that office, no matter how distinguished. So it was too with James' self-set task of communicating an understanding of our shared past so that we know who and what we are in remaking the present and with Faul's conception of a fully just and compassionate social order. To understand the directedness of these lives is to recognize that they all remain incomplete. Their directedness points beyond the particular goods that were their goals.

From time to time, however, rational agents need to take stock of what end or ends it is toward which they will be moving, if they continue to act as they now do. How they reflect on those occasions will depend on what kind of person they have by then become, and it is here that a second aspect of the overall directedness of their lives has to be considered. For as they move toward the achievement of various goods, they too change, developing and strengthening some traits, while losing others, so that there is a story to be told about how their desires and their reasons for desiring what they desire became whatever it is that they now finally are. They will, insofar as they understand themselves, recognize that the changes in their desires and so in themselves have had and have an overall direction, although on this too the self-awareness of agents may continue to need correction by the judgments of relevant others. Here once again the examples of the four agents whose lives I have narrated may be misleading. For although all four were at times or in some respects unaware of some of their limitations, all four came to have remarkably few illusions about themselves, their desires, and their reasons for desiring as they did. They learned earlier or later to see themselves as relevant others would have seen them and how to think truthfully about themselves.

Directedness of these two kinds is then a mark of lives lived well. But directedness toward what? Certainly toward some set of attainable goods, ordered as reason dictates, a set that characteristically changes as agents move from adolescence to middle age and beyond. Yet does this mean that someone who dies before attaining whatever were in her or his case the most notable of those goods must have somehow failed, must have fallen short of perfecting or completing her or his life, so that we may judge that, if only she or he had lived longer, then they might have perfected or completed that life? To think in this way is, as I argued earlier, to misunderstand. To live well is to act so as to move toward achieving the best goods of which one is capable and so as to become the kind of agent capable of achieving those goods. But there is no particular finite good the achievement of which perfects and completes one's life. There is always something else and something more to be attained, whatever one's attainments. The perfection and completion of a life consists in an agent's having persisted in moving toward and beyond the best goods of which she or he knows. So there is presupposed some further good, an object of desire beyond all particular and finite goods, a good toward which desire tends insofar as it remains unsatisfied by even the most desirable of finite goods, as in good lives it does. But here the enquiries of politics and ethics end. Here natural theology begins.

Index

Ross, W. D., 14
Rothko, Mark, 202

Sartre, 23, 232–233
satisficers, 184
Savage, L. J., 102, 108, 184
Schroeder, Mark, 19
Schueler, G. F., 19
self-perception
  and impact of social relationships on, 162–163
  and importance of third person standpoint,
    153, 157–158, 159–162
self-rule, 126
Seligman, Martin, 194
share fishing, 178–180
shared cultural inheritance
  and influence of in life of C. L. R. James,
    274–275, 287–291
  and influence of in life of Denis Faul,
    297–299, 301, 303, 308–309
  and influence of in life of Sandra Day
    O'Connor, 265–266, 271–273
  and need for in Caribbean, 286
  and social prejudices, 112
  and the importance of accumulation of
    wealth, 89–92
shared culture, 183
shared deliberation
  and right action, 291–292
  and the determination of common goods,
    56–57, 314–315
  and the politics of common goods,
    177–178
  and Thomistic Aristotelianism, 215
  as a method to reduce human error,
    191–192
Shiller, Robert, 104
Simon, Herbert A., 184
Smith, Adam, 91–92, 168, 191
social justice, 106–110
social order
  and Aristotelianism, 99–100
  and conflicts over Marxism, 100–101
  and expression of in everyday life, 211–213
  and impact on happiness, 199–200
  and the impact on feelings and desires,
    147–148
  as a requirement for human flourishing,
    271–273
sociological self-knowledge
  and rational justification, 210–213
  and theoretical enquiry, 112–113
Sons and Lovers, 149
Soviet revisionism of war, 253–254, 256–257
Stalin, Joseph, 244–245, 253

Stalingrad, battle of, 254, 258
Stalinism
  and constraints placed on writers, 245,
    247–249, 251, 253
  and determination of good, 245, 246, 263
Steiner, Hillel, 78
Stevenson, Charles L., 17–19
Stoicism, 21
storytelling. *See* narratives
Strawson, Galen, 239–242
Summa Theologiae, 89
surplus value, 96–97
Sutherland, Graham, 144

Tarantino, Quentin, 234
Taylor, Shelley E., 191
teleology, 226–231, 295
telos (Greek), 86
Tengely, Lázló, 238–239
Thackeray, William, 277
*The Black Jacobins: Toussaint L'Ouverture and
  the San Domingo Revolution*, 278–279
*The Needs for Common Goods for Coastal
  Communities*, 178
The Rainbow, 147, 149
The Theory of Moral Sentiments, 92
the virtues
  and influence on rank ordering of goods,
    189–191
  and the human condition, 216–220
  qualities needed in the development of,
    311–312
theoretical enquiry, 110–113
theoretical inquiry. *See* theoretical enquiry
Thomas, Alan, 19
Thomism, 106–110
Thomistic Aristotelianism. *See also*
  NeoAristotelianism
  and double lives, 166–168
  and shared deliberation, 192–193
  and the human condition, 215–217
  and the need to blend theoretical and
    practical enquiry, 206–209
  and the political dimension of rational agents,
    182–183
  philosophical justification of, 209–211
Thompson, E. P., 83
Thorupstrand (Denmark), 178–180
thumos (Greek), 80
tilfreds (Danish), 199
torture, 116
transitivity condition, 185
A Treatise of Human Nature, 79
Trotskyism, 245, 247
Tversky, Amos, 191–192